THE GREAT CANADIAN BUCKET LIST

ROBIN ESROCK

ONE -OF-A- KIND TRAVEL EXPERIENCES

SECOND EDITION

DUNDURN
TORONTO

For my kids, Raquel and Galileo,
and every generation of traveller.

Front cover images: EWM; Gord Vaaderland/EWM; EWM; Robin Esrock; Moraine Lake Lodge; EWM
Back cover images: EWM; Neil Mumby/EWMEWM; Gord Vaaderland/EWM; EWM; Robin Esrock; Moraine Lake Lodge; EWM
Printer: Friesens

Esrock, Robin, 1974-, author
        The great Canadian bucket list : one-of-a-kind travel experiences / Robin Esrock. -- Second edition.

Previous edition published by: Markham, Ontario: Thomas Allen Publishers, 2013.
Issued in print and electronic formats.
ISBN 978-1-4597-3938-3 (softcover).--ISBN 978-1-4597-3939-0 (PDF).--ISBN 978-1-4597-3940-6 (EPUB)

1. Travel--Canada. 2. Canada--Description and travel. 3. Canada--Guidebooks. I. Title.

FC38.E86 2017   917.104'73   C2017-901262-2
                                                       C2017-901263-0

1   2   3   4   5   21   20   19   18   17

Conseil des Arts du Canada   Canada Council for the Arts   Canada   ONTARIO ARTS COUNCIL CONSEIL DES ARTS DE L'ONTARIO an Ontario government agency un organisme du gouvernement de l'Ontario

We acknowledge the support of the **Canada Council for the Arts** and the **Ontario Arts Council** for our publishing program. We also acknowledge the financial support of the **Government of Ontario**, through the **Ontario Book Publishing Tax Credit** and the **Ontario Media Development Corporation**, and the **Government of Canada**.

Printed and bound in Canada.

VISIT US AT

 dundurn.com |  @dundurnpress | dundurnpress | dundurnpress

Dundurn
3 Church Street, Suite 500
Toronto, Ontario, Canada
M5E 1M2

CONTENTS

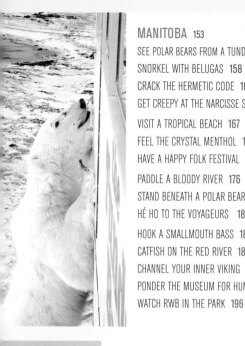

INTRODUCTION

bucket list: *A list of things one hopes to accomplish in one's lifetime.*

B ucket lists are a game of whack-a-mole. Each and every fortunate time you tick off a dream destination or activity, others will
inevitably pop up. For one of the greater truths of travel is that the
more you explore, the more you want to discover. Certainly, this
has been the case in my decade-long quest to over 100 countries on
seven continents in search of the world's most unique experiences,
and even more so in my home and *adopted* land. Born and raised
in South Africa, it took me some time before I could appreciate the
scale and distinctness of Canada. The culture, the history, the people, the astonishing natural beauty.

My own bucket list was kick-started by an unfortunate bike accident and the resulting broken kneecap. There is nothing like a brush
with mortality to remind you it's time to start living. I received a
$20,000 insurance settlement, quit my job, sold my stuff, and went
travelling for a year. The blog I created to keep friends and family
updated morphed into newspaper and magazine stories, and a globally
syndicated television series. With an unexpected enthusiasm for capturing moments in words, video, and photographs, I dedicated myself
to going everywhere in an attempt to do … well, just about everything.
And no matter how many moles I hammered, my own bucket list
never emptied, especially when I turned my attention closer to home.

Inspired by a newspaper column I wrote for Canada Day, the
first edition of *The Great Canadian Bucket List* took me to every
province and territory in search of extraordinary experiences that
define the nation. Following its publication and success, I continued

my journey by returning to each region in all seasons to seek what I'd missed. Even though this new edition contains dozens of new experiences, there's plenty of room for many more. That's par for the course in the world's second largest and most beautiful country.

Spanning nature, adventure, culture, history, and food, the new edition you hold in your hands (or on your device) has been fully revised and updated. Like the first, it is not intended to be a comprehensive guidebook, although it is accompanied by an extensive companion website. I bet my career that when it comes to travel, inspiration is just as vital, if not more so, than information. I appreciate that knowing costs and the best time of year to visit *is* important, but I asked myself the question: Why would someone want to tick this experience off their bucket list in the first place? That's what this book is about: capturing the moments, the feelings, the characters, and the contexts that make you want to learn more, read more, or better yet, follow in my footsteps.

I define a bucket list experience as one that ticks off four very subjective criteria:

1. Is it *entirely unique* with its place and people?
2. Is it *instantly memorable*?
3. Is it something *everyone can actually do*?
4. Finally, will it make a *great story*? A story to tell your friends and family, a story to warm you on cold winter nights, a story that would keep readers of a book about Canada's best experiences inspired and entertained?

This weighty tome is testament to Canada's rich bucket list bounty. From coast to coast to coast, there is inspiration in these pages for everyone, of all ages and all interests. You will meet characters who breathe life into each experience and into the country itself. There will be boats, bikes, cars, trains, and planes, as well as unique wildlife encounters, vibrant festivals, unusual meals and daring (but always safe) thrills to get your maple heart pumping.

During the course of my research, my own bucket list changed dramatically. Shortly after we got married, my Brazilian wife joined me on the legendary train journey from Vancouver to Toronto. Nine months later, our daughter was born, our first-generation Canadian. Three years later, her brother arrived (this time I credit the romance of the B.C. interior). As the children of immigrants, we hope our kids will always appreciate the incredible wonders and opportunities of their home and native land. That they contribute to the bright future of a  country that is dynamic, progressive, and welcoming to all. As for what remains on my own bucket list? "Be an inspiring and loving Dad" feels like the most important tick of all.

Devising a nation's bucket list is an immense responsibility, and one I do not take lightly. Whether you're in high school or enjoying your empty nest, a couple chasing adventure or a welcome visitor, join me as we explore each magnificent province and territory. Canada isn't going anywhere, but each passing year reminds us that we most certainly are.

Robin Esrock
robin@robinesrock.com

USING THIS BOOK

You will notice this book includes little information about prices, where to stay, where to eat, the best time to go, or other travel tips. Important stuff, certainly, but practicalities that shift and change with far more regularity than print editions of a book. With this in mind, I've created online and social media channels to accompany the inspirational guide you hold in your hands. Here you will find all the information noted above, along with videos, galleries, polls, maps, and more.

By visiting **www.canadianbucketlist.com**, you can also join our community of bucket listers, find exclusive discounts for many of the activities discussed in this book, win prizes, and debate the merits of these and other adventures. When you register, unlock the entire site by entering the code **BUCK3TL15T**, or access each item individually with the **START HERE** link at the end of each chapter.

DISCLAIMER

Tourism is a constantly changing business. Hotels may change names, restaurants may change owners, and some activities may no longer be available at all. Records fall and facts shift. While the utmost care has been taken to ensure the information provided is accurate, the author and publisher take no responsibility for errors or for any incidents that might occur in your pursuit of these activities.

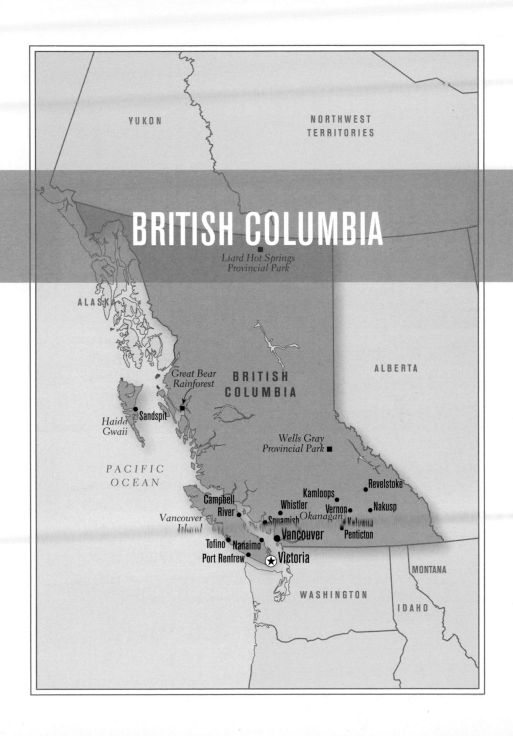

BRITISH COLUMBIA

SAIL IN HAIDA GWAII

West of British Columbia's west coast, beyond the boiling water of stormy dreams and on the knife's edge of the continental shelf, is a 280-kilometre-long archipelago of unsurpassed myth and beauty. A region of mountains, creeks, and towering trees, these Pacific islands are inhabited by a culture whose uniqueness means its art is instantly recognized, and the language of its people found nowhere else on Earth. When I set off to discover the best of Canada, I asked fellow travel writers what tops their own national bucket lists. More often than not, the answer was Haida Gwaii.

Flying into the sleepy village of Sandspit, I catch a ferry over to the $26-million Haida Cultural Centre to give the adventure some context. Here, I learn about the two Haida clans — Eagles and Ravens — and how they balance each other in marriage, trade, and even death. I learn about the importance of western red cedar, how imposing "totem" poles were carved to tell legends, honour people, and identify homesteads. I learn how this proud warrior nation, whose seafaring and ferocity have been compared to that of the Vikings, was all but exterminated after a century of European contact in a deadly cocktail of disease and cultural genocide. Of the Haida who thrived on these islands, 95 percent disappeared, but their descendants are staging a remarkable comeback. First they reclaimed their art, which is recognized worldwide as a pinnacle of First Nations cultural expression. Next they reclaimed ownership of their land in an unprecedented deal with the federal government, so that the Queen Charlotte Islands became Haida Gwaii (Place of the People). Now they are relearning their language, before it, too, becomes a ghost echoing in the forest. It gives me a lot to think about as the Moresby Explorers' 400-horsepower Zodiac speeds down the coast into the vast protected realms of Gwaii Haanas Marine Conservation Area Reserve and Haida Heritage Site. I am late for a date with Bluewater Adventures' 21-metre-long Island Roamer, on which I will join a dozen tourists from around the country on a week-long sailing expedition. This 1,500-square-kilometre national park reserve, unique in its stewardship from mountaintop to ocean floor, can only be accessed via boat and float plane. Only 2,000 visitors are allowed each season. Founded in 1988, the reserve was a hard-fought victory for the Haida over political roadblocks and multinational logging companies busy shearing the islands of their forests. I hop on board to find new friends, deeply fascinated with the culture, wildlife, and beauty, and relishing the comfortable yacht in which to explore it. The islands of Gwaii Haanas boast 40 endemic species of animals and plants, are a haven for 23 types of whale and

dozens of seabirds, and are covered with dense old-growth temperate rainforest. Sailing the calm waters between the coves and bays of the park's 138 islands, we spot humpbacks, seals, sea lions, and a large family of rare offshore orcas. Bluewater's Zodiac and kayaks deposit us onshore to explore forests of giant western red cedar, hemlock, and Sitka spruce, the ground carpeted with bright green moss and fern. We walk among the ruins of an old whaling station in Rose Harbour and pick up Japanese garbage on Kunghit Island, blown in with the raging storms of the Pacific. In Echo Harbour, we watch schools of salmon launch themselves from the sea into the creek and a huge black bear (Haida Gwaii boasts the biggest black bears found anywhere) lick its lips in anticipation. We do the same on the

yacht, with chef Deborah serving up fresh coconut-crusted halibut and other delights from her small but fully equipped galley.

As an eco-adventure, Gwaii Haanas deserves its reputation as a "Canadian Galapagos." Yet it's the legacy of the Haida themselves that elevates this wild, rugged coastline, a history best illustrated by the remarkable UNESCO World Heritage Site on Anthony Island, now known as SGang Gwaay. Haida lived here for millennia, but after the plague of smallpox, European trade, and residential schools, all that remains, fittingly, are eerie, carved cedar mortuary poles. Facing the sea like sentinels with the thick forest at their backs, they make it an unforgettable and haunting place to visit, and all the more so for the effort it takes to do so. The five Haida village National Historic Sites in Gwaii Haanas — Skedans, Tanu, Windy Bay, Hotspring Island, and SGang Gwaay — are guarded by the Watchmen, local men and women employed by the community and Parks Canada. James Williams has been a Watchman at SGang Gwaay for over a decade, showing visitors around and enthusiastically describing the history of the village and the legacy of the poles. He tells us how the Haida attached supernatural qualities to the animals and trees that surrounded them; hence their culture borne out of tales featuring bears, ravens, eagles, killer whales, otters, and cedar. Unassuming in his baseball cap, James discusses violent battles with mainland tribes, the Haida acumen for trade, canoe building, and their interaction with European sea-otter traders, which ultimately killed off the animal and very nearly finished off the Haida themselves. Today, these weathered ash-grey mortuary poles are maintained to honour a tradition that once thrived and shows signs of thriving again. Tombstones that seem older than their 150-year-old origins, they remind me of the stone heads on Easter Island, the stone carvings of Angkor. Trees rattle in the onshore breeze as the forest slowly reclaims the remains of abandoned cedar longhouses. Isolated for months, James gifts us with some freshly caught halibut as he welcomes some arriving kayakers. With Watchmen having to live in solitude for months at a time, it is not so much a job as a calling.

Each abandoned village is different, and each Watchman reveals more about this rugged West Coast wonderland and the people who call it home. By the end of the week, both the land and its stewards have woven a spell over us. Designed to last the length of a single lifetime, old Haida totem poles will not last forever. Fortunately, the protection of Gwaii Haanas, by both the Haida people and Parks Canada, along with the deep respect paid to both by operators like Randy Burke's Bluewater Adventures, ensures this magical archipelago will remain on the Canadian bucket list for generations to come.

START HERE: canadianbucketlist.com/haida

HIKE THE WEST COAST TRAIL

I'm overjoyed I experienced the West Coast Trail, but happier still that one of the world's great hikes didn't kill me. Hikers come from all over the world to challenge themselves on this rugged 77-kilometre trail. Shortly after I left the trailhead, I was convinced every one of them must be insane. Case in point: the few wild animals you might encounter are those most likely to eat you — bears, wolves, and cougars. The path is treacherous, the weather notorious, and every year about 100 hikers are evacuated with injuries. Born out of a life-saving trail created alongside the Graveyard of the Pacific, where more than 1,000 ships have run aground, the West Coast Trail is nonetheless a true Canadian challenge, in all its hurt and glory.

Snaking up the Pacific Rim National Park from Bamfield to Port Renfrew, you're far removed from roads, stores, or civilization. That's

Tips for the Trail

Rub Vaseline on your feet every morning to avoid blisters.
Pack more hot chocolate.
Bring tea bags.
Bring wraps to make meals go further.
Plastic bowls work better than plastic plates.
A walking stick and gaiters are essential.
Bring fire gloves for the campfire.
Instant mash and rice works great as a meal.
Don't bother with towels, a sarong will do.
Bring knee or ankle guards if you think you might need them.
Fruit bars are worth their weight in gold.
A small bottle of hot sauce goes a long way.
Bring an extra battery for your digital camera.
If weather permits, take a day off and relax.
Do your research.
Speak to other hikers as you go for more info. ➤

why park rangers patrol in helicopters and boats looking for wounded hikers suffering from sprains, slips, and hypothermia. Given that 15 centimetres of rain can fall in just 12 hours, the well-marked trail can quickly become a quagmire of thick mud, sharp rocks, and slippery boardwalks. So why would anyone actually add this to their bucket list? To find out, I joined a group of seven hikers, allocating our supplies according to our body weights. All our trash would have to be burned or carried out, while lunch would consist only of GORP (granola-oatmeal-raisin-peanut) and energy bars. Within the first exhausting hour, evacuation didn't seem like such a bad idea. The rain was holding off, but the path was streaked with roots and knee-deep mud pools. Then came the wooden ladders, some of which climb as high as 25 metres.

With my knees creaking under the weight of my 25-kilogram back-pack, I stumble into camp seven hours later, collapsing in a heap.

"The nice thing about hurting your ankle is you forget how much your back and feet hurt," says my friend Andrew, who is dealing with a sprained ankle and receiving absolutely no sympathy. Each man's pain is his own. The key to success, according to Kyle, our veteran hiker, is preparation. We have all the essentials: walking sticks, gaiters, camel packs, dehydrated food, good tents, a water pump. "Inexperienced hikers are usually the first to go," a park ranger tells me. "This is not the trail to break in new boots."

We build our campfires beside driftwood benches and bathe in freezing streams. All food is locked in communal bear lockers over-night, and one morning we awake to find fresh wolf prints next to the tent, just in case we thought we were alone. Halfway into the week-long hike, my pack begins to lighten and my muscles harden. I stop kvetching long enough to admire the massive Douglas fir trees, sea arches, limestone cliffs, waterfalls, sandy beaches, and crystal tidal pools bristling with luminous purple starfish and green anemones. The camaraderie with fellow hikers from around the world, met along the way or in camp, tops up this natural inspiration. Sharing tips on what to expect up ahead, we're all pushing our mental and physical limits. Each day we hike between 11 and 17 kilometres of challenging terrain.

At the end of the week, food consumed and camera batteries low, I trudge along the final 12 kilometres to the end, grateful for the extra-strength painkillers. Our group is haggard, dirty, sore — and utterly elated. "Few finish this adventure pain-free," reads a popular hiking website.

Why is the West Coast Trail on the bucket list? For the challenge, the beauty, the communal spirit, and the opportunity to say, "Yes, I did it, and it didn't kill me!"

START HERE: canadianbucketlist.com/wct

DIVE A SUNKEN BATTLESHIP

With the press of a button, I descend into the cold, dark murk of the Pacific. It's a far cry from the warm, turquoise waters of Papua New Guinea, where I learned to scuba dive among hundreds of tropical fish. Yet the waters off the coast of Vancouver Island are renowned for offering some of the best diving on the planet, with no less an authority than the late Jacques Cousteau rating B.C. as the second-best temperate dive spot in the world, behind the Red Sea.

To see if he was right, if emerald oceans can compete with sapphire seas, I will have to adapt. In these cold waters, dry suits are

a necessity, as they allow you to remain dry in an airtight bubble, which adjusts with descent and ascent through air valves. This kind of diving also requires extra training, which is why I call on Greg McCracken, one of B.C.'s top instructors, to introduce me to the submersed wonders of Canada.

What makes the diving so special in B.C. is how big everything is. Orange sunflower starfish the size of dinner tables, forests of bright white plumose anemones, giant octopus, wolf eels, and big-eyed cabezons. Forget the tropics; divers in B.C. immerse themselves in the clear, clean waters of another planet — and you can keep your jeans on. Greg picked out one of the most spectacular dives on offer: the sunken destroyer HMCS *Saskatchewan*, sitting upright on the ocean floor not far from the ferry port of Vancouver Island's Departure Bay. The Artificial Reef Society of B.C. is a world leader in the art of creating environmentally protective reefs, having sunk six ships and one Boeing 737 in B.C. waters. Such reefs attract indigenous marine life, creating a sustainable and attractive destination for scuba divers.

It's a crisp early morning when Sea Dragon Charters' dive boat anchors to a buoy alongside a slither of rock and sand called Snake Island, home to 250 harbour seals. Two huge bald eagles soar above us. We suit up, bulked by our layers, resembling alien superheroes attached to all manner of pipes and tanks. Even though the water is a

British Columbia's Top Dives

Greg and Deirdre McCracken, two of the province's most respected divers and owners of B.C.'s Ocean Quest Diving Centre, list their Top 10.

1. Browning Wall (boat dive) – Port Hardy
2. Skookumchuck Rapids (boat dive) – Egmont
3. Steep Island (boat dive) – Campbell River
4. Renate Reef (boat dive) – Barkley Sound
5. Dodd Narrows (boat dive) – Nanaimo
6. Race Rocks (boat dive) – Victoria
7. HMCS *Saskatchewan* (boat dive) – Nanaimo
8. Wreck of the *Capilano* (boat dive) – Comox
9. Whytecliff Park (shore dive) – Vancouver
10. Ogden Point (shore dive) – Victoria

brisk 7°C, I'm surprised at how insulated and comfortable dry suits can be. After descending 20 metres, we see the first anemones, rocking in the breeze of the ocean currents. A huge lingcod is perfectly camouflaged against the reef. I soon realize the reef is, in fact, metal, part of the 111-metre-long Mackenzie-class destroyer. Our flippers propel us forward, and I see the old cannons, now exploding with marine life. There are huge spiky copper rockfish, purple California sea cucumbers, assorted sculpins, and thousands of dancing brittlestars. Two hundred and thirty officers once lived aboard this ship. Since it was sunk in 1997, local marine life has gladly taken the officers' place.

We swim through the control deck, descending to 29 metres before making our way back to the midship buoy, keeping an eye on our air supply. After making the required safety stops to avoid decompression sickness, we climb on board the boat elated. "The size and abundance of marine life in B.C. really sets it apart," explains Greg over hot chocolate. "You experience things underwater here that you just can't experience anywhere else."

Just a few hundred feet away from the battleship is another artificial wreck, the world's second-largest upright reef and one of B.C.'s most popular diving locations. The HMCS *Cape Breton* is a 134-metre-long Second World War Victory ship, built for action in 1944 but converted into an escort and maintenance ship soon after. After languishing for decades, she was cleaned up and sunk upright onto a flat seabed off Snake Island in 2001. Once again we suit up, check our air pressure, add weights to our belts. The *Cape Breton* is a massive wreck to explore and cannot be done in one dive. You feel like a budgie exploring a double-decker bus. Greg hand signals to a long corridor, and I follow him through it, peering with my flashlight into various rooms, noticing the fish, plants, and sponges that have moved in. We hover over the engine room skylights, but as much as I'd like to explore the playground below, Greg warned me that this area is only for technical, well-trained divers. When you're 30 metres below the surface connected to life by an oxygen tank, it's best not to argue.

A half-hour later, we ascend once more to the warm tea and smiles of the Sea Dragon crew. They're used to huge smiles lighting up the faces of divers emerging from the depths of British Columbia.

Note: Diving should only be attempted with the proper training, available across the country. If you have chronic ear problems, as I do, look into a product called Docs Pro-Plugs. These handy vented plugs are worth their weight in underwater treasure.

START HERE: canadianbucketlist.com/scuba

SURF IN TOFINO

Canada may be a cold northern country, but Canadians can still live for the surf, philosophize about the rhythm of the ocean, and call each other "dude." Tofino is not Malibu or Haleiwa, but then, Vancouver Island is not California or Hawaii. This laid-back surf town demands a commitment to the waves, not sun-bleached hair and bikinis. When you surf in a full-body wetsuit, pretentiousness dissipates.

The town sits on the wild west coast of Vancouver Island, battered by volatile weather that washes up debris along its long sandy beaches, shredding trees in the surrounding Pacific Rim National

Surf's Up

After renting your gear and taking a lesson with one of Tofino's six surf schools, head to one of these popular surf spots:

Cox Bay: One and a half kilometres long, facing west, the most consistent break in the area and probably the most popular surf destination in the country.

Florencia Bay: Five kilometres long, facing mostly south, one of the quieter beaches, with a steep shoreline offering protection from cold westerly winds.

Chesterman Beach: Popular beach with locals and families, with forgiving swells that make it one of the best beginner breaks on the continent.

Wickaninnish Beach: Located at the south end of the 16-kilometre (and aptly named) Long Beach, it faces west and has an epic coastline. ➤

Park. Storm watching is a popular pastime in the spring and fall, best enjoyed from the large picture windows of the Wickaninnish Inn, one of the finest hotels in the country. Tofino offers whale watching, hot springs, artisans, and hikes in old-growth forest, and for Canadians embracing surf culture, there's no better place to be. Although the climate can be extreme, the surf community is unusually friendly. The beach break is kind to beginners, and one of the most popular local surf schools is called Surf Sisters. Visitors from southern surf towns enjoy the fact that territorial testosterone is kept to a minimum.

Insulated from head to toe, I enter the 10°C water. Although waves can reach up to 10 metres, today is a gentle introduction to the art of riding them. Just several metres into the waters of Cox Bay, I sit on board and admire the unkempt beach cradled by a wind-battered forest. There are no bars, clothing stores, or hard bodies glistening in the sun. Instead of birds in bikinis, a bald eagle soars overhead.

It's my first time on a surfboard, and while the waves may be timid, I still spend the afternoon wiping out, falling off my long board with the grace of a flying ostrich. When I do stand up, for just a moment, the heavens sing hallelujah and an eagle swoops by to give me a congratulatory wink. Maybe I've swallowed too much of the Pacific and I'm not thinking straight. What does it matter? Without the attitude and pushiness, sans the ego and tan lines, surfing the wilderness of Vancouver Island keeps your soul warm just as surely as a wetsuit. Even if you don't manage to get up.

START HERE: canadianbucketlist.com/tofino

ON THE OTHER COAST

Surf the cold, wild Atlantic off the 1.5-kilometre-long Lawrencetown Beach, located about a half hour's drive from Halifax. Legendary local surfer Lesley Choyce tells me sea-ice often freezes to the face, and it's definitely not a place to learn in winter. But Lawrencetown is a friendly community, dedicated to the Atlantic and the waves that peel off in perfection on magic, glassy-clear days. Surfers also congregate at Martinique Beach, and further north near Cape Breton at Ingonish Beach. ➤

TRACK THE SPIRIT BEAR

Pacific Northwest Airlines' amphibious Grumman Goose splashes down, and clearly the Great Bear Rainforest is in good spirits. Absent on this fine mid-September afternoon is the notorious West Coast weather, replaced by a beaming sun striking the Pacific Ocean like a spotlight on a mirror ball. What's more, the familiar face I'd seen at the Vancouver airport's south terminal is coming along for the ride, a man who passionately knows this area, and its conservation, better than most: David Suzuki, Canada's most respected environmentalist.

ON THE BUCKET LIST: Wade Davis

Todagin Mountain is a wildlife sanctuary in the sky that anchors the nine headwater lakes of the Iskut River, main tributary of the Stikine. Todagin is home to the largest concentration of Stone sheep in the world. Because the herd is resident in all seasons, the mountain is also home to an astonishing number of predators: grizzly and wolf, black bear and wolverine. So rich are the wildlife values that hunting by rifle has been forbidden for decades. Unfortunately, open-pit copper and gold mining on the very flank of the mountain threatens to bury pristine lakes in toxic tailings. See Todagin while you still can, and if enough Canadians do, perhaps we might still stop this egregious violation of the Tahltan homeland.

Wade Davis

Author, Explorer in Residence

National Geographic Society

Guests are arriving from around the world to explore this unspoiled temperate rainforest, stretching 70,000 square kilometres from northern British Columbia to the Alaska border. Within its boundaries are hundreds of islands, dozens of First Nations communities, vast amounts of wildlife, and one peculiar animal that has long captured the public imagination — a bear with a coat as white as snow that roams the forest creeks like a mist in search of substance. A bear so rare that fewer than 1,000 are said to exist, and with a spirit so powerful it has never been hunted or trapped. This rare kermode bear, commonly known as the spirit bear, has a recessive gene that gives this subspecies its distinctive white coat. Not an albino, not a different species, just a family of black rainforest bears that pass on a trait that gives them a distinct appearance, like a tribe of redheads living in the Amazon. We settle into our fishing lodge, pampered by staff, enjoying outstanding cuisine, gorgeous views, and cozy wooden surroundings. Some of us have arrived with the hopes of hooking giant halibut or hiking into the mountains among the old-growth trees. Others are here to see the hundreds of hump

back, orca, and fin whales that feed in the rich sea channels. We can also visit the Gitga'at, the closest First Nations community, to meet elders and learn about their fascinating culture in Hartley Bay. Or pop over to a unique, isolated whale research station to hear eerie hydro-phonic songs of local migratory whales. But a different mammal is the star attraction at this time of year. Each September, when millions of salmon begin their final journey up the very creeks in which they were born, the great bears that give the region its name come out to feast. It's an hour-long boat ride along the tidal zone of Princess Royal, crossing the whitecaps on the channel that separates it from our destination: Gribbell Island. Docking against the rocks, we are greeted by a man who has lived and worked with the spirit bears his entire life. Marven Robinson is the go-to guy for the kermode, the man who introduces film crews, tourists, and journalists to this magical animal. Marven personally constructed wooden platforms along Riordan Creek in places that least disturb the bears but still allow visitors to observe them in their natural habitat. "I'm here to protect the bears," he says, "not the people."

Supplied with sandwiches and hot soup, we begin the wait. Marven talks about his passion for protecting the bears and how hunting black bears with recessive genes is a major threat to the kermode. David Suzuki tells me about the fight to save the region from becoming an oil supertanker highway, and how, despite huge financial incentives, the First Nations have joined conservationists to say enough is enough: protecting the Great Bear's natural resources is more important than a short-term paycheque. All this happens in jarringly beautiful surroundings, reminding me of those idyllic photo wallpapers so popular back in the 1970s, the kind that depicted the tranquil forest of your dreams. Below us, hundreds of pink salmon are spawning, squirming against one another, darting upstream. It's the abundance of this food source that Marven knows will draw the bears, eventually. In the meantime, we talk *sotto voce*, swatting the bugs away from our faces. Finally, I feel a ripple of excitement. A large black bear is making its way downstream. It stops, swipes a mouthful of salmon from a pool, and tears it to pieces. Slowly, the bear ambles along the river, stopping right beneath our platform, oblivious to our quiet presence. Privileged to be a guest at a spectacle that takes place all over the coast, I hear the sound of memory cards filling up, and then an excited whisper: "There it is!" A large kermode male, all 135 kilos of him, six years old by Marven's reckoning, is following in the footsteps of the black bear. Ethereal, pink-nosed, with cream-white fur at odds with the earthy tones of its surroundings, the kermode chases salmon in the pools, spraying drops of water that reflect the early afternoon sunlight. Suddenly, the black bear charges aggressively, sending the kermode into the mossy bank adjacent to our platform. Unperturbed, it re-enters a few metres downstream and continues its hunt for, as I'm told, as many as 80 fish a day. Finally, both bears wander off, leaving us spellbound by our good fortune. There's no guarantee you'll see the spirit bear on any given day, and more than once on my Canadian journey, I've found myself facing the wrong end of the barrel of fortune. But not today.

Welcome to New Caledonia

I once visited a friend on a little slice of France located 16,000 kilometres east of Europe, in the South Pacific. Governed from Paris, New Caledonia has tropical beaches, strong cheese, great wine, and locals who can't quite believe their luck at having been born in such a place. It could have been ours … the name anyway.

Simon Fraser originally wanted to call the new British Crown colony on the Pacific coast "New Caledonia," since the mountains reminded him of the Scottish Highlands. Alas, Queen Victoria nipped that idea in the bud, as Captain James Cook had already claimed his New Caledonia in the South Pacific. ➤

The First Nations have always protected the spirit bear, believing it has a powerful effect on all who are lucky enough to see it. My encounter left me inspired by the power of true wilderness, along with all the creatures that inhabit it, protect it, and nurture its future. Creatures like the Gitga'at, Marven Robinson, David Suzuki, and our local guide George's granny (with her "sixty-five-plus grandkids"!). Creatures like the kermode, which radiates magic, bring it all together.

START HERE: canadianbucketlist.com/spiritbear

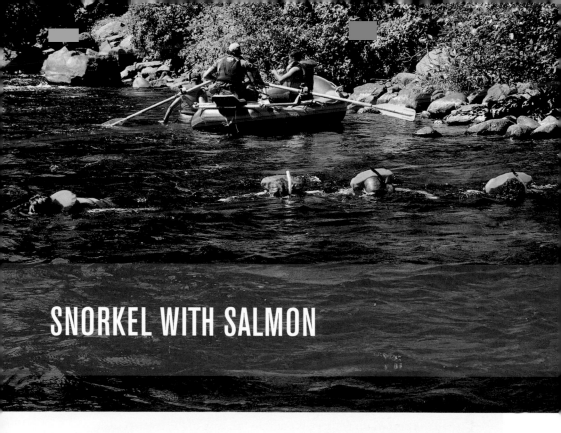

SNORKEL WITH SALMON

Next time you order sushi, spare a thought for the miracle of Canada's Pacific salmon. Half a billion of them, returning from a 5,000-kilometre journey in the open ocean, ready to spawn in the very gravel, in the very river, where they themselves once hatched. In the process, they must survive a who's who of salmon addicts — seals, sharks, eagles, sea lions, bears — and, of course, humans. Leaping from pond to pond, battling predators, starvation, suffocation, overcrowding, and fierce interspecies competition, their backs hump, their noses hook, and their skin turns red as finally they are ready to mate. Having accomplished this extraordinary feat of derring-do, they promptly die.

Why these kamikaze pilots are drawn to the rivers of British Columbia is still something of a mystery (Atlantic salmon don't die after mating), but it certainly has something to do with B.C.'s

abundance of fresh water, filtered by its wealth of temperate rainforest. As the spent bodies of salmon wash downstream, they continue to feed up to 200 species in the forest. Some 80 percent of the nitrogen found in forest soil can be traced to salmon, nitrogen vital for hemlock, spruce, and cedar to grow.

Delicious as they may be (smoked, barbecued, fried, or grilled), there simply wouldn't be a B.C. without its annual salmon run. A salmon run you can witness first-hand, underwater, each year with Destiny River Adventures in Campbell River. Suiting up in full-body wetsuits for a two-hour journey downstream, Jamie Turko and his crew transport us on whitewater rafts to the base of the river. A hydroelectric project regulates the Campbell River's water supply, making it a particularly safe river in which to do what we're about to do. Which is this: hop in the water with masks and snorkels, point our arms downriver, float with the current, and immerse ourselves in this little-seen world of salmon — hundreds of thousands of them.

Jamie, who has run salmon snorkelling tours for over two decades, explains the differences between the five species: the mighty chinook, the chum, the sockeye, coho, and pink. We'll mostly be seeing pink salmon today, interspersed with giant chinooks, along with opportunist rainbow and steelhead trout (yet another predator for nature's ultimate survivors). This enormous bounty of fish means we won't be alone. Locals line the banks with their rods, catching their seasonal quota, or catch-and-releasing in hopes of hooking a

Acquiring the Taste of Salmon

Packed with protein, omega-3 fatty acids, vitamins, and minerals, salmon is considered to be extremely healthy. Salmon is cited as being beneficial for everything from arthritis and dry skin to heart disease and Alzheimer's. But when it comes to cooking, the five species of Pacific salmon are not created equal. Ask any local and they'll tell you: the firm, pink, and oily sockeye swims way ahead of the pack. ➤

true beast (a 32-kilogram chinook was caught in the area). Locals watch us with a mix of curiosity and envy, for once we enter the brisk current of the river, we can see exactly where the fish are. And boy, they are everywhere.

Wetsuits suitably disarm the 10°C water as we enter the river. From above, I had seen streaks of grey darting in the green-brown water. Underwater, there are salmon everywhere — walls of them, floors of them, cities and towns and planets of them. Despite the obstacles that began the moment they were born, in just one corner, I see enough survivors to assuage a feeling of guilt. Certain stocks are threatened, and the debate over farmed salmon versus wild rages on, but today there seems to be a fish for every Tom, Dick, and hungry Harry.

We raft over some gentle rapids and enter another section of the river, where the current carries us into more schools with a feeling that is part buoyancy, part flying. For a moment, I feel like a fish myself, nervously watching for rocks, large predators, and deceptive bait. Most of all, though, I'm just having fun, in awe of a fish that deserves credit for shaping the environment of the West Coast; a fish that, against all the odds, finds itself on the Great Canadian Bucket List.

START HERE: canadianbucketlist.com/salmon

BRITISH COLUMBIA ↑

25

SURVIVE A COLD SAUNA

You, too, can enjoy the health benefits of freezing to death. And benefits there must be; otherwise, guests wouldn't pay for what they're paying for at Sparkling Hill, a pretty, Austrian-style resort located near the interior town of Vernon. Owned by the Swarovski family and adorned with $10 million worth of their crystals, Sparkling Hill has an ambience that is distinctly Old World luxury, even with the crystal fireplaces, stunning pools, and themed steam rooms in the award-winning KurSpa. I'm wooing my wife with these facts in the four seconds it takes before her panic attack sets in. To be fair, we are half naked in a small room with the temperature a frosty -60°C. Sorry, that's the second room; her real panic attack hit in the third room, at -110. Hey, she's Brazilian; they freeze to death quicker than the rest of us.

A visit to North America's first cold sauna provides a treatment in something called cryotherapy, which activates biochemical, hormonal, and immune processes to give your circulatory and nervous systems a healthy kick-start. Sports stars apparently swear by it, whereas I was just swearing, deeply, under my breath, while my

eyelashes froze and my nasal passages turned to ice. Strictly monitored, my wife and I are told to wear bathing suits, supplemented with gloves and slippers. In order to prevent any humidity, we enter the cold sauna through three separate rooms: the first a balmy -15°C, the second -60°C, and the final corker -110°C. Here we must walk in small circles for three minutes, encouraged by a bundled-up spa worker. Ever jump into a freezing-cold lake? Multiply the shock by 10, and go ahead and punch yourself in the neck for good measure. My wife freaks out, and the spa worker quickly ushers her out to safety.

How We Freeze to Death

As soon as your body gets cold, blood moves away from your skin and extremities to protect your core. Shivering is a mechanism to generate warmth, and it gets intense once your core temperature begins to sink. Welcome to hypothermia.

The good news is that hypothermia is typically associated with moisture (our bodies lose heat about 25 times faster in water than in air), which is why the cold sauna is so well insulated, air-current free, and perfectly dry. When the body temperature drops from its normal 37°C, horrible things start to happen. Lose five degrees and you'll lose consciousness. Once you hit 21°C, your lights might go out permanently.

Inside Sparkling Hill's cold sauna, sticking around longer than the prescribed and therapist-monitored three minutes is a bad idea. Just two to three minutes in, your body surface temperature plummets to −2°C, but your core remains comfortable. Once your time is up, relief, warmth, and comfort are just steps away. ➤

Meanwhile, I continue walking with three elderly ladies in a tight circle, all of us trying not to touch each other in case we fuse. Bob Marley is blasting from in-sauna speakers, "stirring it up," as it were, with images of frozen corpses washing up on the beach. As I twitch with cold, nipples ready to break off, my testicles having retreated deep into my pancreas, the three minutes come to an end and we rush out of the chamber. Time may fly when you're having fun, but when you're freezing to death, a single Bob Marley song can sound like a James Joyce reading. Here's the best part: once you exit the cold sauna, you are not allowed to hop in a hot tub or steam room. I assume it's because the rush of blood would explode your head like a champagne cork. Rather, we are told to rest in our robes and drink a warm cup of tea.

While you need multiple treatments (sold in blocks of 10) for the cryotherapy to be effective — flash-freezing muscle inflammation, improving joint and muscle function, and relieving skin irritation — one visit was perfectly adequate for my purposes. My wife did (eventually) forgive me, and once again, I learned that what doesn't kill you only makes you appreciate the bizarre things people pay good money for.

START HERE: canadianbucketlist.com/coldsauna

EXPLORE AN OLD-GROWTH FOREST

These days, it's hard to impress kids who have grown up on PlayStation, music videos, and TV cocktails spiked with attention deficit disorder. Show them a great mountain, a sweeping beach, a lush forest, and chances are they'll be glued to their text messages on the smartphone you regretted the minute you bought it for them. Fortunately, Mother Nature still has some tricks up her foliage when it comes to impressing children, and it's doubtful cell coverage will interfere at all. Yes, they're just trees, kids. But look at the size of them!

The giant red cedars, Douglas firs, hemlocks, and spruce trees that survive in the old-growth forests of British Columbia are truly impressive. Somehow, these trees have survived the colonial building

BRITISH COLUMBIA

29

Canada's Biggest Trees

According to the Ancient Forest Alliance, the town of Port Renfrew is the go-to place if you're looking for the biggest trees in Canada. Near this Vancouver Island town, you can find the planet's biggest Douglas fir, two record-sized spruce trees, the country's finest red cedar stand in the endangered Central Walbran Valley, as well as Canada's biggest tree, the Cheewhat Giant (a red cedar). Located within the Pacific Rim National Park Reserve, the Cheewhat is 56 metres high, six metres in trunk diameter, and has enough timber volume to create 450 regular telephone poles' worth of wood. ➤

boom and the modern logging industry, and now range in age from 250 to more than 1,000 years old. "This tree was here before Marco Polo explored China, before Shakespeare ... *em*, before Harry Potter!"

Fantasy is an apt means to capture a kid's imagination, because standing between 800-year-old Douglas fir trees — some towering up to 75 metres in Cathedral Grove in Vancouver Island's MacMillan Provincial Park — you can't help but feel you're on another planet. The forest moon of Endor comes to mind, although I'm dating myself with *The Return of the Jedi*. Perhaps the kids will prefer Avatar Grove, 15 minutes away from Port Renfrew, so named for this ancient red cedar and Douglas fir forest's resemblance to the planet Pandora in the blockbuster *Avatar*. Surrounded by a drapery of fern and moss, with a soundtrack of chattering woodpeckers or babbling brooks, a spell of peace and space envelops adults, as well. When the kids get tired of trying to hug a trunk that can accommodate the linked hands of eight people, bedazzle them with a contorted red cedar known as "Canada's Gnarliest Tree." Keeping with the theme, it looks remarkably like Jabba the Hut.

According to the Ancient Forest Alliance, a B.C. organization working to protect these natural wonders (and to support sustainable forestry practices), less than 25 percent of the old-growth forest on Vancouver Island still exists, and only 10 percent of the biggest trees that you might find on a valley bottom. Some studies have shown that conserving old-growth trees might be more economically viable than slicing them down for furniture. A successful campaign by the (Rebel?) Alliance resulted in provincial protection for Avatar Grove, but the few remaining stands in the province are still threatened with clear-cutting. The emotional and childlike wonder that accompanies hiking an old-growth forest certainly belongs on our bucket list. Unfortunately, we have to add the caveat "while they still exist."

START HERE: canadianbucketlist.com/oldgrowth

GO HELI-SKIING

Welcome to a place where a person's worth is measured in vertical feet. It is surrounded by mountains, waist-high powder, and the *whomp-whomp* sound of a helicopter. Heli-skiing has been on my bucket list ever since I discovered how much fun it is to strap on a plank of polyethylene and launch oneself off a mountain. Having gone through the meat grinder of learning to snowboard, the idea of being dropped off at the top of the world to float over virgin snow seems a just reward. Thus I found myself at the Canadian Mountain Holiday's K2 Rotor Lodge in Nakusp, among a group of Americans on a mancation, folks proudly addicted to the "other" white powder. How else to explain the guy celebrating his six-millionth vertical foot with CMH? Or the sole Canadian who has visited every one of CMH's 11 heli-skiing lodges? Using a helicopter as a makeshift ski chair doesn't come cheap, with trips costing north of $6,000. "My wife goes on cruises, I go to the mountains," explains Mike. One guy has flown in from London, England, for four days of powder. That's if the weather plays ball.

Tips for Heli-Skiing

The more fit you are, the more fun you will have.

- Start training as early as possible, focusing on cardio and muscle strength.
- Make sure your boots are worn in and comfy. This is not the place to break in a new pair. And make sure you pack them in your carry-on luggage, just in case.
- Canadian Mountain Holiday veterans sing the praises of yoga classes as having increased core strength and flexibility, improving their skiing.
- Drink water on every heli-run. Keep those muscles hydrated and prevent fatigue.
- The free stretch classes before breakfast are gold. Warm up and iron out the stiffness before each day begins.
- Book off enough time to get used to the powder and physical demands, so you can truly enjoy the magic heli-skiing delivers. ➤

It's late February, and the avalanche risk is high. The snow is plentiful, but conditions mean "we only have an area about eight times the size of Whistler available to us, as opposed to 100 times," explains affable mountain guide Rob.

We watch a safety video, which pretty much explains all the ways heli-skiing can kill you: avalanches, tree wells, decapitation by skis. We practise avalanche drills and rescue, get fitted with receivers, radios, and shovels, and finally head to the Bell chopper we will come to know so well. I see grown adults behave like little kids, clapping their hands with glee. Wind, visibility, and terrain dictate where the helicopter can land, but it appears to be able to settle gently on pretty well anything. We exit, the chopper taking off right over our heads, and the Selkirk Mountains surround us in blue-sky mountain glory.

I strap in, barely containing my excitement, and proceed to have the worst run of my life. Powder, I discover, is not a groomed ski hill. Heli-skiing and snowboarding require new techniques, new muscles and instincts. My group of heli-veterans patiently pull me out of tree wells, traverses, and snow burials. Every muscle is burning as I battle my physical demons, determined to master the challenge. This is why you don't go heli-skiing for one day. Besides bad weather that can ground you for days, you need several days to enjoy the diversity of runs and snow, and to progress in your ability. We ski runs called Drambuie and Cognac, In Too Deep, Lobster Claw, and, my favourite, Little Leary. I had expected just a few rides in the helicopter, but we average about 10 a day, the pilot somehow landing the copter just a few feet from our heads for the return flight to the top of the mountain. Like the skiing itself, it's a thrill that doesn't get tired. We whoop and bird-call through the forest, making sure nobody is lost, over fresh powder that stretches in every direction.

By day three, I've found my groove. Early morning stretching classes (and fabulous food) at the lodge help the muscle woes, and now I'm carving in deep pow, slaloming pine and hemlock trees. "That was the best run so far," says the guy from England after just about every run. I'm taken with the routine of each day: wake up, stretch, eat, ski, soak in natural hot springs, drink beer, eat dinner, retire early. No wonder these guys keep coming back and work so hard to be able to afford to do so.

Atop a mountain on the final day, crystals glittering in the air as skis click into their bindings, I soak in a post-adrenalin, post-exhaustion, sense-of-achievement high. It's been a once-in-a-lifetime week of sport, companionship, and natural beauty. A highlight on the Great Canadian Bucket List, and my first 50,000 feet of CMH vertical. Strap in, there's still a long way to go.

START HERE: canadianbucketlist.com/heliski

STOP AND SMELL THE ROSES

Receiving around one million visitors each year, Vancouver Island's iconic Butchart Gardens is a National Historic Site and a stunning depiction of flora as art. Set on 55 acres of privately owned land near Victoria, the gardens date back to 1904.

Having exhausted a limestone quarry for the family's successful business, matriarch Jennie Butchart was determined to restore the natural beauty of the area. Anyone who steps into her ivy-coated Sunken Garden can see just how seriously she took the task. Today, more than 50 gardeners maintain the immaculate Butchart Gardens, well-deserving of their world-renowned reputation. Open year round, its flowers and bulbs change with the seasons, blossoming

Top 10 Places to See Flowers in Western Canada

Have a fancy for the floral? Water your passion with these options in western Canada:

1. Butchart Gardens, Victoria, B.C.
2. Vancouver Cherry Blossom Festival, B.C.
3. Tulips of the Valley, Seabird Island, B.C.
4. Waterton Wild Flower Festival, Alberta
5. Manning Provincial Park wildflowers, B.C.
6. Bradner Daffodil Festival, Bradner, B.C.
7. Queen Elizabeth Park, Vancouver, B.C.
8. Prairie Gardens, Edmonton, Alberta
9. Nikka Yuko Japanese Garden, Lethbridge, Alberta
10. Dr. Sun Yat-Sen Classical Chinese Garden, Vancouver, B.C.

by the thousands in spring, glowing in summer, radiating red and gold in the fall. Most visitors spend about 90 minutes exploring the various gardens, but if you're not in a rush, take a blanket with you and stop to relax in the sunshine, surrounded by dancing bees and a riot of colour.

START HERE: canadianbucketlist.com/butchartgardens

POWDER DOWN IN WHISTLER

When it comes to North America's largest and most highly rated ski resort, one word comes to mind: epic. Epic terrain, Epic snow. Between Whistler and the adjacent mountain, Blackcomb, you've got 8,100 acres of skiable terrain linked by the world's longest and highest lift system, the 4.4-kilometre-long Peak 2 Peak. That's over 50 percent more terrain than any other ski resort on the continent, and the reason you'll find long lineups with visitors from around the world.

To ensure the first line of the day will be mine, I pick up a Fresh Tracks ticket, which offers a breakfast buffet and early loading privileges

Canada's Top 10 Ski Resorts

Scott Birke, editor of Snowboard Canada Magazine, *drops in the ultimate Canadian ski and snowboard destinations.*

1. **Whistler Blackcomb, B.C.:** For its two massive mountains with over 200 runs, world-class terrain parks, and some of the best slackcountry in the world.
2. **Red Mountain, B.C.:** Since you can drop in anywhere 360° from the top, and as long as you don't go below the mid-mountain cat track, you're good to go.
3. **Whitewater, B.C.:** The trees over on Glory Ridge are so perfectly spaced and free of people that you'd think you're out of bounds.
4. **Fernie, B.C.:** Big bowls, tons of gullies to slash, and lots of snow? No-brainer here.
5. **Lake Louise, Alberta:** For some of the most majestic views ever and its great expansive terrain.
6. **Le Massif, Quebec:** For its super-snowy microclimate, steep West Coast–like terrain, and killer views of the St. Lawrence near its widest point.
7. **Kicking Horse, B.C.:** Sixty percent of its runs are rated black and double-black. 'Nuff said.
8. **Revelstoke Mountain Resort, B.C.:** At 5,620 feet of vertical, it's the highest drop in Canada. Oh, and it gets tons of snow.
9. **Marble Mountain, Newfoundland:** It's a gem on the East Coast with enough great runs and charm to make the west of the country jealous.
10. **Mont-Tremblant, Quebec:** Party. Where else do people dance on tables in bars and not get thrown out by the help … ➤

at the top of the mountain. I've still got egg in my mouth when I hear "The runs are open!" This initiates a school bell–like atmosphere as everyone grabs their gear and races off to Emerald Express.

Having only discovered snowboarding in my late twenties, I still get a kick taking lift rides surrounded by shark-fin alpine peaks. Among the kids are adults with permission to behave like children,

whooping at the top of the world and then bulleting down the mountain on planks of carbon fibre. I'm not one for throwing myself into the challenging double-diamond bowls, although there's plenty of that to go around. Rather, I choose to glide down the blues, in seventh heaven on my favourite runs: Harmony Ridge, Peak to Creek, the Saddle, and Spanky's. Riding the impressive Peak 2 Peak Gondola can be unnerving, especially in the glass-bottom carriage. But the reward is worth it. Blackcomb offers heaps of snow, with accurately named runs like Jersey Cream and, yes, Seventh Heaven.

The entire experience has a tendency to make other resorts pale in comparison. No wonder so many visitors return year after year, or simply pack up and move here for good. Factor in the nightlife, festivals, world-class restaurants — Barefoot Bistro's nitro ice cream is something to experience on its own, as is their $1.4-million wine cellar — along with endless backcountry Nordic trails and thrills like bobsleigh at the Whistler Sliding Centre, and it's always a powder day for Whistler on the Great Canadian Bucket List.

START HERE: canadianbucketlist.com/whistler

FLY LIKE A SUPERHERO

Ziplining typically takes place through forest or canopy and is safe enough for your grandmother (if she hasn't tried it already). Superfly, located just an eight-minute drive from Whistler Village, elevates the thrills. With some of Canada's longest ziplines, Superfly lets you fly backcountry-style between the soaring peaks of Cougar and Rainbow Mountain. Even better, all the lines are tandem, so you can share the experience with your partner, parent, or child.

Using a comfortable harness more familiar to hang gliders, hold on to the bar or go hands-free as you clock speeds of more than 100 kilometres per hour. Breaking free of the forest or jungle canopy, the scenery is astounding, the flight unforgettable. Is it a bird? A plane? No, it's just you!

Also in Whistler, North America's longest zipline is Ziptrek Ecotours, "The Sasquatch." Operating in summer only, this "hairy" zipline spans 2.2 kilometres, allowing you to reach speeds in excess of 100 kilometres per hour as you soar across the valley between Blackcomb and Whistler Mountains. Dual lines let you share the moment (albeit one that lasts up to two minutes) with someone special.

START HERE: canadianbucketlist.com/superfly

STROLL THE SEAWALL

"Can you imagine, some people actually live here?"
I overheard that comment from one of the eight million people who visit Vancouver's Stanley Park every year, during my very first stroll along its 8.8-kilometre paved seawall. When the sun is beaming, the park — and the city — has that effect on people. Today, it's the first place I take visitors to Vancouver, the first and most powerful impression I can give them.

One second we're surrounded by apartment buildings in the West End, and the next we're in a tranquil coastal rainforest, with stellar views of the North Shore Mountains. If you look at the view of downtown and Stanley Park from across the Burrard Inlet on Spanish Banks, Stanley Park looks almost exactly the same size as downtown, the perfect balance of nature and city. With a half-million trees, 200 kilometres of trails, and attractions such as Vancouver's

Sea Vancouver

Vancouver joins Cape Town, Sydney, and Rio de Janeiro as one of the world's most beautiful cities. If you don't want to walk around Stanley Park, you can take a hop-on hop-off bus, harbour cruise, float-plane flight, or visit the Vancouver Lookout Tower. If you don't mind being out in the elements, I recommend Sea Vancouver's Zodiac tour. Well-priced, with the fun bonus of bouncing over waves, the 90-minute ride covers Coal Harbour, English Bay, False Creek, and Stanley Park. Weatherproof cruiser suits are provided, but wear layers for the wind. ➤

START HERE: canadianbucketlist.com/seavancouver

world-class aquarium, some of the city's best beaches, manicured gardens, teahouses, Pitch n Putt, and concerts under the stars in Malkin Bowl, there's plenty to do in Stanley Park. This is why it has repeatedly been named the number-one park in the world by Trip Advisor, beating out the likes of Central Park in New York, Golden Gate Park in San Francisco, St. James Park in London, Guell Park in Barcelona, and the Singapore Botanical Gardens. Illustrious company to be sure and something to ponder as you explore it by foot, bike, rollerblade, horse-drawn cart, car, or trolley. In fact, some might argue — under their breath during hockey season — that this is Lord Stanley's greatest legacy. Our bucket list wants you to breathe in the view of the mountains, city, ocean, birds, and people. This can be done in all weather and all seasons, but be warned: on a warm, glorious summer day, it will probably make you want to live here, too.

START HERE: canadianbucketlist.com/stanleypark

CROSS A WILD SUSPENSION BRIDGE

The post read: "13 Breathtaking Places Guaranteed To Make Your Stomach Drop." It's a typical headline you'll see these days in the frenzy of social media, although at least it wasn't accompanied by "It blew my mind" or "#5 made me laugh so hard I peed my pants." Naturally, I clicked on the link, where I found images from truly scary spots in Norway, China, Zimbabwe, and Spain, many of which I'd been to. But it was #10 on the list that stood out for me, for one very simple reason: it's one of the most popular and accessible tourist attractions in Vancouver.

Stretching 137 metres across North Vancouver's Capilano Canyon, the Capilano Suspension Bridge was originally built of hemp rope and cedar planks way back in 1889. Since then, it has been completely reconstructed as the centrepiece of a West Coast outdoor eco-tourist theme park, which includes a treetop platform path built amidst 1,300-year-old Douglas-fir trees, traditional totem

Flyover Canada

Want to fly but afraid of heights? Vancouver's Flyover Canada is a fear-friendly simulation ride that puts you at the centre of a huge screen dome. Safely strapped into your chair, the floor drops away, and soon you're whooshing through the Rockies, over cowboys in the prairies, then the coastal rainforest, and into Niagara Falls. Engaging the rest of your senses, this 4D eight-minute ride allows you to smell the scents and feel the mist and the wind. It's delightfully overwhelming; after all, Canada's beauty is nothing to scoff at. ➤

START HERE: canadianbucketlist.com/flyover

poles, forest hikes, interpretation stations, and a series of cantilevered and suspended walkways constructed against a striking granite cliff.

Still, it's the suspension bridge that has attracted visitors for more than a century, swaying with every step, 70 metres above the Capilano River. Technically, there are longer suspension bridges that are not as high and higher bridges that are not as long. But few bridges are run like this slick tourism operation, with its heavy tour-bus traffic in the summer. Personally, I love the cool, clear nights of winter, when the bridge and treetop walkways are illuminated with Christmas lights, creating an experience that is just magical. Not that it needed the boost, but now that the Capilano Suspension Bridge has gone viral on social media, it's certain to remain on bucket lists for generations to come.

START HERE: canadianbucketlist.com/capilano

TASTE THE OKANAGAN

I'm on an electric-assist bike scooting alongside vineyards, the wind in my hair. It's a honeymoon of sorts, but since my wife and I cannot afford jet-setting to Tuscany, we drove four hours from Vancouver into the B.C. interior for our very own Canadian wine adventure. Certainly, there is nothing in Tuscany that remotely resembles the sparkling 135-kilometre-long Lake Okanagan. Neither do Tuscan wines benefit from the "lake effect" — a cooling of the temperature caused by the lake's deepness. Wines in the Okanagan's Lake County more accurately resemble those produced along the Rhine in Germany. Yet, as in all great wine regions, the caramel-coloured countryside here has the fragrance of a farmers' market. Summers in the Okanagan routinely bake the landscape above 40°C. And while the rest of Canada deals with harsh nine-month winters, Okanagan summers last from April to October. This might explain why the region's largest city,

Wine in B.C.

British Columbia produces over sixty types of varietals, the most popular reds being Merlot, Pinot Noir, and Cabernet Sauvignon, and the most popular whites Pinot Gris, Chardonnay, and Gewürztraminer. The province boasts five wine regions: Okanagan Valley, Similkameen Valley, Fraser Valley, Vancouver Island, and the Gulf Islands. ➤

Kelowna, has become one of the fastest-growing cities in North America, attracting everyone from tech start-ups to celebrity chefs.

Visiting over the years, I've always been surprised by just how beautiful this part of the world is and how good the wine can be. A sommelier at Mission Hill, the region's biggest vineyard, tells me that the enjoyment of wine is all about context: where you are, how you feel, and whom you're with. Years earlier, I romanced a girlfriend in the Okanagan by visiting wineries in the back of an immaculately restored apple-green 1953 Cadillac convertible. It was one of a hundred classic cars owned by Garnet Nixdorf, who offers chauffeured tours to vineyards around Penticton. Talk about context!

There are more than 120 wineries in the Okanagan, many opening their doors for summer tastings, with patio restaurants and artisan stores. Everyone has their favourites: Gray Monk, Burrowing Owl, Summerhill, Cedar Creek, Sumac Ridge, Dirty Laundry, Red Rooster, the rock 'n' rollers at Ex Nihilo. Wine is a taste to be acquired, and the Okanagan provides ample opportunity to do so.

While you're in the area, consider renting a houseboat to float on Lake Okanagan, complete with wet bar and Jacuzzi. On a sweet summer day, lounge on the thick carpet of grass below Mission Hill's watchtower with a chilled glass of white wine. It's balm for the soul. And a lot cheaper than flying to Italy.

START HERE: canadianbucketlist.com/okanagan

SEE THE SOCKEYE RUN

Every year, Pacific sockeye salmon swim up from the ocean into the very rivers and tributaries where they were once hatched. Then they proceed to find a mate, spawn, and die. Millions of them — even more during the dominant run, which takes place every four years.

Given the large numbers, it's worth noting that each female salmon will lay about 4,000 eggs, of which only two will survive to fulfill the promise of this remarkable migration. Once the breeding is complete, the salmon's bright-red spawning colour will fade to grey and, with their strength exhausted, the fish will die and float downriver. You could snorkel with the salmon on Vancouver Island (see page 23), but if you prefer to stay dry, you can still experience this amazing natural phenomenon up close. Each Thanksgiving, as many as 250,000 people visit the Salute the Sockeye Festival on the Adams River, located about a one-hour drive from Kamloops. The crowds are here to see the world's largest return of sockeye salmon to a single river: a migration of people, drawn to the migration of a species that people love to eat.

Highway 5 (a.k.a. the Coquihalla, a.k.a. the Yellowhead Highway) is one of those drives you don't forget in a hurry. The scenery east of Hope is simply staggering (especially in the mountains of Coquihalla Pass and most notably in the fall). With good weather and multiple lanes, it takes me less than four hours to drive from Vancouver to Kamloops, where I immediately stop in at one of my favourite brew pubs in the province, The Noble Pig.

One basket of crispy fried pickles and several more flights of beer later, I feel suitably inspired for a round of foot golf at the Sun Rivers Golf Course. Yes, foot golf is a real thing, as are the muscular bighorn sheep that roam this scenic 18-hole course overlooking the city. Talk about natural hazards: I dribbled past a birdie and saw an eagle, but that's just par for the course.

But I came for the salmon, and to the salmon is where I shall go. So I wake up early the following morning to begin my drive along the Trans-Canada toward Jasper, turning off in the direction of Roderick Haig-Brown Provincial Park. Traffic is already lining the streets, so I keep going until I reach Shuswap Lake Provincial Park, where I meet up with Barb from Shuswap Unique Adventure Tours.

Barb leads off-road Segway tours into both provincial parks, and if you've never zipped around on a Segway, trust me, the best way to do it is among fall foliage, alongside a sparkling lake, and through leafy tree tunnels.

Barb provides me with some invaluable local information for viewing the blood-red salmon in their mating death throes. To see the fish clearly, polarized sunglasses are a must. Also, don't worry; everyone is struggling to take good photos. Having a polarized camera lens helps, or you could join the keeners, some of whom have travelled from as far away as Europe to don expensive wetsuits and underwater cameras. Despite the crowds, it's a lovely stroll along the riverbank, with plenty of space for everyone, and no shortage of salmon to observe.

Sockeye endurance is remarkable, but that doesn't stop me from craving some wild cedar-planked salmon when we return to the city. I feel terrible, but they are delicious, and humans are but one of the 200 species that rely on the annual runs. All in, it is a rather unique natural experience for a sunny fall weekend. Even better if you can visit during the week and avoid the crowded parking lot.

START HERE: canadianbucketlist.com/sockeye

FIND YOUR INNER OUTLAW

I was not born to be wild. Never listened to heavy metal, thunder terrifies me, and any attempt to grow a goatee yields an unkempt weed patch. Although I've got my motorcycle licence, I've only ridden a real bike a couple of times (scooters don't count). Yet cruising a Harley-Davidson on the world's most scenic roads feels right for a bucket list. As my car heaves up the Coquihalla Pass from Vancouver to Kamloops, questions cloud my mind like lines on a paisley bandana. Of all bikes, why am I drawn to the loud, obnoxious one? What do the roads of the B.C. interior offer that others do not? Am I going to kill myself with a growling 1690cc air-cooled, twin-cam engine, with steel laced wheels and less fuel economy than a Fiat 500? Is this an experience that belongs on the Great Canadian Bucket List? Questions, and no shortage of nerves, too.

Few machines inspire emotional attachment like a Harley. In the lobby of the Kamloops Sheraton hotel, a rider shows me the serial number of his first bike, which he has tattooed across his arm. It's the weekend of the annual B.C. Poker Run, which attracts 750 Harley bikers from across the province. I expect to see aggressive bearded gangsters, tattoos, leather, bad teeth, and chains. Yet when I gaze across the Valleyview Arena, where bikers have gathered for a muscular dystrophy fundraising event, I instantly recognize this crowd: bucket listers — people of all shapes, colours, and income brackets, drawn to a dream and the promise of a Harley-Davidson. It's the promise of renegade freedom, delivered with every throttle; the promise that lets imaginary urban outlaws ride into town on powerful steel horses. Wanted … not dead or alive, but back in the office on Monday morning.

Barnes Harley-Davidson rents bikes by the day or week, while the town's tourism board has handily created five road trip itineraries showcasing the back roads and attractions of the B.C. interior. It's an attractive package that demands investigation, even if my previous hog was a tin-can scooter, one I mangled in a bike accident 10 years ago. That accident led directly to my career as a travel writer, so who knows where this bike will take me?

As soon as the sassy rental manager hands me a black leather jacket and lets me pick out my choice of bike, my excitement accelerates. Straddling a Heritage Softail, it's difficult not to buy into Harley's visceral connection to danger. My eyes squint, my beard grows. With my extremely limited bike experience, I expected a raging bull I'd have to throttle under control. Instead, the Softail is simple to operate, stable, and incredibly forgiving. Japanese bikes might have more bells, whistles, and reliability, but Japanese bikes don't inspire delusions of rebellious grandeur. Plus we're in pioneer country, pockmarked with copper mines and ghost towns. The right kinda bike is calling for the right kinda road.

"B.C.'s interior has some of the most curvaceous roads in Canada," explains James Nixon, an editor at *Cycle Canada* magazine. "The East Coast is a close second, but B.C.'s roads are in better condition, and you can't beat the scenery." James has rented a Road King for the week, but is devoted to his BMW back in Toronto. "Harleys want to conquer riders' hearts," he explains, "but it's not always the bike that succeeds, it's the ride itself."

Kamloops is one of Canada's sunniest cities, boasting more parks than any other city in the province. Straddling the Thompson River, it has an average temperature of 27°C all summer, and is surrounded by scenic hills and valleys. It's a perfect launch pad for a road trip, even when an unseasonal storm blows in. I see lightning strike the valley below, which seems appropriate as I blaze out toward the Clearwater Corridor. I notice plenty of bikers on the road, passing each other with a casual wave, the camaraderie signal motorists never see. The highway meanders through rolling countryside, with traffic enjoyably light. Fuelling up before Highway 24, the same route fur traders used centuries ago, I cross into the Cariboo Chilcotin region of British Columbia. Mirror lakes reflect the moody sky, my engine roars in fifth gear, a blustery wind slams against my leather armour. It's only the start of a five-day road trip, but bliss has found me early.

Bikers may look rough, but bucket list bikers shouldn't rough it. I didn't expect to find authentic Italian cuisine at the rustic Lac des

Rochoo Resort, but here it is, al dente. The route turns south onto the twisty twin-lane blacktop of Highway 97, past the impressive Painted Chasm, and on to the towns of Clinton and Ashcroft. I roar alongside the Highland Copper Valley Mine, the largest open-pit copper mine in the country, continuing south toward Merritt and the historic Quilchena Hotel. The Softail is opening up to me, revealing her secrets. She's most comfortable at 90 to 100 kilometres per hour, but even on a steep uphill, she's got plenty to give. And she gives it on Highway 5A, returning through Kamloops on my way to Lytton. If the Icefields Parkway (see page 84) is the world's most beautiful drive, then British Columbia's Highway 5A, together with Highway 33, must be among the most beautiful rides. On the bike, I smell the pine, taste the wind, and see the beauty of British Columbia's interior Salome, slowly peeling off her layers.

It can be difficult to know what we don't experience. What I thought was an outlaw, crime-soaked subculture is actually the domain of the pleasantly normal, give or take a few fermented apples. With my limited experience on a bike, what I expected to be dangerous was perfectly safe, provided I took it easy, employed common sense, and used the right gear. Harleys, I discovered, are much like their riders — seasoned, full of character, and more bark than bite. Kamloops proved an ideal gateway to explore the natural beauty of B.C.'s Thompson Okanagan and Cariboo Chilcotin Coast, and a rented Harley was the ideal vehicle from which to do it. Cars will do just fine, too, as will bicycles and RVs. Whatever revs your engine, this is bucket list country.

START HERE: canadianbucketlist.com/interior

CLIMB A MOUNTAIN WITH NO EXPERIENCE

Here's what we like about mountain climbing: the epic views, the physical challenge, the pristine mountain wilderness. Here's what we don't like about mountain climbing: the danger of slipping, falling, and dying, or worse, having to use a penknife to cut a trapped arm off. Fortunately, there's a place to meet in the middle.

A *via ferrata* (Italian for "iron road") is a secure climbing route that allows you to clip safely into staples hammered into the rock, using your carabiner and harness to get to spots even traditional climbers can appreciate. Originally developed in the Alps to help soldiers scale mountains, *via ferratas* have become increasingly popular in mountainous regions, and British Columbia is no exception. The longest *via ferrata* in North America is CMH Summer Adventures' Mount Nimbus summit, accessible for guests at its helicopter fly-in, Bobby Burns Lodge.

As you scale a sheer rock face along the spine of the mountain, relax knowing that the iron-rung ladders and 60-metre-long rope

More Via for Your Rata

If you're lacking the daring (or more likely budget) to attempt Mount Nimbus, there are other options. Consider the four-hour *via ferrata* adventure to the top of Whistler Mountain, open to everyone over 14 years of age. Banff National Park now has its own 300-metre *via ferrata* above the Cliffhouse Bistro on Mount Norquay. Custom Outdoor Adventures operates a *via ferrata* on the 182-metre rock face between Nordegg and the Icefields Parkway, open to everyone 10 years of age and up. ➤

suspension bridge are designed to take 10 times the amount of weight you're putting on them. Relax knowing you're in the perfectly capable hands of expert guides and high-level gear. Relax knowing … oh, who are we kidding? Just because you're perfectly safe clinging to the rock face 1,000 metres above the ground, doesn't mean you won't be quaking with fear. Still, one step in front of the next, and before you know it, you will be king (or queen) of the world.

Canadian Mountain Holidays, which runs 11 heli-ski lodges in the winter (see page 32), has another *via ferrata* near its Bugaboos Lodge called the Skyladder. Once again, the views are extraordinary, and hey, even your teenage kids can do it.

START HERE: canadianbucketlist.com/mountnimbus

CONQUER THE GRIND, HIKE THE CHIEF

Vancouverites have a special place in their hearts for physical pursuits. These are people obsessed with the outdoors, since it's among the best cities in the country, weather-wise, in which to enjoy it. Despite the "granola with my yoga" reputation, Vancouver also offers more demanding physical challenges. Take the Grouse Grind — "Mother Nature's Stairmaster" — running 853 metres up the side of Grouse Mountain over a distance of exactly 2.9 kilometres.

At some point in your life, you've been physically exhausted — leg muscles burning, sweat stinging your eyes, mind full of blame. Well done, you've just reached the soul-crushing *quarter-way* sign on the Grouse Grind. People weep when they see that sign. For some, the Grind is a walk in the park; and by walk I mean slog, and by park

I mean mountain. In front of and behind you, you'll see others stuck in the same manual elevator from hell, but not to worry, everyone is too polite to panic. What's more, many will be dressed in form-fitting stretchy pants, because the Grouse Grind is not only a natural workout, it's become an unlikely pick-up joint for yuppies hell-bent on maximizing the tone of their glutes.

Among the 100,000 people who undertake the Grind every year, count on seeing at least one of the following during your visit:

- A young parent seriously regretting the idea that doing the Grind with their toddler on their back would be fun.
- Asian tourists who heard about one of the city's most popular hikes and had no idea what they were getting into. Typically wearing Hello Kitty sandals.
- A fit hiker well into his or her seventies who seems to be having no trouble whatsoever.
- Walkers arriving at the sad realization that there's no view, and nowhere to go but up.

Regular Grinders time themselves, with the average being about 90 minutes, and the current record an astonishing 23 minutes 48 seconds. My personal best up the 2,830 uneven dirt stairs is 55 minutes, but to be fair, I was drunk that day and in the mood for self-loathing. The reward for your calorie-decimating workout is typically beer and nachos at the Grouse Mountain bar. Take off, put on. Fortunately, it's only $10 for the gondola ride down to the parking lot, where you'll find a mix of exhausted, sweaty hikers and tourists reaching for their noses. If a

The Sea to Sky Gondola

Hikers of the world, relax. Squamish's $22-million Sea to Sky Gondola not only preserves the Chief hike, it opens up astounding views of Howe Sound, Sky Pilot Mountain, and the mighty Chief itself. The 849-metre-long gondola ride takes you right to the top of an adjacent mountain, where you'll find a 65-metre-high suspension bridge and scenic walking loops, as well as new hiking and biking trails. Celebrate the commendable execution of one of British Columbia's latest attractions with a craft beer on the sunny patio of the Summit Lodge.

START HERE: canadianbucketlist.com/seatosky ➤

Vancouverite asks to take you on the Grind, be prepared for a physical gauntlet. Or lie, with the reliable excuse, "I've done it, just over an hour, isn't it a bitch of a hike? Wow, once was enough!"

Alternatively, there's another climb that's just a fraction less admired by Vancouverites: the Stawamus Chief, or, simply and respectfully, the Chief. This giant granite monolith sits 700 metres above the Howe Sound, overlooking the town of Squamish on the Sea to Sky Highway between Vancouver and Whistler. World-renowned among climbers who scale its impressive rocky face, hikers and day walkers can go around the back and climb to the Chief's three summits, where they'll find a truly staggering view of the fjords and coastal mountains. The well-maintained trails can be rugged and steep, with handy iron chains and ladders adding to the sense of adventure. Pack a picnic for the top, and marvel at the beauty that stretches out in every direction. You don't have to rough it either. Opened in 2014, the adjacent Sea to Sky Gondola (this page) offers a restaurant, coffee shop, and an easy way down.

START HERE: canadianbucketlist.com/grind

GET A THAI MASSAGE IN THE CARIBOO

Echo Valley Ranch is a bucket list retreat that snags our attention for its striking location and unusual Asian influence, an altogether different ranch vacation from the one we'll tick off in Alberta (see page 80). Think less manure, more tranquil massage. Less hardened cowboy, more affable Englishman.

The ranch is the home of Norm and Nan Dove, and for an international Boutique Hotel Award winner, it feels remarkably like the dream home of a friend who has invited you for a visit. It's family owned and operated, so I was thrilled to bring along my own for the adventure, including an aunt and uncle who were visiting from California.

Guests can retire to their tastefully appointed rooms, suites, or cabins, or gather in the main Dove Lodge for a gourmet meal, a chat around the fireplace, a cozy reading session, or activities in the games room. Each evening, Mark, the head wrangler, asks us what activities might be of interest. A horse ride into the dense forests of

↑

BRITISH COLUMBIA

the Cariboo? A bike ride or hike into the valley? How about an authentic Thai spa, massage, or body treatment?

You can also join Norm for some epic flight-seeing in his leather-seated Cessna 206, which is exactly what I decided to do. The problem was that my dad and I had to look after my two-year-old daughter, Raquel, while my wife, aunt, and mom went galloping in the forest. "No problem," says Norm, "just bring your daughter with."

I get the feeling Norm says "no problem" quite a lot.

Subsequently, Norm's once-in-a-lifetime flight-seeing trip over the stunning glaciers, gemstone lakes, and Grand Canyon-esque Fraser Valley also becomes Norm's Toddler Nap Service. Little Raquel fell asleep shortly after take-off and woke up two hours later after we safely touched down. Between my daughter cradled in my arms, the jaw-dropping views, and my dad flying the plane for a few minutes (ticking that one off his own bucket list), it became one of the most memorable flights of my life.

Horses rarely look this healthy. Vegetables — picked daily from the greenhouse or gardens — rarely taste this good. On the lush green lawns outside our homey cabin, Raquel plays Frisbee with Echo, one of the ranch's half-dozen border collies. My wife is stretched out on the soft grass, soaking up the warm late-summer sun. On the patio, my mom is raving about her Thai massage in the striking wooden pagoda. Born and raised in Thailand, co-owner Nan's Asian influence here is unmistakable.

When the dinner bell sounds, we gather with the other guests for another outstanding meal, at which Norm and Nan entertain the guests. While life is never quite as simple as it appears, I've decided that the Doves

have figured life out: retire with success, operate a passion project hotel, meet interesting people from around the world, live with all the comforts one can imagine, and fly your own plane with an international airport just an hour's flight away. It's as good as it gets.

My dad and I enjoy a single malt Scotch on the cabin's patio as we watch my daughter take a ride on pony named Moonwalker. Initially reluctant, Raquel is beaming, and my wife is literally fist-pumping the sky, celebrating that our daughter has embraced the saddle and will likely be a lifelong horse fan as a result. My mom is playing cards with my aunt, while my uncle takes an afternoon nap. "These are the days of our lives," says Dad.

I'm often asked how I would describe a bucket list experience. Well, it has to be unique (like a luxury family ranch/Asian spa). It has to be realistic and something everyone can do (Echo Valley accepts reservations online). It has to make a great story, and it has to be memorable (like moments in the plane or on the patio described above).

Checking out with warm handshakes and hugs, Norm asks me what I thought of our stay at the ranch.

"Bucket list, Norm. Bucket list."

START HERE: canadianbucketlist.com/echo-valley-ranch

BRITISH COLUMBIA ↑

Soak in the Liard Hot Springs

Thermal activity beneath British Columbia has gifted the province with outstanding hot springs. Located a 25-minute drive south of Radium, Fairmont is the country's largest — renowned for healing waters devoid of the sulphur stink.

Size may or may not matter (depending on who you speak to), but I prefer Canada's second-largest springs, an altogether wilder affair. The Liard Hot Springs are located adjacent to one of the few campgrounds open year-round on the Alaska Highway. Instead of hotels and shops, campers and tired drivers will find the pool via a raised wooden boardwalk across a swamp. Wildlife is known to gather from the surrounding boreal forest, and it's not uncommon to spot a moose. Stairs lower you into the spring, with temperatures ranging between 42°C and 52° C, depending where you sit. Breathe. Soak. These rugged springs are absent of tour buses or hordes of kids contributing to the liquid warmth. For its therapeutic benefits on mind, body, and soul, Liard Hot Springs soaks its way into our Bucket List.

START HERE: canadianbucketlist.com/liardhotsprings ➤

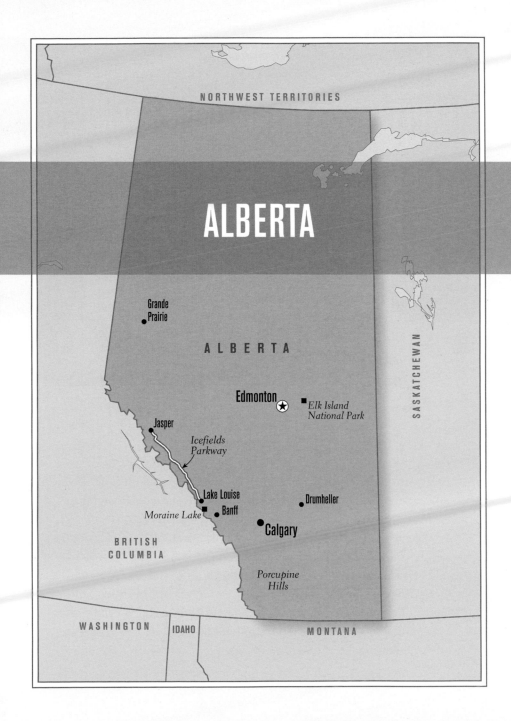

NORTHWEST TERRITORIES

ALBERTA

Grande
Prairie

ALBERTA

Edmonton ★ ■ Elk Island
National Park

Jasper

*Icefields
Parkway*

SASKATCHEWAN

Lake Louise
Moraine Lake ■ Banff

Drumheller

Calgary

BRITISH
COLUMBIA

*Porcupine
Hills*

WASHINGTON | IDAHO | MONTANA

EXPERIENCE THE CALGARY STAMPEDE

It may be many things to many people, but there's no denying the Calgary Stampede — that 10-day Cowtown spectacle — is something to experience before you die. For those who have been, or locals who live it, no explanation is necessary. For the rest of you, take it from a city slicker who came to love his inner yahoo and to wear his white hat, buckle, and boots with pride. Here's why:

The festival attracts millions of people, from Western Canada and beyond. Among them are party animals, herded through gates into wild nights at Cowboys, Nashville North, and other venues around town. They see the Stampede as an excuse to drink beer, dance on sticky floors, flirt with the opposite sex (in boots) and perhaps go home with them, wake up, hate themselves, and repeat it all the following day. Strangely enough, older celebrants don't stray

Tips for a Stampede

1. If you don't have boots, get a pair at the Alberta Boot Company, which has been furnishing cowboys and their accountants for more than 30 years. That pain you feel breaking them in makes you a better person.
2. Pick up the traditional Calgary White Hat at Smithbilt, official hat-maker for the event, and for the stars. Do not take it off, even when you sleep.
3. Never say Yee-haw. It's Yahoo. Remember that, or face a world of shame.
4. Line up for free bacon pancakes and festive chit-chat each morning at Flour Rope Square. Do not make fun of the clowns.
5. Win a prized item from China along the midway. Donate it to a kid, but not in a creepy sort of way.
6. Ride the abnormally fast Ferris wheel, pet an animal, visit the exhibitions, watch a miniature horse show, eat lunch in the Big 4, and gear up for the rodeo.
7. Stay for the Big Show and fireworks.
8. After that, interact with local wildlife at Cowboys, Nashville North, or Ranchman's. ➤

too far from the above, perhaps preferring smaller venues such as Ranchman's or bigger concerts like the Round Up. It's one of the world's biggest parties, if you're into that sort of thing, which the Stampede is more than willing to provide you an excuse to be.

Next, the Stampede is the World's Richest Rodeo. Before I understood exactly what the rodeo is, how it works, and who's behind it, I always rooted for bulls and horses. I'd yell at my TV set: "Throw that bastard off you and trample him in the mud!" I'm sure I'm not alone, but that changed when I decided to actually see what was going on for myself. Interviewing riders, judges, farmers, and vets, I found myself busting one rodeo myth after the next. No, the testicles of the animals are not strung up to make them buck. No, rodeo animals seldom get hurt and receive the best possible medical attention when they do. (Riders have the utmost respect for the animals and bear the brunt of the injuries.) No, the animals are never overworked, but are bred for their bucking ability and live out their days like champions in the pasture. And yes, it's dangerous, as even a mechanical bull can snap your wrist. It's always difficult to lift a veil of assumptions, but having finally learned more about the rodeo, I see a timeless confrontation

between man and beast, in fierce but relatively harmless battle, catering to and supported by the very people who work with animals in their daily lives. Animal rights activists may still want to string me up by my testicles, but I'll say this: go check out the rodeo, meet the people, see the animals, and form an educated opinion.

Finally, there's Cowtown itself: Calgary. Over the years, I've visited the city during the Stampede, and I'm always impressed with the community spirit behind the event. The free pancake breakfasts. The parades. The exhibitions. The Young Canadians. The volunteers who make the event tick, taking unpaid leave from work in order to do so. "Any time you can give back to the community, and help them out a little bit, you get something out of it," TV's Mantracker Terry Grant tells me. He's been a volunteer at the Stampede for years.

During my second Stampede, I was hell-bent on breaking in a pair of boots and never left the hotel without my white hat. Before that, the only time I'd ever dressed like a cowboy was at Halloween parties, but here I can slot right in. Boots make me stand taller, puffing out my chest. The cowboy myth (see Ranch Vacation, page 80) still holds power in our modern age.

Certainly there are those who avoid the Stampede like a warm pile of cow droppings, but there's no denying the sheer energy that shakes up the city. Boots and hats are everywhere, kids have cotton-candy grins, the midway is buzzing. Like many items on the Great Canadian Bucket List, the Stampede is likely a saddle that fits some better than others. But as a true Canadian celebration of western roots and community spirit, you can't miss it.

START HERE: canadianbucketlist.com/stampede

SKI INSIDE A UNESCO WORLD HERITAGE SITE

Canada has 18 UNESCO World Heritage Sites, and it's safe to say that visiting them all should be on the national bucket list. After all, these are places of unique physical and cultural significance worldwide. Still, a bucket list should transcend the thoughts of a committee, even if they get it right, and especially when they get it wrong. Some World Heritage Sites I've visited around the world consist of little more than historical rubble. Some sites are miss-them-if-you-blink-really-that-was-it? And some, like the Canadian Rocky Mountain Parks, are just so staggeringly gorgeous they belong in another category altogether.

In any season, Banff National Park is the picture postcard of Canada. Vast carpets of forest, gemstone lakes, and mountains with views waiting to kick you in the plexus. It took genius, and considerable Canadian elbow grease, to set up three different ski resorts in

ALBERTA ↑

the park: Lake Louise, Sunshine, and Norquay. Come winter, you can literally slide down the wilderness that surrounds you.

Lake Louise, the third-biggest ski resort in Canada, is View Central. Enjoying the resort's runs, I often had to stop and plop my butt in the snow simply to admire the vista. I was determined to hit every lift in one day, which I did, and was not disappointed. Thanks to its location inside a national park, respect for the environment takes precedence over the ambitions of a leisure corporation. Perhaps this is why Lake Louise is owned by one family, with patriarch Charlie Locke being the first guy to scale all 10 peaks in the area. Here is a mountain for people who love mountains: million-dollar views, not million-dollar condos.

Closer to Banff town centre is Sunshine, a smaller resort famed for its champagne powder. Staying at the Sunshine Mountain Lodge,

Banff's only ski-in, ski-out boutique lodge, it's easy to awake each morning to catch "first chair" and reap the rewards. For skiers and snowboarders, simply catching first chair is one for the bucket list, anywhere, especially with a dozen centimetres of fresh snow on the ground. Sunshine has the kind of snow that makes your skis smile. This from a guy who grew up in Africa, who first saw snow as a six-year-old during a freak storm in Johannesburg, and was told to hide under his school desk in case it was ash from nuclear fallout. True story.

For all the snow in Canada, and the resorts that offer world-class conditions without even trying, what's the big deal about the UNESCO designation? You probably won't ski among moose and elk (although one instructor tells me his girlfriend once saw a wolverine). Sunshine, Norquay, and Lake Louise — the Big Three, as they co-market themselves — look like typical resorts, with lifts and quads and young Australians sweeping chairs in exchange for a season pass. There are après-ski bars serving craft beer and knee-high plates of nachos.

So how is this different, you may ask? It could be the views from the chairs at Lake Louise. It could be the snow at Sunshine. It could be the hominess of Norquay. It could even be the proximity of iconic and grand Canadian hotels: Fairmont's Banff Springs and Château Lake Louise. On investigation, I can confirm it's all of the above, wrapped in a shell of deep respect for its surroundings — safe, protected, but available to be enjoyed.

START HERE: canadianbucketlist.com/skibig3

HUNT FOR DINOSAURS

Oh, what irony that the fiercest creatures ever to roam the planet have been unearthed, literally, in Canada. Here, in the land where the mighty *Tyrannosaurus rex* roared, we now honour the beaver. *T. rex* would use beavers as tennis balls — assuming dinosaurs played tennis or coexisted with beavers. Regardless, their old bones, discovered in southern Alberta's badlands, have been found in the world's richest fossil bed. Like most kids, I was fascinated by dinosaurs, reciting their long-winded *saurus* names and taking extra time to look at today's tiny lizards, wondering where it all went wrong. Or, given the rise of mammals, right. Unfortunately, by the time I arrived at Dinosaur Provincial Park, I was just another jaded adult too consumed by maturity to appreciate the fact that I had just plucked a 70-million-year-old dinosaur bone directly from the ground. The kids around me, however, went berserk.

ON THE BUCKET LIST: Professor Philip J. Currie

The world's foremost dinosaur expert (think Sam Neill in Jurassic Park, who was partially based on Dr. Currie) digs into the national bucket list:

The Milk River Canyon north of the American border is Alberta's deepest canyon and is also in the most sparsely populated region in the southern half of the province. The unhindered view of prairie grasslands is augmented by a great bowl-like depression that slopes down toward the canyon, offering a spectacular view of the mysterious Sweetgrass Hills on the south side of the border. The badlands have produced some of the most interesting fossils from the province, including embryonic duckbilled dinosaurs within eggs and a superbly preserved skeleton of the ancestor of *Tyrannosaurus rex*!

— Professor Philip J. Currie, world-renowned palaeontologist,
  founder, Royal Tyrrell Museum of Palaeontology

All it takes is a little imagination. Seventy-five million years ago, the Red Deer River valley was as lush and tropical as Central America. Huge beasts roamed about, looking very much like giant lizards, or birds, or museum skeletons, depending on which theory you choose to believe. When the dinosaurs woke up to the Worst Day Ever, and promptly died, their bones settled on the riverbed, were covered by soft sandstone and mudstone, and were all but forgotten until the 1800s, when the fiercest creatures on Earth, humans, now wore funny hats. During the last ice age, a glacier had removed the top level of dirt, exposing hundreds of bones from more than 40 types of dinosaurs, including Tyrannosauridae, Hypsilophodontidae, and Ankylosauria (you know, the ones with thick ankles).

Today, this UNESCO World Heritage Site is more than just Dinosaur Central Sure, the visitor centre and interpretation drives are interesting, and you can drive a couple of hours to the Royal Tyrrell Museum of Palaeontology in Drumheller to see what the fossils look like cleaned up and bolted together. But it's the landscape itself that struck me, dare I say it, like a meteor.

The badlands are so called because the soil makes this land terrible for farming but wonderful for filming science fiction.

Cracked grey earth resembling the skin of an elephant is tightly wrapped around phallic rocks called hoodoos. Rattlesnakes shake among the riverside cottonwoods, while the much smaller descendants of dinosaurs fly overhead or bask in the sun. Taking it all in, it's hard not to appreciate the scale of our planet's history, and the paleontological riches of Alberta.

A couple of years later, I find myself extracting an articulated bone from a fossil bed cut into a steep cliff, an hour outside Grande Prairie. I am almost 1,000 kilometres north of the badlands, at the site of yet another remarkable discovery. Here, among oil and gas platforms, lies one of the world's next-richest fossil beds, as palaeontologists from around the world work each summer in sun and rain to extract one fossil after another. One of the world's most famous dinosaur guys, Canada's own Professor Phil Currie, is spearheading the charge, complete with a $26-million namesake museum to house new-found treasures unearthed from the area.

Oil and gas beneath the earth have made Alberta Canada's richest province. Yet its earth continues to yield riches that give us profound insight into the past. Whether you're into history, museums, or just unusual scenery, join the hunt for dinosaurs in Alberta. At least before a meteor comes out of nowhere, causes a deep impact, blocks out the sun, wipes out life, and forces you, inconveniently, to wait another 70 million years for the opportunity.

START HERE: canadianbucketlist.com/dinosaur

HELI-YOGA IN THE ROCKIES

If you place the prefix *heli* in front of any other word, the result can only sound impossibly and incredibly cool. Heli-shopping! Heli-badminton! Heli-dating! We've already covered heli-skiing in B.C., so let's get creative as we climb aboard a whirlybird to witness one of the very best views one can possibly see: the peaks, spires, glaciers, lakes, and valleys of the snow-capped Rocky Mountains.

I'm Lululemoning my way into the mountains for an afternoon of Rockies Heli Tours' heli-yoga. It's the perfect blend of Western Canada: the healthy lifestyle choices of British Columbia wrapped

ALBERTA ↑

in the big ideas and money of Alberta. I meet my hatha yoga instructor, Martha McCallum, who is also a certified hiking guide, wildlife biologist, and wellness coach. Like most yoga teachers I've encountered, she speaks with a voice as soothing as lip balm, edging me on to find my centre and connect with the earth, or in this case, the mountains. She's well aware of the irony of using jet fuel for an elevating mind–body exercise, but it does bring us closer to nature without having to build any roads or destroy any shrubs. It's also a lot easier than hiking with a yoga mat.

Travel writers use the adjective *breathtaking* with far too much gusto (myself included). Breathtaking is when someone punches you in the stomach, or you're about to bungee jump. The view of the Rockies from a helicopter is simply awful. As in "fills one with awe," like the word was originally intended. *Awesome* is only some awe, but here, we're talking full, as in "to the brim." Our pilot banks through the canyons, glides over sharp peaks, and hovers over bighorn sheep and a lone wolf that should probably make the sheep nervous. From above, I feel like a kid who has skipped all his vegetables and gone straight to dessert. With no long hikes to the top, heli-touring is instant gratification.

We land on a site called the Wedding Knoll (what, you've never been to a heli-wedding?), where Martha safely ushers us out with mats and a picnic basket. The helicopter takes off just as smoothly as it landed, and we are all alone, 2,700 metres up, embedded in wilderness. She lays out the mats, using rocks to keep them grounded in the mountain breeze, and begins the first pose. The goal of yoga is to meditate to a point of perfect mind-body tranquility. Usually, this is done in a room with polished hardwood floors, mirrors, New Age music, and a dozen ladies wearing stretchy pants that flatter their buttocks. On the mountain, we still wear stretchy pants but have either far more or far fewer distractions, depending on your love for nature or for the behinds of yoga practitioners.

After the 45-minute class, we dine on Martha's homemade organic sandwiches and follow that up with a short heli-hike along the spine of the mountain. I decide that all hikes in the mountains should start at the top and then just stay that way. Our helicopter returns, and the reward for this strenuous day of exercise is another fly-by through the mountains. *Namaste!*

It is certainly not essential to combine yoga with your heli-flight-seeing experience in the Rockies. Not all of us are in pursuit of mind–soul nirvana, and not all of us want to stretch into a pretzel. Seeing the Rocky Mountains from above, on the other hand, is a must. Heli-hiking, heli-poker, heli-cooking — just add the prefix *heli* and you've got a winner, flying high on the Great Canadian Bucket List.

START HERE: canadianbucketlist.com/heliyoga

HIKE THE SKY

Widely regarded as the best hike in the Rockies, over half of Jasper National Park's 44-kilometre Skyline Trail is above the treeline. Expect spectacular views as you cut across ridges that overlook crystal lakes, alpine meadows, and Tolkien-esque valleys. Be aware that hiking this high up also means greater exposure to the elements, particularly along Maligne Ridge, where strong winds and whipping rain can make life particularly miserable for trekkers. When in doubt, channel Frodo … he always kept going.

Depending on your level of fitness and sense of purpose, the Skyline Trail can be completed in anywhere from two to six days, and there are well-serviced campsites along the way. If you're lucky, you might see some of the animals that roam the high valleys looking for food, such as wolves, grizzly bears, and mountain lions. You'll feel even luckier if you're carrying bear spray.

Due to the unpredictable weather, you'll want to invest in quality gear, including fine hiking boots (I'm a long-time KEEN fan) and a camping stove, since no fires are allowed on the trail. Tour companies in Jasper offer a shuttle service between the trailheads of Maligne Canyon and Maligne Lake, with most hikers choosing to start at the lake, avoiding a nasty early ascent. As it's one of the best-known hikes in the Rockies, booking ahead is essential. For those who would rather sit than walk, look into one of the horseback riding trips to the backcountry lodge that sits midway along the trail.

START HERE: canadianbucketlist.com/skyline

A Tramway and a Gondola

Banff and Jasper, the two towns that serve Canada's oldest national parks, boast a world-class gondola and tramway. There are many technical differences between gondolas and aerial tramways. Tramways work like elevators, with a counter-balance car, whereas gondolas can leave more frequently, like ski lifts. The Banff Gondola Mountaintop experience is an eight-minute ride to the top of Sulphur Mountain in a four-passenger cabin, climbing to an elevation of 2,281 metres. At the top you'll find a restaurant, the Cosmic Ray Station National Historic Site, and a short, self-guided interpretative Skywalk. Running up Whistlers Mountain, the Jasper Tramway is the longest and highest guided tramway in Canada, giving visitors spectacular 360° views of six mountain ranges, glaciers, alpine lakes, and the town of Jasper itself. On arrival at 2,300 metres, boardwalks and hiking trails lead to the summit the mountain.

BE THE COWBOY ON A RANCH VACATION

Cowboys date back to the 1700s, the name being a direct translation of the Spanish *vaquero*, a person who managed cattle by horseback. Cattle drives, averaging around 3,000 head, were managed by just 10 men or fewer, each with several horses, battling the elements to literally drive the meat to market. The cowboy, often poorly paid, uneducated, and low on the social ladder, had many tasks to perform. These included rounding up the cattle; sorting, securing, and protecting herds from thieves and wild animals; breaking in horses; and birthing and nursing sick animals.

The hazardous and strenuous nature of the work created a breed of hardened men and terrific fodder for the romance novels eagerly snapped up by urban readers fascinated by the call of the Wild West.

Despite Hollywood's portrayal, there were relatively few violent confrontations with Native Americans. Instead, most chiefs were paid

in cattle or cash for permission to drive cattle through their lands. Another aspect glossed over in the folklore is that, according to the U.S. census of the time, 30 percent of all cowboys were of African or Mexican ancestry. Giddy-up, amigo! When railways replaced cattle drives, modern cowboys began to work on ranches and show off their skills at competitive rodeos.

Our bucket list is now singing that old eighties song. "I Wanna Be a Cowboy." Who am I to argue?

Bill Moynihan talks with a throat of gravel, as if he's been chewing on the bones of Jack Palance and needs a can of oil to wash them down. He may be in his seventies, but the patriarch of the 120-acre Skyline Ranch is as tough and grizzled as any bootstrapping cowboy. Located in the Porcupine Hills, Skyline offers ranch vacations where guests can assist with daily chores, including feeding the 300 head

of cattle, roping up steers, and patrolling for wild animals. The area, captured beautifully in Ang Lee's *Brokeback Mountain*, sweeps up to the Rocky Mountains on the horizon. Bill's kids and grandkids are all involved in the family operation, a working ranch where you can leave your hat on and get your hands dirty.

Bill's moustache looks like an army guarding his upper lip. The former boxer, bush pilot, cop, and rodeo cowboy sizes me up. I'm a regular cowpoke, as alien to life on a ranch as I am to life in the Himalayas. I select a white horse named Barry (ahem) and saddle up for my first roundup. Here's what they don't tell you about Angus cows: they're big, and they can be rather belligerent. My cutting horse, bred for sudden stops and bucking cows, isn't fazed. Bill lassos a young calf and I assist with tagging it on the ear, nervous about its 600-kilogram mom who seems endearingly protective. Next I feed heifers some grain and dispense hay from an industrial tractor. While I barely manage to heave a bale of hay to the shed, Bill walks past carrying two on each hand. When the zombies attack, I hope I'm around a guy like Bill.

Skyline guests can also go hiking, fishing, biking, and horse riding in the hills, but ranch work is where the action is. Moving hay, shovelling shit, feeding the animals: farm life is physically tough and yet satisfyingly simple. You know what has to be done, and you do it.

That evening, over cold cans of Lucky Lager, I share stories with Bill and his son Reid, learning about the respect one has for the environment when one actually lives in it. "When the stars are out, you can see just about every one of them," explains Reid, feeding the firepit. The chain bonding ranching to nature is thick, and the Moynihans have a deep appreciation and respect for the animals and the land that provide their livelihood.

They also like to have fun. When Bill teaches me how to lasso, the only thing I succeed in lassoing is my eyeball. City slickers are always good for a laugh around the fire.

The following day, I succeed in sticking my arm deep inside a pregnant cow's vagina, verifying all is ripe for birthing. Yes, I've come a long way in a couple of days. We saddle up for a ride to the property fences, making sure nothing is damaged and looking for signs of predators. A strong, icy wind blows across the foothills.

"The biggest thing you can do in life is pass on the thing you love to somebody else," Bill tells me. He is not a man of many words, but cowboys don't have to be. I try to grunt, but it comes out like a squeak.

The word *dude* technically refers to someone who doesn't know cowboy culture but pretends otherwise. You can also refer to a dude as being "all hat and no cattle." A dude like, say, me. Yet the hospitality from these earthy folks was wonderfully warm and genuine, and the values of the modern-day cowboy seem to be alive and well. As it rides its way onto our bucket list, ranch life remains as real and alluring as the cowboy myth that promotes it.

START HERE: canadianbucketlist.com/ranch

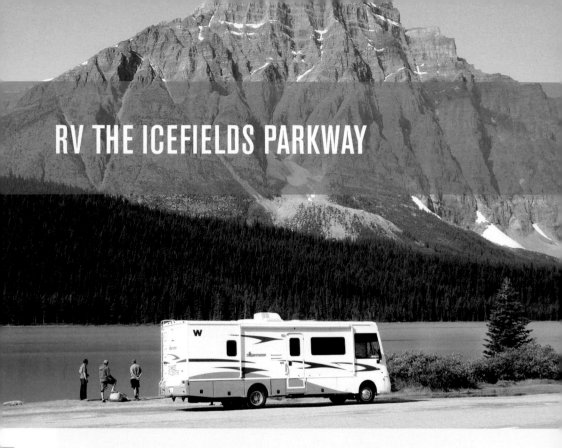

RV THE ICEFIELDS PARKWAY

The first time I hauled a backpack around the world, I had a wonderful sensation of independence. I'd packed everything I needed: clothes, toiletries, an iPod, books, cash, and most importantly, the right state of mind. My daily challenge was deciding where to sleep and use the toilet. The first time I went on an RV adventure, I felt that familiar gush of independence, only the daily challenges were flushed away with the black water.

My dad, my brothers, and I had rented a nine-metre Winnebago for a week's mancation to the Rockies. We would become just one of over a million RVs on Canadian roads that summer, the others hopefully driven by people with more experience than us. With a complete kitchen, two television sets, a bedroom, and a bathroom, the RV

Canada's Top RV Destinations

GO RVing is an organization representing RV dealers, manufacturers, and campground operators that helps to promote the freedom, flexibility, and fun of the RV lifestyle. Here's a list from their Top Destinations to RV in Canada:

BC Ashnola River
      Bella Coola

AB Banff National Park
      Beauvais Lake Provincial Park/
      Waterton Lakes National Park

SK Douglas Provincial Park
      Duck Mountain Provincial Park

MB Spruce Woods Provincial Park

ON Algonquin Park
      Bronte Creek Provincial Park

QC Bannick, Ville-Marie
      Gaspésie

NS Aspy Bay, Cape Breton
      Cabot Trail

NB Fundy National Park
      Littoral Acadien

PE Cavendish Sunset
      Twin Shores, Darnley

NL Gros Morne
      Twillingate

YK Kluane Lake
      Tatchun Lake

rattled and rolled its way out of Vancouver, wobbling in the wind with the aerodynamics of a cement brick. I was driving; my brothers were yelling: "Too close to the side!" "Watch the lines!" "You almost hit that car!" Ah yes, just a few hours in and I could feel our mancation easing my stress … right up behind my eyeballs and straight to the back of my throat.

My dad has always been in love with mountains, but since emigrating from South Africa, he'd never had the opportunity to see the Rockies. For the full effect, I steered our

ALBERTA ↑

roadworthy beast to Highway 93 — a.k.a. the Icefields Parkway — a 232-kilometre stretch of road between Lake Louise and Jasper. It is, without a doubt, one of the world's most spectacular drives, a gee-whiz postcard moment waiting for you at every turn. The visual impact of the mountains and glaciers that line the highway rivals that of the Himalayas, but boy, the Rockies are a lot easier to get to. Passing turquoise lakes and glacier-cut mountains, we craned our necks from side to side to capture the view out of the large windows, like we were watching a game of tennis. The overall effect, especially for someone who enjoys mountain beauty, can be as rich as overly cheesy fondue. "It's too much," I heard my dad reporting to my mom on his cellphone. "But in a good way."

Rock flour, crushed and carried by glaciers, makes mountain lakes glow in luminous shades of blue and green. We visit Moraine Lake on a postcard-perfect day, getting our group photo in front of one of Canada's most popular and sought-after views. By the time we reach Peyto Lake, farther up the highway, our camera batteries need refuelling from the RV's generator. The RV's height, big windows, and ease of movement made it the perfect vehicle from which to gawk at the mountains, if not always to park. Thank you, Parks Canada, for the extra-long parking bays at all the major sites. Parks Canada protects our wilderness, and they park Canada, too!

We pop into the Athabasca Glacier, where monster customized four-by-four buses take us directly onto a six-kilometre-long ice floe in the Columbia Icefields. Out on the ice, I scoop up melted water, drinking the taste of nature at its purest.

Bookending the Parkway are two of Canada's most iconic wilderness areas: Banff and Jasper national parks. No surprise that we come across a bear chewing berries alongside the road, or huge elk stopping traffic in its tracks. During the week, we take the Banff Gondola and the Jasper Tramway, barbecue steaks in an RV park, play a terrific round of golf at the Jasper Park Lodge, rent Harley-Davidsons to rocket up Mount Edith Cavell, and even swim in the ice-cold waters of a glacial lake. It is, in short, an epic mancation, immersed in true Canadiana. We even manage to keep the RV in relatively good shape, although on the last night of our journey, we realize that nobody has been paying too much attention to the instructions on how to empty the black water. Push a few buttons, pull a few knobs, and the next thing we know, the tube comes loose and drenches my brother and me. Truth be told, black water looks rather yellow. My dad would have wet himself laughing, but of course, we'd already beaten him to it.

I've been on the Icefields Parkway several times since, yet the RV trip stands out. Travel magic is not about what you're doing, it's about who you're doing it with. Wise words to remember when crossing off any item on your bucket list.

START HERE: canadianbucketlist.com/icefields

ALBERTA ↑

CANOE ON MORAINE LAKE

J ust 15 minutes from Lake Louise is one of the most magnificent views in all of Canada. The jewels of the Rockies gather in one magical spot — dramatic snow-capped peaks, emerald evergreen forest, a turquoise lake, and an easy-to-access lookout point — sparkling together on a crown of natural beauty the entire nation can wear with pride.

It took less than a decade after its discovery in 1899 for tourists to start arriving at Moraine Lake, which was soon serviced by a teahouse and later by tents and log cabins. Today visitors will find luxury accommodations in the form of the Arthur Erickson–designed Moraine Lake Lodge, which is open each summer.

After feasting in the restaurant on gourmet dishes, such as bison carpaccio and deer tenderloin, head down to the mirror-like, glacier-fed lake to rent a canoe. On a sunny day, with the Valley of the Ten Peaks reflected in the water, you just might think you've died and gone to heaven.

START HERE: canadianbucketlist.com/moraine

A-BERTA

STEP OVER THE ROCKIES

Mind-blowing views: the Rocky Mountains — and the Icefields Parkway in particular — have no shortage of them. Yet there's always room for more, especially if we can add in the term *knee-shaking*. Inspired by the Grand Canyon Skywalk, the folks behind the Columbia Icefield glacier tours spent $21 million to build a horseshoe-shaped glass-floor observation deck extending 35 metres around and 300 metres above Jasper National Park's Sunwapta Valley. Opened in 2014, the Glacier Skywalk is another meaty mouthful of natural beauty in a region that won't stop dishing it out until you explode — or at least unbuckle your belt.

With the environmental blessing of Parks Canada, your experience begins at Brewster's Glacier Discovery Centre down the road. A shuttle departs every 15 minutes from existing parking lot facilities, ensuring no additional paradise paving was necessary. The short bus ride is further symbolic since it was a company bus driver who

ALBERTA ↑

originally conceived the idea of a suspension bridge across the valley. Architects went one better, creating the steel-and-glass structure that places you right into the view itself. First you must walk through six interpretative stations, revealing the natural history, ecology, wildlife, and geology of the area. Suitably informed, you approach the awaiting giant glass horseshoe.

Glass is a funny thing. Even when it's reinforced, 9.67 centimetres thick, and capable of withstanding the weight of two Boeing 747s, it still seems woefully inadequate. Especially when you take your first steps off a cliff and see the ground disappear between your feet. Some people just don't do heights — be it bungee jumping or glass platform observation decks. I'd suggest they take the Columbia Icefields Glacier Tour while the rest of us walk nervously forward to the apex of the platform. Immediately apparent: the Skywalk jiggles slightly when you walk. Engineers designed the platform to withstand metres of heavy snow and sway safely in strong valley winds. Suspended high above the valley floor, you'll eventually be able to tear your eyes (and cameras) away from your feet and look out at Mount Andromeda, the Snow Cone, and its surroundings. You might even spot a bighorn sheep on the valley floor below. Standing on that platform is a bucket list moment, one that some visitors will want to experience for as long as they can. Others will be more than happy to take a few pictures and return their feet to solid earth.

START HERE: canadianbucketlist.com/skywalk

VISIT AN OASIS OF WILDLIFE

North America's largest terrestrial mammal, the bison, once roamed the plains in the millions. Indigenous people hunted the huge beasts for meat and skins, and there was more than enough to go around. The arrival of European hunters, however, quickly took the species to the brink of extinction. Today, wild bison are protected in enclaves of national parks, the most famous and certainly the largest being Wood Buffalo National Park.

Far more accessible, and just as significant, is Elk Island National Park, located an hour's drive east of Edmonton. The country's only entirely fenced national park, Elk Island is a haven for free-roaming bison, not to mention elk, deer, moose, and more than 250 species of birds. Here, Canada's largest mammal shares its habitat with Canada's smallest — the pygmy shrew.

ALBERTA ↑

91

By the year 1900, there were as few as 1,500 plains bison remaining. Early conservation efforts saw the establishment of Elk Island in 1906, with several hundred purebred plains bison shipped up from Montana. Their numbers rebounded, and the park was eventually successful in relocating bison throughout Canada, the United States, and even as far as Russia. Elk Island also contains the most genetically pure wood bison remaining, as the two subspecies — plains and wood — have interbred everywhere else. The two are kept separate in the park, with wood bison on the south side of the Yellowhead Highway and plains bison on the north side. On either side, visitors can leave their cars to hike or hit the mountain-biking trails in summer, and snowshoe or cross-country ski in winter. On these treks, it's not uncommon to encounter grazing bison herds and other wildlife. Today there are more than 800 bison in the park, the number controlled so as not to overwhelm their sanctuary. Parks Canada's interpretation and conservation efforts are an encouraging sign that bison will remain a wildlife encounter on Canadian bucket lists for many years to come.

START HERE: canadianbucketlist.com/elkisland

HIKE OR SKI IN TO SKOKI LODGE

In 1931 Swiss mountain guides and members of the Banff Ski Club decided to build western Canada's first commercial ski lodge. With thousands of kilometres to choose from, they settled on a place called Skoki, selected for its scenic beauty, quality of snow, proximity to a creek, and safety from avalanches. Today, one of the oldest and highest backcountry lodges in Canada is an 11-kilometre hike from the groomed ski slopes of the Lake Louise Resort, and I'm feeling every step of it.

It's my first time on cross-country skis, slipping and sliding forth with surprising ease. A strip of material under each ski, called the skin, grips the snow as I edge my way through pine forest, over

ALBERTA

The Royal Throne

When the newly married Duke and Duchess of Cambridge needed time alone on their first royal visit to Canada, Skoki Lodge was the perfect fit: miles away from the paparazzi, relaxing, and in the bosom of the Rockies. Skoki's staff worked with royal handlers to keep the destination mum and prepare it for the future king and queen of England (and Canada). This meant the no-running-water, no-electricity charm of Skoki would need a little polish.

A helicopter brought in a modern bathroom, complete with flush toilet, bathtub, and sink, painstakingly installed to the bemusement of long-time staff, who have always found other ways to make do. Everything went off splendidly, even if the royal stay was less than 24 hours. As for the bathroom, it was hastily demolished and cleared away. Since Skoki is a wonderful slice of rustic history, guests are directed to the outhouses, as perfectly serviceable a throne as any. ➤

frozen lakes, and across windy mountain passes. Every guest must ski, hike, or snowshoe in, unless you're the Duke and Duchess of Cambridge, in which case, Parks Canada will organize a helicopter. Skoki made headlines for attracting the newlywed William and Kate on their Canadian honeymoon. No electricity, no cellphone or internet coverage, no running water, no paparazzi — Skoki provided a rustic royal break from the media frenzy. It wasn't the first royal connection, either: one of the lodge's first guests was one Lady Jean, a lady-in-waiting to Queen Victoria, who visited Skoki with her travel-writer husband, Niall Rankin. While the Rankins used the outhouse like regular guests, William and Kate had a specially built bathroom constructed for their visit, which was hastily destroyed afterward, lest regular guests get any fancy ideas.

Skoki strives to be as authentic a backcountry experience today as it was in the 1930s. That means candles, blankets, and late-night

stumbles to the outhouse during blizzards. It's one of the best winter adventures in North America, with an emphasis on adventure. You'll know this as you make your way up Deception Pass, a steep uphill that keeps going, and going, and going. By the time I arrive, covered in sweat and snow from too many downhill tumbles, the fireplace is surrounded by guests enjoying hot homemade soup. The lodge accommodates up to 22 guests, and we each feel we deserve our place on one of the sink-in couches. Among the guests are two Norwegians, a ski club from Manitoba, a couple returning for the ninth time from the Northwest Territories, a birthday party, and a couple on their second honeymoon (staying in the Honeymoon Cabin, of course). Will and Kate, who signed the guest book like

everyone else, preferred the Riverside Cabin, close to the creek. I
offload my gear in a cabin called Wolverine, named for the wolverine
that got stuck in it and almost tore it to shreds. Although Skoki's original builders took refuge in a special bear tree, the bears, cougars, and
wolves that roam Banff National Park nowadays keep their distance.
The most bothersome creatures appear to be pine martens, porcu-
pines, and exhausted travel writers.

Skoki itself is the launch pad for hiking and skiing trails, which
most guests explore on their second day. Two-night stays are typical,
giving you just about enough time to recover from the 11-kilometre
trek in order to do it all over again. Nobody can expect to lose much
weight, however. The chef and staff somehow prepare gourmet

meals, such as coconut-crusted Alaskan halibut, marinated tenderloin served with candied yams, avocado Caesar salad, and fresh home-made bread. That everything is packed in by snowmobile (horses in summer) and prepared using propane stoves makes it all the more impressive, and appreciated.

The discussion by the fire revolves mostly around Skoki's beauty, history, and legacy. One couple sifts through the guest books until they find the last time they signed it, in 1974. Another guest plays the piano, helicoptered in sometime in the early 1980s. I read an old book about Western Canadian outlaws, play with Lucy and Bill (Skoki's resident Jack Russells), and let the fresh air and exercise sink into my pores. On my final night, the moon is so full I can read without a headlamp. Miles away from anything, protected by a world of mountains, forest, and snow, Skoki is the perfect escape, for royals and the rest of us.

START HERE: canadianbucketlist.com/skoki

VISIT A SITE FOR ALL EYES

The Rockies rock in all seasons, which is why you can't go wrong, whenever you choose to visit. If it's warm and sunny, you hit the hikes. If it's cold and snowy, you ski the slopes. Or, in the case of Maligne Canyon, explore the ice. Despite the shadowy roots of its name (from the old French word for "evil"), Maligne is Jasper National Park's top-rated attraction.

In the summer months, a river barrels through crevices in the limestone canyon, some as deep as 50 metres. This rush of water is best viewed from the well-trodden footpath and a series of six bridges, accessible via an easy two-hour round-trip walk with the welcome refreshment of pure glacier waterfall spray. Exit, as always, through the gift shop.

In winter, the gushing water freezes on the canyon floor, ideal for a guided ice-walk both alongside and through the canyon. Tour operators provide the cleats, headlamp, and interpretation of the canyon's unique topography. (It sits above the largest karst cave system in North America.) Spikes of ice like candle wax cover the rocks. Walking among the crystals of the canyon's flash-frozen waterfalls never fails to impress, nor does the site of water still flowing beneath the ice in some sections. Ice chutes create natural slides, which are particularly popular with the kids. They might want to break off an ice pick for an all-natural glacial-ice lolly — there's plenty to go around — and unlike stalactites, it won't take 1,000 years to grow them back.

Whether you're chasing raging torrents, sparkling ice, or just the chance to immerse yourself in the beauty of one of Canada's most famous national parks, Maligne Canyon is a bucket list item for all seasons.

START HERE: canadianbucketlist.com/maligne

Get In the Spirit

Surrounded by snow-capped peaks, glaciers, and unspoilt boreal forest, Maligne Lake is one of the most popular attractions in Jasper National Park. Located 48 kilometres from the town, it is the world's second-longest glacier-fed lake, attracting over a million tourists a year, particularly to the 90-minute scenic boat cruise to Spirit Island. Alternatively, hop aboard a canoe for a two- to five-day paddle along the shores, camping at one of two campgrounds along the way. Watch for bears and moose, fish for trout, and take your time enjoying the spectacular scenery. ➤

BOARD THE ROCKY MOUNTAINEER

All aboard for one of the world's great train experiences, a genteel affair, smothered in five-star service, tasty libations, and views of the Rockies in all their splendour.

Running on four routes going both east and west, the Rocky Mountaineer is North America's largest private rail service. National Geographic called it one of the World's Greatest Trips, and Condé Nast Traveler listed it among the Top 5 Trains in the World.

I hopped on board at the station in Vancouver for a two-day journey up to Banff. You don't sleep on the Rocky Mountaineer. The 1,000-kilometre journey takes place during daylight so you can enjoy

the views, with passengers staying overnight at the company's hotel in Kamloops. Guests are seated in a two-level, glass-domed coach with panoramic views, drinks service, and a helpful, unnervingly cheery attendant pointing out places of interest along the route.

On the way out of B.C., we pass over Hells Gate, the narrowest point of the Fraser River, and spot a bear walking across the tracks behind us. We enter the engineering marvel of the Spiral Tunnels and are halfway through a game of cards when Mount Robson, the highest mountain in the Rockies, comes into view. That deserves another Caesar.

There's an excellent gourmet meal service and optional activities such as wine-tasting to put you nicely in the groove of the rocking train. Of course, like many of life's great luxuries, the comfort comes with a price tag. The trip is ideal for Vancouver cruise shippers extending their journey, seniors, or anyone looking for a little bit of romance. All can relax, soak in the views, and appreciate that the Rocky Mountaineer is all about the journey, not the destination.

START HERE: canadianbucketlist.com/rockymountaineer

ALBERTA ↑

Swallow a Prairie Oyster

The chef invites me into the restaurant kitchen, and pulls out his balls. Buzzards Restaurant has been offering its infamous prairie oysters on for two decades, served as a special treat during the Calgary Stampede. In order for cattle farmers to control their stock, male calves must be castrated. Some of these testicles roll their way to Buzzards, which has thought of creative means to cook, grill, and sauté prairie oysters for the adventurously hungry. Each year the dish is given a new name and recipe. I was served the Crown Jewels, in which Crown Royal whisky was added for flavour. In my travels I have been fortunate to sample crickets (legs get stuck in the teeth), termites (taste nutty), deep fried guinea pig (stringy chicken), fermented horse milk (acidic), and crocodile (less stringy chicken). In the end, culture determines what we find acceptable to consume and what we don't. Eating the gonads of a bull, which carry flavour rather well, might be unacceptable for the same folks who will happily nosh on pig feet, liver, rump, and halibut cheeks. The bulls get the snip either way, which keeps the coyotes, farmers, and daring diners on the bucket list happy.

START HERE: canadianbucketlist.com/balls ➤

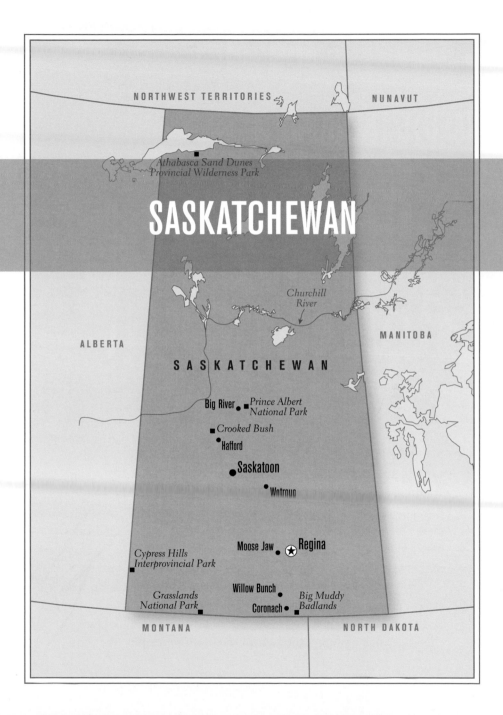

NORTHWEST TERRITORIES

NUNAVUT

Athabasca Sand Dunes
Provincial Wilderness Park

SASKATCHEWAN

Churchill
River

ALBERTA

MANITOBA

S A S K A T C H E W A N

Big River ■ Prince Albert
National Park

■ Crooked Bush

Hafford

Saskatoon

Wotroug

Moose Jaw ★ Regina

Cypress Hills
Interprovincial Park

Willow Bunch

Grasslands
National Park

Big Muddy
Badlands

Coronach

MONTANA

NORTH DAKOTA

SALUTE THE RCMP

The Red Serge is such a Canadian icon that the Mounties have trademarked it. After all, this is a police force on which others around the world are modelled. I want to understand just what the Royal Canadian Mounted Police is, who these people are, and what makes them so great. I want to chase cars and shoot guns and catch bad guys. I want to be RCMP. So it's off to Regina's Depot, the very soul of the RCMP, the mother from which all cadets are birthed.

The excellent Arthur Erickson–designed Heritage Centre can answer my questions, but I want to get inside the organization's skin. So I continue driving, through the security gate, warned that I might encounter live training exercises. At the clothing facility, the Stores

Person, Sean Lussier, measures me up: I am freckled, accented, with a streak of anti-authoritarian tendencies. Mind you, he's got tattoos, piercings, and a waxed moustache. Sean pulls out his pencil and tape measure. I am fitted with formal and casual wear and handed a pair of leather boots that need to be polished for 25 hours before they attain the appropriate sheen. He tells me new cadets tear up when they try on the Red Serge for the first time. I slip on the red blazer and immediately feel three inches taller.

It's off to the barber, where, from a selection of short, shorter, and eight ball, I really begin to look the part. In the morning I am taking the Physical Ability Requirement Evaluation (PARE), an obstacle designed to challenge the bodies and minds of incoming cadets within the first two weeks of their arrival. New cadets must complete four circuits of the course in under 4:45, plus tackle a weight mechanism. If they fail, they are given three days to give it another go. Failing that, they are released from duty, dreams and all. To graduate from Depot, the PARE must be completed within four minutes.

Cadets sleep on average just five hours a night. They will pack in studies equivalent to a four-year degree in just 26 weeks. Speaking to some of them at breakfast in the canteen, I learn just how determined they are to make it, and how proud they are to be RCMP. I eat lightly before nervously making my way to the gym for the PARE test. Prior to the attempt, each cadet's blood pressure is checked as a precaution, which only succeeds in rocketing the nerves.

I am shown how to jump over this, hop over that, up the stairs, around the orange cone, on my back, on my front, again, again, again. The clock starts, and I keep an even pace.

They Always Get Their Man

- The RCMP is the provincial police force for all provinces except Quebec, Ontario, and Newfoundland and Labrador. It provides additional policing services to 200 municipalities in Canada and nearly 200 Aboriginal communities.
- The Red Serge, which is worn only at civic ceremonies, celebrations, and memorials, consists of a scarlet tunic with a low-neck collar and brass buttons. The pants are black riding breeches with a yellow stripe down each leg. Spurs accompany brown leather riding boots.
- The Dempster Highway was named after RCMP inspector William John Dempster, for his service to the North.
- Charles Dickens's son served as a member of the North-West Mounted Police, a precursor to the RCMP.
- Women first graduated as RCMP members in March 1975.
- The last RCMP dog patrol was in 1969.
- The RCMP served in the Boer War, and the First and Second World Wars.
- Only Canadian citizens can join the RCMP.
- There are currently over 27,000 members and employees of the RCMP. ➤

It doesn't seem too difficult at first. By the second lap, I am breathing heavily. Cadets are starting to cheer. By the third lap, my body feels ambushed. The jumps seem longer, my steps heavier. Fourth lap, the cadets are cheering, "Go, Robin!" I can't let them down. If they see me fail, they'll be discouraged, and here is a room full of future peace officers, people who will save lives. I'm choking for lack of breath but continue to the weight machine, where I must thrust my body forward and pull weights in a fluid semicircle. My heart tries to rip itself out like the creature in *Alien*. Still, the cadets are cheering, and their cheering keeps me going. Suddenly, I understand why home ice is so important.

I finish the task and pick up a 36-kilogram bag, carefully carrying it around a cone and returning it in complete control. The sergeant announces my time: 3:50. I collapse in exhaustion, the cadets

cheering. Already they are beginning their rotations, so I am whisked out of the gym. Who needs media at a time like this? Corporal Dan, the communications officer showing me around, is impressed. I'm coughing up intestine, tasting the iron of blood at the back of my throat. "That's the PARE cough," says the corporal. "You'll have it for a couple days."

No time to recover. I rush off to formation marching and the daily Sergeant Major's Parade, where I am picked on by a mean-looking corporal who makes me fully aware of his garlic-heavy diet. Cadets stand to attention as stiff as trees in a pine forest. Then it's off to the Police Driving Unit, where Corporal Darcy Jacksteit allows me to join him for the day's exams. We play out various scenarios in his Crown Victoria, as I learn about RCMP policies and just how stressful it can be behind the wheel. After some evasive-driving procedures, I'm dropped off at a firearms unit, where I learn that guns are the last-ditch attempt and should always be aimed for maximum impact. Cadets will spend a minimum of 52 hours at the range.

Finally, I visit Sergeant B.J. Landry's Simulator Training Unit, where high-tech cameras and simulators allow me to play out life-and-death scenarios in safety but under scrutiny. Police forces from around the world train at the Depot, sometimes adopting

SASKATCHEWAN ↑

RCMP policies. No other country has a national police force charged with performing so many roles — from policing to drug enforcement, immigration and borders to anti-terrorism. A movie made the maxim famous: "The Mountie always gets his man." This, unfortunately, is not always the case. Yet, despite the clobbering the organization gets in the news media, its standards and traditions are of the highest calibre.

Growing up in South Africa, we were afraid of police. They were very often just as crooked as the thieves they were supposed to catch. Not so in Canada. It might not be on everyone's bucket list to put themselves through a crash course of cadet training. Yet everyone needs to visit the RCMP Heritage Centre and learn about this vital Canadian institution — to try on the Red Serge and see how it fits.

START HERE: canadianbucketlist.com/rcmp

CLIMB CASTLE BUTTE IN BIG MUDDY

Scramming from Regina south on a straight-as-a-church-choir highway, we're leaving the RCMP Depot in the dust in search of the Big Muddy Badlands. It is a region famed for its outlaws, and it's their spirit I blame for flooring a Ford Explorer, which growls its distaste for the 100-kilometre speed limit. Like many highways in Saskatchewan, this one seems purposely built for land-speed records. Turning left onto SK-36, the smooth highway becomes cratered and cracked, as if an attacking squadron of fighter jets has strafed it.

"How do you like our road?" asks the lady at Coronach's Co-op pump, clearly unimpressed with the provincial highway commission. By the time you read this, we're all hoping the road to Coronach is as smooth as the gravel country roads that surround it. Either way, it all adds to the adventure of seeking out a place where tumbleweed is blown by the ghostly breaths of lawlessness. For a while, the Big Muddy Badlands epitomized the Wild West, where rustlers eluded pursuing posses, and rogue outlaws demonstrated the charm and gunmanship touted in nineteenth-century romance novels. Even today, you can hear the sound of six-shooters whistling in the strong prairie breeze.

"Oh, people visit us from around world," explains Big Muddy's welcoming guide Trish Manske. We pick her up at the modest Coronach Visitor Centre, from which daily summer tours to the badlands depart. Trish has lived on a ranch nearby for decades, and she's eager to show us why Big Muddy belongs on every Canadian's bucket list. Van tours take place in July and August, but we're here for a private tour in spring. The Long Tour is a 180-kilometre round-trip visit to eight separate sites. A ninth could be added if you factor in the scenery. For while the drive to Coronach was one of flat and endless wheat fields, once we enter the valley, fields drop into sandstone valleys and buttes of elephant skin–like sedimentary rock rise from the valley floor, recalling glacial action some 65 million years ago. Thousands of bison once feasted on the valley's grassland, supporting numerous First Nations. Neither remained after the influx of European hunters and ranchers.

Located within sight of the Montana border, this is where the Land of the Living Skies (Saskatchewan) meets Big Sky Country (Montana). Running along this porous international border is a fence, although word on the prairie is that some rocks are actually hidden cameras and drones patrol overhead. Our first stop is the valley's most striking natural landmark, Castle Butte. Think of it as Canada's Ayers Rock. Jutting 60 metres out of the valley like a camel's hump, it is 500 metres in circumference and offers those brave enough to climb up an outstanding view of the surrounding valley. Aboriginal people used it as a vantage point to spot bison herds roaming the plains. The North-West Mounted Police (the forebears of today's RCMP) used it to spot outlaws.

"Can I climb it?" I ask Trish.

"That's what it's for," she replies.

You can't do that at Ayers Rock.

It's a quick scramble to the top. Eroding sandstone provides plenty of footholds up the steep banks, although I'm a little nervous about the sinkholes, some of which are the size of manhole covers, and deep as a well. The brisk prairie wind is howling, the 55-kilometre valley stretches below. Legend

has it that when the glaciers melted, one could paddle from Big Muddy all the way to the Gulf of Mexico. No one was around with a canoe back then, but by the late 1800s, ranchers had settled throughout the valley. Far removed from the reach of the North-West Mountain Police, Big Muddy attracted a different sort of settler.

"Dutch Henry was the ringleader," explains Tamela Burgess, matriarch of the nearly 20,000-acre Burgess Ranch. Tammy has become the go-to badlands historian, penning a book about the bandits, tracing photographs, researching tales long buried in the dust. She's built an outlaw gallery on her ranch, the same ranch that hosted the first detachment of mounted police in 1902. She has drawn portraits of Big Muddy's principal characters — the ranchers, the law, and most intriguingly, the outlaws. It didn't take long for smooth-talking, likeable horse wranglers to see the thieving potential of the badlands. Not only would the international border deter chasing posses, but the region's caves provided natural hideouts for

The Giant of Willow Bunch

Highway 13, on the way to Coronach, passes through a small community called Willow Bunch, which at one time happened to be the home of Canada's tallest man. Edouard Beaupré was born in 1881, and, before the age of nine, he stood six feet in height. Due to abnormal amounts of natural growth hormones, Eduoard eventually towered over his peers at seven feet eight inches. By all accounts a gentle giant, Edouard toured North America as a circus freak and strongman to earn income for his family. (He would raise large horses on his shoulders.) He died of tuberculosis when he was just 23 while working for the Ringling Bros. Circus at the 1904 St. Louis World Fair. For decades, his mummified remains remained at the University of Montreal, until they were finally returned to his hometown in 1990, where they were cremated and laid to rest outside a museum that continues to honour the Giant of Willow Bunch. ➤

both men and horses. This is why Butch Cassidy and the Sundance Kid, immortalized by Paul Newman and Robert Redford in the film of the same name, chose Big Muddy as Station One in an outlaw trail that stretched all the way from Canada to Mexico.

A station might consist of a friendly (or fearful) rancher who would provide shelter and food, or a hideout safe from the pursuing law. Dutch Henry's Wild Bunch would steal horses from the United States and rebrand them to be sold to Canadian ranchers. If Canadian ranchers thought they were getting a good deal, they underestimated the cunning of the gang. Their own horses would be stolen and re-branded for another cross-border swap. The Wild Bunch was even known to sell stolen horses back to their original owners. Integral to the scheme were co-operative ranchers, and integral to this co-operation was an atmosphere of fear. This is where notorious thugs

like Sam Kelly and Bloody Knife came in: dead-eyed men with reptilian blood and a thirst for violence. They even murdered one of their own — a fellow outlaw who botched a train job south of the border. Legend holds that Sam Kelly dehorned a steer with his rifle from 100 metres away.

Tammy eagerly shares the stories of these and other characters, explaining how the intimidated ranchers finally stood up for themselves and how the area improved when Big Muddy at last received a full Mountie detachment. Ironically, Sam Kelly never went to jail, and lived out his days in the region. Various theories abound about the fate of Dutch Henry, an enigmatic character begging for the Hollywood treatment. Tammy's portrait of Henry makes him look like a 1970s-era Burt Reynolds.

We leave the Burgess Ranch with a real feel for the characters that put the bad in badlands and an appreciation for Tammy's enthusiasm to share their stories with visitors each summer.

A few miles away, Trish unlocks a heavy gate and swings it open. We drive along a natural spring to find a sign boldly revealing the twin Sam Kelly Outlaw Caves. One was for the men, the other for the contraband horses. Adjacent is a pyramid-like hill that provided an ideal lookout for police or posses. The caves have been reinforced

with wood beams, but there's not much more to them than holes in a hill. It's not hard to imagine the cowboys whittling away on branches, rolling tobacco in stony silence. Now the tour veers toward the artifacts left behind by the First Nations who once hunted bison in the valley, including an 18-metre-wide stone circle, and bison and turtle effigies.

The origin of these effigies remains a mystery, but the views across the valley from here are astounding. The Long Tour takes in the Heritage School House, the Big Beaver Nature Centre, and Aust's General Store. ("If we don't have it, you don't need it.") A shorter half-day tour takes in the highlights; the stories are infused with the landscape.

We know the Sundance Kid sent postcards from Big Muddy. (There's no evidence that Butch Cassidy was in the area, although everyone believes it was highly likely). We know that the rancher who hosted the first North-West Mounted Police detachment was in the pocket of the Wild Bunch, and re-branded the stolen horses right under the noses of the law. We know about the Mountie's wife who rustled horses on the side. Stories of law and order forever at odds in the badlands of Saskatchewan.

START HERE: canadianbucketlist.com/bigmuddy

BUST THE CHICAGO CONNECTION

Visiting Saskatchewan can feel like a game of cops and robbers. We visited outlaw caves in Big Muddy, put on the Red Serge at the RCMP Depot, and now we've taken a 45-minute drive west of Regina to Moose Jaw in order to get our gangster on, *capisci*? For most of the century, Moose Jaw authorities denied the existence of an underground labyrinth beneath the buildings on the city's Main Street. After all, nobody is fond of revealing skeletons in closets located in secret rooms. Unless, of course, those skeletons can intrigue tourists, in which case, bring out the bone polish!

The Tunnels of Moose Jaw recreates the city's infamous history with two 50-minute underground tours: the first one (Passage to Fortune) explores Chinese immigration in the early twentieth century, and the second (The Chicago Connection), the role Moose Jaw

played during the Prohibition years. Re-enactors lead us through passage-ways and hidden rooms renovated to recall both periods, explaining how the tunnels were used — first as access corridors for steam engineers, then as a safe haven for Chinese migrants fearing for their lives, and finally by boot-leggers and gangsters. Although there's no physical evidence he ever visited "Chicago North," Al Capone's ghost is everywhere here. Gangster history of that era is soaked in rum, myth, and hearsay. What is known for certain is that Moose Jaw was an important distribution centre for rum-runners smug-gling booze into the United States on Canadian Pacific Railway's Soo Line. During this period, local law enforcement consisted of a chief of police by the name of Walter P. Johnson, a man firmly in the pocket of the gangsters. Exchanging envelopes stuffed with cash for peace, Capone's men essentially had the run of the town, operating gambling, booze, and prostitution rings in the refashioned tunnels, safe from prying eyes. When prohibition ended, the tunnels were abandoned, their existence either denied or forgotten. That is, until their reopening in 2000 as a lively historical tourist attraction.

At the entrance on Main Street, old newspaper clippings and exhibits immediately set the tone for an underground adventure that takes visitors back in time into the city's seedy past. Two re-enactors lead us across the street to where the tour will begin. We enter a saloon to the sounds of honky-tonk piano. Our guide, Miss Fanny, a vivacious lady of dubious profession, sets the mood. It is 1927, an era of temperance. Alcohol has been outlawed in the United States, creating rich opportunities for Canadian liquor operations close to the border. Speakeasies are doing a roaring trade, but the fear of police and FBI raids permeate the air along with cheap perfume and cotton-wool clouds of cigarette smoke. Even with the law in their pockets, for gangsters on the lam, the tunnels of Moose Jaw are the perfect place to operate. We walk down a narrow staircase, Miss Fanny passing us off to a young Wise Guy with a thick "Joisey" accent. He shows us where the boys gambled, sent and received radio communications, hoarded booze, and stockpiled their Thomson submachine guns, all the while reminding us to "fogeddaboutit!"

It's fun and hammy, and the entire time I'm thinking, "Really, this is happening each day beneath the streets of downtown Moose Jaw?" By the end of the tour, I'm pulling my hat low and my collar up. Walking onto Main Street, there's a jarring feeling when we return to the present, to our own era of law and order. Although the truth was probably less glamorous, Moose Jaw's gangster history smuggles itself onto the Great Canadian Bucket List. No questions about it, *capisci*?

START HERE: canadianbucketlist.com/moosejaw

SUPPORT RIDER NATION

The first time I heard the word *Roughriders*, I thought it was a brand of condoms. Immigrants to Canada have to face these sorts of challenges, such as learning how to pronounce *Saskatchewan*, or following the puck, or believing that a place called Moose Jaw actually exists. It took me some time to understand that Canadian football is different from American football, and that the most rabid fans in the CFL, if not the country, belong to Regina's own Roughriders. Indeed, when you visit Saskatchewan, you are actually visiting Rider Nation, where you'll no doubt get swept up in a frenzy of Rider Pride. This is why it's really important you don't tell anyone you once thought Roughriders was a brand of condoms. They might just stick a watermelon on your head.

It's game day for the Riders. Even though they didn't qualify for this year's Grey Cup playoffs, the fans are ready to brave sub-zero temperatures to show their enthusiastic support for the team. The Riders are far from the most successful team in the CFL (they've only won a handful of trophies after more than 100 years of chasing the ball), but fans of Canada's biggest sports franchises have a high threshold for failure. I'm throwing myself into the mix, donning the

Why the Watermelons?

Visitors to a Roughriders game will notice the colour green, lots of beer, and people with watermelons on their heads. This is especially strange, because watermelons don't grow in Saskatchewan, and can be hard to find when the season extends into the cold months of October and November. Ask five fans why they're wearing watermelons and you'll get six answers, and a cold beer. Some believe it's a statement that the Roughriders are so good they can wear fruity helmets for protection. Some believe it's because they're cheap to buy and fun to carve. There's a legend of some local students inventing the craze, and another that claims placing sticky watermelons on the head is the perfect way to cool down on a hot summer day. My research led me to someone else's research, which told of a couple of kids who went to Winnipeg to support the Riders in 2001, covered themselves in green, and capped it off with a watermelon. Their antics attracted local media, which in turn attracted the marketing department of the Roughriders, who promptly encouraged the fashion, much to the delight of local watermelon suppliers. This may or may not be the winning theory, but when it comes to supporting Rider Nation, results rarely count for much anyway. ➤

Green and White, painting my face, applying temporary Rider tattoos, putting on green bug glasses and a bright green wig. Covering it all is a thick jacket; otherwise, all the swag will freeze to my skin. Initially, I thought I'd overdone it, but as I walk from the Hotel Saskatchewan to Mosaic Stadium, I am snug among the faithful. I ask some locals to explain the passion for the Riders.

"Well, we haven't got a heck of a lot going on besides the Riders," says one chap.

"They're the best thing we got going!" yells another.

I begin to sense a theme. Without a hockey franchise, Saskatchewan has only one team to represent the province in the media limelight, and come snow or freezing rain, they're going to support them every yard of the way.

It's the last game of the season, and a game of meaningless consequence. The opponents are the Hamilton Tiger-Cats, who sound like characters from a Saturday morning cartoon. It's my first ever CFL game and a real glimpse into a Canadian sport determined to differentiate itself from the strikingly similar, much more popular version of the game just south of the border.

Canadian fields are larger; the team has one extra player; there are only three downs instead of four; and the game has all sorts of strategic, tactical, and rule differences. For a newbie like me, both sports provide an opportunity to watch large armoured men slam into each other while fetching women with pompoms do backflips — therefore, a grand day out, whatever side of the border you happen to be on. I take my seat and immediately scream "Go Riders!" at the top of my lungs. I probably should have waited until they finished singing the national anthem.

Mosaic Stadium holds 30,000 people and is neither covered nor heated. This is important to note should the playoffs extend into November, when Regina has recorded temperatures as low as –37°C. If you can survive watching a football game when the thermometer retreats well below zero, you deserve to support the best team in the entire universe, of any sport, period.

As the game proceeds, I do as the locals do: yell at the visitors ("Tiger-Cats, more like Pussy-Cats!"), yell at the referee ("I don't know what rules you're following, but only Riders rule!"), crack open hand warmers in my pockets, and drink copious amounts of beer. This endears me to fellow fans, and I receive not one but two fluffy key-chain toys of Gainer, the Riders' lovable gopher mascot. I am told Gainer pioneered the art of beating stuffed lions and tigers in the middle of a football field.

After an awful season and against all odds, the Riders emerge triumphant, providing some consolation for Canada's most festive fans. Another season is over, but there's always next year, when the mighty Riders will charge for the Cup yet again. Time your visit to Regina to coincide with a game and you'll see why Rider Pride scores a touchdown on the Great Canadian Bucket List.

START HERE: canadianbucketlist.com/riders

DROP THE HAMMER IN SASKATOON

*D*ays *of Thunder* was a cookie-cutter early-nineties Tom Cruise
vehicle. Determined, somewhat arrogant underdog gets humbled, taken under the wing of a wise mentor, works hard, takes risks,
and is rewarded with a heroes welcome/court victory/beautiful girl/
checkered flag — or any combination of the four. Having grown up
with the more sophisticated Formula 1 series, *Days of Thunder* was
my first introduction to NASCAR. As with many of Tom Cruise's
films, I wasn't particularly impressed, but it nevertheless left a lasting
impression on the power of auto sport and the appeal of redheads
(i.e., Nicole Kidman, who was soon to be "Mrs. Cruise").

The possibility of *actually* racing on a speed track that *actually* hosts
a NASCAR event stoked my bucket list engine, and clearly stoked

the engine of our Ford Explorer as my dad and I tore along prairie back roads from Calgary to Saskatoon. These are roads seemingly designed for speed tests, and we had to test the mettle of the governor, the name of the software that locks the top speed of most modern cars. Dad was *only* travelling at 144 kilometres per hour when we were pulled over just outside of Harris, SK. The real injustice was the fact that the polite RCMP officer told us the speed limit was 100 kilometres per hour. This on a road that would have the electrocardiogram of a corpse. Humbled by a $384 speeding ticket, we eventually pulled up to the Wyant Group Raceway, located two miles north of Saskatoon.

At last, we could legally drop the hammer ("NASCAR speak" for flooring the accelerator) and drive as fast as our four wheels could spin.

Canada's only member-owned and volunteer-run raceway, the Wyant Group Raceway is an oval track that hosts stock cars, pro-trucks, super-late models, and one of only two official NASCAR events in Western Canada.

Alex "Mad Cat" Leschenko has been racing since 1975 and has competed in every division there is. I get into the passenger seat beside him for a couple of white-knuckle runs in our street SUV, and I ask him about the racing concept of BYT (that is, doing any-thing "beyond your talent") as Alex inches closer and closer to the wall with each straightaway. It is proving to be a challenging workday for our governor.

Next, I am invited to suit up and climb into a 350-horsepower Caprice stock car that seems to have only two speeds: fast and faster. Alex buckles me in to the crash cage, shows me how to put the car in gear and install the removable steering wheel, and then wishes me luck. The engine growls menacingly. I manoeuvre the Caprice out into the centre of the raceway and floor it with such force I have to do another 360-degree loop just to collect my eyeballs. I toy with the possibility of letting the banged-up Caprice rub the walls, since, as Tom Cruise explains in *Days of Thunder*, "it's just a little rubbing, and rubbing's racing!"

My 10 laps are exhilarating, immensely fun, and, most importantly, something that anybody with a licence can actually do. Racing a stock car on a NASCAR speedway is made accessible to the general public here. Several times a year, the Wyant Group Raceway holds introductory sessions where the public can show up and drive 10 laps with an instructor and 10 laps at the wheel solo. Or you might get addicted and end up signing up for more instruction. The next thing you know, you're screaming at Mad Cat Leschenko in your headset that you're going to drop the hammer! It's a beautiful dream, and it stays with you long after you exit the raceway.

Just remember to adhere to the speed limit when you return to the roads of reality.

START HERE: canadianbucketlist.com/stockcar

FLOAT IN CANADA'S DEAD SEA

Before you die, you really should experience the wonders of the Dead Sea. With its banks being the lowest place of dry land on Earth, and with waters 8.6 times saltier than the ocean, one floats without any effort, cradled by the lifeless yet legendary therapeutic waters. The Dead Sea splits Israel and Jordan in the Middle East, which is a little far to travel even by Canadian standards. So it's Saskatchewan to the rescue, with its own lake, unique in the western hemisphere, located just a 90-minute drive southeast of Saskatoon.

Twelve thousand years ago, a receding glacier trapped a lake at the bottom of a valley. Hemmed in by the valley walls, water was prevented from seeping away by pressure caused by groundwater aquifers. Thousands of years of evaporation later, the result is Little Manitou Lake, with waters three times saltier than the ocean and laced with all sorts of wonderfully helpful minerals. As in the Dead Sea, you can float, you can heal, and you can smother yourself in goopy mud that international spas could market for small fortunes.

Having visited the Dead Sea a number of times, I admit I am skeptical. Surely, if such a lake existed, it would be on the world map, or at least North America's. Driving through the prairie, passing small towns and potash mines, I have a sinking feeling (*ahem*) that Little Manitou will not live up to the hype. Although few people outside the area know about it today, it was immensely popular in the 1950s.

"Canada's Carlsbad!" reads an enthusiastic wooden sign as I enter Watrous, the nearest town. It's sleepy and quiet, but then again, so are the towns that service the Dead Sea. I check in to the Manitou Springs Hotel and Spa, my room offering a lovely view of the calm lake mirroring a big prairie sky. A few people are taking a dip, but nobody is floating on their back. Downstairs, the "rich golden colour" of the heated indoor mineral pools looks suspiciously like dirty tea, even if it is 100 percent natural.

I walk across the street to find adults sunbathing among rows of kids playing on the coarse sandy beach. I try to imagine Cree peoples on these same banks, discovering, to their surprise, that drinking and bathing in the water cured deathly fevers and painful rheumatism. Legend has it a group of sick men were left for dead here, only to recover thanks to the water's healing properties. When they returned to their tribe, they were initially thought to be ghosts.

Chemically, the water is rich: magnesium (helps regulate body temperature, tones skin); potassium (antibacterial); sulphate (aids nervous, blood, muscular, and lymph systems); calcium (great for the skin);

silica (skin tone, bone and nail growth); sulphur (for aching joints and collagen synthesis) — all of which should easily take care of the uric acid, as contributed by the small kids playing in the shallow areas. Unlike the suitably named Dead Sea, there is life in these waters: brine shrimp, bugs, and a sticky green weed the kids are collecting to make messy wigs.

I walk to the edge, dip in my toe-thermometer, lie back, and expect to sink like a stone. Instead, the water makes me buoyant, and I find myself easily floating on my back. Admittedly, the liquid is not as supportive as the Dead Sea, but it's comfortable enough, in that one would have to work very hard to drown oneself.

After applying and rinsing off the mud, I find my skin wonderfully silky and shiny, making me wonder why Dead Sea mud sells for big bucks while Manitou mud is unheard of. Watrous, there's cash to be made here!

The Dead Sea undoubtedly benefits from that repetitive Trio of Important Rules: location, location, location. Manitou, on the other hand, literally means "Great Spirit" in Cree, a godly lake blessed with healing, recreational, and definite bucket list qualities.

START HERE: canadianbucketlist.com/manitou

VISIT A HAUNTED GROVE

Driving out of the city, Saskatoon dissipates into a string of strip malls, homesteads, farmsteads, and finally no steads at all, just endless flat fields of wheat. An ominous sky hovers above the autumn chill.

My destination is a mysterious grove of deformed aspen trees that locals believe might be the freakiest trees in all of Canada. It begs investigation and provides a neat excuse to drive north into the prairie to see for myself. Crooked Bush is not on any maps.

Once I pass through the small town of Hafford, I stop and ask for directions at a gas station. It looks as if it could easily be the location for the hit Canadian sitcom *Corner Gas*. Fortunately, the pimply kid behind the counter knows exactly what I'm looking for. Apparently, "Y'all ain't the first stranger driving these parts lookin' for trees."

He hands me a one-page sheet containing information about Crooked Bush. "The Crooked Bush is a group of wild aspen trees that … twist, loop, and bend into the eeriest of forests. Courage of stone is necessary to visit it at night." Fortunately, I've planned my visit during the day, although I score extra points for making it the week of Halloween.

With no help from the pamphlet's awfully confusing directions, I get lost within 10 minutes of turning off the highway. When in doubt, follow those in front of you. I hope the pickup truck in question is also seeking the strange and unusual, and not, say, a tractor part. Ten minutes later, a lopsided wooden sign, written in what can best be described as witch scrawl, points right. A small clearing leads to a wooden boardwalk with a sign boldly indicating that I've arrived at a legendary botanical mystery.

Exiting the car, hunched up against the cold, I take a few steps, stop, and start yelling into the bitter wind. "Tim! Tim? Are you there?" Only director Tim Burton's warped mind could possibly have created the trees that knot themselves over the boardwalk: silver-flecked branches with black scars, tangled and twisted, like the claws of a goblin or the dislocated legs of a giant spider. While university researchers have determined that some form of genetic mutation

Spooks in Saskatchewan

1.   The St. Louis Ghost Train is a steady white glow followed by a red light, a mysterious oncoming locomotive that never arrives. While some believe it to be car lights, local legend attributes the ghostly lights to a decapitated conductor.

2.   In 1938, a mysterious bouncing light startled a resident walking through the Tabor Cemetery near the town of Esterhazy. Accompanied by a chill in the air, other residents saw it, too, and soon enough, the Tabor lights captured the nation's attention.

3.   Haunting the abandoned mines between the towns of Bientait and Estevan are the *rugaroos* — mean-mannered, shape-shifting ancient First Nations spirits with glowing red eyes and a penchant for mischief.

4.   The community of Brickleigh was notoriously haunted for half a century, until the 1980s, when a farmer unearthed a human skull. It is thought to have belonged to a murdered railwayman, whose ghost has since been quiet.

5.   Fleeing a Blackfoot raiding party, three Assiniboine women are said to have drowned in Old Wives Lake. On calm days, locals claim they can still hear screaming across the water.

6.   An elderly female ghost, said to be the kindly spirit of a former nurse, haunts the hallways of Regina General Hospital. Meanwhile, the ghost of Howie, a cook who died in the mansion in the 1930s, is said to haunt Government House. ➤

causes the trees to grow as they do, mystery still surrounds what led to the mutation in the first place, and why forests of perfectly normal, straight aspen trees surround the grove.

Locals in the area claim to have seen UFOs, while others point fingers at meteorites, contaminated soil, or overzealous imaginations. My favourite theory belongs to the farmer who claims to have seen an alien urinate in the area before the trees began to grow in the 1940s. This might explain another creepy forest in Poland, where pine trees are deformed at 90-degree angles. After all, even little green men gotta go when they gotta go.

The boardwalk is not very long, and there are a few standout rock star trees that hog attention. Another couple arrive, telling me they've heard about the trees for years. On Halloween, the goth inclined are known to throw creepy parties here, and they're welcome to it. There's definitely something strange in the air, an energy charged by aliens, meteors, or an arboreal sense of humour.

The chill is piercing my fleece, and my wife has run back to the car to catch up with her imagination. A few minutes later I join her for the return drive to Saskatoon, as the late-afternoon sun peeks out from under the clouds, brightening up the wheat fields. The drive is straight, long, and unmistakably beautiful. No verdict on whether Crooked Bush is, in fact, one of the most haunted spots in Canada. But for providing an excuse to drive into the prairie on a fun, hare-brained adventure, it deserves its spot on the Canadian bucket list.

START HERE: canadianbucketlist.com/crookedbush

STARGAZE IN A DARK SKY PRESERVE

Many years ago, human beings navigated their past, present, and future by the stars. The movement of these celestial bodies determined the seasons and festivals, the direction in which to point foot, wagon, or ship. Constellations gave birth to the mythology of gods, immortalized in pinpricks of light in the darkest of skies.

For those of us who live in cities, it's a rare night indeed when we can observe the full glory of space. *Sky glow* is a term used for powerful urban light sources that surround a city — from the street lights, buildings, and stadiums. It creates an orange haze scattered by reflections in the dust, airbrushing out the darkness of night. We don't see the Milky Way or the movement of planets and constellations: the

Starbathing in the City

If you can't get to a Dark Sky Preserve, visit the University of Saskatchewan's Campus Observatory in Saskatoon. Each clear Saturday night, the observatory focuses its three-metre refracting telescope on planets, clusters, galaxies, and the occasional unsuspecting comet. Admission is free. ➤

nightly reminder of how little we know and how small our problems really are. This light pollution protects us from ourselves, a comforting blanket to warm us against the chill of insignificance. It is also an illuminated bandit that robs us of a view that is, literally, out of this world.

Fortunately, Canada is a country that leads the way in the creation of Dark Sky Preserves, areas protected from artificial light, promoting astronomy while allowing for the study of the impact of darkness on wildlife. As of this writing, Canada has 20 of the 49 Dark Sky Preserves that have been established worldwide and the tightest controls to ensure they remain true refuges of night. Saskatchewan has two Dark Sky Preserves: the Cypress Hills Interprovincial Park it shares with Alberta and the 900-square-kilometre Grasslands National Park.

Grasslands is Canada's darkest Dark Sky Preserve and has the highest rating on the Bortle dark sky scale, a nine-level Richter-like measure for nocturnal darkness. Here you can see faint traces of Earth's airglow, the weak emission of planetary light, while parts of the Milky Way actually cast shadows on the ground. Parks Canada holds free stargazing events, guided by astronomers from the Royal Astronomical Society of Canada. High-powered telescopes are available to the public. So clear are the stars that you can see the

Triangulum Galaxy with the naked eye, a galaxy three million light years away. Even a pair of binoculars will serve as an able telescope. The best places to view the stars in the park's West Block are at the Belza Viewpoint or the Two Tree Trail Access Road. McGowan's Campground and Dawson's Viewpoint are ideal in the East Block.

It took a while for my eyes to adjust and for the sheer spectacle of the night sky to manifest itself. Satellites and shooting stars are abundant, almost overwhelming. Lying down, wrapped warm in a blanket, I have to remind myself this isn't a planetarium, but that I'm perfectly safe to enjoy the dark dome above me, exposed and vulnerable on the soft prairie grassland.

When it's time to leave, I check the time on my cellphone and the backlight stings my retinas. Rays of car beams cause me to squint. Slowly, I reacquaint myself with this world of illumination, even as the stars above disappear in the wake of the halogen.

Canada's Dark Sky Preserves are a welcome reminder that we all need to look up more.

START HERE: canadianbucketlist.com/darksky

ZIP THROUGH THE CYPRESS HILLS

Straddling the border between two provinces, Cypress Hills Interprovincial Park contains the highest elevation to be found between the Rockies and Labrador. Not mountains, mind you (we're in the Prairies, after all), but healthy hills that invite downhill mountain bikers as well as hikers, paddlers, and campers. Open year round, the park is a designated Dark Sky Preserve, contains twisted lodgepole pine forests and rare wild orchids, and includes a former whiskey trading post that is now the Fort Walsh National Historic Site.

When it comes to ziplining, I've found the experience is only as special as the environment in which you do it. This makes flying with Cypress Hills Eco Adventures particularly interesting. Operating May through September, their 25-metre-long sky bridge and six zips let you fly 10 metres above the forest floor, through and over the

forest. With a treetop adventure park, treetop drop, and climbing wall, this award-winning company believes in pushing your boundaries, just like any self-respecting bucket lister.

While you're in the area, you can stroll through the beautiful acreage of the Cypress Hills Vineyard and Winery and also pop over to the town of Eastend to visit a local character, somewhat long in the sharp tooth. The country's most complete skeleton of a *Tyrannosaurus rex*, nicknamed "Scotty," was discovered by a local high school teacher in 1991, and is now on display in the town's excellent T.rex Discovery Centre.

START HERE: canadianbucketlist.com/cypresshills

EXPLORE NORTH AMERICA'S LARGEST SAND DUNES

Twenty thousand years ago, 97 percent of Canada was covered by a thick sheet of ice. As the glaciers retreated, they left behind spectacular natural phenomena, including the Bay of Fundy, Newfoundland's Gros Morne, and an area in northern Saskatchewan that looks very much as if the Sahara has relocated to the boreal forests of Canada. The Athabasca Sand Dunes extend 100 kilometres along the southern edge of Lake Athabasca. They are the result of

Where to Find Canadian Scorpions

Athabasca's dunes may look like a desert, but for the real thing, you have to head to the warmth of the west. Forests, prairies, mountains, lakes: in Canada, a tiny desert has to fight for respect. Osoyoos, B.C., is the only recognized semi-arid desert in Canada. It has the country's lowest rainfall, highest recorded temperatures, and warmest lake. Located in the South Okanagan, this desert zone is home to 100 rare plants and 300 rare invertebrates, and it shelters the country's only tarantulas and scorpions. Being Canadian, these fearsome critters tend to apologize for causing any inconvenience. ➤

glaciers depositing bedrock into a delta, receding, and exposing the remains to thousands of years of erosive wind. Local Dene nations, on the other hand, believe the dunes were created by a giant beaver, which does seem more patriotic. Winds continue to expand the dunes, by as much as 1.5 metres a year, earning Athabasca the title of the largest active sand surface in Canada — a sandpit the entire country could play in.

This is not a desert. The dunes look over a huge freshwater lake, which is fed by streams, steady rains, and winter snowmelt. The water table can be come high enough to foster productive nurseries for grasses, trees, and shrubs, attracting birds, animals, and insects. Standing at the top of a 30-metre-high dune, gazing south, certainly plays tricks on the mind, like finding an outdoor ice hockey rink in central Saudi Arabia. Canada does have true deserts: the semi-arid Osoyoos and the soft sand in the Yukon's Carcross, recognized by Guinness as the World's Smallest Desert. Yet the size of Athabasca makes it look like a desert and not a freak of nature.

SASKATCHEWAN ↑

Athabasca Sand Dunes Provincial Wilderness Park is protected by legislation, although its way-out-there location is just as effective. The province's most remote park is only accessible via float plane and boat, and according to the official website, it contains "no communities, permanent residents, services, facilities or roads of any kind." That last bit is important, in case you expect communities of Ewoks, sky-roads, and underground toilets. That being said, the Fond du Lac First Nation have a reserve adjacent to the park, and they use the dunes to hunt, trap, and collect medicinal plants, as they always have.

The area is ecologically unusual and extremely fragile, containing 300 plant species, including 10 endangered plants you simply won't find anywhere else in the world. Hard-core wilderness lovers can fly in and camp in six designated camping areas, packing everything in and out so as not to disturb the natural environment in any way. Float planes deposit visitors at Canterra Lake, or you can boat into Thompson Bay. It's a day hike to the sand giants that make up the William River dune fields, through subarctic forest and plants adapted to this unique environment. Since no camping is allowed among the dunes themselves, you must return to your campsite, where you can be alone in absolute wilderness, give or take a billion bugs or two. As someone who's hiked in dunes before, I can assure you the fun wears off just as quickly as your shoes fill with sand. Still, there's something to be said for climbing a tall, kilometre-long sand dune, and something even more wonderful about doing such a thing in Canada.

START HERE: canadianbucketlist.com/dunes

HORSE RIDE WITH BISON

Highway 12 slices through the wheat fields north of Saskatoon, a never-ending runway as flat as a boardroom table. Our destination is Prince Albert National Park, less than three hours as the crow flies or, more accurately, plucks road kill from the highway. The speed limit on these roads is 100 kilometres per hour, a perversely slow clip for a mid-size rental sedan, or any horseless carriage for that matter. It's memories of galloping horses keeping me awake at the wheel: the time I raced across the green plains of Mongolia; that day I cantered on a Bedouin's horse in the Jordanian desert; exploring Lord of the Rings locations on horseback in New Zealand; learning to ride a unicorn Lipizzaner in the training rings of Slovenia. The Great Canadian Bucket List is kicking for an equine adventure, and Sturgeon River Ranch is ready to put us back in the saddle.

SASKATCHEWAN ↑

A Brush with Extinction

For a beast so large, it's frightening to think that North American bison almost went the way of the passenger pigeon, once among the most abundant birds on Earth but hunted to extinction in the late 1800s. It is estimated that 20 to 30 million bison once roamed the plains of America, but after decades of unchecked and wholesale slaughter, largely by fur traders, bison numbers had decreased to just over 1,000 by the late 1800s. Today, there are around 500,000 bison in North America, of which only 15,000 can be found roaming in their natural range. ➤

We turn off Highway 55, driving 26 kilometres on a dirt road through the West Gate entrance of the 3,874-square-kilometre national park. Across the river are three generations of Vaadelands, a family that settled here in 1928, the same year the park was founded. Operating cattle, land, and horses, Gord Vaadeland took a different route when he founded Sturgeon River Ranch as a horse riding and adventure operator, successfully integrating both his business and his family's farms with Prince Albert's star attraction: Canada's only herd of free-ranging plains bison, roaming within their historic range.

Gord is waiting for us, with his trademark wide-brimmed black cowboy hat and red checkered shirt. Two bold black horses will pull our supply wagon. Along for the ride are Gord's trusty sidekicks, Glen (hangdog moustache, slow prairie drawl) and Beckie (chef, bison naturalist, trail mom), and my dad, eager to believe that riding horses is like riding bicycles. It's been 30 years since he hopped in a saddle, and we're both hoping he can stay on it.

My horse is a tall, brown speckled stallion named Applejack. He's got the race champion War Admiral twice in his lineage, but Gord assures me this apple has fallen miles from the tree. After years of commercial riders, Applejack is addicted to grazing on the same abundant sweet grass attracting the bison. Still, the stallion is certainly a step up from my usual brand of trail horse, with names like Haystack or Lego, as in "always falling apart."

Saddled up, we head into a dense forest of trembling aspen and wild hazelnut bush. Gord calls this the "Mantracker Trail." When the hit TV series filmed a couple of episodes in the area, Gord was the on-camera guide, while his horses tracked down the "prey." No crazy chases are expected for our overnight trip, but still, we're on a hunt: somewhere in the meadow clearings ahead are herds of wild bison, and our horses will help us find them. Wildlife viewing on horseback is ideal, explains Gord. The park's animals don't get spooked, and our horses will detect any wildlife long before we do.

As we plod along in single file, the landscape quickly proves there's so much more to the prairie than flat farmland. Jackson, Gord's feisty horse, perks up his ears. Up ahead is a black bear, oblivious to our approach. With the wind in our favour, we ride closer and closer, until the bear suddenly realizes we're just feet away and quickly darts into the forest. Next is a lone bison bull, a tank of a beast, grazing in a meadow. We approach quietly and carefully. Having grown up in these woods, Gord knows never to corner a bison and the value of keeping your distance. "They can probably outrun your horse," he whispers. Especially Applejack, who would probably stop for a snack in the middle of a stampede.

Two hundred years ago, there were millions of bison in North America, migrating across the plains. Their meat and fur supported First Nations tribes for millennia. But when European fur traders arrived, they hunted the bison to the verge of extinction. In 2008, there were 450 bison roaming Prince Albert. By 2014, that number had been reduced to just 240, the result of illegal poaching, increased wolf predation, and disease. While farmed bison are plentiful (their meat is a healthy alternative to beef), the genetic future of these wild bison is constantly under threat.

Riding through aspen and Jack pine forest that at times seems almost impenetrable, we arrive a few hours later at our tipis and campsite. As a licensed operator and wildlife consultant, Gord has special permission for his guests to spend the night here. Wagon unloaded, cots set up in the tipis, we sit around the fire, baking bannock on sticks to accompany Beckie's delicious wild elk stew. Gord pulls out a bottle of bourbon (a bison is on the label), the five of us enjoying a night of true prairie wilderness. As the fire crackles, the horses tense.

"Over here, quick!" says Glen.

Just across the river, 100 feet away, a herd of 30 bison have wandered into a clearing to graze in the twilight. It's one of those magical, unexpected wildlife moments, when everything comes together: the people, the landscape, the weather, the animals. When it gets too dark, we sit around the fire, listening to the herd make its way upriver. Retiring to the rustic comforts of the tipi, we hear the patter of raindrops on the soft walls, the howl of a wolf in the distance.

Thinking of the area's glittering lakes, fun characters, wild animals, and even wilder summer celebrations at Ness Creek, I fall sound asleep in little doubt that the plains of central Saskatchewan have much to offer the Canadian bucket list.

START HERE: canadianbucketlist.com/princealbert

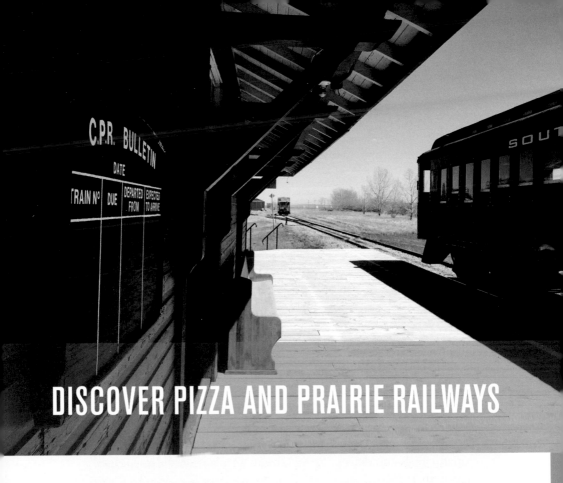

DISCOVER PIZZA AND PRAIRIE RAILWAYS

Everything is on track in Ogema, Saskatchewan. This town of fewer than 500 people offers visitors a chance to ride on a unique full-sized railway and to devour what is quite possibly the best wood-fired pizza in Canada.

Originally located at the end of a railway line, the first settlers wanted to name the town *Omega*, the Greek word for "end." Unfortunately, another town had already beaten them to the name, so they decided to go with Ogema instead.

Surrounded by seemingly endless flat prairie farmland, Ogema is the last place you'd expect to find authentic Italian pizza and pasta. But while travelling in Costa Rica, Marco de Michele, a young

SASKATCHEWAN ↑

143

man from Naples, fell in love with a Canadian backpacker named Tracey, who happened to be from a small town called, you guessed it, Ogema. After living in Turin for a while, the pair relocated to Tracey's hometown to start a family and indulge Marco's lifelong obsession of making the perfect pizza. His goal wasn't just to create the best pizza in Saskatchewan; it was to make the best pizza in the world! He would spend six months building a wood oven to exact Naples specifications, perfecting the dough (thin and crispy) and importing authentic ingredients from the boot of the Mediterranean itself.

And so Solo Italia, fine purveyors of authentic Italian pizza, pasta, coffee, sausage, and sauces, was born.

Walking us through his small kitchen as it churns out pasta for supermarkets and delis in Regina, Marco explains to me in his thick accent that "Mozzarella … it can taste like gum in North America," and he's deeply concerned that anyone should have to eat gum on their pizza. He goes on to explain the history of marinara and margherita, and why pizzas should *never* be loaded with too many toppings.

His obsession is clearly paying off; visitors are showing up at Solo Italia from all over Saskatchewan, and even as far away as Montana. The deli doesn't even have seats.

I explain to Marco that he clearly succumbed to Canada's lesser-known international trade strategy: send attractive Canadians abroad to lure ambitious young men and women back to our small towns in order to create thriving businesses!

Satiated with a perfect slice of pizza, I set off to catch the train.

Like the settlers of the Prairies before them, the Ogema Agricultural Society had a dream: to enhance the heritage experience of the community. Since the town's birth was connected to the railway, the society decided it would be a great idea to reconstruct a pioneer-rail excursion for visitors to enjoy. Since Ogema's original Canadian Pacific Railway station had long since given way to the forces of progress, an identical station was found, purchased, and transferred from the town of Simpson, Saskatchewan. Volunteers cleaned it up, painted it, and restored it to its original glory.

Now all they needed was a locomotive and passenger car. Operating as the non-profit Ogema Heritage Railway Society, they purchased a 1944 General Electric Diesel Locomotive from New Hampshire (which ironically had to be transported by truck since it could not ride modern railway tracks). Meanwhile, a 1922 Pullman 70-passenger coach was brought to Ogema from Gettysburg, Pennsylvania. The train and passenger car were carefully restored, and 15 years after its conception, the Southern Prairie Railway opened for business.

From June to September, various tours take passengers from Ogema out into the expanse of the big-sky prairies. The Heritage Train lets you visit an authentic grain silo from the 1920s, while the Robbery tour involves enthusiastic re-enactors attacking the carriage and fleecing passengers of their wealth (with all proceeds going to worthwhile charities). The Rum Runner takes you back to the days of Prohibition — a dress-up affair with passengers dining on Solo Italia's delights (of course). Watch out for Bonnie and Clyde.

There's also a package tour that takes you to a farmers' market and others offering a murder mystery and live music. Located about an hour-and-a-half drive from Regina, Ogema is a small town with some big, delicious surprises for your bucket list.

START HERE: canadianbucketlist.com/ogema

MEET THE FIRST NATIONS

Tyrone Tootoosis, the former curator and manager of cultural resources at the Wanuskewin Heritage Park, squints his eyes looking out over the valley corridor. "When I grew up, we didn't have air conditioning ... just a cold wife," he says.

"But I guess that made her a hot wife in winter," I reply.

"Yes, Robin, and you know, back then, Running Water was just somebody's name."

I'm laughing at the joke, but I'm laughing with gratitude, too. Tyrone's humour has put me at ease as I wrap my head around the

First Nations of Canada. Aboriginals? Natives? Indians? I've seen their legacy across the country, but I've come to Wanuskewin, a short drive from Saskatoon, to finally understand who these Canadians are, what they believe in, and why the scars run so deep.

Tyrone's long black hair is braided and parted in the fashion of the Plains Cree. He's got the look of a noble actor (he's appeared on screen), earrings and beads shaking from a waistcoat. Over a delicious pulled bison sandwich at the park's restaurant, Tyrone immediately puts things in perspective. "When people say, 'Tell us about the First Nations,' it's like arriving in Europe and saying, 'Tell us about the white man.'"

There are some 700,000 First Nations people belonging to more than 630 communities spread out across the country — communities

with different languages, cultures, and customs. One of the challenges for the Wanuskewin Heritage Park, a National Historic Site located on land with 6,000 years of Aboriginal history, is to help visitors understand this. Another is to create a community where old wounds can heal, for all people of the Northern Plains, and forgotten traditions can once again thrive.

"We have the responsibility to tell our own story, and not necessarily through history. Aboriginal tourism is not just something to tick off, it's about discovering a comfort zone," says Tyrone. A comfort zone I didn't know existed.

We take a walk along one of the paths on the almost 600-acre grounds. Tyrone explains what a powwow is: three days and three nights of dancing and singing. "If people want Indian culture, they should visit Bombay. We're the First Nations," he says proudly. Nations that communicate in a language of nature and spirits, where everything is connected to everything else. Nations that believe they have always lived on these lands — before the ice age, before Europeans arrived, before the residential schools that were cruelly implemented to annihilate their culture. Tyrone's grandfather was a "radical" and raised his family away from the Canadian government's shocking attempt to rip apart the fabric of First Nations culture. Tyrone never went to the schools, and he grew up proud.

We look at the remains of a medicine wheel as old as Stonehenge. So much oral history has been lost, nobody is quite sure what it was designed for. Back in the park's galleries, which host schools, training sessions, festivals, and events, we watch a young man (and two young boys) perform a mind-boggling hoop dance. A special exhibition honours the horse, known as Mistatim; literally, "big dog." Tyrone explains to me the importance of elders, the custodians of the community, and leads me to an elder named Norm McQuill. I've been encouraged to ask the difficult questions. "Why are the First Nations seemingly so down and out? How come there's so little integration? Where does all the government money go?"

It's a lively discussion, and Norm's answers surprise me. With so much pain in the past, Norm believes the First Nations must take responsibility for their own futures. He rues the corruption of tribal councils, the breakdown of First Nations values.

Tyrone brings over a young man who has overheard us in the gallery. "Sorry to interrupt, but this is important," he says.

The young man presents two cigarettes to his elder, according to the tobacco tradition, and begins to tell his story. He was sent away to a residential school, lost all touch with his family and culture, and is visiting from Alberta to begin the long journey home. He asks Norm if he knows of some of his relatives, and it turns out that Norm does, indeed. In fact, Norm is a relative, too. The young man trembles, his eyes riding waves of tears, the swells of happiness

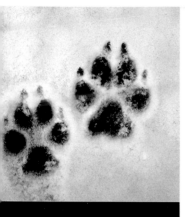

Track a Wolf

The Prairies meet the boreal forests in Prince Albert National Park, which is bordered by dense forests of birch, aspen, and spruce, creating beautiful panoramas in an area that hosts one of the most elusive creatures in Canada's wildlife pantheon — the grey wolf. The largest of the wild dog species, the grey wolf can travel up to 70 kilometres in a day when hunting. They tend to live in packs of between 5 and 12 wolves, ruled by an alpha pair that generally mates for life. Spotting wildlife is always a gamble in Canada, which tends to have a lot of space for too few animals. Still, Prince Albert National Park is one of the world's best places to encounter wolves, especially during the winter. Guided sled-dog or vehicle excursions will often discover hand-size wolf prints, scat droppings, or yellow patches of urine in the snow marking territory. The fortunate among us might see wolves along a road, or better yet chasing prey across a frozen lake. Alternatively, visit in summer and join the wolf howl — when park interpreters lead a caravan of cars to the forest's edge for a man-beast conversation.

START HERE: canadianbucketlist.com/princealbertnationalpark

and disaster. It's an honour to witness a moment nobody has prepared for. An honour to be allowed a glimpse into a vibrant and rich world that has so much to offer, even for just one afternoon. One doesn't have to visit Wanuskewin to embrace First Nations culture in Canada. Yet the heritage park's exhibits, history, land, and personalities make it a great place to start.

START HERE: canadianbucketlist.com/wanuskewin

SASKATCHEWAN

Portage in the Prairies

Traversing a famed Voyageur route along the Churchill River is a true bucket list canoe adventure. The river itself flows over the Precambrian Shield, into a series of lakes linked by rapids and falls, and crosses forests and rocky outcroppings. Enjoyed by both seasoned pros and beginners, this particular trip takes you 105 kilometres from Sandfly Lake to Otter Rapids, navigating nine portages up to 300 metres in length. Churchill River Canoe Outfitters arrange for equipment, transportation, and cabins on either end of the journey. And there'll be plenty of time to view wildlife, see ancient rock paintings, and feast on shore lunches and campfire BBQs. As for the water, it's so clean that some paddlers drink it right out of the river.

START HERE: canadianbucketlist.com/churchillriver ➤

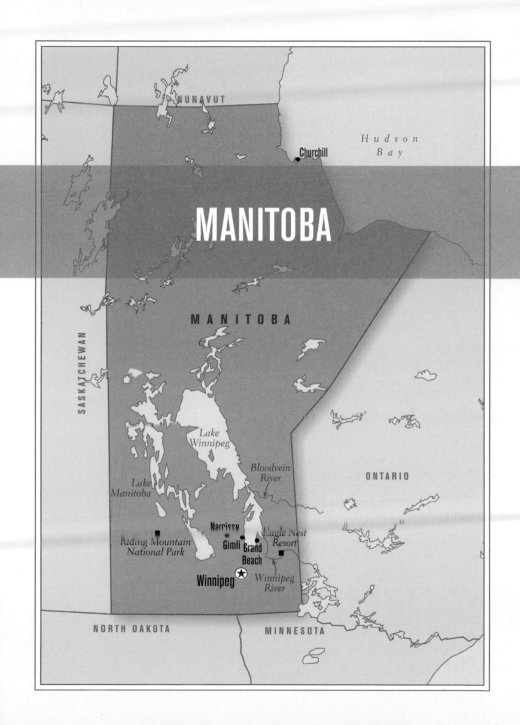

NUNAVUT

Hudson Bay

● Churchill

MANITOBA

M A N I T O B A

SASKATCHEWAN

Lake Winnipeg

Bloodvein River

Lake Manitoba

ONTARIO

Narcisse ●

Riding Mountain National Park ■

Gimli ● Grand Beach ■

Eagle Nest Resort ■

Winnipeg ★

Winnipeg River

NORTH DAKOTA

MINNESOTA

SEE POLAR BEARS FROM A TUNDRA BUGGY

Standing on the outdoor viewing platform of one of Frontier North's customized Tundra Buggies, I gaze at the permafrost of northern Manitoba. Two polar bears are on their hind legs, sparring like boxers, oblivious to the fact they are providing one of the most spectacular animal encounters you can experience anywhere. I'm wearing two thermal under-layers and a layer of fleece beneath my parka, but what does it matter if my nose is an icicle? Watching the largest carnivore on Earth in its natural habitat lights a fire under my soul.

Although polar bears can be encountered in Churchill during summer months, each October and November sees them gather and socialize along the southwest coast of Hudson Bay. Waiting for the

POLAR BEAR ALERT

STOP

DON'T WALK IN THIS AREA

sea to freeze, the bears are eager to head north on the ice in search of food. Cool ocean currents in the bay freeze these waters early, making the small bayside community of Churchill the most southerly point for humans to encounter polar bears. The 900-plus bears that annually migrate through this region are joined by thousands of tourists, scientists, media, and students, all excited by this unique wildlife encounter. It is not uncommon for bears to wander directly into town. Surrounded by bear traps, Churchill is closely monitored on camera, and famously has a jail for offending bears that continue to pose a problem.

We're advised to stick within certain town limits, with polar bear warning signs reinforcing the message. Considering that Churchill's population shares the landscape with hundreds of hungry bears, it is remarkable there haven't been any human fatalities for decades. In fact, Churchill has become an example of how humans and wildlife can safely live together. We're not 10 minutes from the airport, seated in a school bus shuttle, when we spot our first bear. Fellow passengers around me explode into action: cameras, whoops, sighs, even tears. A solitary sub-adult male bear is ambling over rocks close

MANITOBA ↑

Is That a Pizzly or a Grolar Bear?

Melting polar ice caps are sending polar bears farther south, just as human development is pushing grizzly bears farther north. While the two species would have encountered each other in the past, there's evidence that for the first time, these two different species are mating to produce hybrids: white bears with larger heads, grizzly humps and brown streaks; and brown bears with white patches, known to feast on seals. DNA testing on a pizzly shot by a hunter confirmed it was indeed a hybrid. A half-dozen wild pizzlys (also known as grolars, prizzlys, or nanulak) have been spotted on Victoria Island, and as the Arctic continues to melt, scientists anticipate the numbers will grow. Since pizzly bears are not considered polar bears, they are not protected from hunters. ➤

to the bay. He stands on his hind legs like a giant meerkat, observing us with curious eyes. Although the bear has yet to feed after a long summer, there's no doubting he is a magnificent creature: shag-carpet hair the colour of a vanilla milkshake, round furry ears, a black button nose. Polar bears look too cuddly to be hungry carnivores, but a loaded rifle above our driver's seat reminds us otherwise. These bears can run up to 40 kilometres an hour, and with one of the best noses in the animal kingdom, can smell prey from miles away. Camouflaged against the snow, these ruthless hunters are perfectly adapted to be at the top of the Arctic food chain, with no natural enemies — save humans and the rapid disappearance of their habitat.

Elated from our first sighting, we transfer to a Tundra Buggy for the 90-minute drive to Frontier North's Tundra Buggy Lodge. The 40-passenger buggy sits on 1.7-metre tires above a customized fire truck chassis. Heated by a propane furnace, it has anti-fog windows,

↑
MANITOBA

an eagle-eyed driver, and a handy latrine at the back (it's way too dangerous to step outside, and besides, good luck finding a tree on the tundra). The "road" is a rough, bouncy mud track, but all discomfort vanishes when we spot several more bears, anxiously waiting for the ice to freeze. Hundreds of photographs are taken as we observe them for a half-hour. Docking to the impressive 100-metre-long lodge on wheels, we settle into the bunks, kitchen, and lounge for the next few days. Since the lodge is located at a particular gathering point for bears, the onboard crew don't touch ground for the entire eight-week season. The price of the excursion is steep, but nobody is complaining about sharing quarters. We're here for one reason — polar bears — and fortunately, nobody is going home disappointed.

For the next three days, we spend eight hours a day roaming the tundra and are treated to a polar bear extravaganza. Multiple male pairs spar just metres from our windows, exerting their dominance for the winter to come. Large, curious bears stand up on their hind legs against our buggy, their warm breath literally fogging up our camera lenses. A lone bear walks across a frozen lake, backlit by the low afternoon sun. It's a photographer's dream, and pure heaven for a polar bear enthusiast. Arctic foxes, hares, and gyrfalcons also make an appearance, as do boxes of wine, great food, interesting presentations, and wonderful company.

The bears around Churchill are among the most threatened of the estimated 20,000 polar bears remaining in the Arctic. They're also the most accessible. Frontier North's Tundra Buggy adventure is without a doubt something to experience before you die. Although, sadly, with melting sea ice, rising sea levels, and the increasing threat to their natural habitat, you might want to act before the polar bears surrounding Churchill beat you to it.

START HERE: canadianbucketlist.com/polarbear

SNORKEL WITH BELUGAS

You can thank two large white animals for putting Churchill on the map: the most southerly population of polar bears and the thousands of beluga whales that gather where the Churchill River pours into Hudson Bay.

Snorkelling typically involves bright coral, tropical fish, and at least one kid surrounded by a suspicious yellow haze. Well, we're in Canada now, and in Canada our experiences are big, bold, and bucket list–worthy. That's why, when the weather is favourable, we'll don thick wetsuits, head into Hudson Bay on a Zodiac, and search for a particularly inviting pod of belugas. Fins, heads, humps, and tails are everywhere, and with their doe eyes and flexible necks, belugas seem particularly friendly and curious.

Hopping into the frigid 5°C water is something of a shock to the system, but since hundreds of whales are in our general vicinity, it's a shock we can deal with.

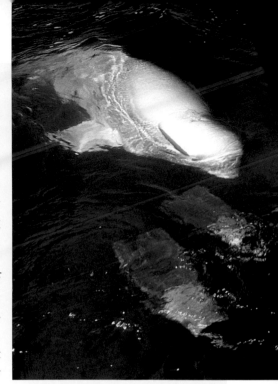

We hold on to a rope attached to the raft. The shade of the water is less Caribbean-blue and more Arctic-murk. With our affable guide on the lookout, the belugas swim around us, gazing with their prominent melon heads, singing with distinctive canary-like calls, diving deep or breaching above.

Given the abundance of whales, the responsible practices of the tour operators, and the relative scarcity of snorkellers each summer, whale biologists do not believe the animals are negatively impacted by the human presence.

With the limited visibility, you won't really know where to look, or where the next grinning whale might suddenly appear. Depending on the beluga activity (and your ability to withstand the extreme cold), your underwater excursion might last mere minutes or up to an hour.

Sure, we won't find Nemo snorkelling in Hudson Bay, but our bucket list far prefers this once-in-a-lifetime encounter with a one-of-a-kind animal, anyway.

START HERE: canadianbucketlist.com/beluga

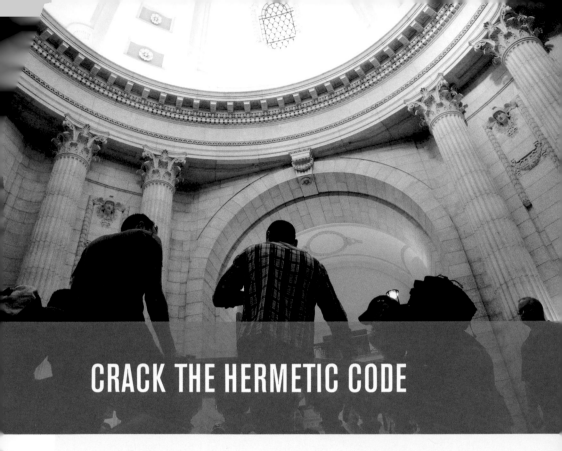

CRACK THE HERMETIC CODE

Things you may not know about Winnipeg:

- It was the first city in the world to introduce the 911 emergency response system.
- Its residents consume the most Slurpees in the world.
- Winnipeggers inspired James Bond and invented the cellphone.
- It hosted the biggest gold heist in Canadian history.
- The Manitoba Legislature is actually a mysterious temple with codes and clues that have been deciphered to reveal 6,000 years of architectural magic.

A local academic named Frank Albo expects you to scratch your head at that last one. He'll also appreciate the symbolism in my choice of five, not four or six, factoids about Winnipeg. A long-time student of the esoteric, Frank initially noticed some architectural weirdness on the sphinxes guarding the Manitoba Legislature. He decided to investigate, and 10 years later, he cracked a century-old code built into the imposing government building that reveals far more than anyone could possibly have imagined. Frank has since become an expert on Freemasonry, architectural symbolism, and the occult. While his bestselling book *The Hermetic Code* opens the doors of perception, his evening tours personally invite you to join him at the Legislature, swallow the blue pill, and follow him down the rabbit hole. Since he introduced the Hermetic Code Tour in 2009, more than 10,000 people have done exactly that, and today, joining two dozen tourists, I will be one of them.

A handsome, slim, dark-haired Frank arrives fashionably late, wearing torn jeans and well-worn boots. Given his academic prowess, everyone was expecting a bookworm. Frank's enthusiasm for the subject, and his skill in bringing life to the stone, is immediately apparent. "I assure you, you will never look at architecture the same way," he tells us. "On the surface it's a house of government, but this building is a Sudoku puzzle in stone, built by grand masters and keepers of ancient secrets."

These are heady words, and Frank challenges everyone to question, to not believe. He knows how flighty these claims sound if not supported by physical evidence. It is the physical evidence, as solid as the Legislature's imposing concrete pillars, that makes this 90-minute tour un-missable.

FACT: Every person involved in the construction of this building was a Freemason, as were nearly a century's worth of consecutive Manitoba premiers.

FACT: The Freemasons were traditionally custodians of the design of the original Temple of God, which was passed down through the ages under great secrecy.

FACT: The architect, Frank W. Simon, was a master Freemason, a professor of architecture, a man who placed nothing by ornament and designed everything with utmost thought given to the hermetic principles of numerology, astrology, geometry, and alchemy.

Frank walks us outside and points to the statues overlooking the entrance. They are infused with special significance representing two deities, Manitoba and Winnipeg, based on ancient gods, Hermes and Aphrodite. Even the pillars are measured to temple specifications. And as for the famous Golden Boy on the top? Surrounded by the four elements is Hermes himself, placed as the alchemic fifth essence, the quintessential symbol of enlightenment, and the hero of the architectural craft. It's heady stuff, but Frank's obvious passion, clear voice, and sense of humour keep everyone fully engaged.

Inside the entrance, he points out more ancient temple similarities: guarding bison, protective amulets energized with sunlight, and the repetition of the significant numbers 13, 8, and 5: there are 13 lights on every floor, 13 stones in the archway, 3 sets of 13 steps, and 8 pointed stars. The details would require a book (hence Frank's bestseller), but symbol after symbol, fact after fact, prove that Simon's building is a Rosetta Stone of mystical architecture, challenging Winnipeggers to decipher its accurate recreation of the biblical temple, chiselled in concrete, hidden in plain view. There is even a Holy of Holies, in this case, the lieutenant governor's office, off limits to outsiders, protecting a symbolic Ark of the Covenant behind purple curtains. Like the original Holy of Holies, it is accessed on just one day of the year.

Frank peppers his tour with entertaining anecdotes, such as how he convinced the premier to support his research, how members

of the Assembly thought he was bonkers, and how he was accosted one night while doing research in his pajamas. When he discovered Simon's own writings about the creation of a symbolic altar over marble with veins specifically aligned to symbolize blood, even he got a little spooked.

After shattering the traditional understanding of the Legislature's large mural, we head downstairs and stand in a circle around the Pool of the Black Star. During the day, government officials cross this star with scant regard for its intense symbolism and architectural genius. "Architecture is frozen music. You can read dimensions like notes. With the large dome visible through the 13-foot altar above your head, at this spot, you're speaking in fifths, literally speaking with the power of Hermes." His voice echoes and booms through the empty building. He invites us each to stand in the star and try for ourselves. It feels as if I've entered a sound bubble; my voice deepens, swells, and reverberates around me. Six thousand years of architectural mystery unfold, and my neck hairs stand up.

The great architect Frank W. Simon took his design secrets to the grave, and so the symbolism at the Legislature would have remained a complete mystery, an anomaly, another quirk in a quirky city. One man spent 10 years figuring it out, and he's absolutely right: after standing in the Pool of the Black Star, you will never look at buildings the same way again.

START HERE: canadianbucketlist.com/hermetic

GET CREEPY AT THE NARCISSE SNAKE DENS

I used to be petrified of snakes, a condition many a reader will relate to. Even though we are much bigger than all but the biggest of serpents, and even though most of them are completely harmless (not to mention painfully shy), they nevertheless instill terror at the very thought of them. Slithering, fork-tongued, sharp-fanged, poisonous killers waiting in the shadows to strike! I'm convinced our fear of these reptiles has something to do with the Bible, where the snake was picked out early as representative of a far greater evil.

In any event, I've found a way to conquer the fears that hold us back. Afraid of heights? Go skydiving. Claustrophobic? Go caving. Afraid of sharks? Jump into a cage and swim with a great white. Afraid of snakes? Adopt one as a pet. Which is what I did, in my early

Relax, This Isn't Australia

Red garter snakes are perfectly harmless. This isn't Australia, which has the top 11 most venomous snakes in the world, and that doesn't include Matrix actor Hugo Weaving. Canada has 24 species of snake, the largest of which is Ontario's harmless black rat snake, which grows to more than two metres in length. Vipers such as the massasauga and western rattlesnakes can be nasty, but encounters are so rare you're in far more danger of getting stung by a bee. ➤

twenties — a metre-long North American corn snake. To be honest, I never quite got over my fear of old Aquarius the Dog, as she was named, which might explain why she attacked me frequently. Corn snakes are constrictors, and although she could wrap herself tightly around my arm, she could do no more harm to me than an infant with a plastic toy. She could, however, strike for no reason, quickly, with a cold-blooded stare, sensing my fear and pouncing on it. Aquarius went missing one day, and we found her three weeks later living in my bedroom hi-fi speaker, inches from my head. After that, we named her Sony. Snakes make great pets: they're super low maintenance, increase in value with age, and scare the bejesus out of any intruders. Strangers don't knock on doors with Beware of Snake signs.

All this to say I was delighted to learn that 130 kilometres from Winnipeg lies the largest congregation of any vertebrate species on Earth. Twice a year, a natural phenomenon takes place that blankets the wetland region of Interlake with tens of thousands of snakes. In spring, typically late April or early May, males literally crawl over themselves in an effort to impress one female. The result is a landscape writhing and bubbling with serpents — in the crevices of their limestone dens, in the trees, on the rocks. Managed by Manitoba

Conservation, a three-kilometre-long interpretive trail has been established so visitors can watch all this from the comfort of the other side of the fence. Researchers believe there are up to 150,000 snakes living in these dens, located six kilometres from the town of Narcisse, off Highway 17. To prevent the automotive slaughter of thousands of snakes, tunnels run under the roads to funnel garters away from harmful traffic. Visitors are allowed to pick up the snakes, so long as they are gentle and release them unharmed. Red garters are quite thin and don't grow much longer than your arm.

Under a pile of 100 male snakes might be one female, noticeably larger than the boys on her back. Rubbing their chins all over the female, the males are courting amidst stiff competition, creating what scientists call a mating ball (a similar phenomenon might be observed on the dance floors of nightclubs). The female will select only one lucky male, and then, together with the rest of the snakes, disappear into the wetlands for the summer to gorge on frogs, insects, and other unlucky participants in the wetland food chain. Come autumn, the snakes return to their dens in another brief period when you can watch this reptilian phenomenon. The snakes survive the freezing Manitoba winters by huddling up by the thousands in these limestone sinkholes, slowing their metabolisms down and turning their blood to the thickness of mayonnaise in a process known as brumation.

Come on, Esrock! Is this really something to see in Manitoba before I kick the bucket?

Look, let's not snake around the issue: this is as unique and squirmy as it gets. Plus, Canada is not Australia, which is cursed with many of the world's deadliest snakes. You can't pick up taipans or black tiger snakes, since they are not nearly as polite as a red garter snake. True Canadian snakes, then, involved in a truly unusual natural spectacle.

START HERE: canadianbucketlist.com/snakes

VISIT A TROPICAL BEACH

As a travel journalist, I receive over a dozen press releases each day asserting the outstanding qualities of destinations, often from countries claiming to have it all. Well, as large as Canada is, we do have to face some facts. We don't have jungles or savannahs or large salt deserts, and as anyone who has been to the Caribbean will tell you, nor do we have tropical white-sand beaches. Unless, and somewhat bizarrely, you live in southern Manitoba. Here you'll find the cocaine-powder sand of the suitably named Grand Beach on the eastern shore of Lake Winnipeg.

At less than a 90-minute drive from Winnipeg, I admit I have my doubts about it. This is the prairie, after all, and comparing a lake beach to the finest sands of Belize, Brazil, and Barbados is a mighty bold statement. Yet that's what Winnipeggers are apt to do. As the car makes its way along the flattest of highways and through the sleepy town of Grand Marais, I brush up on the grand history of Grand Beach.

In 1916, the Canadian Northern Railway opened a line connecting the town, and adjacent Victoria Beach, to the boom town of Winnipeg. With a boardwalk, shops, and the largest dance hall in the British Empire, the town attracted tens of thousands each summer, who flocked daily to the sunny, sandy shores of Lake Winnipeg. Eight trains a day, packed to the rafters, depositing passengers on this unlikely beach of dreams.

I pop in for breakfast with Ken and Luise Avery, who have been living in Grand Marais for 30 years, running their lovely B&B, Inn Among the Oaks. With the wind blowing in a sweet fragrance from the garden, Ken fills me in on the history of the area, handing me a book with sepia photos recording a glorious yesteryear. One picture shows the beach and water so packed with people it's hard to distinguish the beach from the bodies. When the dance hall burned to the ground in 1950, and Winnipeg's boom began to dim, the railway discontinued their service and the area declined, until the province bought the land and turned it into Grand Beach Provincial Park in 1961.

Today's Grand Beach may not have the Atlantic City–like draw of its heyday, but it still attracts thousands of sun worshippers in the summer, particularly on weekends. When Winnipeggers strip off their layers of winter, they're a good-looking bunch, too. No less an authority than *Playboy* magazine named Grand Beach one of its Top 10 Beaches in the World. There's still a boardwalk, a campground, a couple of flea-market stalls, and popular hiking, biking, and bird-watching trails. (Grand Beach is home to several pairs of the endangered piping plover.) Warm water and strong winds attract kite-surfers from around the world. "Why be pickled in salt water when you can have white sand with a freshwater lake?" Ken says, laughing.

I bid the Averys farewell, envious of their indoor hot tub, and drive to the beach itself. On their advice, I head to the fourth parking lot, keeping the sand dunes, some as high as 12 metres, on my left.

It's a scorching summer day, but it's early, before the crowds show up. At this point, I confess, I'm still dubious. I've been to some of the best beaches in the world, on six continents, and with no disrespect to the locals, this is a lake beach. So what if the lake is the sixth largest in North America?

Well, I should know better by now. Grand Beach lives up to its reputation. Talcum white, it squeaks when I walk, the sand as fine and white as any tropical beach I've ever seen. It stretches for three kilometres, cradled by lapping water and sand dunes, a pleasant breeze blowing onshore. Day trippers begin to arrive with their umbrellas, beach balls, and sand buckets. Who can blame them? Canada may not have the world's best beaches, but with our slice of paradise in the Prairies, we've definitely got one that is unique.

START HERE: canadianbucketlist.com/grandbeach

MANITOBA ↑

FEEL THE CRYSTAL MENTHOL

MANITOBA ↑

Several years ago I was in Finland investigating a story about saunas. The Finns take the sauna ritual very seriously, so much so that they invented the word. The sauna is a place to relax, to reconnect, to cleanse, and to meditate. The heat itself is a spirit, called the *löyly*, which is to be admired and respected, discussed and adjusted. I entered a traditional smoke sauna outside of Rovaniemi, just shy of the Arctic Circle, and I melted inside a public sauna in Helsinki, where old naked men sat high on benches, enduring heat intense enough to burn the tongue of Beelzebub. (Finns use another word, *sisu*, to describe the inner strength and courage one possesses, presumably in order to survive a public sauna.)

I expected that was to be my most intense sauna experience, but that was before I visited Thermëa, a spa complex in Winnipeg. The spa is owned by the same company that owns Nordik Spa-Nature, the largest Nordic-inspired spa in North America, located in Chelsea, Quebec. These are people dedicated to the art of relaxing, and their latest complex is just gorgeous.

Bring forth the eucalyptus and orange steam rooms, pools of varying temperatures, relaxation rooms with headphones and ergonomic heated benches, an on-site restaurant, and a host of massage

Float On

Located a 15-minute drive from downtown Ottawa, Nordik-Spa Nature bills itself as the largest spa in North America. With seven outdoor baths, eight beautiful saunas, silence zones, and a fine-dining restaurant and lounge, it is a temple to pampering oneself. A particular highlight is Källa, an underground salt-water pool dug into the rock and outfitted with low lights and otherworldly cement pillars. Due to the addition of Epsom salts, the still water has a 12 percent salinity, allowing you to float effortlessly, a soft trace of new age music wafting beneath the water. Resting on a neck pillow, I was lulled into a blissful and entirely unique aquatic sleep. According to Nordik-Spa, Källa's salt water improves circulation, heals wounds, reduces stress, and stimulates creativity. Your robe is waiting. ➤

treatments. Nordic spas want you to heat up and cool off in succession, recharging your senses and delivering a range of benefits. Let us remove our robes and take the top bench in the Finlandia sauna, authentic enough to bring a tear of sweat to any Finn's eye. Although it is winter and pushing −30°C outside, my spells in the steam rooms and pools make the cold inconsequential. Sure, if I had long hair, I might have been able to pull off a frozen-hair pic, but this is a place to relax, not win the internet. A towelled sauna master invites everyone to take a seat on the wooden benches. He advises us to simply walk out of the room if it gets too intense. Hey, pal, I got flogged with birch branches in a Siberian sauna and stared down the scrotum of a Finnish grandpa in Helsinki. I can take it!

"Today, we are going to use crystal menthol," he explains. I'm not sure what that is exactly, but it's got a damn fine name, nonetheless.

Placing perfectly round balls of snow on the rocks, the sauna master adds a spoonful of tincture to the balls and flattens them with a wooden spoon. Next, he ceremonially waves a towel, distributing the heat around the room. When it hits me, combined with the intense menthol rush of the essence, it grips my lungs in a chokehold. Eyes burning, I have to go deep within myself and find my *sisu*, and when I do, the *löyly* kicks the crap out of it. It is intense, it is a rush, and it is incredible. The bucket list is all about chasing unique moments of magic, moments that stay with you for the rest of your life. How amazing would a sauna have to be to make it one of those moments? Thermëa amazing.

Once the sauna is over, I get to relax in the hot pools outside, overcome with a sense of relaxation, of cleanliness, of sound mind and body. Hot damn! That Thermëa experience took me places, a hot rush of cool crystal menthol to the head.

START HERE: canadianbucketlist.com/thermea

HAVE A HAPPY FOLK FESTIVAL

The Winnipeg Folk Festival is one of the world's most popular music festivals, a bold statement backed up by its enduring legacy, its global reputation, and the participatory nature of the community to which it belongs. A local named Don Greig, visiting for his thirty-seventh year, puts it succinctly: "There are comfort foods, and what we have here is comfort entertainment." Bea Cherniak, here on her thirty-ninth consecutive visit, typically hates crowds, but she loves the fest. "It's gotten bigger over the years, sure, but its heart is still Folk Fest."

The heart of which she speaks takes no time seducing me. As I walk around the nine stages, meeting areas, food lanes, beer tents, and campgrounds, the atmosphere is enchantingly welcoming. Strangers greet each other with big smiles and a "Happy Folk Fest!" The sound of acoustic instruments — guitar, horns, strings, even piano — permeates the air. There are 2,950 volunteers donating a combined 55,000 hours of their time to make it happen, directed by

MANITOBA

just 50 full- and part-time and contract employees. Volunteers share the backstage tent with the performers, all fed by a volunteer-staffed kitchen that produces more than 9,000 meals a day. Every effort is made to recycle, following a model green policy that keeps the grounds of Birds Hill Provincial Park in immaculate shape over the five-day event. Of the roughly 16,000 people who visit each day, 6,000 will be camping on-site on grounds that have turned into a destination unto themselves.

The camping atmosphere here is so fun, inviting, and creative that I easily understand why some campers don't even make it to the main stages. Festival-supported animation areas allow amateur musicians to perform, while others can rest in hammocks, drum in tipis, play giant board games, dress up, and join jolly daily parades. I pitch my tent with the Castle Boys, a dozen guys and girls with a reputation for throwing the wildest parties and building the most striking installations. It's difficult to tear myself away from their party and make the 10-minute walk to the main grounds. The festival also offers an RV and caravan section, along with a quiet camping ground better suited for families.

Although it is much smaller in scale, the Folk Fest embodies a spirit I first discovered at Burning Man, a massive cultural event in the Black Rock Desert in Nevada. It's a feeling that makes you believe in humanity and goodwill, and that everything is going to turn out just fine, after all. I tell a reporter it feels like Burning Man in the Prairies, and I am surprised to see my quote on the front page of the *Winnipeg Free Press* the following day.

As much fun as the camping is (the limited spaces sell out quickly), performances by some of the best musicians on the planet are still the primary draw. Under the clear prairie sky, sweetened with the tang of a tangerine sunset, I watch as singer-songwriters capture the audience's attention with their songcraft, politically minded lyrics, and simple charisma. The weather is smashing, and with the successful introduction of mosquito-chomping dragonflies, Manitoba's legendary summer biting insects are blessedly absent. An eight-piece Latin band kicks up the energy, the music swinging from salsa to jazz to pop to soul. With more than 70 acts, the organizers ensure there is something for everyone. Many of these artists will also collaborate through improvised workshop performances on the day stages, leading to some of the best musical experiences of the entire event.

K'naan, a Somali-born Canadian rapper-poet, rocks the crowd and wraps up the main concert, but the party continues until way after sunrise, especially atop Pope's Hill. It was built by the Catholic Church for the 1984 visit of Pope John Paul II, but I enjoyed its reincarnation as a venue for watching dreadlocked drummers beat tribal rhythms as thousands dance and drink in the new day. Not quite the spiritual communion the hill was built for, but for many, it's an ecstatic religious experience nonetheless.

Canadian summers are a time for outdoor celebration. The folk festivals of Edmonton, Vancouver, Yellowknife, and Regina do an incredible job of allowing people of all ages and musical tastes to come together, listen, party, interact, and get involved. Winnipeg, that beating heart of culture in the middle of Canada, hosts the granddaddy of them all. Leaving Birds Hill Provincial Park for the short drive back to the city, I tell the Castle Boys I'll be back, with a lot more folks in tow.

START HERE: canadianbucketlist.com/folkfest

PADDLE A BLOODY RIVER

A 300-kilometre-long river that flows through unspoilt virgin boreal forest and is called the Bloodvein conjures up strong images of violence. Its name may refer to a bloody skirmish between local First Nations or simply to the veins that can be seen in the ancient red granite rocks and riverbed. Either way, rafting or canoeing down this remote Canadian Heritage River is an adventure that paddles (and portages) its way onto our bucket list.

Rafters take anywhere from a week to 15 days to complete the journey, with some choosing to float plane in and out of certain lakes, carrying in all their gear as there is no road access. The Bloodvein corridor is a series of pools and drops, and as a result, it can be tackled in either direction, although most paddlers will go with the flow to exit at the Narrows on Lake Winnipeg, about 200 kilometres northeast of Winnipeg. The river favours those paddlers with experience. There are more than 100 rapids, unmarked and wild enough to send you downriver on the wrong side of the canoe. Reading whitewater is a handy skill, one you'll almost certainly have developed by the final stroke.

Glaciers scoured the area during the last ice age, and due to its in-accessibility, the Bloodvein was not used for trade or settlement. The result is virgin landscape, full of old-growth forest and wildlife that ful-fill the promise of the Great Outdoors. Marshes, forests, lakes, and the ancient rocks of the Canadian Shield host an abundance of animals, several of which are rare and endangered. Besides the usual suspects — black bears, moose, deer, otters, beavers — you're in the domain of wolverines, great grey owls, white osprey, and woodland caribou. Surrounding you is some of the oldest rock on the planet, and beneath you swim trophy-sized northern pike, walleye, lake trout, and sturgeon. During your paddle, you'll also see signs of ancient human history, archaeological sites from hunter-gatherers dating back 6,000 years, and red-ochre pictographs in Artery Lake drawn between 900 and 1200 CE. The Ojibwa people did use the river as a trapping area, and their des-cendants still live in the community of Bloodvein, at the mouth of the river, operating a lodge that greets paddlers at the end of their journey.

Paddlers will tackle the river from spring until fall, with July and August being the most popular months. That being said, you won't find that the campsites located on the spits and shores of Atikaki Provincial Wilderness Park and Ontario's adjacent Woodland Caribou Provincial Wilderness Park are crowded. There are no facil-ities or services, and the remoteness that has largely protected the Bloodvein from human history will continue to reserve it for those seeking a water-bound wilderness experience. Fortunately, guided tours are available to help us novices navigate the river channels, the whitewater, and the challenges of a multi-day canoe trip. For a name steeped in blood and battles, the Bloodvein offers just the sort of rugged adventure by which to experience the true peace of nature.

START HERE: canadianbucketlist.com/bloodvein

STAND BENEATH A POLAR BEAR

Churchill hogs Canada's polar bear glory, although not everyone has the time or the resources to hop aboard a tundra buggy. Fortunately, there's another polar bear experience in Manitoba that can scratch your *Ursus maritimus* itch. The not-for-profit organization that runs Assiniboine Park, a sprawling 395-acre park on the shores of the Assiniboine River, spent $90 million on the Arctic enclosure and Polar Bear Conservation Centre at its popular zoo. Part of an extensive $200-million upgrade over 10 years, the zoo has become a world-class fixture for anyone hoping to connect with the great animals of the north: wolves, snowy owls, Arctic fox, moose, cougars, elk, caribou, and, of course, polar bears.

Residing along a scenic walkway called The Journey to Churchill, animals might live in large enclosures, but they still stop visitors in their tracks. Several readers might feel queasy about animals in captivity.

MANITOBA ↑

Think about this: all but one of the six polar bears at Assiniboine Park was rescued from certain death in the Churchill wilds (the other was born in captivity). A fed bear is a dead bear, and so is a cub abandoned by its mother. Whether you believe the bear should have died in the wild or is better off being fed and nurtured in a zoo is a matter of personal taste. My own thoughts: a well-run zoo plays a vital role in the conservation of wildlife, serving as a crucial tool in our education and interaction with species we share this planet with.

Nature documentaries are wonderful, but observing an animal in the flesh makes them real. Critical to my bold statement is the adjective *well-run*. Bruised in my memory is a visit to Cairo Zoo many years ago, where I had the misfortune to see polar bears locked in a tiny, filthy enclosure and elephants chained to a stump. Outraged, I wrote a letter to the World Wildlife Fund to protest these conditions, knowing my verbiage would make scant difference. But that was a world away from Winnipeg, where the enclosures are spacious and the animals seem to be treated better than household pets. There's enough space for bison to chase each other around and wolves to disappear over the hill. Clearly, the animals' comfort and health is of primary concern. I believe we easily succumb to anthropomorphism — attributing human qualities to animals that don't have them. Would a polar bear be happier in the wild, battling each day for survival in a constant struggle for food? Is that fed bear/wolf/moose happier in the zoo? Can a moose be happy in the first place? Until we start talking to the animals, like Dr. Doolittle, we can't say for sure.

In the meantime, the animals of Winnipeg look healthy and content. There's no denying the contentment of visitors when they enter the Arctic centre to find themselves standing beneath a pair of swimming polar bears. The three-metre-wide, six-inch-thick transparent acrylic tunnel puts an O-ring on the mouths of believers and opponents alike.

Polar bears are stunning to observe on land. Wait until you see them gracefully gliding underwater or resting their powerful paws just above your head. With their creamy, off-white hair bristling like an aquatic hairbrush, never have polar bears appeared so charming, magical, and accessible. It makes you want to know more about their habits, their habitats, and the challenges they are facing due to climate change.

Information is offered through the excellent use of interactive displays and interpretation boards. As for the bears, they interact when they feel like it, though they are particularly active in the winter months, when Winnipeg's climate more closely resembles that of Churchill.

For those heading to Churchill, a visit to Assiniboine Park is a fantastic introduction or epilogue to the world of Arctic wildlife. For the rest of us, and families in particular, it's a marvellous day out on the Canadian bucket list.

START HERE: canadianbucketlist.com/assiniboine

FORT GIBRALTAR

HÉ HO TO THE VOYAGEURS

A solemn candlelight procession departs from the Canadian Museum for Human Rights. It doesn't take long for the icy whipping wind to extinguish my flame, which I tried pitifully to protect with a plastic cup. Hundreds of people continue across the Esplanade Riel and right at Tache Avenue, shuddering forward beneath the old ruins of the original St. Boniface Cathedral. As church bells chime, we pay homage at the gravesite of Louis Riel before continuing on toward Voyageur Park. Even if the temperature has dipped below −40°C with the wind chill, and even if I am still coming to grips with Prairie French-Canadian and Métis culture, it is an earnest bucket list moment. Best of all, we're just moments

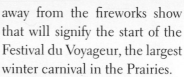

away from the fireworks show that will signify the start of the Festival du Voyageur, the largest winter carnival in the Prairies.

With long days and back-breaking work in an environment as hospitable as a rabid python, the voyageurs paddled their way into Canadian lore as the toughest of men. Organized fur traders for the North-West Company (a fierce competitor of the Hudson's Bay Company before being swallowed by it), these rugged French-Canadian woodsmen had a reputation for hardiness, industriousness, and a certain *joie de vivre*. In the early nineteenth century, these men canoed down raging rivers transporting the furs from the animals they'd trapped up north to trading posts in the south. Eventually, these adventurous voyageurs were phased out with the invention of the railway and the decreasing demand for furs, but their legacy lives on with their descendants, the Métis people, celebrated during this vibrant 10-day annual festival.

Winnipeg's St. Boniface boasts the largest French-speaking community west of Quebec. Each February, the neighbourhood's Voyageur Park attracts hundreds of thousands of revellers with music performances, contests, parades, food stands, and family-friendly activities. Having warmed my blood up with a sweet, fortified

beverage called caribou (served in an ice glass), I find myself in the main tent eating poutine, chewing on freshly poured maple taffy, and foot-stomping along to a jig. A terrific band called the Dead South take the stage with a now-familiar greeting of "Hé Ho!" — the festival's boisterous rallying cry. I didn't think it possible for the temperature to drop more, but that isn't stopping the ice sculptors scraping the finishing touches into their creations outside or the lineup of people waiting to get into the tent. Voyageurs playing a game of Nine Men's Morris in their trading posts would have been proud. Fort Gibraltar was a fur-trading post originally built in 1810 at the Forks — the point where the Red and Assiniboine Rivers meet. It has been impressively reconstructed upriver in Voyageur Park as a living historical site, complete with costumed actors recounting tales from the daily lives of the voyageurs. For these men, no portage was too long, no dried pemmican too foul, and no bag of fur too heavy, even for the pittance they received in return, which was barely a

MANITOBA ↑

living wage. The spartan living conditions at the trading posts were reminiscent of prisons. Through trading and intermarriage with Aboriginal populations along the trading routes, the voyageurs established the province of Manitoba.

Outside the fort, artists from 10 countries admire their snow sculptures, sparkling in the morning sun. I strap on snowshoes for a guided walk along the Red River, but ditch them later for a thrilling toboggan track. Activity tents provide suitable refuge from the chill, but locals are only proving what I've long believed: you can't do Canada if you can't do cold.

While their role in society was phased out, the voyageurs' ability to enjoy life in any conditions has surely been passed down to their descendants. How else can you explain the festive atmosphere and outdoor carnival spirit when Winnipeg's thermometer falls below "my nose is an ice sculpture" level? No matter how cold it gets, bundle up for the maple taffy, snow cones, flapjacks, and festivities. And if the lineup gets too long, draw on the spirit of the voyageur (and put some toe warmers in your boots).

START HERE: canadianbucketlist.com/voyageur

HOOK A SMALLMOUTH BASS

"Our float plane takes off as I hold my cup of piping hot coffee." According to my friend Scott, an editor at *Outdoor Canada*, that opening sentence right there is your typical cliché for any remote fishing lodge story. Since I'm no angler journalist, I figure I'll stick with it. Only there is no piping hot coffee, and I am breaking speed limits I shouldn't be in a Ford F-150 rocketing across the flat Manitoban prairies en route to Adventure Air in Lac du Bonnet. Through fate and circumstance, I have been invited to Eagle Nest Lodge, a fly-in fishing lodge on the Winnipeg River. At this point, I should note that I did, indeed, hold a cup of piping hot coffee as the float plane took off. My previous fishing experience included:

- hooking a barracuda and wahoo in the Cook Islands
- hooking dying sockeye salmon on a river in Alaska
- hooking piranha in Venezuela and Brazil.

Barracuda tasted best; the piranha was way too bony. The pursuit of trophy fish is a serious business, and much like jocks and football players, anglers judge one another by the size and weight of their tackle. The abundant waters of the Winnipeg River, cutting channels through hundreds of islands, are a world-class fishing destination. Eagle Nest, a family-owned lodge in operation since 1966, offers 18 staff for its 40 guests, serviced by two-dozen boats, fully equipped cabins, gourmet meals, and hard-won knowledge on the best spots to hook the local attractions: smallmouth bass, northern pike, walleye, sauger, perch, and, to a lesser extent, sturgeon.

Fred Pedruchny, who took the lodge over from his parents in 1977 and has been here every summer since, tells me the largest pike caught in these waters was a 127-centimetre monster. But it's not just about catching fish. Escaping the city, being in the wilderness, hanging out with friends and family — this is Manitoban wilderness, where at any point, you'll be at least an hour's boat ride (or 20-minute float-plane ride) from anywhere.

Jason, one of the sun-bronzed fishing guides, says there are only two things you need to pack when you go fishing: a raincoat and sunglasses. When it rains, the water whips across our boat. In the sun, my fair skin sizzles. Rain or shine, mosquitoes and horseflies are determined to take their pound of flesh.

In the capable hands of the fishing guides and my far more experienced new fishing buddies, it takes no time before I catch my first walleye. Sport fishing is strictly catch and release, but we are allowed to hold on to a right-sized walleye for our shore lunch. Pike flesh is not as desirable, so we throw them back, even the ones large enough to feed half of North Korea.

I learn to jig, cast, and troll. Comedian Demetri Martin was right: fishing should be called tricking and killing. Or tricking and letting go. But there's a healthy respect here for the fish: barbs are pinched to minimize physical damage. My trophy of the day is a 78-centimetre pike. Despite my inexperience, I haul in several species of fish, including a healthy-sized and much-prized smallmouth bass. Trust me, this says more about the number of fish in the Winnipeg River than about my fishing skills.

In the early afternoon, we all gather on an island for lunch, our guides making short work of filleting the fish, which are rubbed in spice or dunked in flour and cornflakes, deep-fried, and served with fire-roasted potatoes. Fish, to me, has never tasted better, or fresher.

As one of the world's largest flowing rivers (by volume), the Winnipeg River boasts abundance. An abundance of water, clean enough for hardier anglers to drink and warm enough for late afternoon dips. An abundance of fish. An abundance of good times. Eagles fly overhead; mink, bear, and deer roam the shores. Casting off the dock with my fishing buddies at sunset, I share Fred's sentiment: for all its tall tales and trophies, fishing is something to keep you busy while you ponder life with good friends under an enormous prairie sky.

START HERE: canadianbucketlist.com/eaglenest

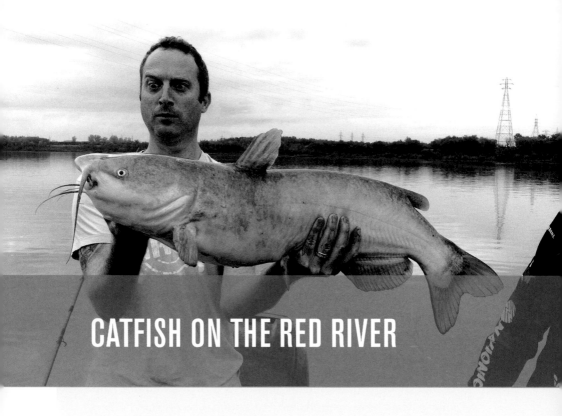

CATFISH ON THE RED RIVER

If you think pike resemble fearsome prehistoric monsters, wait until you encounter the formidable channel catfish that trawl the bottom of the Red River. Each summer, fishing guides at City Cats will take you out on the river, using onboard GPS to find the creatures lurking below. The fish average 7 kilograms each; all you need to do to declare yourself a master angler on the Red River is hook one that's 86.5 centimetres. Given the abundance of cats in the channel, this is not as rare an event as it would seem, but that doesn't mean it's easy. My first catch of the day was 71 centimetres. Reeling it in, I almost pulled a muscle in my groin before inventing a creative technique that involved jamming the rod in the bend of my chair. Beyond their girth and weight, catfish put up a tremendous fight. I heed the sound advice of Manitoban outdoor expert Shel Zolkewich:

Step One: Listen to your guide.
Step Two: Put on your big girl panties and suck it up.
Step Three: Reel in that cat, and hold on.

Muscles burning, I finally get the slippery beast to the boat, where my guide Cameron scoops it up with a net, measures it, and hands it over for my prerequisite proof-of-conquest photo. Catfish over nine kilograms are protected in the Red River. I respectfully release the beast back into the muddy river, to grow into an even bigger monster for others to enjoy.

START HERE: canadianbucketlist.com/catfish

MANITOBA ↑

CHANNEL YOUR INNER VIKING

Gimli is so much more than a dwarf warrior in *Lord of the Rings*. Billed as the second-oldest continuous cultural festival in North America, Manitoba's largest lakeshore community's annual Icelandic Festival (or *Islendingadagurinn*) is a celebration for, and by, the largest Icelandic population outside of Iceland.

This translates into music, parades, competitions, and re-enactments of famous Viking battles. I tried wrestling with a particularly large chap who pillaged my thigh out of my hip socket, then gave me a beer and a bear hug. Here you can also feast on traditional dishes like *rullupylsa* (sausage), *vinatarta* (Christmas cake), *ponnukokur* (pancakes), and enter the locally invented Fris-Nok tournament.

Avenge the Vikings and invade Gimli. (Just remember that Vikings never wore horns on their helmets.)

START HERE: canadianbucketlist.com/gimli

PONDER THE MUSEUM FOR HUMAN RIGHTS

All human beings are born free and equal in dignity and rights. It is a simple concept, elegant in truth, yet tainted by history. From biblical times to the present day, great thinkers have recognized that, despite physical and ideological differences, every individual deserves universal respect. The Golden Rule is one of the primary teachings of all great religions: Do unto others as you would have them to do unto you. And yet ... And yet, thousands of years of suffering, misery, massacres, abuse, torture, pain, repression, violence, and cruelty demonstrate humanity's inability to implement the idea. It remains a struggle to apply the concept of human rights to the everyday machinations of our existence.

Discussion, reflection, and debate are essential to leap over the barbed wired of ignorance that continues to jail our collective rights. How is one person's freedom fighter another's terrorist? How does one

MANITOBA ↑

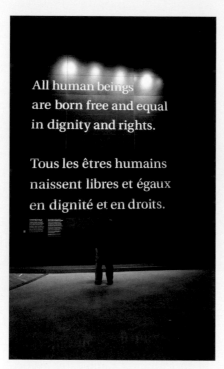

All human beings are born free and equal in dignity and rights.

Tous les êtres humains naissent libres et égaux en dignité et en droits.

move beyond injustice, transcend revenge, and avoid the yo-yo of hate that has plagued society's evolution? Given the exposed nerves bleeding between these and many other questions, any space that encourages such conversation is bound to feel the hot breath of controversy.

Bundled in layers against the icy chill of winter, I walk into Winnipeg's most striking building somewhat apprehensive. Would this be a holier-than-thou exhibition in a country, indeed a city, with a history of Aboriginal conflict? How can a museum possibly encapsulate everything from the horrors of genocide to gay rights? I check my expectations in with my coat, and begin in the dark and cavernous Bonnie and John Buhler Hall.

Ambitious in scope, bewildering in budget, outstanding in execution — the Canadian Museum for Human Rights (CMHR) is the first national museum built outside the capital region of Ottawa. First conceived by media mogul Izzy Asper as a museum to celebrate tolerance, it took 15 years and $351 million in private sector, federal, and provincial money before the doors opened to the public in late 2014. Based on the ambitious designs of American architect Antoine Predock, the building's construction costs spiked higher than its

23-storey Tower of Hope. Then the 2008 recession bit as viciously as a winter wind blasting down the Red River. Predock's unusual design and his insistence on using Manitoban stone and glass, Spanish alabaster, Mongolian basalt, and white-painted steel ignited the critics, creating construction nightmares. Then — despite the efforts of history and human-rights academics and extensive public engagement — came the protests: Why a permanent exhibit about the Holocaust and not the Holodomor? When discussing cultural genocide, there was a demand by Aboriginal leaders to include Canada's treatment of its First Nations. Reassuringly, a museum that celebrates the positive power of protests welcomed the debate, fully aware its curators will never be able to please everybody.

I walk up the first in a series of seemingly endless glowing ramps to the first gallery, a stunning space that explores the concept, history, and value of human rights. It is easy to see how the millions were spent. Exhibits here and throughout the museum use state-of-the-art technology to create an immersive multimedia experience. There are hundreds of video clips and thousands of images, most of which are accessed through interactive tablets inviting personal investigation. A 360-degree theatre shows a short film about Aboriginal perspectives, leading to Canadian Journeys, the largest gallery in the museum. Stations along the rim of the large hall reveal all aspects of human rights in Canada's history. Gay marriage is celebrated with a chandelier of moving wedding photos, selected from thousands solicited from the public. I learn about residential schools and the fight for language rights, religious rights, gender equality, disability rights, and workers' rights. A large group of children are being guided in the centre of the room, interacting on a digital canvas. While many battles are still being fought, in Canada and around the world, each station represents a victory. Each station suggests these kids are now growing up in a better world.

Glowing alabaster ramps continue to the next level, looking like a science-fiction movie set. Indeed, I expect it is only a matter of time before Hollywood arrives to take advantage of these distinctly futuristic walkways. Just how controversial human rights can be is explored in an interactive exhibit that lets visitors vote on Supreme Court decisions. Should a young Sikh boy be allowed to carry a ceremonial knife to school? After hearing the arguments, it's no easy decision. A real-time poll shows that 60 percent of today's visitors had voted yes, 40 percent no.

Level four's permanent exhibition on the Holocaust is outstanding. As a Jew — as a human — I find the subject deeply personal, evoking complex emotions of rage, pain, sadness, and vengefulness. Having visited Holocaust museums in New York, Jerusalem, and Berlin, as well as Auschwitz in Poland, it is still impossible to grasp the scale of this genocide. Some museums use symbolic art. Others use shocking footage. The central display here focuses on complicity, the brutal fact that the Nazi's industrial killing machine needed accountants and secretaries and architects. It asks: Are we complicit in today's atrocities? Are we also just going with the flow, following orders, believing what we're told? This leads us to a gallery entitled Breaking the Silence, which examines genocides throughout history. A large digital display case lets me scroll through the ages, examining the causes, evidence, and result of humankind's darkest hours. One can spend hours in this room alone. Having learned about the horrors, we now move on to Hope: life-sized digital displays introducing individuals whose actions have changed the course of history: Ghandi, King, Mandela, Suu Kyi, Malala, and many others whom you might not have heard of. A bold display showcases the Universal Declaration of Human Rights, and we ramp up to the final floor, which explores the complexity, challenges, and heroes of the fight for human rights today. A glass elevator shepherds me to the late Izzy Asper's Tower of Hope and grants those ascending a view of the open-plan offices of the researchers, curators, and academics

who work to keep the museum current, while using it as a beacon for human rights across the globe.

I meet some friends back on level three amidst the pillars, pools, and glass of the Garden of Contemplation. Prairie sunlight bathes us through the glass walls and sky-high ceiling. We have an earnest discussion about our experience, a need to make sense of it all. Some feel the technology and architecture got in the way. Others were moved to tears. We all agree that the CMHR is more than just a museum. It is more than the legacy of a media mogul or hubris of a rock star architect, and more than just the most striking building in the Prairies. On a personal level, visitors of all ages and backgrounds might connect with the space, the stories, the art, and the technology. They will surely connect with the message. For while some exhibits reveal the horrors of humanity at its worst, this is a space reassuringly infused with hope. Despite controversies that have plagued its development and content, the mere existence of the CMHR speaks volumes about the desire of Canada to transcend its own sordid history. It proudly declares that vital conversations must continue to take place, and that they can start right here in the Prairies. Most of all, it is a strikingly physical reminder that if we don't learn from the mistakes of our past, we are forever doomed to repeat them.

START HERE: canadianbucketlist.com/cmhr

MANITOBA

Watch RWB in the Park

Ask yourself: how is it that a city in the Canadian Prairies boasts one the world's most respected, sought-after, and watched ballet companies? Perhaps the answer lies in the fact that two out of every three people who see the Royal Winnipeg Ballet do so outside Winnipeg. As a financial necessity, the RWB began touring the world in the 1950s. The result is that many people's first exposure to ballet came through this company, which pirouetted in popularity in the ensuing decades. The Winnipeg Ballet got its Royal designation in 1953, and today is the longest continuously operating ballet company in North America. Its program has always leaned on the populist side — something classic, something modern. An institution since the 1970s, the annual free performance at the outdoor Lyric Theatre in Winnipeg's Assiniboine Park is perfect for those who want to experience ballet in a relaxed environment. Pull up a blanket, indulge with cheese and wine, and appreciate one of the world's best ballet companies performing for an appreciative home crowd.

START HERE: canadianbucketlist.com/ballet ➤

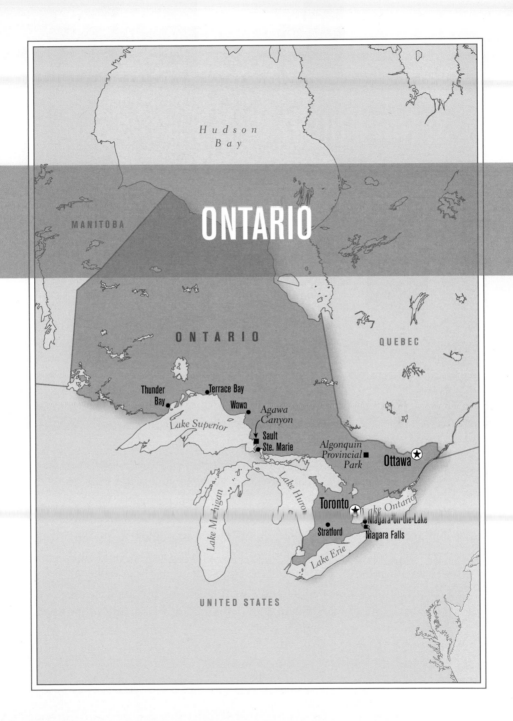

ONTARIO

Hudson
Bay

MANITOBA

ONTARIO

QUEBEC

Thunder
Bay

Terrace Bay

Wawa

Agawa
Canyon

Lake Superior

Sault
Ste. Marie

Algonquin
Provincial
Park

Ottawa

Lake Michigan

Lake Huron

Toronto

Lake Ontario

Niagara-on-the-Lake

Stratford

Niagara Falls

Lake Erie

UNITED STATES

SPEND A NIGHT IN JAIL

On a personal list of dubious achievements, being incarcerated for something silly does have a certain appeal. Perhaps it shows that even honourable, noble lives have roguish moments. Perhaps it's because one night of prison reaffirms the benefits of freedom. Perhaps it's just something interesting to say at a dinner party, provided the words "misunderstanding," "no criminal record," and "that was an adventure!" are used in the story. Of course, the reality of prison is entirely devoid of charm. There's nothing fun about being locked away in an institutional cell, denied the joys of modern life, surrounded by people who actually deserve to be there. Still, our bucket list demands adventurous transgressions, and fortunately, I found a prison cell where I could leave with my reputation, and clean criminal record, healthily intact.

"When they chained up the naked prisoners on the cement floor in pure darkness, were they on their backs?" This is the kind of question that arrests my curiosity as I stand outside the "Hole" cells in the basement of the III-Ottawa Jail.

For 110 years, the thick-stoned building on Nicholas Street was known as the Carleton County Gaol, an imposing hell designed to imprison the city's most notorious offenders. Built in 1862 as a "model" British prison, the reality was far less respectable: tiny cells crammed with both men and boys (as young as five years old), reeking of excrement, the floor crawling with bugs and rats.

The jail was eventually shut down in 1972 due to inhumane living conditions, but it reopened the following year as a refurbished youth hostel. The new owners clearly knew the lengths to which backpackers will go to save a buck. Today, budget travellers spend the night bunking in the original cells, drink beer in the canteen that once fed prisoners slop, and wake in fear with blood-drained ghosts hovering over their beds.

Okay, I made the ghost part up, but just barely. Ghost Walks Ottawa holds nightly prison tours in the old jail, guiding the public and hostel guests to some of the original, unrestored sections of the prison, recounting trials and tales, and revealing why this has been called one of the world's most haunted buildings. After touring the punishment cells, my Ghost Walks guide, Adriane, leads me to the eighth floor, still in its original state.

The cells are punishingly small. She paints a vivid picture of life for a nineteenth-century prisoner and explains the sad, short life of

Patrick J. Whelan, the man who murdered Thomas D'Arcy McGee, one of the Fathers of Confederation. Whelan met his maker at the jail during the last public execution in Canada. I'm led to the actual gallows, thoughtfully decorated with a hangman's rope. Five thousand people desperate for entertainment watched Whelan squirm for 10 minutes.

Even though Adriane has been guiding tours in the old jail for over a year, she's edgy and freaked out as we wander through death row. She nervously tells me about doors slamming, disembodied voices, guests reporting ghosts at the edge of their bunks. Seriously! I bid her adieu, retire to my cell, slam the iron bars shut, and make sure it's locked from the inside. Lying in my bed, I try not to think about the poor, miserable bastards who rotted away in Cell 4. It's deathly quiet, save for the snoring of someone in an adjacent cell. Although the walls are thick, the vaulted ceilings were designed to carry sound so guards could hear even the faintest of whispers.

I somehow fall asleep, but wake up in a cold sweat at 4 a.m. Worse, I need to pee, which means I have to leave the safety of my cell and walk down the long, dark hallway. At the point of bursting, I muster the courage to rise and walk to the bathroom, but decide to film the whole thing, just in case I become the first guy to catch a ghost on camera. Relieved, I return to my cell, toss and turn for hours, and thank God, Jesus, Buddha, Allah, and Elvis that I'm a free man, condemned to spend but one night in Canada's only prison hotel.

START HERE: canadianbucketlist.com/jail

PAY YOUR RESPECTS

Several readers will feel that celebrating Canada Day on Parliament Hill is an experience that belongs on the nation's bucket list. Touring Parliament might be another, and I'm not one to argue. The building itself is as grand as any of the great halls of power. With its imposing Peace Tower punctuating the sky like an exclamation mark, Parliament is a landmark that oozes grandeur.

I personally found the most moving spectacle in the capital to be Remembrance Day, taking place each November 11. It's a solemn affair, brightened only by flowered wreaths and red poppies pinned to lapels. Canadian veterans march to the National War Memorial, where they are greeted by the prime minister, the governor general, and a Silver Cross Mother — a mother who has lost a child in battle. Wreaths are placed at the steps of the memorial, a children's choir sings, and, if the weather permits, Royal Canadian Air Force jets crackle across the sky.

I watched as a Second World War veteran, motivated by the power of his memories, stood up from his wheelchair and marched forward proudly. The haunting bugler played "Taps," signifying the last call, and the sound echoed off the surrounding buildings. Thousands of people — soldiers, veterans, locals, and tourists — lined the streets, showing quiet respect. At exactly 11:00 a.m. on every Remembrance Day, a sunbeam pierces through a single window in the Canadian War Museum's Memorial Hall, illuminating the headstone from the grave of Canada's Unknown Soldier.

It's powerful stuff: a moving reminder of so many young lights extinguished before they had the opportunity to tick off their own bucket lists. An important reminder of how fortunate we are to be able to tick off our own.

START HERE: www.canadianbucketlist.com/remembrance

Lest We Forget

From its earliest armed skirmishes to the latest peacekeeping efforts, Canada's military history is on full display less than two kilometres from Parliament. Ottawa's bunker-like Canadian War Museum holds an incredible three million artefacts, including fighter jets, tanks, art, uniforms, documents, and a range of permanent and rotating exhibits. The museum's distinctive architecture includes one of North America's largest grass-covered rooftops, and a fin with small windows that spell "Lest we forget" (and "N'oublions jamais" in French) in Morse Code.

VISIT THE HOCKEY HALL OF FAME

"Please, for the love of God, can someone explain to me what's going on?"

It's my first week as an immigrant in Canada, and I'm staring at a TV set broadcasting 12 millionaires on ice skates. My older brother, who moved to Canada a few years before I did, has already forgotten our childhood sports of cricket, rugby, and soccer, and is now wearing a Vancouver Canucks hockey vest. His conversion to Canada's national religion took less than a year, but my love for cricket bats and rugby balls will not allow me to yield quite as easily.

First, how can anyone take seriously a team called the Canucks? Blackhawks, Predators, Sharks, Devils, Flames — those are some badass-sounding teams. But Canucks? Canadiens?

Senators? Maple Leafs? *Oooh, I'm trembling.* Second, hockey to the uninitiated is too fast to watch, too difficult to understand, and too painful to listen to, especially when a guy named Don Cherry gets on his soapbox. Further, the fact that I skate like an ostrich on Rollerblades clouds my understanding of the skills and talent needed to distinguish oneself in the National Hockey League. I'm not proud of it, but when I arrived in Canada, a "puck" was a character from Shakespeare.

During the regular season, when it felt as if the Canucks played a game twice a day, I never quite got what all the hubbub was about … until I visited the Hockey Hall of Fame. Standing on the corner of Yonge and Front Streets in downtown Toronto, the HHOF is located in what was once a Bank of Montreal office, a grand-looking building sculpted with gravity and pomp. To get inside, you have to walk through a shopping concourse, which may be symbolic of the commercialization of the sport or a practical way to control the daily crowds. And they come from far and wide, these worshippers of the vulcanized rubber puck, ready to open their wallets and drop their jaws at exhibits of the game's great knights and stand before the Holy Grail itself: Lord Stanley's Cup.

With 16 different exhibits, I'm not sure where to start, so I head to the Hartland Molson Theatre to watch an introductory movie. If you edited the most stirring scenes from *Rocky*, *Hoosiers*, and *The Natural* with *Gladiator* and *Braveheart*, you might approach the spirit of this sweeping, epic journey through Canada's great game. A frozen pond, wooden sticks, men with pencil-thin moustaches, and the recipe for legends. The film explains the development of the game, the teams, the rules, and culminates in the quest for the Stanley Cup.

I leave the theatre inspired to learn more, to meet the heroes of the game: Cyclone Taylor, Ken Dryden, Gordie Howe, Bobbie Orr, Mario Lemieux, and a goal machine they call simply the Great One. After the exhibits in the NHL Zone, I wander over to the scale replica of the Canadiens' dressing room from the Montreal Forum.

Canada's Official Sports

The unusual contradiction that Canada's most wildly popular sport wasn't its official national pastime was finally laid to rest in 1994. Up until that point, a game originating with Algonquin tribes along the St. Lawrence Valley was Canada's official game. In fact, lacrosse was the country's most popular sport until hockey usurped it around 1900. When politicians sought to resolve the situation, they agreed on a compromise whereby lacrosse became Canada's national summer game and hockey its national winter game. Any attempt to play either sport typically leaves me sprawled out in a bloody pulp. ➤

It's the first time I hold a stick and feel the weight of a puck in my palm. In the Dynasties exhibit, I learn about the dominance and great rivalry of the Canadiens and the Maple Leafs from the 1950s to the late 1970s, the emergence of the Oilers, and the dearth of Canadian domination ever since. In a large section called the World of Hockey, I'm amazed to see that the game extends beyond just northern countries to teams in Australia, Turkey, Mongolia, and, yes, even my old South Africa. Women play hockey, kids play hockey ... I leave the exhibits knowing the world is hockey mad, with Canadians the maddest of all.

The Great Hall of NHL trophies is approached with reverence. Here are the game's most sought-after pieces of silverware, including the original bowl donated by Governor General Lord Stanley, and the Stanley Cup itself. I'm told it's the hardest trophy to win in world sports, but fortunately, it's easy enough to stand next to and get someone to take a snapshot. Finally, I'm drawn to the interactive section of the HHOF. The Be-a-Player Zone allows me to put on some kit and play the goalie in a life-sized net. In the Slapshot Zone,

ONTARIO ↑

Cheer for the Jays

I'm going to say this right off the bat. I grew up watching cricket, which tends to bowl out North Americans
the way baseball throws a curveball at cricket fans.
Still, I can appreciate that the Toronto Blue Jays are
no grandstanding bush-league team. They're the only
Canadian team in the major leagues, and the only part
of the world outside the States that currently qualifies
for the World Series. Supporting the Blue Jays on a
summer night under the retractable roof of Toronto's
Rogers Centre is an activity all bucket listers can hit out
of the park. The bases are loaded, let's play ball! ➤

I learn that shooting is difficult enough, never mind scoring. In the
Broadcast Zone, I give a live play-by-play of a recorded game, then
convince a kid to play some table hockey.

By the time I leave the Hall of Fame, my conversion to Canada's
national religion is complete. It's game night, and the Habs are playing the Canucks. I head over to a bar, order a pint, and, for the first
time, anticipate where the puck will go, understand how the rules
work, and thrill at just how big the hits can be.

When a tourist innocently wanders in front of me, I say, "For the
love of God, move outta the way, I'm trying to watch the game!"

START HERE: canadianbucketlist.com/hhof

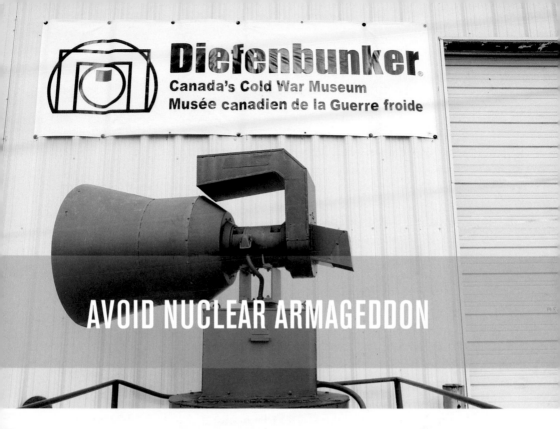

AVOID NUCLEAR ARMAGEDDON

You haven't lived until you've seen just how close we all came to dying. About 30 kilometres outside Ottawa is a bone-chilling, fascinating, and entirely unique glimpse into a time when geopolitics tightroped along a knife's edge. Two superpowers were headlocked in the Cold War, armed with atomic and hydrogen bombs capable of wiping entire cities off the map and poisoning anyone lucky enough to survive the nuclear Armageddon. Canada recognized that the end might indeed be nigh and set to work on a top-secret military bunker that would ensure the survival of its government. Commissioned by Prime Minister John Diefenbaker, 9,300 square metres of Ontario countryside were excavated to make room for a four-storey-deep underground fortress, using 5,000 tons of steel, 25,000 cubic metres of concrete, and $22 million of 1960s taxpayer dollars.

How I Learned to Worry and Fear the Bomb

A visit to the Diefenbunker wasn't my first exposure to the highly niche world of atomic tourism. In Ukraine, I visited a former top-secret nuclear missile base and was given a tour of its underground control station by a former Soviet general who once had his finger on the button. Men like him were trained — and carefully monitored — to destroy the entire planet on an order. Several times in history, that order was almost given, typically as the result of a computer glitch.

In Canada, Prime Minister John Diefenbaker authorized the construction of 50 Emergency Government Headquarters around the country. Smaller regional "Diefenbunkers" were built in Nanaimo (B.C.), Penhold (Alberta), Shilo (Manitoba), Borden (Ontario), Valcartier (Quebec), and Debert (Nova Scotia), along with other communication sites. While some are still active military installations, most were sold off or destroyed. ➤

The Diefenbunker, as it became known, was a full-service facility in which 535 lucky bureaucrats would have had the task of somehow rebuilding whatever was left of Canada. These appointees were selected based on their profession, not their personal qualifications. No family members were included, and, rather naively, no psychological considerations were taken into account. A large group of mostly men would emerge weeks later into a world of ashes and radioactive zombies. These, apparently, would be the lucky ones.

Fortunately, none of this happened. Despite several near misses (you know about the Cuban Missile Crisis, and you might want to search Able Archer), the Iron Curtain smelted, the world evolved, and children no longer have to memorize how to duck and cover under a fireball. The Diefenbunker functioned as a military telecommunications base until the 1990s, at which time it was decommissioned and turned into a Cold War museum. Due to the increasing sophistication of nuclear weapons, there simply wouldn't be time today to relocate government to the base, and at no time was the Diefenbunker used for its intended purpose. The only PM to actually visit the base was Pierre Trudeau, who promptly cut its operating budget.

Today, anyone can enter the 115-metre-long blast tunnel, cross through intimidating 36-centimetre-thick bank-vault doors, and explore the fully equipped world below. I'm greeted by Mike Braham, the former director of Emergency Preparedness Canada and now an enthusiastic volunteer at the museum. Mike was one of those chosen to survive in the Emergency Government Situation Centre. Shaking his head in disbelief, he reckons the real victims would have been the ones trapped inside the bunker. "With no psychological preparedness, these people would have gone nuts," he tells me.

The bunker was designed to withstand a five-megaton blast up to a couple of kilometres away. That's 250 times more powerful than Hiroshima. Its air would be triple filtered and, in theory at least, supplies would last up to 30 days. "People couldn't see beyond 30 days of nuclear war," explains Mike.

He leads me through the decontamination area and the medical and dental centres that have been transformed into excellent Cold War exhibitions. School kids might giggle at relics such as rotary phones and 1.5-metre-high computers. Adults have an entirely different reaction. "We came close, but we felt, we hoped, that common sense would prevail," says Mike.

I sit at the prime minister's desk, peering at his mounted toilet, and learn about the escape hatch, canteen, and Bank of Canada vault. Today, the Diefenbunker hosts parties, offers spy programs for kids, and even shows spy-era movies in a theatre. Hollywood has used its facilities, and the nearby small town of Carp has benefitted from the tourism. Other bunkers around Canada have been destroyed, but much larger and still-operational facilities exist in the U.S. and Russia. We may live in a safer world, but as long as we possess the tools of our own destruction, the threat of Armageddon will always exist. For its unfiltered, radiation-free fresh air of much-needed perspective, the Diefenbunker is one for the bucket list.

START HERE: canadianbucketlist.com/diefenbunker

UNRAVEL A MYSTERY IN ALGONQUIN

Algonquin Park's rugged beauty has inspired an art movement, a mystery, countless wilderness adventures, and a surefire hit on the nation's bucket list. Quite an achievement considering Canada's oldest provincial park lacks the gee-whiz landscape of the Rockies or the wind-swept vistas of the coasts. With all the tenacity of a blackfly, Algonquin's beauty burrows under the skin, seducing visitors by demanding that they, too, must burrow inward — no motorized boats, no planes or cars. In this park of 2,500 lakes, one enters the realm of the canoe, one of the First Nations' best gifts to the world. The canoe is a technology so perfect that European explorers ditched their boats and took up the paddle as is. Our bucket list wants us to pick up the paddle, too.

After a four-hour drive north from Toronto, I enter Algonquin's Access Point #1: the park's 7,630 square kilometres of wilderness can be accessed via 29 access points, your entries to 1,500 kilometres of canoe routes. On Canoe Lake, the park's busiest access point, wilderness lodges and fishing outfitters have done a roaring trade for over a century, but I've arrived in early June, with the busy season yet to kick into gear. Voyageur Quest has guided visitors into Algonquin from the northern Access # 1 for more than 25 years. They're happy to take me — a complete canoe newbie — several portages deep to Craig Lake. I don't know the correct way to hold a paddle, and my 67-year-old dad — a man who has never gone camping before, or even slept in a tent — is my canoeing companion. Adding further spice to the adventure pot is the fact that it is peak Bug Season, with a capital B. Bucket lists seldom shy away from taking one outside one's comfort zone, although I'm sure there are readers who have camped their entire lives and can start a fire by rubbing their fingers together, set up a tarp with the power of thought, and tie knots with the dexterity of a surgeon. I'm determined to prove a canoe trip in Algonquin is for everybody, although it certainly helps to have one of those outdoorsy fellas handy, someone like our affable guide Matt Rothwell. He's got that gleam in his eye that shows he's truly in love with the bush, and the demeanour of a welcoming host. Matt demonstrates the canoeing basics for us at Voyageur Quest's outfitting shop: the paddler up front provides the power, drawing forward, inward, or cross-bow drawing away. Paddler in the rear steers with movements called prying or sweeping. Canoes are surprisingly stable and can carry a lot of gear. Voyageurs — those hard-as-tack toughs who blazed the trail into Canada's interior — paddled up to 12 hours each day, carrying as much as two tons of supplies in their canoes.

We gather our tents, sleeping bags, food, and cooking gear, and it's all packed into waterproof bags and centred in the canoe. We'll need just two sets of clothes: one for paddling (which might get wet)

Howl at the Wolves

In the park's earliest days, Algonquin authorities set out to exterminate bears and wolves. After all, you can't have predators ruining an uptight, civilized Canadian's day in the park, can you? Fortunately, the hunters failed in their task and, today, Algonquin's more than 30 resident wolf packs are one of the park's star attractions. Each Thursday in August and September (until Labour Day), Algonquin Provincial Park hosts an unusual sing-along. More than 500 cars line the side of Highway 60 for a public wolf howl.

After a presentation about the wild eastern wolves found in the park, naturalist staff lead the procession to a location with the best chance of success, instructing participants in the art of wolf howling. The humans call; the wolves respond. Wind, rain, and other factors can dampen the evening, but 1,500 people howling into the Algonquin darkness is worth the free admission. Arrive early, dress warmly, and make sure your gas tank is full. ➤

and one for camp (which should remain dry). Crucial to the success of our mission are the following: bug jackets, bug dope, hats, cameras, sun block, rainwear, comfortable sandals, and 12-year-old Glenfiddich. It also helps to have some background on Algonquin's most famous explorer, Tom Thomson.

Largely credited with inspiring the birth of Canada's greatest art movement, Thomson was a park ranger and guide who often disappeared into the thicket with his canoe, emerging days later with paintings and sketches that not only illustrated the park's natural magic but sparked the imagination of what would become the Group of Seven. These seven artists put Canada on the global art map, restlessly breaking from European tradition to capture a true north aesthetic. It was Thomson who introduced them to Algonquin, and it was Thomson who drowned in Canoe Lake under mysterious circumstances. His death, which preceded the formation of the Group of Seven, has spawned books, films, and no shortage of conspiracy theories.

"Look, there's no question about it. Thomson was murdered by Shannon Fraser, with a paddle … or maybe a candlestick, in the basement, dressed as a butler," I tell Matt over the fire. Flames are licking a pot sitting on the burning wood, a strong wind sending firebug-like sparks into the early evening sky and blessedly blowing the biting bugs away.

Algonquin is comprised of a seemingly endless string of lakes, and our first day had consisted of several paddles and portages. For those unfamiliar, portaging involves balancing a canoe on your shoulders and hiking with it across land to the next put-in location. (It also involves a return trip to pack in the rest of the gear.) Canoes are designed for just such a task, and well-maintained portage trails are wide enough to accommodate them. I quickly got the hang of it, discovering that canoes make great echo chambers to sing motivational songs when traipsing through the forest. Each portage took us farther and farther away from civilization, deeper into the wilderness, deeper into the joys and challenges of canoeing. We felt as if we had earned our lakeside campsite, the cool swim in the drinkable tea-brown water, Matt's fabulous spicy-chicken pasta dinner, and one of the most gorgeous sunsets I've ever seen. A storm front rolled past, leaving in its wake the kind of starry night where the Milky Way drips its dust all over you. My father is somewhat bewildered by his first night camping in the woods. He says "magnificent" a lot. A pair of loons yodel their distinctive call, and it might just be the wind, but we're convinced the wolves of Algonquin are howling their approval, too.

Voyageur Quest's customers typically opt for a three-day canoe trip, pampered by guides like Matt, with his honed campfire cooking skills (fresh bruschetta, salmon wraps, apple crumble, vegetable stir-fry, and gourmet sandwiches) and knack for storytelling, including Aboriginal legends surrounding the stars, trees, and fire. When the wind chill settles in, Matt promptly builds a makeshift sweat lodge around some of the hot rocks, steamed with water and soothing cedar leaves. If only every outdoor experience had a Matt.

After a sunrise paddle that serves up a muscular bull moose munching on lilies, we pack up camp and float to another lakefront site that instantly earns our approval: even the exposed wood latrine seems scenic. A couple of days is all one needs to acclimatize to nature, where everything takes longer, tastes better, and feels more alive. No wonder Thomson and the Group of Seven called Algonquin their spiritual home.

Returning to the access point, we decompress in Voyageur Quest's rustic yet comfortable island cabin, enjoying solar-powered comfort, warm beds, a rejuvenating floating sauna, and a 360-degree view of Kawawaymog Lake. Suitably calibrated by our canoe trip, the scenery appears more vivid, the sound of lapping water as soothing as lip balm. I can only imagine what all this is like in fall, when the foliage explodes into a riot of colour, attracting visitors from around the world.

Mind you, the paintings of Thomson and the Group of Seven do it for me. At the peaceful McMichael gallery, located in Kleinberg, just 40 minutes north of Toronto, I see the now-familiar jack pine, spruce, cedar, and birch trees standing tall among the rock of the Canadian Shield and reflected in Algonquin's dramatic skies and calming waters. Like the lingering taste of an unforgettable meal, the famous art of Algonquin is already calling us back. Back to the lakes. Back to the wild. Back to the canoe.

START HERE: canadianbucketlist.com/algonquin

ICEWINE AND DINE IN NIAGARA

Canadians didn't invent icewine, but we sure perfected it. A notable achievement, considering this sweet elixir is one of the riskiest, toughest, and most labour-intensive wines to make. Healthy grapes must be frozen on the vine, then hand-picked and pressed within a matter of hours, squeezing out those sweet, valuable, and industry-scrutinized drops.

Niagara is Canada's largest wine region, famed for its Riesling and Chardonnay. As in B.C.'s Okanagan and Nova Scotia's Annapolis Valley, the seductive allure of life among vines has led to a boom in wineries and first-class restaurants. Niagara, blessed with ideal climatic conditions created by Lake Ontario and the Niagara Escarpment, feels like a fat grape bursting with goodness. No wonder other varietals are making their mark: Merlot, Pinot Noir, Baco Noir, Sauvignon Blanc.

↑

ONTARIO

Canada's Best Wine

After a humble start, Canadian wines now compete on the world stage for quality and taste. Angela Aiello, a wine expert, wine writer, and founder of the popular social wine club iYellowWine Club, (iyellowwineclub.com) raises a glass to her Top 10 Canadian wines:

1. Flat Rock Cellars Twisted, VQA, Twenty Mile Bench, Ontario
2. Huff Estates Winery South Bay Chardonnay, VQA, Prince Edward County, Ontario
3. Mission Hill Reserve Merlot, VQA, Okanagan Valley, B.C.
4. Henry of Pelham Baco Noir Reserve, VQA, St. Catharines, Ontario
5. Inniskillin Vidal Icewine, VQA, Niagara-on-the-Lake, Ontario
6. Closson Chase Chardonnay, VQA, Prince Edward County, Ontario
7. Benjamin Bridge Nova 7, Gaspereau Valley, Nova Scotia
8. Le Clos Jordanne Village Reserve Pinot Noir, VQA, Twenty Mile Bench, Niagara, Ontario
9. Thirty Bench Riesling, VQA, Beamsville Bench, Ontario
10. Château des Charmes Equuleus, VQA, Niagara-on-the-Lake, Ontario ➤

My Segway rolls gently along rows of Cabernet Franc as Daniel Speck, one of three brothers behind Henry of Pelham Estate, explains the magic. Warm wind rolls off the lake and gets trapped by the escarpment, circulating to allow grapes to reach their full potential. Among some of the healthiest vines I've ever seen, he points out the wind machines that have revolutionized wine in the region. Essentially stationary helicopter turbines, the blades suck in warm air from higher altitudes, rotating it across the vines to prevent devastating frost in emergencies. It all helps with the consistency needed to produce quality product, and to further Canada's claim as a major winemaking country.

Segway tours, offered at the estate, scoot between vines as I learn about Henry of Pelham's long history and the brothers' devotion to their craft. It makes the icewine tasting back in the dark, cool cellars all the more enjoyable. Niagara introduced the world to a Cabernet

Franc icewine — light ruby-red heaven. The first drops on my tongue explode with notes of sweet strawberry jam. The Riesling is more complex, departing with a citrus aftertaste. Vidal, a sturdy grape that is the most popular icewine variety in Niagara, is a pounder, a deliriously delicious full-frontal assault of velvet.

"We need to think of icewine as a condiment, a side dish," explains Daniel. "It should be enjoyed at the start of the meal, paired with spicy and salty dishes, or just enjoyed as dessert on its own." Drinking icewine after a rich, sweet dessert can throw your appetite a life vest made of concrete. Icewine before lunch, on the other hand, is rather decadent, so I head off to Beamsville's Good Earth Restaurant and Cooking School, driving past rows of grapes basking in the sun. My wine philosophy is simple: the bottle is never as important as whom you're sharing it with — in this case, Good Earth's firecracker owner-operator, Nicolette Novak.

Having grown up on the farm before chasing adventure in the city, she moved back to open the region's first cooking school, creating an intimate space in which to pair her favourite things: food and wine. Today the restaurant attracts both locals and visitors, who are drawn by

ONTARIO

217

Karen's Ice House Slushy Recipe

Icewine is magical to share, and here's a fantastic recipe to spread the love around. Since I discovered it, it's become my go-to at dinner parties.

6 to 10 ice cubes
200 mL Vidal icewine

Blend, adding ice cubes until frothy.
Toasts 8 to 10

her exceptional dishes, such as house-smoked salmon with home-grown asparagus on flatbread and a lobster and shrimp burger. There's also the orange-hued romantic ambience to be enjoyed under the summer umbrellas; the terrific service; aromas wafting from the open-plan outdoor kitchen; and great musical performances by local artists. Good Earth's wit, candour, and laughs dispense with wine's traditional haughtiness — a reminder of the importance of soul on any plate and in any glass.

After stopping off at Inniskillin, Canada's most famous icewine producer and its earliest pioneer, I pull into a small operation called Ice House, run by Jamie Macfarlane, one of the world's most experienced icewine makers. "Life is too short for cheap wine" reads a sign hanging at the door, a reminder that the cost and difficulty of making icewine justify its expense. I'm greeted by Jamie's wife, Karen, beaming with pride at her products. She pairs my tastings with wasabi peas, lime-chili chips from Australia, and dark chocolate. The rich flavour of Macfarlane's icewine explodes on my tongue, revealing complex flavours: a dazzling meal for my senses. "Icewine is the sweetest kiss," muses Karen, who sealed her own wedding to Jamie with a mouthful of icewine. "It asks you, 'Are you special enough to enjoy this?'"

I leave Ice House sipping on a refreshing icewine slushy, the perfect accompaniment to a hot summer day, and wonder how far I can take it. At Peller Estates, one of Niagara's largest wineries, you can take it very, very far, indeed. In the award-winning, family-run estate's restaurant, I start with an icewine cosmopolitan. The meal begins: foie gras, tuna tartare spiced with Cabernet Franc icewine, and green bean salad with truffles, paired with Ice Cuvée Classic, Peller's sparkling wine, topped with icewine for sweetness. Next, icewine-poached lobster-stuffed ravioli, heritage beef served with quinoa and dried berries (rehydrated with icewine, of course). Each course is paired with an excellent Peller wine, building up to the finale: a glass of Signature Series Vidal Icewine. I hold the smooth liquid on my tongue, letting its acidity bloom.

Icewine's freezing origins somehow warm the soul. For its distinctly Canadian flavour — encompassing its food, wine, and people — visiting Niagara's wine region is easily one for the bucket list.

START HERE: canadianbucketlist.com/niagara

HIKE THE BRUCE TRAIL

Realistically, few people are going to complete the entire 885-kilometre Bruce Trail in one shot. Who has the time or stamina to spend a full month hiking 30 kilometres a day? Snaking along the Niagara Escarpment and through Bruce County, Canada's oldest and longest walking trail is a challenge best experienced in stages, a goal for a lifetime. The escarpment's limestone cliffs, waterfalls, and creeks offer plenty of eye candy.

Day hikers might start with the Walter's Fall Loop or stroll to the Devil's Monument in Dyer's Bay. Other highlights include the 2.5-kilometre Rockway Falls trail southwest of St. Catharines and hiking to the old stone furnace found on the Forks of the Credit near Belfountain.

START HERE: canadianbucketlist.com/hike-bruce-trail

LEARN FROM THE ROCKS

People inhabited the so-called New World for thousands of years before Europeans arrived; their legacy is told in the culture, language, and myths of today's First Nations. This makes Petroglyphs Provincial Park, site of the largest concentration of Aboriginal rock art in Canada, all the more important. Nine hundred symbolic carvings of humans, objects, and animals were carved between 600 and 1,100 years ago into a single slab of marble, cherished and used like an ancient photo gallery. Elders would remove protective moss and use the rocks to introduce new generations to the story of the Ojibwa people.

The Teaching Rocks, as they are known, remain a hallowed and sacred site to this day. The park, a National Historic Site, is a 55-kilometre drive from Peterborough. From there, it's a short walk from the visitor centre to the humidity-controlled glass building that protects the petroglyphs.

ONTARIO ↑

ON THE BUCKET LIST: Kevin Callan

Broadcaster and author of the bestselling series "The Happy Camper," Kevin Callan (kevincallan. com) is one of Canada's best-known canoeists and outdoorsmen.

"Hidden amongst the rugged Penokean Hills, north of Elliot Lake, is a cluster of aqua blue lakes and crystal-clear streams, all alive with trophy self-sustaining rainbow — a rarity that only occurs in 1 percent of Canada's waterways. This is one of northern Ontario's absolute gems. Once you explore it for the first time, you'll be returning — guaranteed."

Visitors often feel a peaceful energy and sense of calm inside the park, especially when hiking the surrounding trails. There are information boards and staff available to answer questions. You can also have a seat and watch a 20-minute video in the visitor centre in which some of the legends are revealed. Ontario's Teaching Rocks are a very physical reminder that Canada's cultural history stretches back farther, and is far richer, than it is often given credit for.

START HERE: canadianbucketlist.com/petroglyph

SKATE THE RIDEAU

I'm having coffee with some local friends in Ottawa, and one of the guys at the table starts talking about the Rideau Canal. He's not harping on the fact that it is "the best-preserved slack-water canal in North America, demonstrating the use of European technology on a large scale." Neither of us knows exactly what that means, but that's the quote from UNESCO's website recognizing the canal as a World Heritage Site. It's way cooler to think of this 202-kilometre-long waterway as the very reason Canada is not part of the United States, since this military-built engineering achievement allowed the British to defend the country against the attacking Americans. Some historians believe that if the canal didn't exist, neither might Canada.

Cooler still is the fact that every winter the Rideau turns into the world's largest outdoor skating rink. At 7.8 kilometres, the skateable section that cuts through Ottawa is equivalent to 90 Olympic-sized

hockey rinks. The Rideau used to be the world's longest skateable rink, until Winnipeg took the title with its 8.54-kilometre-long Assiniboine River Trail. Now there's an upstart in Invermere, B.C., hoping to usurp both with its Whiteways Trail system on Lake Windermere. Ottawa's wide, Winnipeg's long. When it comes to the ego of a city, size does matter.

Back to the coffee table in Ottawa. It's a frosty −12°C outside, and the beans taste particularly good. "You know, the Rideau, it's a magical place," says my friend. "Sometimes, at midnight, I put on my speed skates, crank some music on my iPod, and I just go for it. I mean, I just skate fast and smooth, and it feels like I'm flying. Nothing beats that feeling — nothing."

He tells it the way he feels it, with deep respect and awe. His experience axel-jumps over the historical significance of the Rideau. It spirals around the quirky fact that Ottawans skate to work, briefcases in hand. It makes my hair stand up and my heart quicken. I want to know that feeling.

That evening, I walk to Kilometre Zero, not far from the steps of Parliament. I only have one night to chase the experience, but there are some challenges to overcome. The fragrance of fresh-fried

Beaver Tails wafts in the air, demanding a detour. Exquisite ice sculptures on display from the annual Winterlude festival prove an additional distraction. I don't even have skates, but to the rescue are rental booths on the skateway. Everything is set, when the final two hurdles present themselves:

1. I ice-skate with the grace of a duck on skis.
2. The ice is in no condition to be skated on.

Ottawa has enjoyed an unseasonably warm winter, and the result is a skateway cracked and scarred, pockmarked and as uneven as a politician's ethics. The locals know when to steer clear, but poor tourists are discovering that ice is very hard and that an outdoor canal differs greatly from a smooth indoor skating rink. An ambulance flashes and some helpful volunteers cart off a skater. On the way, they tell me I'm mad even to think about being on the ice. The fact that I can barely stand up on ice skates (cut the immigrant a break!) isn't helping.

I close my eyes, take a deep breath, and imagine myself skating at speed, under the bright stars, perhaps an artist like Ottawa's Kathleen Edwards dreamily cooing away on my headphones. Then I slip, land hard on my butt, and quickly decide the only sane place for a tourist in Ottawa right now is a warm pub in the ByWard Market district. Which is exactly where I go. So I never did quite get to skate the Rideau in all its glory. But that shouldn't stop us from adding the experience to the Great Canadian Bucket List.

START HERE: canadianbucketlist.com/rideau

LEAN OFF THE CN TOWER

O ver the years, I've built a reputation as something of a thrill-seeker. Trust me, I never set out to run with bulls, jump out of planes, swing from bridges, and dive with sharks. Yet one thing led to another, and a former desk-jobber morphed into the travel guy with a magazine column called "Thrillseeker." So you're probably thinking: "Of course Esrock would choose to walk outside on one of the world's tallest free-standing structures. It's probably something he does every day." Not quite, although I did walk around the edge of Macau's 233-metre Skytower, shortly before I bungee jumped off the damn thing.

The CN Tower EdgeWalk is over 100 metres higher than that, and the view over Lake Ontario and the city beats anything Macau, much less anywhere else, has to offer. Sucked in by the CN Tower's vortex, I decided to join a group of tourists ranging in age from 23 to 68. Piercing the sky, head and shoulders above anything else, Canada's most iconic building landmark was declared a Wonder of the Modern World by the American Society of Civil Engineers. It is a true engineering marvel, 553.33 metres at almost pure vertical, beautifully illuminated at night to become more than just an observation deck and communications tower. The CN Tower is construction as art, Canadian ingenuity at scale, a soaring symbol of Toronto and beyond. Why wouldn't you want to step outside on its rim, put your toes over the edge, and place the world at your feet?

Danger? Come on, people, this is one of Canada's busiest tourist attractions. Even though we sign the customary waiver, the emphasis on safety is miles ahead of similar attractions I've encountered in Asia and New Zealand. After all, this is the world's highest full-circle, hands free walk, and we will be walking on a 1.5-metre-wide ledge 356 metres above ground on the Tower's main pod.

After taking a Breathalyzer test for alcohol and drugs, we are asked to lock up all loose items — watches, earrings, wallets, necklaces — and slip on a rocket-red walk suit. Our harnesses are checked and quadruple-checked, shoes tightened (twice), glasses attached with string, hair tied up. I see familiar looks of "I don't know why I'm doing this, but I must do it all the same."

You can see every one of the CN Tower's 116 storeys in the elevator as you ascend the external glass-faced shaft. Suddenly, the height becomes real. Suddenly, the only illustrious CN Tower record I can remember is that 360, the restaurant located 351 metres up, holds the Guinness World Record for the World's Highest Wine Cellar.

In a small control centre, alongside a monitor recording wind speeds and weather, we get clipped in (twice, with additional zip ties) to a steel overhead track. You've more chance of spontaneously combusting than of slipping out of this contraption. Our affable guide, Christian, tells me that although he's undergone extensive training, his only qualification for the job was his healthy fear of heights. Empathy with clients is a natural asset.

He leads us onto the metal walkway and invites us to walk right up to the edge, our toes hanging over. Even though I know we're safer up here than the folks in the Hot Wheels–sized cars stuck in traffic below, my mind does its best to convince me that leaning over the edge of the CN Tower is not something my body should do. Fortunately, I stopped listening to myself years ago, so I follow my fellow EdgeWalkers pushing their limits and shuffle up to the edge. We applaud our efforts, swap high-fives and breathe in the sweeping view below.

As the walk continues around the tower, we hit the windy side, with 53-kilometre-an-hour gusts of warm air instantly pickling our adrenal glands. Christian has to holler to point out landmarks. This time he encourages us to lean forward over the edge, on our tip-toes. Each challenge is ably met, so by the time the group returns to the sheltered side, facing the sea that is Lake Ontario on a day so clear I can make out the buildings at Niagara Falls, everyone is comfortable enough to lean back and smile for the photos. Arms outstretched, heels balanced on the edge, we embrace the sky with huge smiles on our faces. You don't have to be a thrill-seeker to benefit from a little edge.

START HERE: canadianbucketlist.com/edgewalk

MOTORBIKE AROUND SUPERIOR

Lake Superior doesn't give up her dead. The water of the world's largest lake by area is so cold that bodies sink to its depths. Mortality was on my mind as I nervously tucked into pancakes in the crowded Hoito Finnish Diner in Thunder Bay.

You have to admit, a writer getting killed in a motorcycle accident while researching a book about things to do before you die has just the sort of ironic twist you'd find in a newspaper story. Granted, I'd already walked face-first off a cliff, scuba dived wrecks, and driven many a long moose-trapped highway, but the challenge ahead was particularly and personally daunting. My wife and my mother were in full fret mode over my plan to research one of the great motorcycle trips of Canada:

ONTARIO

the north shore of Lake Superior. So what if I'd never been on a bike trip before? So what if my saddle hours, including my licence training, could be counted on two fingers? So what if the most powerful bike I'd ever ridden was 125 cc? And so what if a car *had* T-boned that scooter, breaking my knee and cracking my helmet? That accident kick-started my grand escapade, my rebirth as an adventurer!

I've faced so many limit-pushing challenges in the many years since then that I've learned the secret to getting through just about anything. Douglas Adams boldly put it in his futuristic travel book *The Hitchhiker's Guide to the Galaxy*. When Larry Lage, owner of Thunder Bay's Excalibur Motorcycle Works, hands me a jacket and gloves, he doesn't notice that under my thin-lipped smile, I'm muttering my most powerful mantra: Don't Panic.

Riding a motorcycle on the shores of mighty Lake Superior, as I was quick to discover, is one part exhilaration, one part speed, a dash of freedom, and a lime wedge of danger, topped off with camaraderie and natural beauty to make a cocktail of mobile magic. No wonder this 700-kilometre stretch of the Trans-Canada from Thunder Bay to Sault Ste. Marie has such an amazing reputation with bikers. Wavy S-curves on smooth blacktop cutting through forest and rock, always close to sparkling blue lake, the north shore attracts riders from across the continent, some of whom complete the 2,100-kilometre loop around Superior on scenic roads in the United States.

Larry had lent me his Kawasaki KWR 650 dual-sport bike, its odometer a third of the way through its second (or third) rotation. The bike is reliable and experienced, much like my biking buddy Steve Kristjanson. A semi-retired jack-of-all-trades, Steve has seen thousands of kilometres in the saddle, having ridden to the Soo and back in one stretch: a 1,400-kilometre sitting. Our goal is half that in double the time, two days on the road, stopping at viewpoints and attractions along the way.

We start by paying homage to Terry Fox at his memorial just outside Thunder Bay. Here was a boy who was running across Canada, racked with cancer, on one leg. His legacy — hundreds of millions of dollars raised for cancer research — is an inspiration and further steel to arm my own courage for the incomparably lighter challenge ahead.

Still, it doesn't stop me from stalling my bike at a highway intersection, right next to Larry and his bike-instructor girlfriend Diane, who are accompanying us to the Ouimet Canyon. I expect Larry to point me right back to his shop, but he gamely encourages me instead. "Keep your head up, and look where you want to go, not at whatever you're going to hit," adds Diane, like a supportive parent. These guys live and breathe their bikes, a world apart from the annoying twits on decibel-shattering cruisers, content to just parade them. I'm told the biggest dangers are moose and deer, which can run out of the ditches straight into your path. Warning signs line the highway, and I spot the occasional cross in the ground commemorating one who didn't heed them. Steve hit a deer a couple of years ago going 60, broke his knee and killed the animal. He knows he got off lightly.

Visor down, I smooth into the groove of the road. The slightest movement of my hand on the throttle has an instant effect, slowing me down, hurling me forward. We pass through the glowing ridge at Red Rocks, stopping to admire magnificent views of this sea-lake. With a surface area of 82,100 square kilometres, Lake Superior contains a whopping 10 percent of all the surface freshwater on the planet. It creates its own weather system, supports fisheries and tourism, and, each winter, generates waves up to 2.5 metres high, to the delight of some truly hard-core and well-insulated surfers.

After dinner in Rossport, we check out the Aguasabon River Gorge before stopping for the night in the small mill town of Terrace Bay. We ride in on a newly tarred stretch of highway candy, as smooth and black as licorice. Steve lubes the chains, checks the tires and oil, a picture of Zen with his art of motorcycle maintenance. It's a relief to get out of my sweat-soaked biker gear, a relief that my only crash today is in the soft bed of the Imperial Motel.

Thick fog blows in ominously the following morning. Moose had crashed into my anxious dreams. Come on, Esrock, get a grip! Yes, motorcycles are more likely to lead to accidents, and having felt the wind slam against my chest at 100 kilometres an hour, I know there's little room for error. Yet the highway is wide and forgiving, traffic relatively light, and overtaking lanes frequent.

We ride into the spooky fog in staggered formation, brights on, speed down. Droplets of moisture cling to my visor, so I use my gloved hand to wipe it clean. The roar of the engine, the blur of green forest, the steam rising off lakes in the shadows: even in the fog, the adventure is ... superior! Gradually, visibility improves, the clouds providing some welcome shelter from the unusually hot sun. I take a photo in White River, where Winnie, the bear that inspired the children's books, was born. When we reach the landmark Wawa Goose overlooking the valley, I'm still wondering what a Pooh is. The sandy beach and overlooking cliffs at Old Woman Bay are gorgeous, as is the view of the lake islands from Alona Bay.

I'm getting comfortable on the bike, accustomed to the speed, the wind, the vibration beneath me. Next time you find yourself behind a bike on the highway, watch what happens when it passes another bike going in the opposite direction. The left hand points out, wrist slightly twisted, for the friendly biker "wave." Everybody does it, like the secret handshake of some exclusive club. Everyone except three riders on Harleys, whom Steve, riding a rare Suzuki DR800, dismisses as posers anyway.

By the time we reach Batchawana Bay, stopping to enjoy a cold reward beer at Voyageurs, I feel as if I've overcome my own power problems. Other than three deer crossing the road, the risk was benign. Whatever ghosts were haunting my nerves had been winterized in the garage. Lake Superior, with waters that never give up her dead, energized me with a rush of life.

Bike stored outside the hotel in Sault Ste. Marie, I text a biker friend back home to let him know I made it safely. He replies in seconds. "Makes you appreciate your life knowing you can die at any moment, hey?"

No, it makes you appreciate life knowing you can conquer your fears.

START HERE: canadianbucketlist.com/superior

MARVEL AT THE FALL FOLIAGE

As the temperature drops and days get noticeably shorter, maple, birch, poplar, and red oak leaves expel oxygen, beginning a process that will see them wither and drift to the ground. A welcome by-product of this cycle is the incredible array of colour that results from the leaves' death throes. Rich maroons, Cabernet reds, bright egg-yolk yellows, and glowing oranges explode in such spectacular fashion that visitors travel from all over the world just to experience them in all their glory. And the best place to see this autumnal display is in central Canada. You may want to consider these two places:

Agawa Canyon Train Tour, Sault Ste. Marie: Operated by Algoma Central Railway, this scenic passenger train departs daily from Sault Ste. Marie and travels 183 kilometres north through forest, lake country, and along the granite cliffs of the Canadian Shield. The locomotive features large viewing windows, GPS-triggered tour narration available in five languages, and excellent dining. Once you arrive at Canyon Park (accessible only by train or hiking), you have 90 minutes to explore five easy walking trails, including a 76-metre-high canyon  lookout. Fall foliage tends to be best during the last two weeks of September and in the first week of October. Like they did with Algonquin Park (another fall foliage hotspot), the Group of Seven artists captured Agawa Canyon's beauty with a number of famous landscape paintings.

Peterborough: Two and a half hours from Ottawa and 90 minutes from Toronto, Peterborough and the Kawarthas are a popular weekend autumn escape. Here you'll find plenty of cabin and B&B getaways, more than 100 lakes, and the largest wilderness preserve south of Algonquin Park. After freaking out at the foliage, adventurous bucket listers should check out the Warsaw Caves and Conservation Area. Having explored the subterranean activity park, you'll emerge from the dark depths to sparkling reds, oranges, and yellows. Since 1868, the region's Norwood Fall Fair has been a Thanksgiving tradition and is located just a short drive east of Peterborough.

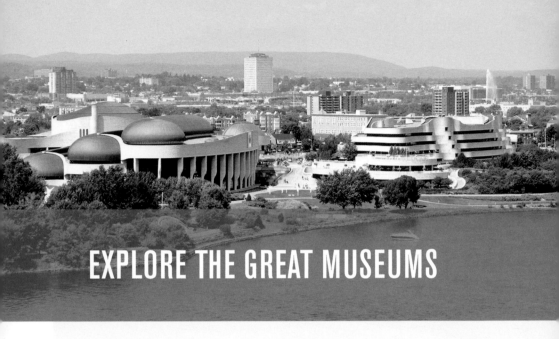

EXPLORE THE GREAT MUSEUMS

The word *museum* sounds awfully like mausoleum — a place where artifacts go to die. Fortunately, Ontario's great museums are anything but, having been revitalized into living temples of knowledge where one can interact with, discover, and journey to far-off places, without ever leaving the building.

Let's begin our brief guided tour in Ottawa, home to a half-dozen national museums, where locals and visitors learn all about Canada and beyond. We start in the National Gallery, the brainchild of renowned Canadian architect Moshe Safdie, housing the country's largest collection of Canadian art. The Great Hall is entered into via a long ramp, designed to put visitors in the right frame of mind to experience the art to come. The Great Hall uses windows and skylights to create an exceptionally light space, cleverly avoiding direct contact with the art itself while offering famous views

ONTARIO ↑

of the Parliament Buildings. Safdie was inspired by the Library of Parliament, so much so that the Great Hall has a volume identical to that of Parliament's stone library, which lies across the Rideau Canal. Besides iconic works from Canadian greats throughout history, the museum also features works by Rembrandt, Van Gogh, Matisse, Monet, Picasso, Warhol, and Pollock. You can't miss the gallery's distinctive glass entrance, or Louise Bourgeois's creepy spider outside.

We then walk across the Ottawa River along the Alexandra Bridge and into Gatineau, Quebec. It takes just 20 minutes to reach the beautifully designed Canadian Museum of History, the most-visited museum in the country. We enter through the Grand Hall, with its view of the river and Parliament Hill, under towering totem poles (the largest display in the world), to Haida artist Bill Reid's original

plaster of his masterpiece *Spirit of Haida Gwaii*. It's a fitting introduction to the first level, the First People's Hall, tracing 20,000 years of Aboriginal history in Canada. With a recent renovation, the former Canada Hall, Canadian Personalities Hall, and Canadian Postal Museum have been combined to create the largest exhibition of Canadian history ever assembled. Inside the Canadian Children's Museum, kids continue to embed themselves in new worlds, literally getting passports as they learn how people live around the world.

Ottawa's other national museums are well worth investigating: the Museum of Nature, the Canadian Agriculture Museum, the

Canadian Aviation and Space Museum, the Canadian Science and Technology Museum, and the haunting Canadian War Museum, with its jarring structural angles and captivating human stories.

Still in Ontario, let's Porter (verb: to fly affordably) to Toronto and take a gander at T-Dot's prized museums. The Royal Ontario Museum (ROM) is the largest cultural and natural history museum in Canada, and the most popular and most visited museum in the city. Star architect Daniel Libeskind's futuristic Crystal looks as if a Transformer crashed into a heritage building — which works to attract more than one million visitors annually to the museum's 40 galleries. With over six million items, the ROM has something for everybody, and plenty left over. I love the Dinosaur Gallery, the giant totem pole, and the creepy Gallery of Birds, forever flying nowhere.

Not far away, on Dundas Street, is the Art Gallery of Ontario (AGO), one of the largest gallery spaces in North America, with a collection of over 80,000 works from the first century to the present. Residing in its Georgian manor premises since 1910, the AGO continues to host some of the world's most important art exhibitions, introducing visitors to the Old Masters and King Tut and the pharaohs, along with priceless works from the Hermitage and India's Royal Courts.

Yes, Ontario's great museums are very much alive, treasured by anyone interested in culture, history, art, and science. Prized and appreciated, therefore, by anyone ticking off the Great Canadian Bucket List.

START HERE: canadianbucketlist.com/museums

FEEL THE SPIRIT OF MANITOULIN ISLAND

On the world's largest freshwater island, they take the Great Spirit very seriously. For the people of the Ojibwa, Odawa, and Potawatomi Nations, Manitoulin Island is a land so beautiful that the Great Spirit, the Father of Life, kept it for himself. Today, they welcome guests with a number of authentic Aboriginal experiences, providing an opportunity to learn about this unique island directly from its people.

The Great Spirit Circle Trail encompasses multi-faceted excursions that include the seven First Nations communities on the island. You can pick local teas, medicinal herbs, fruits, and plants; make bannock over open fires; or hike up a dramatic bluff with incredible views of the island and participate in a traditional tobacco ceremony. Walking tours visit heritage museums and galleries, and there are storytelling and craft workshops, singing and drumming circles, and overnight stays in traditional tipis. Many guests combine an interest in Aboriginal history and culture with the outdoors, taking guided hikes, bicycle rides, and canoe trips on the lake, or horseback riding in the woods. There is nowhere else in the country quite like Manitoulin, a 2,766-square-kilometre island of fascinating culture, stunning natural beauty, and enormous spirit.

START HERE: canadianbucketlist.com/manitoulin

GIVE A STANDING OVATION AT STRATFORD

"We all hope that in your lives you have just the right amount of sitting quietly at home, and just the right amount of adventure."
—Barnaby Tucker in Thornton Wilder's *The Matchmaker*

When a small town falls on hard times, it needs to reinvent itself. Once a railway junction and manufacturing centre for locomotives, Stratford found itself in an economic pickle until a local journalist named Tom Patterson realized that a town named after Stratford-upon-Avon, sitting on its own Avon River, with a neighbouring town called Shakespeare, should have its own Shakespeare Festival. In the summer of 1953, Alec Guinness uttered the first lines of the first play (in a tent, no less), and the Stratford Festival was born.

By the time I visit, 60 years later, Stratford has grown to host one of the largest and most renowned theatre festivals in the world.

During its lengthy April to November engagement, it attracts some of the world's best actors, directors, designers, and theatre talent. The tent has been replaced by four major theatres, pioneering the thrust stage that allows the audience to surround the actors on three sides, as they would have in Shakespeare's day. Enthusiastic audiences arrive from around the world, with the theatre boom resulting in significant economic aftershocks.

Stratford also boasts one of the best culinary schools in the country; an impressive selection of restaurants, hotels, and theatre schools; and the third-largest costume warehouse in the world. It's a town where kids grow up knowing they can make a living in the arts — as actors, stage designers, lighting technicians, or musicians (a fact acknowledged by its most recent celebrity resident, a kid who used to busk outside the Avon Theatre on Downie Street and goes by the name of Justin Bieber). The week before I arrive, Bieber humbly returned to the same spot on the same stairs, guitar in hand, to play a couple of songs. Today, as I enjoy poutine at the Downie Street Burger across the street, a violinist sends his classical notes soaring into the warm summer breeze. Spotless and small, downtown Stratford hums with coffee shops, chocolatiers, boutiques, bistros, and bookstores — the kind of place that leaves one with a whimsical impression and envious of the 32,000 people who live in a town with more culture than many major cities.

Live trumpets at the tent-inspired Festival Theatre signal that it's time for the 2 p.m. matinee of this year's popular farce, Thornton

Wilder's *The Matchmaker*. Non-Shakespearean works were introduced as early as the festival's second year, and today include musicals, comedies, Broadway hits, and classic works of world theatre. *The Matchmaker* was the Broadway hit that inspired *Hello, Dolly!* and contains some of the sharpest wit and most crackling situational comedy ever seen onstage. There are several interweaving story-lines, but I'm particularly drawn to the tale of two shop clerks, trapped in their work, determined, for one day at least, to have "an adventure." It all leads to love, danger, fear, and shenanigans, reflected in blistering one-liners, split-second escapes, and an endearing happy ending. The performances are fantastic, the stage design stupendous, and two hours later, the cast graciously receives a standing ovation from the crowd. On top of the Stratford Festival's many accomplishments, it's this moment of appreciation that bows its way onto our bucket list.

Later, I tour the fascinating costume and prop warehouse, and walk down to the Avon River. Opposite colourful artists displaying their work in the park, swans glide under the scenic arched bridge to Patterson Island. I wonder if Patterson had any notion of the impact his idea would have on the town, its people, and Canada's cultural legacy. Regardless, we can all appreciate the power of reinvention and the special magic that brews when we wake up and decide to chase our own adventures.

START HERE: canadianbucketlist.com/shakespeare

GET SPRAYED IN NIAGARA FALLS

Visiting the tourist zone in the town of Niagara Falls on Canada Day is a classy dream, and by classy I mean tacky, and by dream I mean nightmare. Vegas without the spectacle, the tourist zone is designed for sugar-saturated, over-stimulated kids dragging along bludgeoned parents with their bruised wallets. Theme rides, water parks, lineups, and burger, ice cream, and hot dog joints — on a scorching July 1, it can all seem a bit much. Then I opened the drapes of the honeymooners' suite on the twenty-first floor of the Sheraton to see what had attracted all this madness in the first place.

Never underestimate the impact of seeing Niagara Falls for the first time. This from a guy who's swum in rock pools atop Victoria Falls, speed-boated up the tropical canyons of South America's stunning Iguazu Falls, and showered in the cascades of some of the most beautiful waterfalls on six continents. Once I got past the family holiday madness, the crowds, the crawling traffic, and the 15-minute wait for the Sheraton's elevators, I could see Niagara Falls for what it is: Canada's most spectacular natural wonder, worthy of its draw as one of the world's great tourist attractions.

Draining Lake Erie into Lake Ontario, the American, Bridal, and Horseshoe falls combine to produce the highest flow rate of any waterfall in the world, a volume of water that famously sends mist mushrooming into the sky. It's even more impressive when you consider that massive hydroelectric projects upriver redirect much of the flow before it reaches the 21- to 30-metre drop of the American Falls and the 53-metre plummet at the horseshoe-shaped crest that separates Canada from the United States. Given the hyper-commercialization of the town, I enjoyed simply strolling along the promenade on a warm night, watching spotlights illuminate the water, feeling the refreshing spray as I got closer to the thunderous whirlpool beneath Horseshoe Falls. Before the lake waters disappear over the edge, the falls seem to challenge each visitor with a thought experiment: If I went over the edge, would I survive? Three people have survived after going over unprotected, including a seven-year-old boy, while others have used barrels and protective devices to increase their chances of emerging unscathed. Over the years, some have succeeded, others not. Nik Wallenda's tightrope walk in 2012, the first successful attempt in over a century, becomes even more impressive at the scene of his accomplishment. Illegal as it is to attempt it, people will continue to test the might of North America's mightiest falls, on purpose and by accident. The iconic experience, the must-do-no-matter-how-long-the-lineup, is a gorge cruise. On the Canadian side, Hornblower Niagara Cruises' two state-of-the-art catamarans replaced the iconic *Maid of the Mist* boats in 2014 (the *Maid of the Mist* continues to run from the

American side). Passengers can choose to stay dry or get wet, depending on where they position themselves: on the outer decks, prepare for a cold-mist baptism beneath the Horseshoe Falls.

The boats take up to 700 passengers at a time, doing a blistering trade on the summer's busiest long weekend. Joining the Canada Day mayhem, I expect to be waiting for hours, but the lineup moves quickly and smoothly. Passengers are given pink plastic ponchos and then herded like cattle through various checkpoints before boarding the boat and squeezing onto the upper and lower decks. Soon we're

On the Wire

June 15, 2012, saw the first tightrope walk across Niagara Falls in 116 years. A seventh-generation tightrope walker, Nik Wallenda, walked 550 metres near the base of Horseshoe Falls, watched by millions on television and huge crowds on both sides of the border. Getting permission for the stunt was no easy task, as Canadian authorities in Niagara were worried the stunt would encourage amateurs. Just a few months earlier, an unidentified man had scaled a railing and jumped into Horseshoe Falls, becoming the third person to survive an unprotected fall.

underway, and as we motor along upriver, squeals from the kids greet the first sheet of spray. By the time we retreat from the choppy rapids several minutes later, everyone's head is soaked. Hornblower offers sunrise cruises, cocktails at sunset, and fireworks cruises, too. From the boat, Niagara Falls really looks and sounds like the wild and raging natural wonder it is.

With cash in hand, you can take Niagara Parks' Journey Behind the Falls, or take to the skies with Niagara Helicopter's nine-minute ride, or cross the canyon farther downriver in an old-fashioned air tram, or watch a 4D movie (the extra D means you'll get sprayed with water in the theatre). That's a lot of waterfall action.

I was content to enjoy the exceptional view from my hotel room and watch the nightly fireworks. Could I live without the kitsch attractions and loud, wet kids bouncing around in the elevators? Definitely. Is Niagara Falls something to see before you die? Absolutely.

START HERE: canadianbucketlist.com/falls

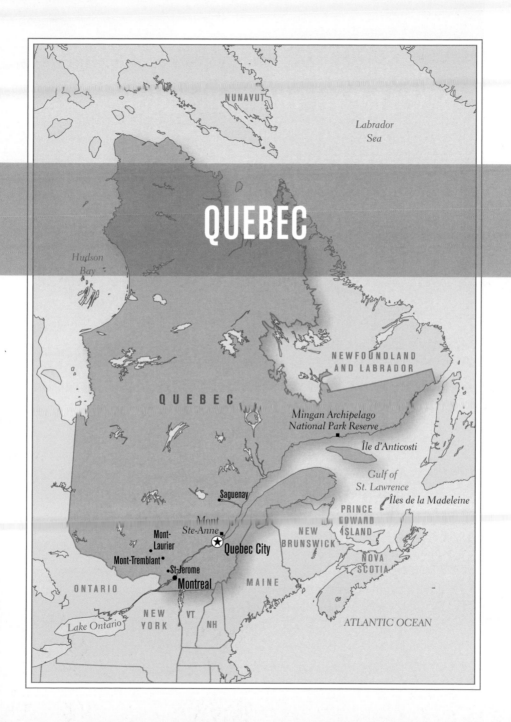

QUEBEC

BIKE LE P'TIT TRAIN DU NORD

Picture this: It's Monday morning. You awake in the comfortable bed of a B&B that puts the charm in charming. Pack your light bags and head downstairs for breakfast, where the owners, inevitably named Jean-Claude or Bernard or Cedric, greet you with a cup of warm coffee, fresh orange juice, and the choice of a large omelette or French toast served with bananas, raspberries, and custard. Figuring you're going to need the calories, you order the French toast and drown it in rich maple syrup for good measure. You leave your bags at the bottom of the stairs, walk outside, and put water, snacks, camera, and sunscreen in the saddlebags of your bicycle.

Across the street is the crushed-gravel pathway of the longest linear park in Canada, a 230-kilometre bike trail in summer — a ski trail in

Even Granddad Can Do It

In 2011, 54-year-old Winnipeg grand-father Arvid Loewin broke the world record for the fastest bicycle ride across Canada, pedalling 6,055 kilometres from Vancouver to Halifax in just 13 days, 6 hours, and 13 minutes. Spending 20 hours on the saddle each day and averaging just two hours' sleep, Loewin raised hundreds of thousands of dollars for street kids in Kenya. ➤

winter — that runs right through the heart of the Laurentians. Bidding your host au revoir, and perhaps meeting some new friends loading up their bikes as well, you pedal to the trail and begin a pleasant, relaxing ride that quickly leaves the village houses behind and splits a landscape of boreal forest, bubbling brooks, rivers, wetlands, and manicured golf courses. The gradient alternates between hardly uphill and lovingly downhill, so while you do work up a little sweat, you're never slogging forth with any serious effort. Passing other bikers going in the opposite direction, you greet them with a friendly "Bonjour!" although they're just as likely to be from Ottawa, Calgary, or even Germany. There are couples, grandparents, students, kids, and occasionally, volunteers biking along in case anybody needs any assistance.

It doesn't take long before you meet lovely people enjoying the scenery just as much as you are, like Guy and Julie from Kitchener. You share camera duties and leave a message scratched in the gravel for Jeff and Katie from Waterloo who can't be too far behind. The trail itself is clearly marked with mileage signs and punctuated every five to ten kilometres with toilets, a shelter, or a small, century-old train station, lovingly restored. At one point, a large deer springs out of the trees up ahead. Speedy chipmunks dart in and out of the dense foliage.

When you pass through the villages, you'll come across cafés or bistros, the kinds of places where the friendly owner takes photos of your group and is so much fun that you ask him to be in the photo as well.

How much biking you decide to do that day is completely up to you — perhaps 60 kilometres, perhaps 40. Your stops are as flexible as your muscles; all you need to do is arrange with the transportation service so that your bags are waiting for you at the next B&B when you arrive. Welcomed by another B&B owner (where do they find these characters?), you lock up your bike for the night, take a warm shower, and enjoy a stroll around the village. There might be a river flowing opposite your B&B, a ceramic arts festival, or a quiet street with cafés and local artists. With four days to accomplish the ride, handily divided into four sections on the easy-to-follow map, chances are you'll arrive at your destination early or mid-afternoon, which leaves you plenty of time to rest before a wonderful gourmet dinner, prepared by an award-winning chef. Your legs are a little tired, and your butt reminds you it's there, but you're also satisfied that you did some exercise today, which helped burn off some of that breakfast! You sleep like a baby.

It's Tuesday morning. Repeat.

Wednesday. Repeat, but your legs and butt are silent.

Thursday, much the same, until you reach Mile Zero in Saint Jérôme, where your car awaits, parked at the hotel. This is where you were picked up four days ago and driven with your bike to Mont Laurier, at Mile 230. The week has flown by in a green blur. Your lungs are blossoming with fresh mountain air.

This was my experience biking Quebec's fantastic Le P'tit Train du Nord. It's the beautiful outdoors, with a little exercise, adventure, culture, and the chance to discover the wonders of small-town Quebec. Your bike is waiting.

START HERE: canadianbucketlist.com/traindunord

DISCOVER QUEBEC CITY

"I'm from Europe," jokes comedian Eddie Izzard, "you know, where history comes from." As much history as there is in Canada, there's no denying that a couple of hundred years here — or, in the case of the West, a couple of decades there — doesn't stack up against the centuries of cobblestone that pave the old towns of Europe. Bienvenue à Quebec City, a UNESCO World Heritage Site, a pocket of old Europe right here in North America, where history comes from as well.

From the 221-metre-high lookout rotunda atop the Observatoire de la Capitale, I see the stone wall that surrounds the Old Town, the archway of Rue Saint-Jean allowing traffic to pass between the

centuries. The fairy-tale turrets of the Château Frontenac loom over tightly-bunched brick buildings like a medieval lord's castle. I see the exact point where the mighty St. Lawrence narrows, an observation that gave birth to the name Quebec itself (which is believed to be an Algonquin word meaning "narrow passage" or "strait"). I see the walls of La Citadelle, a fortress originally built in the 1600s but that obtained its distinctive star shape from British conquerors in the early 1800s. There's the Plains of Abraham, where the French and British battled for what would ultimately be the control of an entire continent. Today, Battlefields Park is a huge recreational area for sport, leisure, and massive festivals in both summer and winter. The impressive Parliament Building towers as parliament buildings often do, while church steeples pierce the sky like the inverted fangs of a vampire. Devoid of billboards and neon lights, the view I see is from another place and another time, reminding me of Riga, or Copenhagen, or Paris. Mirroring my experiences in those cities, I head to the streets with no map book, directions, or itinerary of places to see.

Old Quebec City is small enough to walk on foot within a couple of hours, with pockets of interest lying in wait where you least expect them. I stroll down Rue Saint-Louis, which runs directly to Fairmont's grand Château Frontenac, supposedly North America's most photographed hotel. Like Banff Springs and Lake Louise, this former Canadian Pacific Railway hotel inspires feelings of princely grandeur — a contrast to my own hotel, the modern Hilton, that overlooks the old city like a windowed brick. I walk past statues and churches, little shops selling bric-a-brac, Quebec mainstays such as the clothing store Simons. Lunch is a quick stop at Chez Ashtons, where they make the cheese curd fresh every day to get that vital poutine squeak.

My walk deposits me in Rue du Petit-Champlain, once the city's slum, now easily among Canada's most beautiful urban walkways. It's getting a little brisk out, so I warm up with thick hot chocolate with a dash of spice at La Fudgeric. Cheese, wine, baguettes, chocolate — the city practically reeks of the good stuff. There's a crowd gathered at Place-Royale, where Samuel de Champlain founded the continent's first French settlement in 1608. A beautiful mural paints a vivid picture of the city's history since then.

Up the Funiculaire, opened in 1879 and the only one of its kind in North America, I transition to uptown, past the Dufferin Terrace Slide, where I can't help but spend a couple of bucks to race at 70 kilometres an hour on a sled. The adrenalin buzz makes climbing the 310 steps of La Promenade des Gouverneurs a cinch (the views of the St. Lawrence don't hurt, either). Lost in thought, I arrive at the Musée national des beaux-arts du Québec, where an old prison has been turned into a wing of the art gallery.

My walk is just a brief introduction, and I relish the opportunity to explore the city further. We have a little bit of Europe here, too, Mi Lizard. If you haven't already done so, it's well worth adding Quebec City to your bucket list.

START HERE: canadianbucketlist.com/quebec-city

CAVE BASH IN "THE MAGGIES"

Quebeckers call Îles de la Madeleine — a.k.a. the Magdalen Islands, a.k.a. "the Maggies" — the best-kept secret in the province. Each island in the archipelago located in the Gulf of St. Lawrence is surrounded by soft beach in every direction, sporting brightly painted clapboard houses with massive fairway-cut lawns. Atlantic storms shaped this region both physically and culturally. The eroded soft, red sandstone cliffs shelter countless sea caves and sentinels, while centuries of Acadian settlers and Anglophone shipwrecks have created a unique bilingual island community. Ancestors of many of the 13,000 residents have lived on the island for seven generations, so that surnames are often dispensed with altogether — you are known simply as the son or daughter of your mother or father.

Set deep in Quebec, several of its communities consist of proud Anglos, tracing their lineage to Irish, Scottish, and English shipwrecks. Everyone gets on splendidly.

The economy of the Maggies is dependent on fishing and tourism. Lobster is a prime catch, gathered during a short six-week season. Tourism is the bigger catch, and mostly Québécois visitors arrive each summer by plane, ferry, or cruise ship. Blustering wind has also turned the islands into a global destination for wind sports, with the shallow lagoons providing ideal conditions for kitesurfing, and endless dune beaches being bang-on for kite buggies. Seafood is abundant — smoked, pickled, grilled, poached — and seal is still on the menu, too. There's a view around every corner, and just one main road connecting the eight major island communities of Havre Aubert, Cap aux Meules, Havre aux Maisons, Grosse Île, Brion, Pointe aux Loups, Île d'Entrée, and Grande Entrée. Well-maintained, brightly painted wooden houses overlooking sandstone cliffs recall the finer aspects of the Atlantic coast, but with an unmistakable Québécois twist.

For our bucket list, we can choose from these:

- A carnival of wind: kitesurfing, kiteboarding, and kite buggying
- Cycling on the 100-kilometre-long greenbelt that runs across the archipelago
- Sea kayaking along the red cliffs
- Playing with white-coated harp seal pups on an ice floe, the only place in the world where you can do such a thing.

My personal favourite, though — hence the title of this chapter — is cave swimming beneath the sandstone cliffs of Old Harry's Head. *Cave* and *swimming*: two words that don't do the experience any justice.

QUEBEC ↑

I'm enjoying a warm breakfast at La Salicorne, a popular *auberge* and restaurant in Grand Entrée that runs sea kayaking and other outdoor excursions. It's September, the tail end of the tourist season, but the best time for wind junkies. Canadian kitesurfing pioneer Eric Marchand's Aerosport operation had already introduced me to kite buggying on the 16-kilometre-long Martinique Beach. I was more than happy to let the pilot steer our tandem buggy as it ripped along the sand in 20-knot winds. Today, grey clouds are spitting rain with an unwelcoming autumn chill, and while I'd much rather cozy up indoors by a fireplace, the bucket list is calling. Thus I find myself squeezing into a seven-millimetre wetsuit under the bemused gaze of strapping local lass Sandrine. Joining me is my pal, the well-known hockey writer Lucas Aykroyd, a man of towering height and soothing, modulated voice. Warmed by our thick wetsuits and life jackets, emboldened by the youth of our lovely blue-eyed guide, we reckon we've signed up for a forget-table family-friendly adventure: Hashtag: #weareidiots.

Culinary Quebec

Don't have a taste for fishy-meaty seal salami? You might have better luck with these original Québécois dishes.

Poutine: The province's gift to world cuisine combines fries, cheese curds, and gravy into an anytime hunger buster.

Tourtière: An anything-goes comfort meat pie, typically made with pork, veal, beef, fish, or wild game.

Tarte au Sucre: My sweetie teethie goodness! Who can turn down a pastry smothered with fudgy sugar and maple syrup?

Soupe aux Pois: Traditional Québécois pea soup, served thick and hot on cold winter nights.

Pâté Chinois: Although it translates as Chinese Pie, this distinctly non-Asian recipe is very similar to shepherd's pie. ➤

Sandrine drives us to a beach that is being pounded by huge waves. Our instructions are to follow her. She enters the cold water and veers to the left toward the sandstone cliffs. Lucas and I look at each other with panic in our eyes, "Em   you do see those waves smashing against those cliffs, right?"

"*Oui*, that is cave swimming. Come!" says Sandrine. A swell picks her up, slams her into the rocks, and washes her out again farther down the coast. It looks like one must be an egg short of an omelette to even attempt this, but for some reason, waves buttress the swimmer and cushion the blow. Aided by your buoyant protective wetsuit and life jacket, it appears perfectly safe to let the waves smash you against the coastline. At some points, we scale up boulders for some rock jumping; at others, Sandrine instructs us to wait for a big wave to flush us into a cave, and another to flush us out.

"How is it possible for this to be a commercial family excursion?" asks Lucas, shortly after a huge swell spits him out. I'm too busy screaming with fear and elation to care right then. Apparently, local

island kids used to do this all the time, and at some point, they realized it was safe enough for tourists to do, too.

"Oh, we've had some sprains and bruises, but nothing serious," says Sandrine matter-of-factly. Typically Canadian then: unique, incredible, can't do this anywhere else in world, and you know [shrug] just something we do here for fun.

Two hours later, Lucas and I are deep purple with cold, and not even Sandrine's beaming smile can warm us up. The strong current has pushed us down the coast to a sandy beach, where a guide is waiting with the excursion bus. Later we will toast our courage with a pint of wild herb–scented Belle Saison at the outstanding À l'abri de la Tempête microbrewery. The swells will grow from five to 10, no, 18 feet — not a word of a lie! We will nosh on dried herring and seal salami at Le Fumoir d'Antan, and artisanal island cheese at Pied-de-Vent. We'll meet friendly locals in clapboard *auberges* and explore the historic marina of La Grave. Without Sandrine for company, however, we'll skip the long walks on windswept beaches.

Although there are regular flights throughout the summer season from Montreal and Quebec, the Maggies are often overlooked in favour of their more popular maritime neighbours. Yet with an abundance of history, culture, natural beauty, food, and wild adventures, there's nowhere else quite like it. Lucky for you, I never could keep a good secret.

START HERE: canadianbucketlist.com/iles-de-la-madeleine

BITE INTO MONTREAL'S BEST SMOKED MEAT

When immigrants flooded into Montreal from Europe in the early 1900s, they brought with them passionate quirks and traditional recipes. The Italians delivered their fiery tempers and coffee shops. The Greeks brought their strong family values and their souvlaki. And the Jews? They gave the city a quirky neurosis, along with world-class delis and bagels that have no equal.

The origin of Montreal's smoked meat sandwiches remains a topic of hot dispute. Some say the recipe is Romanian, others Lithuanian, but there's little point fighting while the food's getting cold. The Montreal smoked meat sandwich is a simple creation of edible perfection: rye bread, thinly sliced. Mustard. A pickle on the side. And the meat: expertly carved, melt-in-your-mouth steamed brisket piled so high you can build a fort with it. Choosing where to enjoy such a dish is no simple matter, and locals will let you know exactly why that is. The Great Smoked Meat Hunt has begun.

It starts at 4 a.m. at Dunn's, where I wash ashore at this 24-hour deli after a hard night's research in the bars. Here, a brusque, whip-smart

The Bucket List
Smoked Meat Sandwich Tour

Bring a pen, a camera, and one serious appetite. My conscience demands that I warn you not to try to do this in one day.

1. Schwartz's
2. Lesters
3. The Main
4. Ettingers
5. Smoked Meat Pete's
6. Dunn's
7. Deli Bee's
8. Snowdon Deli

server tells me that Dunn's recipe hasn't changed in 50 years, and that, unlike some of the other shops, Dunn's is still "Jewish owned." Not exactly, since the company now has independently owned franchises around the country. The meat arrives steaming and melts on my tongue. At four in the morning, with food this good, I don't care who owns Dunn's — the sandwich is sensational.

"Dunn's! You can't go to Dunn's for the real experience!" says the father of a Montreal friend, horrified. So he takes me to Lester's Deli in Outremont, where he advises me to order the hot smoked meat sandwich, medium fat for more flavour. Hasidic wives wheel their babies past our table as I tuck into the sandwich, kosher pickle, and a plastic bottle of homemade Montreal spice at the ready. Smoked meat is smoked meat, but under the relieved gaze of a true believer, I confess that Lester's is a mouth-watering notch up from Dunn's.

"Lester's? Are you kidding me!" yells the huge ponytailed bouncer outside a nightclub. He literally grabs me by the collar and pulls me closer. His breath smells of garlic, and his skin like Montreal Old

Spice. "Schwartz's. Nothing touches Schwartz's! If you don't go to Schwartz's, I'll …" And then he lets me go. At this point, I realize that Montrealers take their smoked meat very, very seriously

Schwartz's has been Montreal's most famous smoked meat deli (or Charcuterie Hebraique, as the sign outside says) since 1928. It's inspired a musical, a book, and the interest of Céline Dion, who, together with other investors, purchased the business. Big hunks of smoked meat sit in the window, tempting the hungry lineups that gather around mealtimes. The service is curt, the decor basic. I order a takeout sandwich, and since I can't find anywhere to sit, I cruelly decide to eat it across the street, enshrined in food bliss while the salivating eyes of the lineup look on. Oh YES! It's nirvana for the carnivore, a foodgasm of the first order.

I returned the following day, and the next time I was in Montreal, and every time I've been in Montreal since. Schwartz's uses a secret blend of herbs and spices, marinates the meat for 10 days, and smokes it without preservatives. It's long resisted the urge to grow and take on the fast-food franchises, which explains why the lines are long. But the wait is worth it.

QUEBEC ↑

And I'm not done just yet. Across the street from Schwartz's, close to the bench where I enjoyed my first hit of their smoked meat, is the Main. The meat here is also in the window; there are also dozens of newspaper clippings about the genius of its recipe. By now I've learned about the taste benefits of ordering "old-fashioned" as opposed to the health benefits of ordering "lean." I've debated the origins and recipes of Montreal smoked meat (which writer Mordecai Richler called the "nectar of Judea") and its obvious superiority to smoked meat found in the delis of New York. Who serves the best smoked meat in Montreal is beside the point. Wherever you end up will deliver the goods, a meaty dream that is infinitely better than any other meat sandwich, anywhere in the world.

START HERE: canadianbucketlist.com/meat

DRINK CARIBOU WITH BONHOMME

Canada has no shortage of feisty public celebrations, but there's only space for a handful on the bucket list. They don't come any cooler than the Carnaval de Québec. Buried in my pockets, my hands were literally frozen as well. For over half a century, the world's largest winter festival has attracted millions of revellers bundled up for the snow and ice to enjoy parades, competitions, activities, and parties. Much like Mardi Gras or Rio's Carnival, the tradition dates back to the Catholic festivals preceding Lent. And like my experience at Mardi Gras and in Rio, this translates into alcohol and dancing, with the added bonus that both keep you warm.

The Carnaval's official mascot is Bonhomme Carnaval, a jolly snowman with an unnerving smile. He's a cross between Mickey

Mouse and Elvis Presley, and his effigy in miniature is literally your entrance ticket into the Carnaval grounds in Quebec City's Battlefields Park. I'm greeted by an ice slide, kids being pulled in sleds, food vendors, and deep regret that I didn't add one more layer of long underwear. Well, Rio can keep its wild, sweaty street parties, and New Orleans the plastic beads of Fat Tuesday. This 17-day Carnaval has dogsledding, snow rafts, hot tubs, human foosball, and an ice palace complete with ice discos. Over a dozen teams from around the world work through the night on snow sculptures, and all of this can be enjoyed with your cheap entrance ticket.

I head to the top of the hill for an overview. My immediate impression is that the Carnaval site is smaller than I expected, but since the temperature has plummeted to −15°C, perhaps it's wise that the crowds stick close together anyway. Beneath the Ferris wheel, two men in costumes are leading a Zumba class from the palace stage. It's a direct challenge to winter: snow, ice, wind chill? We'll dance to Shakira!

Ice is cracking on my face as my inflatable raft bounces down a bumpy snow channel. Most activities are family friendly, but there's also a fair bit of drinking going on, mostly in the form of caribou, a hot mulled wine with added whisky. It's perfectly acceptable to buy a Bonhomme cane, twist his head off, and fill up the cane with this hot liquor, a welcome and delicious anaesthetic for the cold.

There are daily events taking place during Carnaval, the most popular of which are the float parades and the ice canoe races across

Make Your Own Caribou

It's easy to make Quebec City's Carnaval drink of choice. Just get your hands on sherry, vodka, brandy, and port. And painkillers for the next morning.

3 oz. (100 mL) vodka
3 oz. (100 mL) brandy
12½ oz. (425 mL) Canadian sherry
12½ oz. (425 mL) Canadian port
Serves 10 (or 7 lushes, 3 bangers, and a partridge in a pear tree).

the St. Lawrence River. If you need proof that Canadians are a parachute short of a skydive, watch dozens of men and women paddle and run over floating chunks of ice in the St. Lawrence. Sometimes they paddle and run over each other, all for prize money that is small enough for teams to drink through in one evening.

Since this is a celebration, I find myself sliding between the ice bars on Grande Allée, a popular evening attraction. Even though snow is piled high on the sidewalks, there's an undeniable spirit permeating the whole city. The *ceinture fléchée*, a traditional French-Canadian sash, adds colour to the waists of locals and tourists. Portraits of Bonhomme are everywhere, and while the jolly mascot initially freaked me out with his dead marshmallow eyes, by the end I'm hugging him, too, joining small kids bundled up like walking pillows.

Canadians live in a northern country where winter is a way of life. Some people deal with it by staying home, others by moving away. Winter Carnaval is correctly revered as one of the world's unique celebrations. If you dress warmly, embrace your inner child, and keep some caribou handy, you won't freeze to death crossing this one off your bucket list.

START HERE: canadianbucketlist.com/carnaval

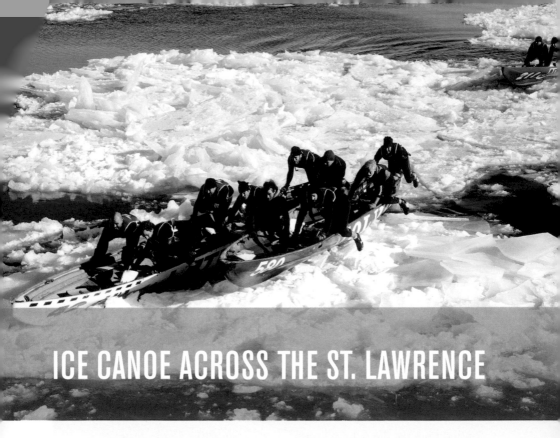

ICE CANOE ACROSS THE ST. LAWRENCE

Imagine you're in a canoe on a tranquil lake. As your paddle creates gentle ripples in the water, you're breathing in the calm, relaxing scent of nature. Ice canoeing in Quebec City is *nothing* like that.

During Winter Carnaval in Quebec City, teams of strappingly fit competitors hoist, haul, push, pull, and paddle heavy wooden canoes across ice sheets and water channels in the freezing St. Lawrence River. Much like dragon boat racing, it is quite the spectacle, except dragon boat racers don't have inch-long screws in their shoes, spikes on the end of their paddles, and sharp chunks of ice ready to splinter boat and bone at any moment. Historically, ice canoes played an important part in the history of the city. Shuttling passengers and goods between the shores of the St. Lawrence, they

served as ambulances, delivery trucks, and mail vans, operating each winter in snow, ice, and freezing rain.

The strong tides of the St. Lawrence add extra challenges, as the pack ice constantly shifts, requiring a combination of strength and sharp navigational skills to successfully make the crossing.

Ice canoe races took place at the city's first Carnaval back in 1894, and today remain a highlight of the world's largest winter festival. A company now offers visitors and locals the opportunity to experience ice canoeing for themselves, and it's just the sort of one-of-a-kind adventure that belongs on our national bucket list — which is how I find myself sweating bullets in the middle of the St. Lawrence, dodging sharp pack ice and the occasional rusty crampon spike.

Although it attracts teams from as far away as France and the United States, competitive ice canoeing is a sport unique to Quebec. With the support of Rowing Canada and the Quebec Port Authority, former race organizer Felix Blanchet-Levesque founded Ice Canoe Quebec to introduce the public to the sport.

We meet at the boat launch located riverside on the Plains of Abraham. After a casual briefing, I'm provided with neoprene socks

and booties, a life vest, shin and knee guards, and slip-on crampons with heavy screws to help me avoid slipping on the ice. Two guides demonstrate the five different positions in the canoe and how to transition from rowing position to "scootering" — the art of pushing the canoe across the ice.

With all the spikes and crampons around, I hope I can avoid shredding clothes (at best) or scarring my fellow racers for life (at worst). When hitting ice, rowers put away their paddles and slide into scootering position (shin and hands in the boat), using the other foot to propel the canoe forward much like a skateboard. Nothing to it if we were on an ice rink, yet it is painfully obvious from the get-go that the St. Lawrence River has never seen a Zamboni. Ice sheets are erratic and sharp, about as unpredictable as a jackal juggling sushi knives. Our canoe tilts and drops with no warning. Legs suddenly sink into dead-cold waters. We wade forward until reaching the next patch of ice, where we must haul the canoe up, only to quickly receive instructions to get back into rowing position.

Our guides, both racing veterans, including the pint-sized Marie-Janick who barely reaches my shoulders, appear have the strength of 16 human beings. Marie explains that men's and women's teams compete with each other each year, and that women's teams do particularly well since they're lighter and often have better technique. As for my own technique, I am clearly the weakest link on our team. Pain quickly sprouts in places I didn't know I had. It takes me ages to figure out how to raise my paddle to jam the spike into thinner ice and how to slide into scootering position without awkwardly tying myself into a thorny pretzel. Fortunately, our race includes plenty of rest stops, hot chocolate, and time to watch the ice packs flow with the tides, with the added bonus of the skyline of old Quebec City sparkling on the south shore.

We finally get our flow right for one stretch, coordinating each push as our canoe carves through the ice. It feels terrific, until we hit our own little Titanic iceberg, lurch to the right, and narrowly avoid capsizing. Stabbing aches in my thigh muscles tell me that giving myself a 4 out of 5 fitness level on the waiver form was outrageously optimistic. While the true race experience is best suited to fitter guests, Ice Canoe Quebec adjusts each excursion to the capabilities of each group, with no experience necessary. Depending on conditions, you'll spend about an hour on the water, with training, gear-ups, and rest breaks taking another two. As for the story about the time you raced an ice canoe across the frozen St. Lawrence in Quebec City? That will last a lifetime.

START HERE: canadianbucketlist.com/icecanoe

SNOWMOBILE IN SAGUENAY-LAC-SAINT-JEAN

Large parts of Canada depend on the snowmobile. Ever since early inventors first strapped skis onto Model T Fords, it's become far more than just a mode of winter transport; snowmobiling is a way of life. Quebec claims rightful ownership of this mode of transportation: local boy Joseph-Armand Bombardier invented the caterpillar track, which soon became a vital system for winter ambulances, school buses, and mail and military vehicles. Today, there are more than three million snowmobiles registered worldwide, and Bombardier is a true Canadian success story — whether on water, in the sky, or out on the snow.

That might explain why Quebec boasts a staggering 33,000 kilometres of snowmobile trails. That's enough terrain to overwhelm anyone's bucket list, so we're going to press the throttle to the region of Saguenay–Lac-Saint-Jean, which is home to nine snowmobile circuits covering a whopping 3,500 kilometres. Huge amounts of snow

fall here every winter, and snowmobilers arrive from around the world to take advantage of it. *Auberges* are polished, bistros are opened, and the trails are groomed and clearly signposted. A seemingly hostile terrain of deep powder, dense forest, and icy lakes suddenly becomes a playground for powerful machines that roar their approval. It's why riders call this part of the world a snowmobiler's paradise.

I sense some of your heads shaking, a thought bubble sprouting: "But I've never been on a snowmobile before. Isn't it dangerous? Don't I need a licence? Aren't they difficult to ride?" *Au contraire.* You don't need a licence to ride a snowmobile. You can go as fast, or as slow, as you want. And danger is often associated with speed and control, and, as with anything — car, bicycle, motorbike, skis — accidents tend to occur when people ride beyond their talent level. Fortunately, snowmobiles are designed to be incredibly forgiving. There's a very fast learning curve as you figure out how to shift your weight to take corners more efficiently and keep your ride smooth. In a region that embraces snowmobilers, there are plenty of gas stations and repair shops if you need them, not to mention friendly camaraderie on the trails. First-timers might want to use the service of a local outfitter like Equinox Adventures, who provides the machines, a guide, a route itinerary, and accommodation for a five-day package. You've heard of ski-in, ski-out lodges. In this part of the world, you sled-in, sled-out.

Quebec's Federation of Snowmobile Clubs charges a trail permit to use their extensive network, primarily to cover the costs of grooming and marking the trails. Online you can find maps with updated conditions to plan your own adventure, or you can choose one of the recommended itineraries (with names like Around the Fjord and the jovially named The Ha! Ha!). Accommodations list which circuit they service, and there are several snowmobile rental shops throughout the region.

Those are the nuts and bolts. But let's get to that moment when you motor up a summit on a blue-sky day. You lift your visor, suck in a mouthful of fresh air, and gaze at a view so extraordinary it revs the horsepower of your heart. Beyond the thrill of gunning a 600 cc machine across a frozen lake or meandering between snow ghosts of trees lies the fact that snowmobiling is part of Canada's winter DNA. If you get the opportunity to ride one, even for a few hours on a commercial joy ride, you'll quickly understand why.

START HERE: canadianbucketlist.com/Saguenay

SCALE A FROZEN WATERFALL

Canyoning, or canyoneering as it is known in the United States, combines aspects of hiking, climbing, rappelling, and, where applicable, not drowning. The goal is to ascend or descend a canyon through pristine wilderness like that found around Mont-Sainte-Anne, Quebec. Although relatively obscure, canyoning is a popular activity in the summer, with various routes open to all ages and fitness levels. I've slid down canyons in Costa Rica, where our guide held everyone back so he could "dispose of" a poisonous snake in our path. New Zealand, Colorado, France — the activity isn't unique in itself, but if we return to the winter ski slopes of Mont-Sainte-Anne, we can find something truly original.

Marc Tremblay's Canyoning Quebec is the only place in North America where you can attempt ice canyoning — just the sort of

QUEBEC

unique activity our bucket list is hungry for. Tall and stringy, Marc is an accomplished spelunker, the kind of guy who gets his rocks off squeaking through caverns underground. He enjoys introducing people to the joys of canyoning and is a pioneer of doing it in snow and ice. He tells me to dress warmly. Drowning is the least of my concerns.

We meet at the ticket office of Mont-Sainte-Anne, where I'm kitted out with ropes, crampons, and a backpack. "The most dangerous things on this trip are crossing the highway and avoiding the snowmobiles," says Marc reassuringly. We hike over to the highway, wait for local drivers hell-bent on creating road-kill, and continue along a snowmobile path where Marc's assistant, Genevieve, keeps watch over a blind hill.

Once we enter the woods, we're in a magical world of snow and ice. A stream flows, barely, carving ice structures along its edges. During the summer this path will be full of hikers, but in winter it belongs to us. Farther down, Marc helps me with my crampons, shows me how to loop my figure-eight hook, and ropes me up to practise my descent. "Keep your legs apart, watch out for the crampons, and just ease your way down," he instructs me calmly. Child's play, which is why even children can do this. I have to watch my harness, though, which has a tendency to trap testicles, initiating a Michael Jackson-esque falsetto.

We continue downstream until we come to the edge of a 40-metre cascade. In summer, you'd descend down the same spot, showering in the flow of the waterfall. This overcast day in February, I hear water barely descending beneath a spectacular frozen formation. Nature has burned 10,000 giant, icy-white candles, and I'm about to lower myself down among the hardened wax.

Crunch! The sharp teeth of my crampons dig into the ice as I do my best to avoid breaking the frozen stalactites. Once I'm over the lip, I stop to admire the view. Limestone caves would take millennia to form these sorts of structures, but out here in winter, every day produces a different show. Goosebumps sprout like mushrooms on my neck. I eventually lower myself to the bottom, where Genevieve unhooks me. I greet her with my favourite one-syllable word: "Wow!"

I can barely recognize the waterfall when I see photos taken during the summer, but winter climes offer an entirely different adventure: an icy, exhilarating thrill that belongs on the Great Canadian Bucket List.

START HERE: canadianbucketlist.com/canyoning

ATTEND THE GREAT MONTREAL FESTIVALS

Montreal has more festivals than there are weeks in the year: arts, children's, music, history, theatre, bikes, fashion, culture — just about everything that tickles your right brain gets the treatment. Other cities — notably Edmonton, Vancouver, Toronto, and Winnipeg — have no shortage of festivals either, so why does Montreal get the nod on the bucket list? Because Montreal does it bigger and sexier than anywhere else.

Take the Montreal International Jazz Festival, the world's largest jazz festival, hosting over 1,000 concerts featuring 3,000 performers from three dozen countries, attracting some two million people to the city, who visit 15 concert venues and 10 outdoor stages. Remarkably, two-thirds of these performances are completely free of charge, which means everyone has the chance to watch artists such

as Norah Jones, Diana Krall, Ben Harper, and Gilberto Gil perform at the huge outdoor, car-free downtown venues.

Typically scheduled at the end of June, the jazz festival's days get going at the site around 11 a.m., when various events specifically appealing to families begin. Kids can build their own instruments at workshops in the Parc Musical, while bands perform on different stages. It runs all day until the heavyweight performers take the stage and continues as the crowd filters into the city's legendary late-night after-parties. The 10-day event transcends jazz; expect world music, rock, fusion, R&B, folk, and a lineup of virtuosos, all drawn to the event like the thousands they perform for.

Come September, the hipsters gather for Pop Montreal, an indie music festival that took on special significance when local artists Arcade Fire exploded to become one of the world's biggest rock acts. From humble beginnings, the five-day festival has grown to present over 600 bands in 50 venues and has diversified with an accompanying design festival (Puces Pop), a music conference (Pop Symposium), Film Pop (for film-related music), Art Pop (visual arts), and Kids Pop. Montreal's "it" factor draws interest and artists from around the world, and while the festival was only founded in 2002, it has fast become one of the coolest cultural festivals on the continent.

Before personal screens allowed a measure of choice, do you remember watching dreary romantic comedies on long-haul flights, if only to alleviate the excruciating boredom? The movie (typically starring Matthew McConaughey's bare chest) would finally end, and

QUEBEC ↑

filling up the hour would be a timeless episode of the prank series *Just for Laughs Gags*. Suddenly, hundreds of people of ridiculously diverse backgrounds were cracking up in unison at the situations — all created, produced, and executed to perfection in Montreal. Humour transcends language.

So it's fitting that every July, Montreal hosts Just for Laughs, the world's largest international comedy festival. It's more than just stand-up from the world's funniest French and English comedians. The event turns the streets of downtown Montreal into a festival, with parades, food trucks, and packed pedestrian-only promenades. Meanwhile, TV execs and producers hunt for the next breakout comedy star. You may have heard of some of them: Jerry Seinfeld, Chris Rock, Tim Allen, Jay Leno, Jim Carrey. Rowan Atkinson did his first non-verbal Mr. Bean performance in front of an audience at Just for Laughs. I ask a cheerful Gilbert Rozon, who founded the event back in 1983, how Montreal has somehow become the funniest place on earth.

"In Quebec, we have a beautiful expression, '*C'est le fun!*' It should be our national slogan, and it's typical about Montreal," he tells me. "Nobody can be against being happy, nobody ever said 'I laughed too much.'" Gilbert reflects on Montreal's legacy as a party town during Prohibition, how it attracted crooners from the 1930s to the 1960s, and how the current festivals uniquely close the streets and offer so many free shows.

Led by its own iconic green Bonhomme, Just for Laughs features comedy theatre, music, dance, and other types of performances. North America's best stand-up stars host gala evenings, usually tele-vised around the world. Outside the theatres, crowds flock to the pedestrian-only St. Catherine Street, enjoying the free spectacle under the lights in the Quartier des Spectacles, which reminds me of the Sambadrome in Rio. Call it a carnival of comedy.

"In the next 30 years, we're going to invest in beauty and build more events around this time, so that you'll have no choice but to want to visit," says Gilbert, like a generous kid who wants to share his candy.

Later that evening, I join the long lineup to see a festival staple: the Nasty Show. Renowned for the vulgarity of its stand-ups — the show's run has featured greats such as Bill Hicks and Denis Leary — tonight's performance is a shotgun of hysterical bad taste. Before you push up daisies, visit Montreal one summer to laugh so hard the tears streak down your face.

START HERE: canadianbucketlist.com/festivals

QUEBEC

SURF A STANDING WAVE

The first time I tried surfing, some bleached beach bums gave me a small board best suited for experts and towed me into a shark-infested meat grinder affectionately known as the Snake Pit. This was in the warm Indian Ocean off the east coast of South Africa. The fangs of the waves repeatedly bit, while the tail of backwash coiled around and sucked the life out of me. Fortunately, the sharks weren't hungry that day.

With an introduction like that, it's no wonder that I still can't get up on a surfboard, although I have tried in other, less hostile environments. There's a draw about surfing that is hard to hang ten on …

a curious blend of nature and exhilaration, patience and full-blown action. It's why people of all ages and interests become hooked, and why it belongs on our bucket list. There's just one problem: we live in the Great White North.

What Canadian surf lacks in weather and waves, it make up for in creativity. Advances in wetsuit technology make the cold swells of B.C.'s Tofino and Nova Scotia's Lawrencetown manageable, while Lake Superior's north shore kicks up encouraging surf in spots like Stoney Point and Park Point.

Those seeking a consistent wave close to the amenities of a major urban city need look no further than Habitat 67. Located close to the iconic building of the same name, the St. Lawrence's Lachine rapids reach as high as two metres, creating one of the world's largest standing waves. These are especially fun to learn on, since you can spend more time learning how to balance on the board, and less time waiting for the right wave to come along and throw you off it. If you don't know where to start, hang in there, dude. KSF, located right by the rapids, is a full-service surf shop offering gear rentals, instruction classes, and stand-up paddle-boarding. No snakes, no sharks, just stoke.

START HERE: canadianbucketlist.com/habitat67

SPEND A NIGHT IN AN ICE HOTEL

F ive hundred tons of ice, 15,000 tons of snow, 36 rooms, and one writer desperately trying to avoid using the word *cool*. The Hôtel de Glace, located outside Quebec City, is North America's only ice hotel. It takes 50 people about six weeks to build the hotel each winter, crafting its rooms, bar, chapel, passageways, slides, and chandeliers. Lit with atmospheric non-heat-emitting LED lights, you'll get plenty of ambience if not warmth standing next to the double-glazed fireplaces. Not to fear, the romance and creative vision of the hotel will warm your heart just as surely as the interior temperature of −5°C will chill your bones.

QUEBEC ↑

At around 9:00 p.m., day visitors are ushered out and the overnight guests gather in the Celsius, an adjacent, blessedly heated building, for the briefing. If you're going to spend the night in a Popsicle, the goal is not to become one by the morning. All guests are required to sit through a training session.

"The two most important things I can tell you," explains our bilingual, dreadlocked guide, "is don't go to sleep cold, and under no circumstances go to sleep wet." Put your glasses on the bedside table (made of ice) and they will soon be part of the installation. Spending the night in a hotel made of snow and ice requires a rather adventurous guest. It becomes clear that those seeking luxury and comfort will prefer your run-of-the-mill thawed hotel.

All guests are assigned lockers in the Celsius, where you'll also find bathrooms and showers. Nothing goes into your room except your pajamas, boots, and outdoor jacket. And while the builders have invented ice glasses to serve chilled vodka cocktails, they haven't invented ice plumbing, so, no, there are no toilets in the ice hotel. Each bed sits on a piece of wood atop blocks of ice, with a carved ice headboard and striking sculptures in the 1.2-metre-thick walls. We are shown how to wrap ourselves in our cocoon sleeping bags, which are designed for −30°C conditions and therefore should have no problem keeping us warm at night.

Slide into the bag liner and then into the bag itself, blow out the candles, and turn off the glow lights with the switch cleverly built directly into your ice bed. Couples expecting a hot, passionate night

in their winter wonderland are in for a disappointment. Exposed skin is simply not a good idea, and the sleeping bags are designed for a snug, solo fit. Although, this being Quebec, a province of passion, the designers merely ask that you get creative. How else to explain the naked life-sized couple staring at my bed? Or the hands grafted onto the headboard, suggesting a night of icy consummation? Perhaps there's a connection between hot thoughts and body warmth.

Before bedtime, there's plenty of time to explore the large public areas. Music thumps in the ice bar, where 400 people can gather to drink and dance and you never have to ask the friendly bartenders for ice in your cocktails. The chapel hosts dozens of weddings each year, with guests sitting on benches covered in deerskin while the doors are covered in fur. There are sponsor exhibits, ice slides for adults and kids, a room explaining the annual theme, and the fresh smell of ozone in the air.

Overnight guests are encouraged to hit the hot tubs and dry sauna before they go to sleep, warming up the body for the night ahead. I arrived after the Celsius kitchen had closed, so the attendant at the front desk, staffed 24 hours a day, ordered me a pizza. I half expected it to arrive in a frozen box.

Light snow is falling when I leave the hot tub, shower, put on my thermal underwear, and get ready for the night ahead. *Please, please, please don't let me need to pee in the middle of the night!*

Everything is locked up, making it exceptionally easy for guests to vacate by 8:30 a.m., staff to collect sleeping bags, and the rooms to open for public viewing tours by 9:30. No housekeeping is required, other than raking the floor and straightening out the fur covers on the bed and benches.

The hotel has been built and rebuilt each year since 2001 and is open from the first week of January until the last week of March. Lying in the deep silence and darkness of my room, I wonder if the builders and designers are heartbroken to watch their efforts melt each spring. Or perhaps they're excited by the potential to start afresh next season? How many other hotels can literally reconfigure themselves each year? Watching the vapour of my breath, I lie awake, wide-eyed and aware of just how unique this experience is.

Ninety-nine percent of overnight guests stay just one night. Dress warmly and prepare for an adventure. One night in one of the world's most unusual hotels is all our bucket list is asking for.

START HERE: canadianbucketlist.com/icehotel

CANOPY CYCLE THROUGH TREETOPS

Bucket lists are all about doing things you've never done before. And while hiking, mountain biking, and ziplining are all worthy outdoor pursuits, you can do them in lots of places. Hang on ... what if we could do them all at the same time?

Just a 90-minute drive from Montreal, near the town of Sutton, is a four-season outdoor resort called Au Diable Vert. Its tree house accommodations are pretty neat, as are its hiking and ski trails, water activities, and shaggy Highland cows. But we're here for a peculiar contraption they call the VéloVolant. Welcome to the world's highest suspended bicycle ride.

Although the line is relatively flat and stays at the same level, the ground disappears beneath your feet once you pedal off the platform, and you'll soon be hovering 30 metres above the ground. Seated and safely strapped in, you'll pass over maple and pine forests, ravines, and waterfalls, listening to birdsong and perhaps encountering some

wildlife foraging below. Fifteen riders are spaced out along the one-kilometre circuit, which takes about 45 minutes to complete. While you can pedal faster to gain some speed, think less zipline or roller coaster and more a gentle cycle in the forest.

A first in Canada; our bucket list applauds the impressive efforts of whoever keeps coming up with these increasingly bizarre methods to enjoy our great outdoors.

START HERE: canadianbucketlist.com/velo

ENJOY THE FALL FOLIAGE

We've already established that central Canada is one of the best places to enjoy the Rastafarian explosion of foliage in the fall. In Quebec, take a leaf out of this book and visit one of the following:

Lanaudiére and Mauricie: Located between Montreal and Quebec City, this regional fall foliage favourite is home to 10,000 lakes and hundreds of forests and parks. There are also a number of attractive small towns and villages to explore in the area. To see the colours, head into the 536-square-kilometre woodland of La Mauricie National Park, where you can drive, hike, walk, or canoe in amongst the foliage. The region also offers various road trip itineraries that trace the heritage of New France, crossing back and forth over Canada's first overland route, the Chemin du Roy.

The Laurentians: It might be getting a little chilly in Mont Tremblant to bike Le P'tit Train du Nord (see page 250), but that shouldn't stop you from heading to the Laurentian Mountains in the fall. This 22,000-square-kilometre region north of Montreal offers up some of the best fall foliage in the country. The mountain air is crisp, the maple groves are glowing, and romance blossoms in the villages, spas, and resorts. Besides enjoying the attraction of the autumn foliage, it's a great time to sample the seasonal gourmet food produced in the area, including fabulous cheeses, wines, ciders, sausages, honey, and maple syrup products.

DEVOUR A PLATE OF POUTINE

Canada has gifted the world gourmet treats well above its station, and any self-respecting bucket list should include a sample of the staples. I'm talking about ginger ale, instant mash, processed cheese, Timbits, and Yukon Gold potatoes fried in canola oil. Back bacon boosts a breakfast, Beaver Tails sweeten up cold days, and maple sugar is our apple pie (and goes great with apple pie, too).

If I were to choose a single Canadian dish that could take over the world, it would be poutine. It takes fries, a universally loved food group served from bistros to trucker bars, and simply makes them better. Poutine — healer for the hangover, sweet gravied taters for the stomach's soul. To foreigners, adding cheese curds and gravy to fries might sound as appetizing as adding clams to tomato juice, but Canadians know how a little creativity can raise the bar.

While several Québécois communities lay claim to its invention and the word itself has been around for ages, poutine only became popular in the late 1960s. In Quebec City, I was directed to Chez Ashton, a franchise that built its fame on the sloppy back of poutine

Canada's Culinary Contribution

Poutine is not the only edible gift Canada has given the world:

1. **Butter tarts:** The sugar-syrup-egg-and-butter delight was once a staple of pioneer cooking.
2. **Nanaimo bars:** A chocolate-custard-wafer sandwich invented on Vancouver Island.
3. **Beaver Tails:** The name of Ottawa's hot sugared pastry continues to confound international tourists.
4. **Fricot:** A hearty Acadian meat stew enjoyed when times were tough, and enjoyed when they weren't.
5. **McIntosh apple:** The crunchy, tart apple discovered by Mr. McIntosh on his farm in Upper Canada back in 1811 provides Americans with the main ingredient for their finest apple pies and was the inspiration for the name of Apple Inc's Mac computers.
6. **Maple syrup:** Canada produces 85 percent of the world's favourite syrup, which works on everything from pancakes to salmon.
7. **Fish and brewis:** Codfish + hard bread + salted pork fat = Newfoundland's comfort food. ➤

in 1972. Greasy as the greasiest spoon, one bite of their hand-cut potatoes smothered in brown gravy and the day's freshly made squeaky cheese curds was better than any poutine I've tried on the West Coast. Served in a foil container it may be, but it's still fit for a king.

Montreal's La Banquise offers 28 varieties of poutine, including La Elvis (ground beef, green peppers, mushrooms), La Kamikaze (spicy sausages, hot peppers, and Tabasco), and La Obélix (smoked meat). Poutine's beauty is that you can't really go wrong with it, but for our bucket list, we're off to Montreal's hip Plateau neighbourhood and a restaurant called Au Pied de Cochon. Celebrity chef Martin Picard is known for his creativity and, as Anthony Bourdain calls it, his "porky and ducky" decadence.

Seated next to me at the bar overlooking the open-concept kitchen are two guys: a bureaucrat who timed his Montreal connection to Ottawa specifically to visit the restaurant and a bartender from Toronto who plans his trips to Montreal around available reservations. Booking is a must, at least a month ahead for large groups, a week for couples. An attractive server walks past with a cooked pig's head on a platter with a large lobster in its

mouth. Behind me, a woman is chewing on a bison rib as long as my forearm. I scan the menu: fresh seafood, handily divided into bivalve, gastropod, echinoderm, cephalopod, and crustacean sections. Pickled tongue. Foie gras hamburger. Duck carpaccio. And there it is: foie gras poutine, calling me like three angels playing heavy metal on their harps.

Foie gras is, of course, a controversial food group, but wise travellers should respect local customs. David, the bureaucrat, orders Duck in a Can, which is so rich and fabulous he breaks out into a joyous sweat, calling it Heart Attack in a Can. Rare duck breast cooked with foie gras and vegetables, marinated in balsamic vinegar, opened and plopped onto mashed potatoes richer than butter. Paul, the bartender, orders a buckwheat pancake with bacon, mashed potatoes, foie gras, and maple syrup from Picard's popular sugar shack. "It's little, but it hits you hard," says Paul, twitching from the excess.

My poutine arrives smothered in a thick gravy, the chips fried in duck fat (of course), with a slab of sinful foie gras on the top. The aroma contains enough calories to feed a village in North Korea. It tastes like winning the jackpot on the first pull of a slot machine and contains the Higgs boson particle of flavour. Another guy at the bar has ordered the same, and while he doesn't say much, his face turns the ruby shade of beet. Our friendly, attractive servers have mischievous glint in their eyes. They've seen it all before, and they'll see it all again.

"Are you enjoying your meal?" they ask.

"It's … to die for," I answer.

START HERE: canadianbucketlist.com/poutine

CLIMB THE DEVIL IN MONT-TREMBLANT

Several years ago I found myself atop a holy mountain in central China, standing on two narrow wooden planks leaning against a wall of solid vertical rock. Below me was a 1,000-metre drop. Trust me when I say I was ill-prepared for this experience, as many others had been before me. To prevent people from inconveniently falling off and dying, Chinese authorities insist all visitors to Mount Hua pay a few bucks for a cheap harness to clip into a static safety line running the length of the "Number One Cliffside Plank Path."

This was my introduction to the exciting world of the *via ferrata* (Italian for "iron road"), a fun adventure for those of us who want to climb mountains without having to risk actually climbing a mountain. We've already looked at Canada's highest *via ferrata* in B.C. (see page 56), but one of the country's most popular is the Via Ferrata Du Diable that soars above Quebec's largest and oldest national park, Mont-Tremblant. I drive into the park on a smooth blacktop road that bends and curves through thick boreal forest, a fun roller coaster in itself. It's mid-morning when I get to the entrance kiosk, signing a waiver in return for a climbing harness, lanyards, helmet, and carabiners. Groups are limited to eight, with the one-kilometre trail divided into three levels of difficulty. I felt bold enough to select the advanced trail, which typically takes about five hours. Sure, one kilometre is no biggie when you're walking on land, but when you have to clip and unclip your way forward against a vertical wall on iron staples with a 200-metre drop beneath your feet, well, it pays to take your time. Our guide, Valérie, shows us how to easily lock into the iron rungs and steel safety line, and we start off with an imposing suspension bridge over the Diable River. Apparently this is enough to make some people turn back, but here's the surefire Esrock Method for Dealing with These Things:

1. Don't Panic.
2. Trust Your Gear.
3. Remind Yourself You're in Canada, not China, and Things Usually Work in Canada.

Designed by conservationists to minimize damage to the environment but overdo the safety aspect for visitors, the line and rungs make their way along the cliff, getting more and more difficult to navigate as we progress. Slowly, I get used to clipping in every few metres. Always make sure at least one of your carabiners is locked in

and it's pretty much impossible to fall more than a couple of feet. I'd say the rest is literally child's play, although kids under fourteen have to turn back before reaching the advanced level.

Here things take a puckering turn as the path moves horizontally against a solid cliff face, the glorious view of the Laurentians and surrounding valley on full display. Standing on an iron rung nailed into the rock, I take my time, breathing it all in — the forest, meandering brown river, the ski slopes visible on the highest peaks. *C'est le fun!* Farther along is a "surprise," in the form of a narrow wooden beam perilously positioned in a crevice. Next is a tightrope bridge, where the braver among the group let go to just hang around in their harness, enjoying the experience of being fully exposed to the elements.

Climbers know it's one thing to hike up a mountain shaded by the trees and another to ascend from the outside, hugging solid rock. If the weather isn't great, you may get lashed with wind and rain, but the view accompanies you all the way to the top.

While it's not for everyone (particularly anyone with a fear of heights, or with weight or fitness issues), I will say this: In China, I recorded a little video about my experience, which has been seen over one million times on YouTube. This devilish, little-known *via ferrata* in Mont-Tremblant might not be as exotic, but it's just as thrilling an adventure.

START HERE: canadianbucketlist.com/tremblant

JUMP THE ROCK

Some people like climbing rocks; others prefer jumping off them. At 61 metres high, Great Canadian Bungee's The Rock is the highest bungee jump in North America. Overlooking a spring-fed lagoon in Wakefield, Quebec (about a half-hour drive from Ottawa), the rebound alone is higher than any other jump on the continent.

You might be wondering why anyone would strap themselves to a heavy elastic band and leap into thin air. Since its invention in New Zealand in the late 1980s (the same country that has given us jet boats and plastic bubbles to hop inside and roll down hills), bungee jumping has proven to be a perfectly safe method of convincing your brain you're about to die, thereby releasing adrenalin and endorphins when your death is rather pleasingly delayed.

I've enjoyed this sensation on four continents, including the world's highest commercial bungee jump in Macau, and I can confirm that at no point does it become any less terrifying. The trick is to jump off the platform quickly, before your brain has time to make the entirely rational argument to back away from the edge and proceed to the nearest bar.

Once you take the leap, you won't be entirely conscious until you're somewhere on the rebound, blood rushing to your head and adrenalin marinating your overstimulated cortex. In Wakefield, you might also find your head wet from the refreshing soak if you requested a water dip.

Few adventures promise to bring you within a hair's breadth of your demise. That relief has created a bungee-jumping industry, and one of the hairier thrills on the Great Canadian Bucket List. Three, Two, One …

START HERE: canadianbucketlist.com/bungee

Boat to the Mingan Archipelago

Five hundred million years ago, a warm tropical sea covered what is today the St. Lawrence Lowlands. It would have been swell to relax on its beach, although good luck finding poutine, cheese, or even potatoes for that matter. Over the course of millions of years, fossils, sediment, and seabed were compressed into rock, which was then exposed when the sea receded, ready to be carved and eroded by ice age glaciers, wind, rain, rivers, and waves. Time-machine forward to the present day and you'll find the largest concentration of erosion monoliths in the country.

Almost a thousand islands and islets lay scattered east to west across 150 kilometres of Quebec coastline, moulded into overhangs, caves, arches, flowerpots, and cliffs. Protected as the Mingan Archipelago National Park Reserve, the area is accessible via boat tours from the north shore of the Gulf of St. Lawrence, from towns such as Longue-Pointe-de-Mingan, Aguanish, and Havre-Saint-Pierre. The boats vary in terms of their size and destinations, but typically visit several of the more dramatic islands, with parks interpreters explaining the festooned cliffs, fossils, tidal pools, and the area's unique geological history.

START HERE: canadianbucketlist.com/mignan ➤

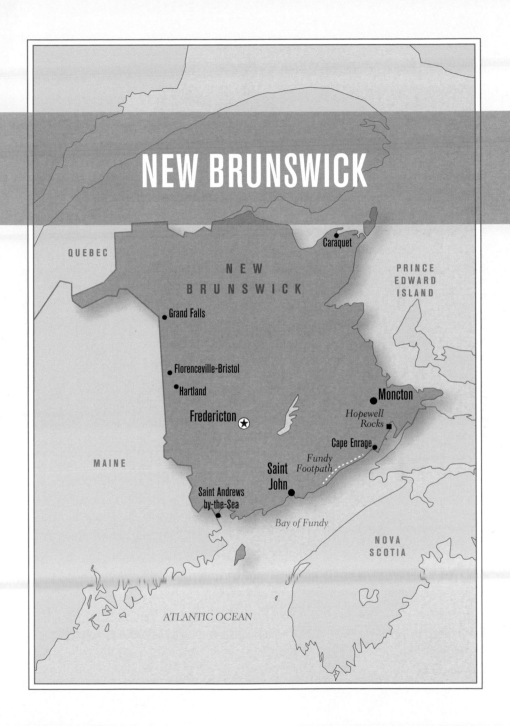

NEW BRUNSWICK

QUEBEC

NEW
BRUNSWICK

Caraquet

PRINCE
EDWARD
ISLAND

Grand Falls

Florenceville-Bristol

Hartland

Fredericton ☆

Moncton

Hopewell
Rocks

Cape Enrage

MAINE

Fundy
Footpath

Saint
John

Saint Andrews
by-the-Sea

Bay of Fundy

NOVA
SCOTIA

ATLANTIC OCEAN

WALK THE SEABED BENEATH HOPEWELL ROCKS

D espite its contribution to my surname, geology has never rocked my casbah. It would have to be spectacular, like the fairy chimneys that poke the sky of Cappadocia, Turkey, the bizarre hoodoos at the Yehliu Geopark in Taiwan, or the basalt columns that explode out of the ground in Iceland. Point is, if it's not a mind-blowing natural phenomenon, chances are I'll take a picture and do what too many tourists do in New Brunswick: floor it for the next province. This is my headspace when I arrive at the Hopewell Rocks, the most popular attraction in New Brunswick. I buy my ticket, walk through an information centre, and meet a site interpreter, who, like all great guides, demonstrates that enthusiasm is infectious — even when it comes to rocks and tides.

Kayak the Rocks

Half the fun is paddling on tides that rise and fall the height of a five-storey building. The other half is paddling along — and sometimes directly through — the striking flowerpots and rock formations that earlier you might have walked right up to. This unique sea kayaking adventure is neither strenuous nor particularly challenging, and therefore a perfect experience for just about everybody's bucket list. ➤

Millions of years ago, a geological shift in tectonic plates produced a valley that was flooded during the last ice age, creating a shallow ocean floor for 100 million tons of water to rush in with the tides, rising up to 16 metres on the shoreline. The Bay of Fundy holds the distinction of having the world's biggest tides. New Brunswickers love this feature of their province (shared only with Nova Scotia), and just about everyone I meet is compelled to describe the tidal phenomenon, which is why I've almost certainly explained it incorrectly. My guide reveals that during low tide, we can literally walk on the ocean floor, among giant rock structures that have been carved and shaped by this daily flush of water. These are the Hopewell Rocks, which didn't excite my imagination until I saw them.

All my travels and experiences have tuned me in to the joy of discovering something truly remarkable, something you just can't see anywhere else. We walk down a metal staircase and find huge brown monoliths, shaped and squeezed like plumber's putty. Among them are natural arches, tunnels, coves, and corridors. In one section I feel as if I'm walking through a giant keyhole, and with green brush on top of the rocks, they do indeed look like flowerpots. The ground is muddy and spotted with seaweed, made all the more fascinating by the fact that twice a day, the very spot where I'm standing will sit more than a dozen metres underwater. Rocks have been christened with names such as Dinosaur, Lovers Arch, Mother-in-Law, and E.T.

More creatively, Mi'kmaq legend holds that whales in the bay once imprisoned some people. One day they tried to escape but didn't make it to shore quickly enough and were turned to stone. Now these giant sedimentary and sandstone pillars guard the coast, staring across the bay at the shores of Nova Scotia. Shorebirds fly overhead as our guide points out a nest to the delight of some international birdwatchers. Blue skies and sun would be great, but Fundy's damp mist and fog adds to the otherworldliness of this strange landscape.

The tide comes in pretty quickly, so we return to the entrance, hopping over pools of water, grateful for our waterproof shoes. Later that day, this influx of water will result in a dramatically different experience, which is why many visitors consult online tide tables to ensure they catch both low and high tides. You can also hire kayaks and paddle between the flowerpots during high tide.

Having amazed a weary travel writer with no prior interest in geology, the Hopewell Rocks are an easy addition to our Great Canadian Bucket List.

START HERE: canadianbucketlist.com/hopewell

ABSEIL CAPE ENRAGE

The road bends and curls on the way to Cape Enrage. By its very name, you can tell this is not the Cape of Good Hope, or Cape Cod, Cape Town, or Cape Point. We're talking about 50-metre-high cliffs that squint their eyes and glare over the Bay of Fundy. Not angry, peeved, or slightly annoyed. No, these cliffs are *enraged*, with a black heart and a permanent scowl. Acadian sailors christened the cape for its exceptionally turbulent waters, boiling at half tide above a reef stretching into the bay.

I arrive on a foggy summer morning, the atmosphere one of moody petulance. Maybe I woke up on the wrong side of the Maritimes, but the terrible weather is enough to make me throw myself off a cliff, and fortunately, that's exactly what I've come here to do.

Since 1838, Cape Enrage has had a lighthouse to warn ships during the thick fog and harsh winter storms — although that didn't

stop ships from wrecking themselves on the reef all the same. When lighthouses were automated in the 1980s, the few battered buildings that stood at Cape Enrage were scheduled for demolition. That is, until a group of Moncton schoolteachers decided to take matters into their own hands.

The owners have worked hard to restore the remaining buildings, creating a non-profit interpretive centre and a commercial business offering kayaking, ziplining, climbing, and rappelling (or abseiling). It's mostly run by teachers and students, and despite the ominous natural surroundings, it's full of sunny Maritime dispositions.

Today I've decided to rappel off the cliff to the bottom, where I plan to hike along the beach, mindful of falling rocks and "tidal miscalculation," which can result in something unfortunate like, say, "drowning." After I slip on a harness and sit through the safety demonstration, it's a short walk over to the platform. Here's what I've learned about rappelling off a cliff: it's a lot more fun than hiking up it. It's also imperative that the, em ... family jewels ... are, how should we say, safely locked up. Fortunately, rappelling is not nearly as scary as other methods of launching oneself off a New Brunswick cliff (see Walk Off a Cliff, page 315), partly because you don't have to look down. You don't want to look up too much either, since heavy falling rocks are your biggest danger.

I kick off from the sheer rock face and slowly descend to the bottom, stopping for a while to swivel around and gaze upon the furious

view of the Bay of Fundy, with the shadowy shores of Nova Scotia in the distance. It doesn't take long before I'm on the beach, the cracked stone of fallen rocks all around me. The tide is coming in, so I don't stick around too long before climbing the much-appreciated metal staircase back up to the top.

An excellent restaurant rewards visitors with locally sourced dishes such as Raging Chowder and Lobster Tacos. By the time I leave, the sun even sneaks a smile from behind the clouds. Quenched in both the adventure and culinary departments, I depart with the satisfaction of having tamed Cape Enrage, another item deserving of its place on the Great Canadian Bucket List.

START HERE: canadianbucketlist.com/enrage

NEW BRUNSWICK ↑

ROLL UP MAGNETIC HILL

If I told you there was a mysterious hill outside of Moncton where you can put your car in neutral and it will roll uphill, would you believe me?

Magnetic Hill has been one of New Brunswick's most popular attractions since the 1930s, a freak of nature that boggles the mind. Once part of the provincial highway, the 1.5-kilometre-long antigravity stretch in question was preserved and today is a quirky roadside attraction adjacent to a popular water park and the largest zoo in Atlantic Canada.

I admit I had my doubts when I paid the five bucks and drove to the bottom of the hill. Yet no sooner had I put the rental car in neutral than, slap-me-with-a-wet-cod, the damn wheels started rolling upward. The illusion is caused by the unusual contours of the surrounding landscape and the lack of a horizon, giving the impression that the car is rolling uphill — as if pulled toward a magnet — when in fact it is rolling downhill. It is called a gravity hill, and there are nearly a dozen of them in Canada alone, Magnetic Hill being the most famous.

Isaac Newton may still be resting easy in his grave, but all the science in the world can't wipe away the wonderfully cool feeling that you're actually sliding uphill.

START HERE: canadianbucketlist.com/magnetichill

BIKE IN A KILT

There are several go-to words for travel writers that make me cringe: Charming. Spectacular. Nestled. I say this because I use those words all the time, and so it pains me to write that St. Andrews is a charming coastal town nestled among spectacular surroundings. And yet that's the truth, and there's no getting away from it.

Canada's first seaside resort community inspires memories of youth and genteel innocence. It's a place where people politely greet one another at the candy shoppe. It doesn't take a day before I'm on a first-name basis with a half-dozen locals, drinking a cold beer on the sun-baked patio of the Red Herring. I've written many times that travel is as much about the people you meet as the places you go, and this held true when two gentlemen greeted me in kilts at the wharf upon my return from a whale-watching excursion on the Bay of Fundy. The minke, humpbacks, finbacks, and endangered northern right whales gather in abundance in the bay, giving you a 95 percent chance of encountering them on a 200-horsepower Zodiac operated by Fundy Tide Runners. Today, however, belonged to the other 5 percent, so these men in kilts were just the sort of silliness I needed to cheer me up.

Off Kilter Bike's Kurt Gumushel doesn't claim to be an ambassador for the village, or for New Brunswick in general; he just is. Considering his pedigree, it's no surprise then that Kurt likes riding

his mountain bike in a kilt, and through his bike company, he shares this peculiarity with tourists throughout the summer.

We bike through tall wildflowers along the coast, into a lush forest, across the rail tracks, and onto beaches of pebble. All the while, I'm regaled with stories about the town, how its 1,500 population swells in the summer months, how the famed Tudor-style Algonquin Hotel wasn't actually the inspiration for Stephen King's *The Shining* though that doesn't stop everyone from thinking so. It's easy to click with locals in New Brunswick, especially when you're riding through gorgeous scenery in kilts and the ride ends up at the Red Herring pub.

The rejuvenating drink of choice here in St. Andrews is a Dooryard organic ale, a local beer served with an orange wedge. On the patio is Kurt's dad, along with some welcoming friends, and right then and there, I decide I, too, would like to have grown up in St. Andrews by-the-Sea. How peaceful to have walked among the original heritage houses barged in from Maine during the Revolutionary War, bought candy at a nineteenth-century corner shop, and practised my swing on the impossibly smooth fairways adjacent to the Algonquin. I could study marine science at the newly refurbished Huntsman Aquarium and Science Centre, and volunteer to keep the manicured Kingsbrae Gardens in tip-top shape. Who wouldn't want to live in a charming town nestled among spectacular surroundings, chomping fresh lobster rolls and slaking back Dooryards in the summer? Of course, my airbrushed dream negates those long, cold Maritime winters, which we'll conveniently overlook as we continue our journey along the Great Canadian Bucket List.

START HERE: canadianbucketlist.com/standrews

APPRECIATE THE GENIUS OF DALI

Art galleries need the right environment, ambience, and lighting to breathe. More life can be added with the help of a knowledgeable guide — someone to explain the nuances, the deftness of meaning, the symbolism behind the strokes. All this comes together as I stand before Salvador Dali's *Santiago El Grande* in the entrance hall of Fredericton's Beaverbrook Art Gallery.

The Beaverbrook serves as the province's official art gallery, a gift from press baron Max Aitken, a.k.a. Lord Beaverbrook. Ontario-born Aitken grew up in Newcastle, New Brunswick, and went on to become a British peer and Fleet Street's first overlord, taking the name Beaverbrook to convey his Canadian roots. As a benefactor in later life, he bestowed handsome gifts on his adopted Fredericton, including the luxury hotel that bears his name, which stands right next to the art gallery.

It is here that I meet local gallery docent and professional storyteller Joan Meade. She sizes me up quickly, in mutual agreement during our conversation that art without meaning is food without taste. I've sleepwalked through many an art museum around the world, lulled by the monotone voice of a bored guide on a still-life audiotape. "Here is our signature piece," says Joan. The museum's iconic painting, taking up a significant section of its gallery allotment, is quite impossible to ignore.

Dali painted his tribute to the apostle Saint James the Great, patron saint of Spain, for the 1958 Brussels World Fair. The four-metre by three-metre canvas depicts the saint on a noble white horse, its forelegs bucking over a liquid blue ocean, with the Ascension of Christ in the top right corner. The painting, regarded as one of Dali's greats, is rife with symbolism. The bottom right corner shows a lady in a monkish robe, a portrait of Dali's wife Gala, who is often present in his works. It is said that she looks at the viewer to see how the painting is being assessed. The horse's neck muscles repeat in the sky, taking the form of angels, the hidden images that are another of Dali's trademarks.

Given the horse's pose, its penis should be quite prominent in the painting. Dali has covered it with an atomic cloud, and the purest of

all flowers: the jasmine. "He proclaimed that further growth of atomic power should be used for good and not for the making of bombs," explains Joan, revealing Dali's newfound interest in nuclear physics and his expression of the relationship between religion and science. Her explanation is far more interesting than my initial conclusion: that Dali covered the horse's dong with a cloud. Joan points out other symbols. The scallop shell, *Santiago El Grande*'s religious icon, can be seen on the horse's neck and again as a protective shell over the saint and the coastline, which resembles the land where Dali grew up.

The painting was a gift of New Brunswick–born industrialist James Dunn, one of Beaverbrook's pals, and is on permanent display in the museum. The Dunns were early supporters and friends of Dali, and they purchased the painting under the nose of the Spanish government after the world fair. There are several other Dali works in the museum, including portraits of the Dunns themselves. Not long after James died, and keeping it all in the family, his widow married Lord Beaverbrook. Passion! Betrayal! Oil on canvas!

Joan leads me through some of the gallery's other masterpieces: the Magritte, the Turner, the haunting Lucien Freud. She knows how to tease the life out of a painting, adding fresh colour to the

Deferring to the Genius of Dali

"There are some days when I think I'm going to die from an overdose of satisfaction." — Salvador Dali ➤

canvas with her words. "A pity you're not there whenever I enter an art gallery," I tell her.

"I could be, if you're buying," she says in a snap.

Art culture in Canada tends to concentrate in the major urban centres: the National Gallery in Ottawa, the Montreal Museum of Fine Art, the Art Gallery of Ontario. Here in Fredericton, up the road from the Old Garrison District and across the street from the impressive legislature buildings, local character fuses with world-renowned genius for an experience even non-arty types will appreciate.

START HERE: canadianbucketlist.com/dali

WALK OFF A CLIFF

I am finally ready to step off a 41-metre-high cliff. While I've rappelled down gorges, caves, and mountains around the world, this will be the first time I'm rappelling face first, clutching a safety rope to my belly, literally walking down a rock face. This is what one does at Open Sky Adventures, the first commercial deepelling operation on the continent.

Deepelling is not bungee jumping, with its quick, what-the-hell-just-happened rush. Neither is it abseiling, where you face the wall and bounce along to the bottom. No, this is a controlled upright descent, with your eyes staring directly at sharp rocks waiting to splatter you over the riverbed. Something funny happens when I'm asked to slowly walk upright off the cliff. My mind refuses to co-operate, but my feet take the first step anyway.

The Australian army developed deepelling (also known as Aussie-style rappelling, or rap jumping) as a technique to prevent its soldiers from being shot while exiting helicopters. Using one hand to control the descent, it not only allowed soldiers to see their enemies, it also kept one hand free to fire back. With practice, you can literally leap off a wall like Spiderman. That practice includes repressing your natural instinct, which will beg, bargain, and plead for you to back away from the edge.

Raymond Paquet's Open Sky Adventures has been running kayak, pontoon, and canoe adventures down the Saint John River for years. When Raymond came across thrill-seekers deepelling in Quebec, he thought it would be a perfect activity for the canyon he owns just a few miles outside Grand Falls. "Babies are born afraid of height," he tells me, tightening up my mountain-climbing harness. "My job is simply to help kids get rid of this fear." His youngest client was seven, his oldest 80, so naturally he's referring to kids of all ages.

The weight of the rope tugs me forward. Raymond has my safety line and can control my fall should I release the rope by mistake. I hold it tight to my stomach, creating a natural lock. To hop down a few metres, all I have to do is release my grip. "You've done many things in the world, Robin, but I promise you'll remember this one," says Raymond behind me.

It's always the first step. Then the second. Actually, the third is just as nerve-racking. Halfway down, it occurs to me I'm walking at a 90-degree angle down a cliff face. Sweat doesn't drip down my forehead, it drips right off it, splashing the ground below. Bending my knees, I launch myself off the rocks and glide several metres in a single hop, like a horizontal walk in zero gravity. Less than a minute

For Those Who'd Prefer to Jump

No aerial adventure matches the pure thrill of plummeting to earth at terminal velocity. A bucket list mainstay, tandem skydiving is safe, unforgettable, and open to all ages. Consider:

Okanagan Skydive, B.C. Jump at 10,000 feet for 35 seconds of freefall, absorbing the spectacular view of sparkling lakes, surrounding ski resorts, and the Monashee Mountains.

Sky Dive Toronto, Ontario: Celebrate bucket lists, birthdays, bachelor parties, and marriage proposals at the longest-established and most experienced skydiving school in Canada.

Edmonton Skydive, Alberta: Offering a 14,000-foot tandem jump with a 60-second, 200-kilometre-an-hour freefall, marinate your brain in adrenalin as you drop over the prairies.

later, I reach the bottom, where I tug hard on the rope, straighten myself up, and land softly on my feet. Like all the best adrenalin activities, it's over too soon, and not soon enough.

Fortunately, the price of admission includes three descents. I walk up the stairs to the viewing platform (easily the most strenuous part of the day), back along the road, and return to the wooden launch platform. Raymond is waiting there with a gleam in his eye. "Isn't that cool?" he says in his thick French-Canadian accent.

"I've never seen or done anything like it. Let's do it again!" I reply, and head back to the edge. It's still a mind killer taking that first step, but this time my jumps become higher and my grip becomes easier on the rope. I make my way down in a matter of seconds, whooping the whole way.

Deepelling has proved so popular that Open Sky also allows you to launch yourself off the walls of its 15-metre-high headquarters, and in all seasons, too. It was developed by the military, so it's not surprising that there's one enemy you can expect to face: the fear in your mind.

START HERE: canadianbucketlist.com/deepelling

CROSS HARTLAND'S COVERED BRIDGE

Before you enter the world's longest covered bridge, they say you should make a wish, close your eyes, cross your fingers, and hold your breath. It's no easy task making it all the way to the other side in this condition. For one thing, the bridge is 390 metres long. Second, if you're driving, you'll probably end up plummeting into the Saint John River beneath you. Chances are your wish isn't going to come true anyway, although many a young man in the early twentieth century still got lucky.

New Brunswick has 61 covered bridges, which provided a safe river covering and an opportunistic spot to escape the invasive eyes of chaperones and parents. For this reason, covered bridges became

known as kissing bridges, makeshift wooden darkrooms for physical romance to finally see the light. Once the horse and buggy reached the other end, scandalous passion would be left behind. I wonder if there's a generation of New Brunswickers who still get turned on by the smell of wood, the creak of floorboards, and the peculiar light that beams from the end of a tunnel.

Inside the Hartland tunnel, my rental car robbed me of the full sensory experience, and my dad, the only other passenger in the vehicle, stole my romantic opportunity as well. Unveiled in 1901, the bridge is still the pride of Hartland, and cars line up on either side of its single-lane entries for the chance to pass through. We cross at a reasonable speed, although I'm sure farm boys slowed their horses as much as possible. Perhaps that's why the townsfolk were so scandalized: they kept hearing "Whoa! Whoa! Whoa!" from the dark depths of the bridge. Sermons once preached the moral decay accompanying such a long covered bridge, a situation that was not helped by rumours that young men had trained their horses to stop in the middle of the bridge for the ultimate smooch spot. Sneaking a snog inside Hartland's covered bridge is a long-standing Canadian tradition. If it's just you and a family member, though, it's perfectly acceptable to grunt and say, "Cool bridge."

START HERE: canadianbucketlist.com/hartland

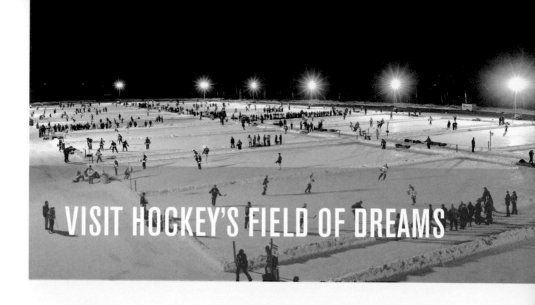

VISIT HOCKEY'S FIELD OF DREAMS

If ice hockey is a religion in Canada, the world's largest pond hockey tournament makes the village of Plaster Rock a bucket list pilgrimage. It is, as one participant describes it, hockey's Field of Dreams. Over the four-day event, 8,000 people will support 120 teams from 15 countries. Here, hockey is played in its purest form — outside, on ice. Players are surrounded by diehard fans of the game, who are bundled up and burning through beers at the bonfire.

The little village of Plaster Rock is reliably cold, the trees bending with snow. Visitors will scratch their heads at the sheer scale of the rinks, and how they remain beautifully maintained throughout the tournament. Traditional music, maritime hospitality, and a warm camaraderie keep players returning and the tournament growing.

This is four-on-four play with no goalies or age categories, the action flowing on the 20 rinks built onto the frozen Roulstan Lake. Occasionally, a pro might even show up; but this is a world away from the slick marketing machine of the NHL. A mecca for any bucket lister who ever skated on a backyard rink, it might get competitive on the ice, but the festivities continue long after the final whistle.

START HERE: canadianbucketlist.com/worldpondhockey

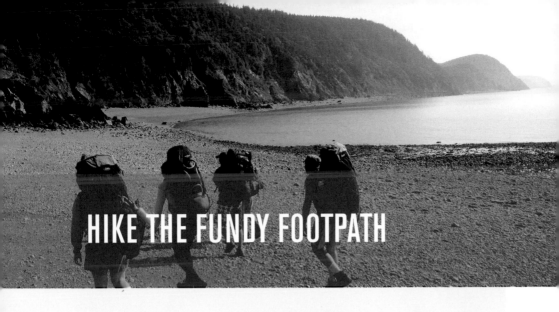

HIKE THE FUNDY FOOTPATH

Much like Vancouver Island's West Coast Trail, this 41-kilometre multi-day adventure tests hikers with its wild conditions and challenging backcountry terrain. Tracing the Bay of Fundy coastline, the footpath begins at the suspension bridge at Big Salmon River and concludes in Goose River, which can only be crossed during low tide. Immersed in the microclimate of the Bay of Fundy, you'll be exploring the Maritime Acadian Highlands, part of the foothills of the Appalachian mountain range. That's a fancy way of saying you'll be knee-deep in fog, steep river valleys, and strenuous switchback trails ready to spook the average day hiker.

While trekking alongside 100-metre cliffs, through old-growth forests, beaches, and streams, the footpath provides a true test for your backcountry wilderness skills. After a half-dozen emergency evacuations one year, volunteers who maintain the trail issued a warning that the footpath is too rugged for novice hikers. That rules me out, but adventurous, experienced hikers will definitely want to add this to their bucket lists. Budget four to five days, and keep your tide chart handy.

START HERE: canadianbucketlist.com/fundyfootpath

ZIPLINE OVER A WATERFALL

Before invading just about every jungle block in Costa Rica, ziplines were a practical necessity in mountainous regions, where they were a means of transporting both goods and people. With the boom in ecotourism, enterprising operators realized tourists will pay good money for the opportunity to slide faster than a monkey through the canopy, learning about the environment as they do so. I've ziplined on four continents, and here's what I've come to realize:

1. Anyone can zipline.
2. Ziplining is only as good as the environment in which you do it.

NEW BRUNSWICK ↑

Usually, the environment consists of trees, which is why this neat little operation in Grand Falls zip-zags its way onto the bucket list. The town is named after the waterfalls it cradles, where the Saint John River drops 23 metres over a rock ledge, creating one of the largest Canadian falls east of Niagara. Eric Ouellette, a local civil engineer with some big industrial projects under his belt, saw the potential and opened Zip Zag for business. It took his team two years to build dual racing ziplines across the gorge, spanning 150 metres above the raging whitewater. He rightly believed that the only thing sweeter than a huge waterfall is ziplining through its spray on a bright, sunny day.

I collect my harness at the Malabeam Information Centre, where visitors learn about the area's history, the hydroelectric project, and how Eric and his team used 2,500 ice blocks to create the world's largest domed igloo, as certified by Guinness World Records. Clearly, here is an impressive man committed to random achievements. The only requirements for zip-zaggers are that they weigh between 25 and 125 kilograms and are capable of walking up stairs.

Eric's wife, Christine, slips me into a harness and gives a brief demonstration, and then we walk to the launch zipline. Ziplining is perhaps the easiest of all "adrenalin" activities, requiring hardly any physical effort and offering the security of knowing you're safely connected to a steel rope over-engineered to take the weight of an elephant. Once I kick off, it takes only seconds to get across the canyon, which is where the real fun begins: the dual lines 23 metres above the waterfalls.

Grand Falls, also known as Grand Sault, is one of only two municipalities in Canada with a bilingual name. Over 80 percent of its population are completely bilingual, including all the Zip Zag guides. This is useful for American customers (the town is right on the Maine border) and Québécois customers driving in from 80 kilometres away. Regardless of whether you whoop in French or in English, once your feet leave the wooden platform, you'll find

yourself gliding along at 30 to 40 kilometres an hour, and with an awfully big smile on your face. A sheet of fine mist gently sprays me as I make the crossing, which is over too soon, as ziplines usually are. While the overall experience might take around an hour, the actual flying time can be counted in seconds. But believe me, those seconds count infinitely more when you're flying over a raging waterfall as opposed to a jungle canopy. There's no practical reason why anyone needs to zipline in this day and age, which is exactly why it's so much fun to do so.

START HERE: canadianbucketlist.com/zipline

PAINT YOUR FACE AT TINTAMARRE

It's August 15, and the descendants of Acadia are eager to make some noise. When the church bells toll 6 p.m., tens of thousands of people erupt onto the streets of Caraquet dressed in costumes, making a right French Canadian rocket with whatever they can get their hands on: drums, bells, horns, buckets, whistles, voices. The annual tintamarre (literally, "clangour") tradition in Caraquet is remarkable for a number of reasons. First, the population of this seaside town is just over 4,000 — so where did the other 34,000 people come from? Second, the tradition of celebrating Acadian culture and history with tintamarre only dates back to 1979. By the enthusiasm on display,

one would think it was part of the 300-year-old Acadian heritage. Third, it's just about the most fun you can have in New Brunswick, with or without the face paint.

The story of Acadia, with its origins in seventeenth- and eighteenth-century French settlement in the Maritimes, is a tumultuous one. Wars, displacement, deportation, and cultural invasion — it's a wonder any culture has survived at all. In 1955, the Catholic Church organized a celebration in Moncton to commemorate the 200th anniversary of the Acadian Deportation, when conquering British armies dispersed the population. The racket that ensued left a lasting impression, although it wasn't until 1979 that tintamarre resurfaced as a massive street festival in the town of Caraquet. The town already boasts an Acadian historical village (the Village Historique Acadien) and Acadian summer festival, so it was the perfect place to celebrate the 375th anniversary of Acadia's founding. Acadia, I should point out, was a part of New France that included much of the Maritimes and parts of Maine. Acadians who resettled in Louisiana became known as Cajuns.

Back to 1979: everyone in Caraquet was invited to participate in the parade, embrace the tricolour Acadian flag, and delight in a doozy of decibels. Although it was supposed to be a one-off event, a year later, folks emerged from their houses with pots, pans, barrels, and sticks. Soon after, costumes and face paint had been added, and visitors were flocking in from all over the province. Community leaders were already talking about holding a "traditional" tintamarre, despite the fact the tradition had barely begun to exist. Today, tintamarre has evolved into a vital expression of Acadian history, culture, and pride. It has spread to other Acadian communities in New Brunswick and to parts of Quebec as a symbol of Acadian identity.

But wait a second, Robin. We're not Acadian, so why should we care?

I'll explain as I paint your face in red, white, and blue, with a golden star around your right eye.

For a start, where else can you make more noise than the kids and be admired for it? Embracing the festival's *joie de vivre* is the kind of fun few should turn down. Unlike Fat Tuesday, this carnival makes an effort to include tourists and visitors, adding everyone into the mix, inviting participation and even home invasions. Tintamarre is the climax of the two-week-long Acadian Festival, featuring hundreds of music concerts, step-dancing, art, competitions, and food. Feast on traditional Acadian fare such as *fricot à la poule*, clam pie, and pulled molasses taffy. If you're historically inclined, 80 percent of the buildings in the historical Acadian village are from the 1770s to the 1890s, relocated to the village for an authentic material reference to history.

But it's the atmosphere and the smiley side of chaos that have made tintamarre one of the biggest festivals in the Atlantic provinces. Besides the party, tintamarre is an opportunity to understand and appreciate a vital cultural element that makes Canada Canada, and not, say, Australia with snow. Make some noise, together with the descendants of the Acadians: "We're here, and we're not going anywhere!"

START HERE: canadianbucketlist.com/tintamarre

JOIN THE POLAR BEAR CLUB

Unlike polar bears and Seth Rogan, human beings do not have thick, insulating fur. However, that does little to deter us from plunging into freezing bodies of water. Polar bear dips take place across Canada, typically on New Year's Day to welcome in the year (and freeze a hangover in its tracks). There's no disputing the fact that a polar bear dip belongs on the bucket list. The question is, where? Vancouver, with thousands of dippers gathered on English Bay? Or at the annual Freezin' for a Reason in Yellowknife, which takes place after the spring thaw? Ottawa has a spring-thaw dip, too, while the Toronto Polar Bear Club raises thousands of dollars for charity with its own January dip.

Our choice combines a defibrillator plunge with one of Canada's natural wonders, and the site is just perfect. Located about a half-hour drive from Saint John, Spa Chance Harbour is a world away from glitzy resorts with panpipe music and the essence of sandalwood. Instead, a crackling fireplace heats up a modest cabin lounge with huge windows that offer a view out over a beach on the Bay of Fundy. The world's highest tides shoot water into an adjacent marsh, where

a freshwater spring flows to meet it through a series of natural cascades. Outside the cabin sits a large firepit, beach chairs, kayaks, and Hula Hoops, which stare across the inlet into a forest. One can only imagine the parties that take place on this secluded beach during the summer. But we're not here for warm-weather shenanigans. A few metres away from the lounge resides the most beautiful wood-fired sauna I've seen anywhere (and that includes Finland and Russia). Huge picture windows allow guests to sweat while gazing across the bay, occasionally spotting moose and bears in the distance. Saunas don't typically have much of a view; this one does.

After raising the body temperature, it's time to join the local Polar Bear Club. This involves a dip in the Bay of Fundy, the adjacent freshwater stream, and a bucket of ice-cold water over your head to complete the trifecta. Because of the tides, the bay doesn't freeze over, and the water sits between 4°C and 6°C throughout the year. I once swam in the ice-cold waters of Lake Baikal in Siberia, waters that are warmer than the Bay of Fundy.

Hydrotherapy uses heat and cold to cleanse your system and kick-start your blood flow. It's the same principle of the cold sauna in B.C. (page 26) — invigorating for the body and invigorating for the mind. I visited Spa Chance Harbour in mid-November, before the true onslaught of winter, but with snow already on the ground. After a meet and greet and the decision to attempt the trifecta is made, I warm myself to the core inside the wood sauna, walk barefoot to the shores of the bay, and slowly enter the Atlantic. Immediately, the cold, salty water produces a prickling sensation, like a thousand leprechauns stabbing me with tiny knitting needles. I rush back to the comfort of the sauna, heat up until I can feel my feet again, then

walk a few metres to the edge of the forest. This time I plunge into the freshwater stream, which somehow feels even *colder* than the bay. I run back and warm up once more in the sauna. Lastly, I tip a bucket of spring water over my head. Hot, cold, hot, cold, hot, cold, and with some relief, hot again in a heated outdoor whirlpool that sits alongside the gushing waters from the adjacent cascade. A new facility at the top of the hill includes massage rooms, a steam room, and a place for couples or friends to stay overnight. In winter, the spa clears a path through the snow to the bay.

Spa Chance Harbour, like New Brunswick in general, doesn't beat its chest with bold claims to be the biggest or best of anything. It doesn't have to. It's unique, unpretentious, memorable, and something everyone should do. Polar bears and Seth Rogan included.

START HERE: canadianbucketlist.com/polarbearclub

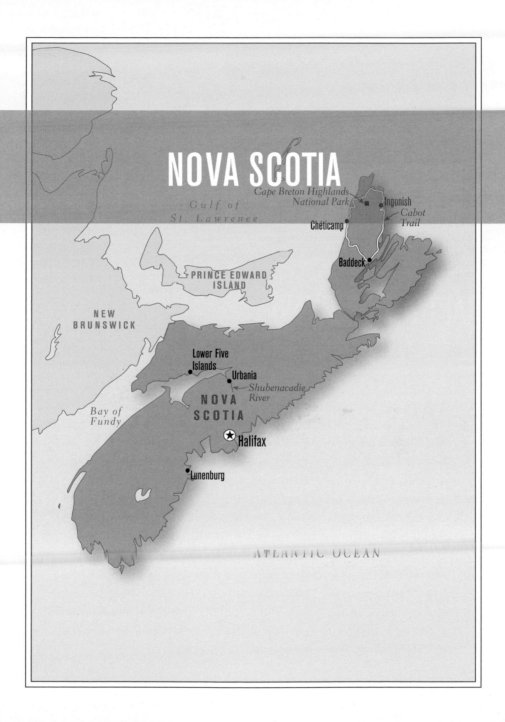

NOVA SCOTIA

Cape Breton Highlands
National Park

Ingonish

Cabot
Trail

*Gulf of
St. Lawrence*

Chéticamp

Baddeck

PRINCE EDWARD
ISLAND

NEW
BRUNSWICK

Lower Five
Islands

Urbania

*Shubenacadie
River*

NOVA
SCOTIA

*Bay of
Fundy*

Halifax

Lunenburg

ATLANTIC OCEAN

RAFT A TIDAL WAVE

When Nova Scotia's largest river, the Shubenacadie (the "Shube"), encounters the rush of tidal water flowing in from the Bay of Fundy, *bore* is not the word that comes to mind. Yet the world's largest tides, reversing into the very rivers that feed them, are called exactly that: tidal bores. It is a true tidal wave (not to be confused with a tsunami), as the leading wave swallows sandbars and marshes in a matter of minutes, leaving a turbulent trail of waves and rapids in its wake.

There are few places in the world where you can experience this phenomenon, much less hop on a high-powered Zodiac to play in it like a theme-park ride. Once a day, rafting companies along the low, shallow banks of the Shube gather clients for the incoming bore, which can bring waves as high as five metres rumbling over the muddy sandbars before harmlessly levelling out.

It's a crisp June morning when I arrive at Tidal Bore Rafting's HQ. Depending on the tide and moon cycle, the bore's size can be classified as mild, medium, or extreme. I've enjoyed the thrill of Class 5 whitewater rafting before (including the world's highest commercial vertical drop, in New Zealand), and so I look forward to today's extreme conditions. The 72-kilometre-long river is brackish and brown, a stream of chocolate milk running through minty green forests and farmland. I'm advised not to wear anything I care too deeply about, and I'm handed a rainsuit, a life jacket, and a pair of old shoes.

Surf Tidal Bores

The tidal bore on New Brunswick's Petitcodiac River has also been creating waves. Two Californian surfers set a North American record, riding a single wave for 29 kilometres. With hazardous rocks and rough conditions, only experienced lunatics need apply. ➤

Our group makes its way to the riverbank, the water running calmly about six metres below the jetty. We squish over thick mud, hop into the Zodiac, and introduce ourselves. I'm with a couple from Halifax, and we're guided by a young pilot named Gillian, who swaps out as a ski instructor in the river's off-season. She pilots the Zodiac upriver, and with the high-tide line clearly marked on the riverbank way above our heads, my imagination starts to run riot. I picture a massive tidal wave, 20 metres high, rushing down the valley and drowning everything in its path, like those water horses conjured by Arwen in *The Lord of the Rings*. Gillian is less concerned, pointing out the first of many bald eagles that have gathered along the Shube in high concentrations to feed on sea and river fish caught in the tides. It's the reason the area is home to the highest nesting concentration of bald eagles on North America's east coast.

Under their watchful eagle eyes, the Zodiac hums along with the current, passing the site of a huge mudslide that took a few trees with it. We're a little early and so we berth on a sandbar, eagerly awaiting the arrival of the bore, occupying our time by submerging our shins in sinking sand. Ten minutes later, Gillian points upriver. In the distance, a harmless white wave approaches. It seems innocent enough, not nearly as extreme as I had imagined. Gillian guns the Zodiac to meet the wave, which we ramp over and then turn back, surfing on its crest. Within minutes the wave will swallow the sandbars and begin its rise to the tide line, high on the cliffs above our heads. The Zodiac pulls out, racing farther upstream. "Are you ready, guys?" Gillian yells. What she knows, and what we don't, is that as the high tide hits sandbars and slopes, the rush of water gets churned up like a boiling soup.

After zooting up the relatively calm side of the river, Gillian makes a hard left and we drop in like unprepared potatoes. *Bang! Ow! Wow! Whee! Bang!* There's not much else we can say as the Zodiac dips and crests through the rapids, lurching our feet in the air, landing us hard with a thud. Keeping our mouths shut is actually a smart idea, as the Shube's muddy water drenches the boat, eager to spoon us with mouthfuls. The rapids are cold, invigorating, and relentless. When they peter out, Gillian repeats the process, skirting the soup close to the shore before turning in for another thrill ride.

Earlier, we had passed a rock formation known as Anthony's Point, which looked like a large boot sitting far above our heads. Now it is completely submerged. We hit the soup again, and again, a concentrated and sustained dose of rapids you just can't find on traditional whitewater adventures. My knees take a beating from the drops as we get pummelled from all sides, almost losing a shipmate at one point. However, with no rocks to worry about, should you fall overboard, it's a relatively safe affair for the boat to find you and haul you back on board. We ride the waves until the riverbanks widen and the bore wears itself out, conveniently close to the jetty we left two hours ago. I can barely recognize its wooden steps, floating above a raging river where before they sat on metres of mud.

A hot shower later, we exchange high-fives and wide smiles, proud recipients of a true Canadian adventure you just can't find anywhere else. Despite its modern usage, the word *bore* comes from Old Norse, meaning "swell" — a word that applies both literally and figuratively to this bucket list adventure.

START HERE: canadianbucketlist.com/tidalbore

STROLL AROUND LUNENBURG

A tlantic Canada's coastline is flecked with seaside fishing villages that recall another era, an age when hard tack fishermen braved rough oceans to haul in cod that would be salted and shipped to all parts of the British Empire. The exceptionally well-preserved fishing town of Lunenburg, founded in 1753, stands apart for a number of reasons. It has been designated a UNESCO World Heritage Site for being "the best surviving example of a planned British colonial settlement in North America, retaining the town's original layout and

overall appearance, based on a rectangular grid pattern drawn up in the home country." I decided to visit the town to understand what that sentence means, because, let's face it, UNESCO doesn't make it sound very exciting.

Driving in on a fine spring day, I'm reminded of an idyllic British seaside resort, complete with busloads of tourists. High season hasn't quite kicked in yet, but the town has tidied itself up after the long winter, eager to welcome new summer guests. My first stop is the excellent Fisheries Museum of the Atlantic, which does a great job breathing life into the legacy of East Coast fishing. I learn about the birth of the industry, the fisherman's lifestyle through the years, the challenges, the science, the equipment, and the rum-runners who made their fortune during Prohibition. There is also an exhibition about the Bluenose — the Lunenburg legend honoured on the back of every Canadian dime. What strikes me most are the stories of clippers lost at sea, many with all crew on board. One fierce hurricane, the August Gale of 1927, sank several ships and claimed 184 souls. A memorial lists the names of local fishermen who never

The Legend of the *Bluenose*

Built and launched in Lunenburg, the *Bluenose* captured the world's imagination as the fastest fishing boat on the seas, holding the International Fisherman's Trophy for 17 years. This hulking ship was a far cry from the sleek modern vessels that race in today's sailing events; it was primarily used for fishing in some of the world's stormiest waters. Immortalized in music and books, on stamps, on Nova Scotia licence plates, and on the Canadian dime, history finally caught up with the old boat. It was sold as a cargo ship in the Caribbean and wrecked beyond repair on a reef in Haiti. Several replicas have been built over the years for promotional and leisure purposes, with a new replica just recently completed in Lunenburg. ➤

returned to shore, from the 1800s all the way up to the present day. We've come a long way from fishermen using single lines to pull in cod, getting paid in cod tongues, and braving treacherous conditions.

Across the bay is High Liner Foods, one of North America's largest fish-processing plants. Modern fishing has made the profession safer but has also devastated fish stocks, and with them, entire communities. All this makes the museum's exhibits seem so vital to Atlantic Canada's history. From the museum, I stroll along the waterfront, admiring the colourful paint jobs on the old wharves and wooden houses.

To get behind the charming facade, I join local guide Shelah Allen for one of her historical walking tours. Storms are threatening when we meet outside the impressive Academy building, built in 1894. The weather doesn't dampen Shelah's enthusiasm one bit, as she begins to tell me stories about the houses, what era they're from, their architecture, former inhabitants, and why they're so well preserved.

"Here's my favourite house," she says, pointing to a large pink Victorian on York Street. Built in 1888, Morash House has overhanging windows, triple bell-cast roofs and a Lunenburg "bump" — large windows facing the ocean so that hopeful wives could watch for ships returning safely to port. Across the street is another old home, painted yellow. "That's actually been rebuilt pretty recently," says Shelah. The town is serious about keeping its heritage well intact. At the end of the block is the oldest Lutheran church in Canada, reflecting the

many German immigrants who made Lunenburg their home.

Each wooden home we pass has a story, until we come to the striking St. John's Anglican Church, faithfully restored after a devastating fire in 2001. An organist is playing inside, adding to the atmosphere. I learn about the many Norwegian fishermen stranded here during the Second World War and taken in by the locals, and the warm relations that still exist as a result. We wander down King Street, past the bright green and orange wooden shops that caused a little stir when the paint dried, ending up at the Knaut-Rhuland House, one of the best-preserved eighteenth-century houses in the country, and another National Historic Site.

Shelah's one-hour tour ends at the pub, because that's just how things work in Nova Scotia. She tells me that Lunenburg is growing with an influx of entrepreneurs, and that this, coupled with the town's ability to preserve and showcase its history, is making the future look pretty peachy. UNESCO's description sounds terribly square — *grid, rectangular, layout*. Rest assured, there's a warm heart waiting to greet you in Lunenburg.

START HERE: canadianbucketlist.com/Lunenburg

NOVA SCOTIA ↑

ARM A CANNON AT THE HALIFAX CITADEL

"Atten-SHUN!"

The kilted sergeant of the 78th Highlanders is doing his best to get our motley regiment into line. Granted, he's actually a paid historical re-enactor, and our regiment consists of confused tourists from Mexico, Germany, and France. Call us the rank and vile. We have signed up to be soldiers for a day at Fort George, Halifax's most iconic landmark, overlooking the city atop Citadel Hill. The year is 1869, when the red-coated and kilted Scottish Highlanders manned the fort that protected the crux of British shipping interests on the Atlantic coast. We've each been given a shilling, which crafty sergeants dropped into the pints of young men who would soon discover they'd

just signed up for a seven-year stint in Her Majesty's Army. Today we'll discover what this might have been like — from barracks to guard posts — breathing fresh life into this National Historic Site.

In the mid-1700s, the British built a fort on the highest hill overlooking Halifax Harbour. It continued to expand until the current Citadel was completed in 1856, designed to be a potent deterrent to American, French, and other aggressors who threatened lucrative British naval interests. With excellent sightlines, thick stone walls, powerful cannons, and even a land moat, the star-shaped fortress was so successful that it never did come under attack — unless you count tourists, penetrating the walls daily to explore this living museum and enjoy its views of the city.

Operated by Parks Canada, the Citadel provides a snapshot of life behind the walls in 1869. Historical re-enactors run through daily chores, inviting visitors to join them through the "Soldier for a Day" program and the Halifax Citadel Experience, which is how I came to be position number five, awaiting the order to transfer a bucket of make-believe black powder to position number three, so that position number two could pretend to stoke a very real cannon to blast non-existent enemies to smithereens. While the Citadel never came under enemy fire, it did witness the tragic Halifax Explosion. In 1917, a munitions ship exploded in the harbour, flattening nearby buildings and killing some 2,000 people.

Back to the present, where, according to the cannon master, we are the worst crew he's ever seen. At least he doesn't have to *hear* our awfulness, unlike the drum instructor, who must listen to my version of a brass shell field drum. Picture Animal, the drummer for the Muppets. *Rat-atat-a-ratatatatata* … Thank you, Robin, someone else, please. Anyone?

Next is the barracks, where we learn how up to 20 men would share these spartan quarters with their families, the kids sleeping under the creaking narrow bed. When winter came, even the hardiest of Highlanders had to wear pants, taking solace in the fact they were made of Mackenzie-clan tartan. Naturally, I ask a soldier if he's a true Scotsman.

"My boots are the only item beneath my kilt," he replies. Minutes later, a gust of wind causes an embarrassing Marilyn Monroe moment, and I can confirm kilts are not nearly as becoming as white dresses.

After visiting the huge waterless moat, designed to turn attackers into sitting ducks, we learn about weapons and watch a demonstration with a working nineteenth-century muzzle. The loud crack of black powder reminds us that these high-calibre bullets would stop an elephant, and certainly ruin the day of anyone on the receiving end. For Queen and Country, the soldiers might say, pulling the trigger, feeling the breeze on their knees. Still, for all its red-coated pomp and glory, it was no fun to be in Her Majesty's Army.

Today, the Citadel continues to guard the city of Halifax like a brawny, protective grandparent. It's well worth a visit, especially now, when even the soldiers are smiling.

START HERE: canadianbucketlist.com/citadel

Twin Tragedies in Halifax

The Citadel has borne witness to two of the early twentieth century's greatest tragedies. In 1912, Halifax was the closest port of call to the *Titanic* disaster. Plucked from the ocean, survivors were taken to New York, but the dead were routed to Halifax. The 150 victims are buried in three cemeteries across the city. Today, the Maritime Museum of the Atlantic houses an extensive collection of *Titanic* artifacts. By the way, the tombstone marked J. Dawson in the Fairview Cemetery has nothing to do with the Leonardo DiCaprio character in the movie (but that doesn't stop flowers appearing around it anyway).

Five years later, an accident in the harbour resulted in the largest human-made explosion prior to the invention of the nuclear bomb. Like many disasters, the Halifax Explosion resulted from a series of unfortunate events. A Norwegian vessel collided with a French ammunition ship in the harbour's narrow strait. A fire attracted thousands of locals to the shore, and 20 minutes later, when it ignited the ammunition, the ship was blasted nearly 300 metres into the air. More than 1,600 people were essentially vapourized, along with every building within a 2.6-kilometre radius. Nine thousand people were injured, and the final death toll topped 2,000. Factor in an 18-metre-high tsunami and raging fires, and you can understand why the Halifax Explosion is still regarded as one of history's greatest disasters. ➤

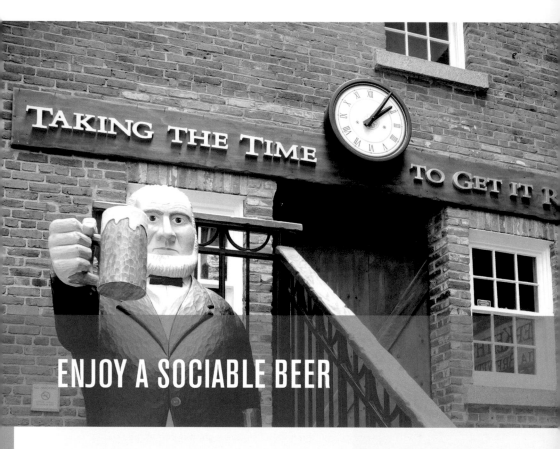

ENJOY A SOCIABLE BEER

It is my custom, on the road, always to order the local beer. The thought of ordering Heineken in Hungary, Miller in Mexico, or Corona in China may be a boon for major beer monopolies, but not for the authentic traveller. Beers taste better in the land of their brewing — except for Budweiser in the United States and Chang in Thailand, which are best enjoyed nowhere. Canada's beer, it must be said, is vastly underrated in terms of its quality. Visit Australia and you'll see how even a committed beer-drinking nation is forced to consume weak, industrial beverages such as VB, XXXX, and Tooheys. Phooey!

Great Canadian Beers

Coast to coast to coast, Canada is blazing a craft beer revolution. I asked expert Joe Wiebe, a.k.a The Thirsty Writer and author of *Craft Beer Revolution: The Insider's Guide to B.C. Breweries*, for his bucket list of beers:

Driftwood Brewery, Fat Tug IPA (Victoria, B.C.). This juicy hop bomb became the flagship beer of the B.C. craft-brewing scene after winning Canadian Beer of the Year in 2011.

Half Pints Brewing, Old Red Barn (Winnipeg, Manitoba). This Flanders Red Ale is barrel-aged for two years!

9 Mile Legacy Brewing, Gose (Saskatoon, Saskatchewan). A delicious, refreshing beer at the most interesting brewery I've visited on the Prairies.

Brasserie Dunham, Saison Cassis (Dunham, Quebec). An unexpected favourite at the Great Canadian Beer Festival.

PEI Brewing, Beach Chair Lager (Charlottetown, P.E.I.). A perfect summer sipper.

Spinnakers Gastro Brewpub, Northwest Dark Sour Saison (Victoria, B.C.). Sample this barrel-aged sour to see why Canada's first brewpub is still a leader of the craft beer revolution.

North Brewing/Stillwell Bar x 2 (Halifax, Nova Scotia). This gorgeous Brett Saison blew my socks off at the Canadian Brewing Awards.

Niagara Oast House Brewers, Barn Raiser Country Ale (Niagara-on-the-Lake, Ontario). A delicious, hoppy pale ale brewed in the midst of wine country.

Dieu du Ciel, Péché Mortel (Montreal, Quebec). This imperial coffee infused stout is widely considered one of the best beers brewed in Canada, if not the best.

Alley Kat Brewing, Olde Deuteronomy (Edmonton, Alberta). A massive barley wine that's great fresh and even better after some time in the cellar.

Four Winds Brewing, Nectarous (Delta, B.C.). Can't get enough of this gorgeous kettle sour from this highly acclaimed brewery.

Left Field Brewery, Cannonball (Toronto, Ontario). Take me out to the ballgame with this Munich Helles–style lager.

While microbreweries have made great-tasting inroads in North America, when I'm Down Under and beyond, I'll take the mass-market Kokanee, Rickard's, Sleeman, Big Rock, and Moosehead over bestselling local brands any day. And then there is Alexander Keith's, purveyors of fine Nova Scotian beer since 1820. Although it's now owned by Labatt (in turn owned by Anheuser-Busch InBev, which owns just about everything else), Keith's holds a special place in the hearts of Nova Scotians. I'm told it is the most widely distributed non-specialty beer in the country, and while I'm not exactly sure what that means, it sounds as if it holds a special place in the hearts of many Canadians, too.

This explains why the Brewery Tour, held in the same brick building on Lower Water Street in which Alexander Keith created his famous Indian Pale Ale, is a popular attraction in Halifax. Historical re-enactors walk you through the history of the man, the beer, and the city before depositing you one hour later in an old-fashioned tavern where you can enjoy the fruits of your labours.

It's a little hokey, and I'm hesitant to say you must take this tour before you die, because, quite frankly, you might have more fun with your mates at the adjacent pub, the Stag's Head. Whatever pub you end up in while in Nova Scotia, ordering a pint of Keith's will endear you to the locals, lubricate new friendships, and possibly turn out to be more fun than any item on this bucket list. Or maybe not, but what is a beer if not its potential to lead to something more, even if it is the gutter? So raise a glass to all of Canada's beautiful beers, and say, like a true Nova Scotian, "Sociable!"

START HERE: canadianbucketlist.com/beer

RUN A RACE OF BIBLICAL PROPORTIONS

We all know the Bible story: Moses leads the Israelites out of slavery in Egypt, chased by the resentful pharaoh's army, to the shores of the Red Sea. Here, Moses raises his staff and one of the great biblical miracles occurs: the sea divides, allowing the Israelites to pass safely across the ocean floor. The pursuing army is swallowed by the sea, and lo, the Israelites are free ... to wander the desert for 10 years.

But that's another story. Now let's replace the Red Sea with the Bay of Fundy, which we already know has the world's highest tides. Instead of the Israelites racing for freedom, picture joggers covered up to their ankles in red mud. For the pursuing soldiers, we'll use time itself, which relentlessly ticks forward until the bay begins to fill, drowning rocks and mud up to 15 metres underwater. Not since

Moses has there been a race against such a powerful foe, hence the name of this quirky and extreme 10-kilometre annual run along Five Islands, Nova Scotia, which is called ... Not Since Moses!

Over 1,000 competitors must race along the ocean floor — over mud, seaweed, rocks, muck, and slime — to reach the finish line before high tide. These conditions make it particularly treacherous, but the well-organized event takes great pride in ensuring that no one is forced to swim to safety. Participants in the 10-kilometre run, or the less frenetic five-kilometre walk, follow a path among five islands that sit off the coast: Moose, Diamond, Egg, Pinnacle, and Long. If you stop long enough to admire your surroundings (and don't slip on seaweed), you'll see eroded muddy cliffs, sandbars, and distinct islands of rock — and probably a jogger knee-deep in sludge, his or her shoes lodged firmly in the mud.

The volunteer-driven event is a festive affair, culminating in live music, hot food, a poetry reading, and a popular children's event. Run times typically fall between 60 and 90 minutes, with the winner clocking in at around 45 minutes and the last runner at around two hours, by which stage the kids are already enjoying a burger, having completed their own Basket Run. Conditions can vary from year to year — strong winds once had competitors wading through a waist-high tidal river — and volunteer stations along the route are known to turn back slow runners. Fortunately, boats are on hand for rescues, since this is not a triathlon — yet. How great would it be to see a race on the ocean floor that starts on foot and finishes with a swim?

Not Since Moses benefits local schools, draws athletes from around the world, and relies on the uncanny ability of Nova Scotians to, well, run with it. Besides the sticky terrain, runners are cautioned to expect strong winds and bring their own water (or alcohol, if that's the fuel you need). It may not be a biblical miracle, but Not Since Moses still crosses the mud-splattered line to finish on the Great Canadian Bucket List.

START HERE: canadianbucketlist.com/moses

A Foodie Escape

Located alongside the Bay of Fundy, the Annapolis Valley is the third most important fruit-growing region in the country, blessed with some of the best weather in Atlantic Canada. Besides the inviting towns and seafront views, foodies will love the culinary choices on offer, particularly fine dining at boutique wineries.

Wine Access magazine named Le Caveau Restaurant, located at the Domaine de Grand Pre winery, as one of the world's 20 best vineyard restaurants. Not far away is the Fox Hill Cheese House, which produces 20 types of specialty cheese, along with yogourt and gelato. Foodies will also enjoy the Wolfville Farmers' Market, which takes place Wednesday evenings and Saturdays during the summer. The farmers' market also presents "Tastes of the Valley," a celebration of local food that has the region's best chefs creating locally sourced dishes. ➤

EXPLORE CAPE BRETON

"I have travelled around the globe. I have seen the Canadian and American Rockies, the Andes, the Alps, and the Highlands of Scotland, but for simple beauty, Cape Breton out-rivals them all."

Thus spoke Alexander Graham Bell, the distinguished gentleman who invented the telephone, the metal detector, and the hydrofoil. This explains why his former Canadian residence is a National Historic Site, and why it is located in Baddeck, Cape Breton. The question is: Why did Cape Breton beat out the Rockies, Andes, Highlands, and Alps? Why do international travel magazines bestow titles on Cape Breton such as "The Most Scenic Island in the World" (*Condé Nast*), "The Number One Island to Visit in Continental North America" (*Travel+Leisure*), and "One of the World's Greatest Destinations" (*National Geographic*)? If Cape Breton casts a spell on its visitors, what lies behind its McAbracadabra?

Aye, the Scottish influence is unmistakable. Upwards of 50,000 Highlanders found their way to Cape Breton in the early nineteenth century, bringing their Gaelic language and culture with them. Centuries later, discovering Scotland in Canada charms the kilt off most visitors, unaccustomed to the distinct Cape Breton accent they encounter in small communities dotting the island. You will also discover some wonderfully preserved Acadian communities — Belle Côte, Terre Noire, Cap Le Moine, Grand Étang, Chéticamp — benefitting from their isolation, adapted to the distinct environmental culture of the Maritimes.

I crossed the island's causeway on the very day a Cape Breton musical legend Buddy MacMaster passed away. Fiddlers would be gathering from around the world, and it is fiddle music I heard just about everywhere, starting at the Celtic Music Interpretive Centre in Judique. Here I would also experience my first *ceilidh* (pronounced kay-lee), a traditional gathering of song and dance. My own fiddle efforts in the museum sounded not unlike a cat sliding down a three-storey chalkboard, claws extended. And let's not get into my Highland dancing efforts.

Cape Breton Island has several immaculate driving routes. Motorbikes, cars, bicycles, and RVs descend in the thousands each

summer to explore the meandering, hilly coastal roads, the cyclists receiving a certain amount of pity and respect when you pass them. There are world-renowned golf resorts, sailing opportunities on the sparkling inland sea of Bras d'Or, and worthy attractions like the Alexander Graham Bell Museum, Glace Bay's Coal Miner Museum, and the Fortress of Louisbourg (see page 356). Kayaking up the North River on a sunny day was entirely memorable, complete with a shower in a local waterfall and a blues jam session with owner/musician Antonio Spinazzola. Islanders have fantastic stories to tell, and even better musical skills for the soundtrack.

The Cabot Trail is an approximately 300-kilometre loop at the northern tip of Cape Breton, running through eight communities (Scottish, Irish, and Acadian), across the Margaree River, and the island's crown jewel, the 948-square-kilometre Cape Breton Highlands National Park. Open year-round, the Cabot Trail could put together its own Top 10 list of how many Top 10 lists it has been placed on. It is a destination worthy of the acclaim. Summers are gorgeous, while foliage explodes each fall for the Celtic Colours International Festival. Shaped by the Gulf of St. Lawrence on the west and the Atlantic on the east, the national park consists of temperate and boreal forests containing bird species you won't find anywhere else in the country.

The Acadian fishing village of Chéticamp welcomes tourists with fiddle music and traditional hooked rugs, while Ingonish, at the east entrance to the national park, touts one of Canada's most highly rated golf courses, the Stanley Thompson–designed 18-hole Highlands Links Golf Course.

But it's the mountains on the elevated plateau that left the biggest impression, rolling into the sea, a million-dollar view waiting around every corner. Some of the park's two-dozen hikes, the most popular being the Panorama, take you right to the cliff edge of the headlands. In Pleasant Bay, I hopped on board Captain Mark's Whale Cruise, and even if 40 pilot whales hadn't surrounded our boat and sung their riddles for our underwater cameras, the views of the highlands rolling into the Atlantic would have been worth it.

Throughout the island, keep your eyes peeled for all-age community *ceilidhs*, delicious lobster suppers, and flowing pints of the local craft ale, Big Spruce. You'll quickly notice this is a place where locals smile with their mouths, eyes, and hearts.

Yes, one can spend a week or a lifetime enjoying Cape Breton, taking in its sights, meeting its people, and experiencing its history. A week or a lifetime to agree with the opinions of nineteenth-century inventors, round-ups in twenty-first century travel magazines, and writers of national bucket lists.

START HERE: canadianbucketlist.com/capebreton

Dram Good Whisky

With Cape Breton's rich Scottish heritage, consider popping into North America's first single malt whisky distillery, Glenora, located on Highway 19. Take a distillery tour before tasting the impact of Cape Breton ambiance on aging oak casks. There's a wonderful inn and restaurant on-site, too. ➤

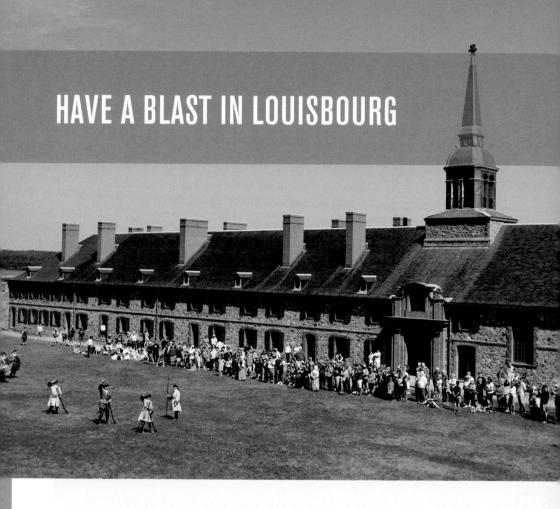

HAVE A BLAST IN LOUISBOURG

You won't understand just how big and ambitious Parks Canada's Fortress of Louisbourg is until you see it. You'll quickly realize why this National Historic Site is the largest historical reconstruction project in North America. Completely rebuilt based on meticulous records kept by the French government, the fortress takes you back to the year 1744, when French soldiers protected a lucrative cod outpost.

Levelled by the British during the Seven Years' War, Louisbourg rotted on the coast for 200 years until the federal government saw it as an

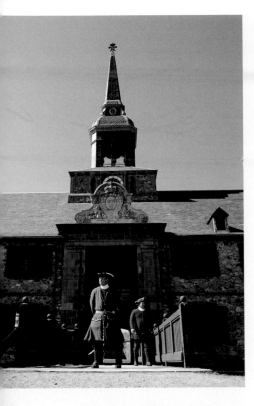

opportunity for unemployed coal miners in the 1960s — and, of course, to reclaim an important part of Canadian history.

Much like the Halifax Citadel, re-enactors add colour to this living museum, helping visitors make traditional cookies on the fire, tend the flock, or light the two twelve o'clock cannons. It's worth paying a little extra for the half-hour Cannoneer in Training program, complete with formal eighteenth-century French army uniforms. Space is limited, so call to book ahead. Regardless of your level of affection for French colonial artillery science, our bucket list has plenty of room for the Louisbourg boom.

START HERE: canadianbucketlist.com/louisbourg

PRINCE EDWARD ISLAND

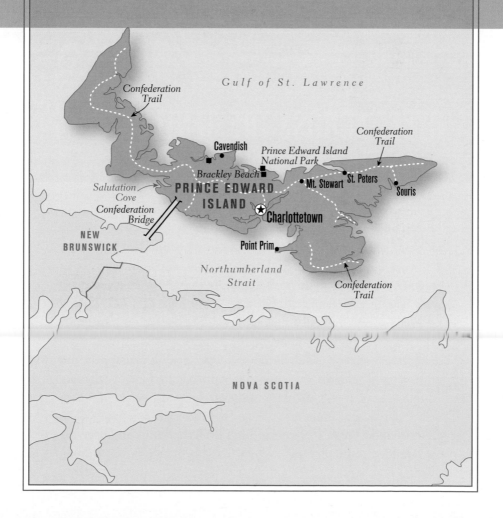

CYCLE ACROSS THE GENTLE ISLE

There's a lot to be said for multi-day cycling trips. Awakening our five senses, we can smell our surroundings, taste the wind, see the trails cut across rolling hills, listen to birdsong, and feel wonderful that we're burning calories in the process. Yet, since I'm nowhere in the kind of shape I should be, the thought of a long bike trip is physically daunting. How many times have I driven past a cyclist huffing up a big hill and thought: "I wouldn't want to be that poor bastard!" I do enjoy cycling, downhill usually, joyrides mostly. A week on a saddle seems like a callused and sore arse waiting to happen, but undeniably it remains an experience worth doing before pedalling off into the sky. If only there was somewhere mostly flat, somewhere with scenic beauty, friendly locals, and delicious cuisine. Somewhere that will allow me to stay in charming B&Bs and inns and have my bags shuttled ahead for me … Somewhere like Prince Edward Island.

Canada's smallest province appears to have been designed for amateur cyclists like me (and for you hard-core folks, as well). Besides its abundant bike lanes, P.E.I. is blessed with a mostly flat trail that snakes from the west coast to the east, a 470-kilometre tip-to-tip marvel known as the Confederation Trail. Arteries branch to coastal communities, linking to paved bike lanes that

skirt some of the most magnificent scenery in the country. Some of you might prefer to plan every step of the way yourself. I contacted outdoor specialists Great Canadian Trails, who make it as easy as coasting down a hill. Together with a highly knowledgeable and immensely likeable islander named George Larter, they offer the ultimate P.E.I. cycling trip. All we have to do is show up. George picks us up from the airport, shuttling us over to the Outer Limit Bike Shop to pick up our rental bikes. If, like me, you have no idea what a pannier is, don't fret. These bike bags are straddled onto comfortable upright hybrid bikes, which in turn are strapped onto George's van to take us to our first stop. Now all we have to do is pedal. George will ensure our luggage is waiting at our next inn, always close to a cold Gahan wheat ale and that famous P.E.I. seafood. Really, it's as simple as riding a bike.

We start in the town of Borden-Carleton, in sight of the Confederation Bridge (see page 381). Replacing a dug-up rail track, the well-maintained Confederation Trail is a car-width wide gravel strip cutting through dense forests, rural villages, and fertile farmland. It's a hot summer day, and our handy itinerary is blessedly

flexible. Since this is only Day One, we let enthusiasts tackle the extra 24 kilometres to Kensington, and instead leave the trail after 18 kilometres for the lightly trafficked shouldered highway that leads to Stanley Bridge. Bright sunshine reflects the countryside off our sunglasses. We see manicured lawns bigger than football fields, sprawling fields of potatoes, lush meadows, and purple lupines cradling immaculate wooden houses. All the peacefulness and beauty of the gentle island floods our five senses. Arriving at the Stanley Bridge Resort, bags waiting for us in large air-conditioned rooms, we're physically knackered, but not enough to deny ourselves the reward of a dozen fresh oysters at the adjacent Carr's Oyster Bar. Day One may have been physical, but it was also a slow seduction into the island's pace. Day Two will clobber us over the head, grab us by the hair, and carry us back to the cave.

It's called the Gulf Shore Parkway, and it is, without doubt, one of the world's most beautiful bike rides. From Cavendish (see page 384), we follow a paved bike path onto the beach, and ride east into Prince Edward Island National Park. Tracing the shoreline, the 50-kilometre parkway takes us to tall sand dunes, windswept beaches, viewing decks, and P.E.I.'s striking red coastline. With postcard-worthy views around every bend, and having had more than enough time to explore them, we arrive in North Rustico elated. That parkway is truly something special. Waiting for us at Fisherman's Wharf is a lobster supper, a wooden boardwalk to bike

off the all-you-can-eat dessert tray, and a smiling George, ready to shuttle us along to Brackley Bay. We could ride there ourselves, but there's no shoulder on the highway and too many hills. Let's save our time and energy for the good stuff!

After a relaxing overnight cabin stay at Shaw's (the oldest business on the island), we continue the following morning on the paved parkway, hop onto some quiet local roads, and re-join the Confederation Trail en route to Mount Stewart. Awaiting us is offbeat accommodation above the homely, rustic Trailside Café. Each room here has a vintage record player and a selection of vinyl chosen by owners Pat and Meghann Deighan, who also happen to own Charlottetown's hippest record store.

"Everyone in P.E.I. tells a good story and plays an instrument," a friend once told me. We hear great stories and incredible music at the café downstairs, which features local and touring musicians each summer weekend. The place is jammed and the staff as welcoming as good friends — which by the end of the night, they are.

Just steps from our antique bed frame, the bike path continues east to St. Peters, crossing pink-painted wooden bridges, peat bogs, bubbling streams, and hardwood forests. The 13 kilometres from Morrell to St. Peters is considered among the most scenic sections of the entire Confederation Trail. Oyster and mussel beds line the inlets. With our legs getting stronger, the kilometres disappear behind us with increasing quickness. That night, we will toast the moon as it lights the gazebo beneath the Inn at St. Peters. Wine will flow. All of us "from-aways" — whether we're travelling by car, motorbike, or bicycle — recognize that a golden P.E.I. summer is worthy of celebration.

The next day it's all trail from St. Peters to the coastal town of Souris: our final stop. A week ago, I'd never have imagined myself biking 40 kilometres in a single morning, much less that I'd have the legs to continue if I wanted (the itinerary includes an optional 47-kilometre circle route to Basin Head Provincial Park).

Adjacent to the historic McLean House Inn in Souris is a local eatery called the Bluefin. We reward ourselves with their surf and turf — an eight-ounce rib-eye steak and a pound and a half of lobster — all for less than 30 dollars.

It has been an unforgettable week relishing the beauty of Prince Edward Island — keeping healthy, making friends, and eating "like a king in France," as the Germans would say. Listening to the wind blowing in from the Gulf of St Lawrence, how could we not fall asleep with a smile on our faces? This is a one-of-a-kind trip for experienced cyclists — and for the rest of us, too.

START HERE: canadianbucketlist.com/bikepei

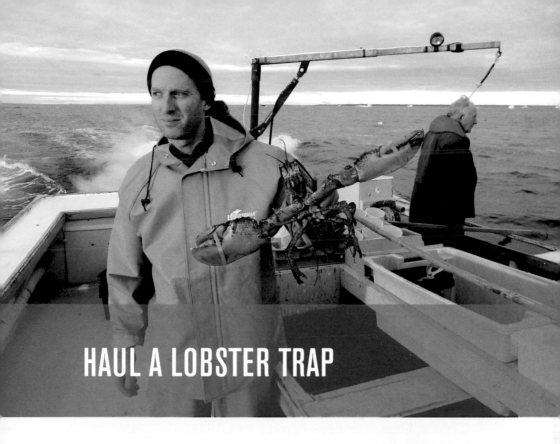

HAUL A LOBSTER TRAP

Lobsters intimidate me. For starters, they look like spider-dragon aliens, capable of slicing your neck off with one swipe of their giant claw, or latching onto your face to impregnate you with acid-dripping offspring. Just look at their undersides: surely that was the inspiration for the *Alien* movies. Spiky legs, sharp edges, and two beady eyes thinking, "If I were your size and you were mine …"

Growing up inland, I never had lobster on the menu, and while I appreciate it is a delicacy for many, so are crickets in Thailand, worms in Venezuela, and deep-fried guinea pig in Ecuador. Also worth noting: for all its status as a high-brow delicacy in higher-end restaurants, lobster was once so plentiful on the East Coast it was considered food for the poor. Farmers would spread lobster meat on their fields as fertilizer. Beef and chicken: now that was the good stuff!

Times change and so do tastes. No self-respecting Canadian bucket list can avoid a culinary-inspired crustacean date with destiny. After all, Prince Edward Island (along with New Brunswick and Nova Scotia) produces the finest lobster in the world.

It's particularly easy to tick this one off the list. Simply walk into one of the island's fine lobster establishments — consider the Water-Prince Corner Shop and Lobster Pound in Charlottetown, Fisherman's Wharf in North Rustico, or the Lobster Shack in Souris — order your lobster dinner, and get cracking. Just about every restaurant is sympathetic to first-timers, with printed placemats or cheery staff providing a helpful plan of attack:

- Remove the claws by twisting them with one hand, holding the body still with the other hand.
- Remove the much-prized tail by pulling it apart from the body.
- Pull the legs apart, sucking the juices …

I'll stop there for the benefit of vegetarians. Plastic bibs are provided because things will get messy, and let's face it, that's part of the fun. Alternatively, order a lobster roll, the quality of which you'll soon discover is a topic of fierce island-wide debate. Too much lemon juice? Too much mayo? Too much roll? As for the hype about tail meat, I find the claw to be firmer and tastier, plus, removing the meat cleanly from a claw without breaking it is especially joyous. Also, while some diners prefer hot butter, I quickly grew fond of a vinegar dip. To each their own, which is why lobster makes such a poor choice for tapas.

To further appreciate your lobster dinner, I strongly suggest sailing with Captain Mark Jenkins of Top Notch Lobster Tours. Lobster has long been in the Jenkinses' blood. A fourth-generation fisherman, Mark and his brother Cody supplement the short fishing season with outstanding tours to introduce us CFAs (Come from Aways) to the lobster fishing industry. A dozen tourists board their boat, which operates throughout the summer, in Charlottetown to head into the calm, cold waters of the Northumberland Strait. Wooden traps with nets, called *kitchens,* are baited with mackerel or other fish. Several lobsters might enter one kitchen, with each trap connected to a buoy and pinned with GPS coordinates. This helps with finding and track-ing traps, and also ensures we're not raiding somebody else's kitchen, so to speak. Mark locates several demonstration traps and invites guests to use a long pole to hook the buoy, which is then attached to a mechanical crane to haul the kitchen out of the water and onto the boat. At first I'm hesitant to stick my hand in a trap. Those claws look sharp and the lobsters are understandably disagreeable. Eventually, intimidation will always give way to familiarity.

Fishermen will work for eight solid hours hauling in more than 300 traps, and at the start of each season, a typical day might net up to 550 kilograms of lobster. Crabs also find their way to the kitchen, but only the largest are collected to be weighed and sold; the rest find themselves sinking back to the bottom of the Atlantic Ocean.

Lobsters with black eggs are immediately tossed back into the sea to produce new yields. The rest are put in a sorting bin to measure their size and determine whether they are classed as premium market or standard "canned." Smaller lobsters are returned to the sea. The aim is to catch old, huge, and heavy lobsters with large claws, the so-called "bone crushers." Market lobsters have their claws banded with small blue elastics to prevent them from damaging one another. New bait is set by placing chunks of mackerel on a spike inside each trap, and it's onto the next trap.

A vital industry for Canada's smallest province, lobster fishing is heavily regulated to ensure there's no overfishing. Cold water and a carefully managed industry ensure a staggering bounty. According to federal figures, Canada exports more than 82 tons of lobster each year, generating over $2 billion in revenue. This is why licences cost well into the six figures, and why fishermen will work six days a week during the season, with high overheads. One boat might spend up to $1,200 a week just for bait. The two seasons (May to end of June and August to October) are short. Catches will be hauled to distribution centres, where they will be promptly flown or shipped off to Europe, Asia, or the United States. Boats will sell their lobsters for anywhere from three to eight dollars per pound, depending on the demand. Consider that the next time you order a $50 one-pound lobster at a restaurant.

As for the island itself, visitors can rest assured that lobster is on the menu year round, and at a reasonable price, too. Of course, it doesn't come any fresher than aboard the *Top Notch* itself, with a traditional lobster meal included in the two-and-a-half-hour afternoon or evening sail. Grab your seafood crackers, hold on tight, and dig deep with those picks. What good is a bucket list if you can't suck the tomalley out of life?

START HERE: canadianbucketlist.com/lobster

SUCK BACK AN OYSTER

P.E.I.'s oysters have a reputation that precedes them. Case in point: without having set foot in Atlantic Canada, some of you might be familiar with Malpeque, Raspberry Point, Summerside, and Colville Bay. Oysters — that delectable bivalve long associated with decadent pleasure — are named after the body of water in which they grow, and P.E.I.'s oysters are prized items on menus across the continent.

Admittedly, some might argue there's nothing delicious about consuming a live, raw animal with the texture of a nasal infection. Once you understand how oysters are farmed, harvested, and best enjoyed on Prince Edward Island, I expect that will change.

I hopped into the boat of local fisherman Erskine Lewis of Rocky Bay Oysters, who took me out into the shallow waters of Salutation

Cove. Oysters here grow in prized abundance. After demonstrating the art of tonging oysters from the sandy depths, Erskine hands me the wooden rake–like tool with stainless steel teeth. I carefully scrape the bottom, jostling the tong to loosen up oysters and hopefully bring in a decent haul. We measure the size of each oyster against a simple measuring unit, returning the ones that don't make the cut. Erskine explains that the difference between choice, restaurant-grade oysters and standard, industrial oysters is simply the shape of the shell. The more round, the more sought-after, and often the less actual oyster to slurp back. Erskine rummages through my haul, selects a choice shell, shucks it right there, and hands it to me. No lemon juice, no Tabasco. P.E.I. oysters are best enjoyed raw, fresh, and on their own. For this is no ordinary oyster: this is the very taste of Salutation Cove, nature condensed into a food group. In just a couple of hours, I develop a deep respect for oysters and the amount of work it takes to harvest them. The typical price of an oyster in a P.E.I. restaurant: $2.50. Being able to appreciate them: priceless.

Visitors to the island needn't get all muddied up among the seaweed, either. Oyster Lovers is a two-hour experience offered by John and Jackie Gillis in lovely South Pinette, about half an hour east of Charlottetown. They harvest wild oysters right in front of their home,

How to Shuck an Oyster

1. Rinse the oyster with fresh water, clearing away muck and mud with a steel brush. Refrigerate until ready to serve, covered with a damp towel.

2. Use a dishtowel or glove to protect yourself as you hold the oyster down on a flat surface, the pointed hinge facing you. Insert the oyster knife into the hinge, pushing it toward the bottom of the cup and giving it a slight wiggle. Twist the knife to pop the hinge.

3. To cut the muscles holding the shell together, slide the knife across the top of the shell. Separate the shell, clear away any mess, and slide the knife under the oyster flesh to detach it from the bottom shell. ➤

giving guests the opportunity to tong and shuck, and finish it off with a helping of Jackie's grilled quahogs and, of course, as many fresh oysters as your libido can handle.

Continuing my quest to appreciate the pearl of P.E.I. seafood, I enlisted the help of a true oyster aficionado. John Bil is a three-time Canadian Oyster Shucking Champion and "one of the greatest oystermen on the continent" (according to the *Globe and Mail*). I caught him on the island before he moved back to Toronto to open his latest restaurant, Honest Weight.

Bil is a chef who believes that the ocean does all the work, while chefs just add the heat. After teaching me how to shuck an oyster and demonstrating his own renowned skill (including shucking blindfolded, behind his back), John educates me on the subtleties of oyster appreciation. Salty, lemony, crunchy, creamy, strong — I begin to taste the coves of each individual oyster, feeling the waves in my mouth.

John Bil started his career shucking oysters at Carr's Oyster Bar, an island institution located in scenic Stanley Bridge. I order a dozen world-renowned Malpeque oysters — tonged fresh from the nearby beds. Each bivalve seems to tell a story of the waters, land, and people of the island. By now I've learned to forego the Tabasco and lemon, to truly taste a delicacy humanity has enjoyed for eons. Or maybe I was drunk on the wheat-honey ale. Either way, these oysters represent bivalves at their finest, and in a fine environment, too. Oyster connoisseurs chasing a more upscale experience must visit local rock-star chef Michael Smith's flame-inspired restaurant, FireWorks, located inside The Inn at Bay Fortune. A pre-dinner oyster hour takes place nightly at 6 p.m., followed by island dishes cooked over an open hearth, on the grill, or in the smokehouse. Gobble your way through world-famous Colville Bay and Fortune Bay oysters.

So why are P.E.I. oysters so revered? "Oysters are like grapes. A Sauvignon Blanc from Ontario is simply not the same as a Sauvignon Blanc from California," explains John Bil. From which I conclude that an oyster tonged and shucked from P.E.I.'s delightful bays is just about as good as the oyster going gets. Shuck up and let's slurp this one down the bucket list.

START HERE: canadianbucketlist.com/oysters

PLAY A ROUND OF GOLF

There are several things I look forward to doing in the autumn years of my life. I look forward to watching all these TV shows people keep talking about, so I can finally visit Westeros and understand why the phrase "winter is coming" is significant. I look forward to a long career in skydiving, weeks spent playing video games, hip replacements, and, most of all, golf. Not all at the same time, mind you, although that would be interesting.

You see, golf demands the supreme patience, time, skill, and budget reserves I don't yet possess. For those who argue the folly of whacking a little ball a long way to get it into a little cup, I say, "Four!" Yes, I spelled that correctly.

PRINCE EDWARD ISLAND ↑

One: Golf gets you outside, in the fresh air, usually in beautiful surroundings.

Two: Golf gets you socially active, because really, it's not all that important whether you score a birdie or an eagle or any other form of bird life.

Three: Golf is a personal challenge, a combination of mental and physical skill that is easy to learn and impossible to master. Just ask Tiger Woods's ex-wife.

Four: Golf is punctuated by ice-cold beverages and ends in a clubhouse with more libations, nachos, and chicken wings.

Prince Edward Island may be Canada's smallest, least-populated province, but the facts speak for themselves: at the time of writing, it claims 10 out of the Top 100 Golf Courses as rated by *Globe and Mail* readers and 5 percent of the Top 350 Courses in North America. The island is branded as Canada's Number-One Golf Destination, and received an award from the International Association of Golf Travel

Canada Best 18 Holes

John Gordon, a member of the Ontario Golf Hall of Fame, has covered golf in Canada for 30 years and is the author of four volumes of *The Great Golf Courses of Canada*. With more than 2,300 courses in the vast country (more than 90 percent of which are open to the public), it is tough to choose a handful for your bucket list. Here are just 10 of Gordon's favourites.

1. **Cabot Links/Cabot Cliffs, Inverness, Nova Scotia**
2. **Highlands Links, Ingonish, Nova Scotia**
3. **Club de golf Le Maitre, Mont-Tremblant, Quebec**
4. **The National Golf Club of Canada, Woodbridge, Ontario**
5. **Devil's Pulpit/Devil's Paintbrush, Caledon, Ontario**
6. **Muskoka Bay, Gravenhurst, Ontario**
7. **Rocky Crest Golf Club, MacTier, Ontario**
8. **Blackhawk Golf Club, Spruce Grove, Alberta**
9. **Jasper Park Lodge Golf Course, Jasper, Alberta**
10. **Bear Mountain, Victoria, British Columbia** ➤

Operators as the Undiscovered Golf Destination of the Year. The island's 33 courses are renowned for their natural beauty, variety, design, and the fact that they're mostly a half-hour drive from Charlottetown.

Take the Brudenell River Golf Club, one of the island's most popular courses, dotted with lakes, ponds, and gardens. Here I have the opportunity to learn a few tricks from LPGA pro and resident island golf expert Anne Chouinard. Considering my experience is mostly limited to hacking the carpet off minigolf courses, Anne is impressed by my enthusiasm. She moved here from Quebec for the fantastic island lifestyle along with the world-class courses, and she recommends anyone with a love of the game do so as well.

We proceed to play a round, the course buttressed against a gorgeous coastline and surrounded by the tranquility of Brudenell Provincial Park. At par-three, I somehow manage to skip my golf ball twice over a water hazard and into the rough. Anne tells me Phil Mickelson did that once on purpose, which I take as a compliment.

PRINCE EDWARD ISLAND

On the sixth hole, I'm pretty sure I scored a puffin, penguin, and pigeon, which is definitely quite the feat. This demands further celebration back at the clubhouse, with nachos and cold beer. Despite Anne's best efforts, I have a lot to learn if I want to master this game. Before I die, there's no place I'd rather master it than on Prince Edward Island.

START HERE: canadianbucketlist.com/golf

RAKE FOR A CLAMBAKE

Between the lobster and oyster, our bucket list in Prince Edward Island is beginning to resemble a seafood buffet. But it would be a travesty to forget the mighty clam, which just happens to be bundled with an experience many visitors have called the highlight of the island. *Oh clam! Pac-Man of the molluscs, chow in the chowder, your two sheepish shells burrowed in the sand to protect your delicious morsel within. Open your secrets for us bucket listers, because believe me when I say, we will dig it!*

"What we do is real, not plastic or mocked up. Even if guests only experience it for a few hours, they will get a glimpse into the life of a real islander," explains Perry Gotell. He showed me exactly what he meant on his lobster boat several years ago, and continues to show others from around the world with his Giant Bar Clam Dig excursion. Perry's

Hail Caesar!

How did a mollusk become the key ingredient in Canada's national drink? It's 1969, and the Calgary Inn is opening a new restaurant called Marco's Italian. Bartender Walter Chell is tasked with concocting a cocktail to presumably bring in the masses, because it's the 1960s, and cocktails still have that sort of power. Inspired by spaghetti vongole, his favourite Italian dish, Chell begins to mix booze with tomato and clams. Three months of experimenting later, he nails the combination that would change Canada Day (and many a hangover morning) forever:

clam-infused tomato juice
1.5 oz. of vodka
2 dashes of Tabasco sauce
2 dashes of Worcestershire sauce
a stalk of celery
a wedge of lime
a celery-salt-rimmed glass

While similar recipes were known to be floating about, it was Chell's "Bloody Caesar" that grabbed the attention of Calgary, western Canada, and eventually, the nation. This boosted the sales of Mott's Clamato (a languishing mix of tomato and clam juice), and today Mott's estimates some 350 million Caesars are consumed each year. Nevertheless, it remains a distinctly Canadian drink, as the mouth-watering Caesar is largely unknown south of the border. Chell did not receive any royalties, and the mixology legend died in 1997. *The Canadian Bucket List* toasts him with a tangy, clammy Caesar in Prince Edward Island. ➤

Tranquility Cove Adventures has been so successful that he's given up lobster fishing altogether to focus exclusively on tourism, winning numerous awards and accolades in the process. Recalling my overalls covered in mackerel guts, I can assure you Perry's experiences are wonderfully and reassuringly authentic. He knows that raking clams is just a part of the stories, culture, people, and coastal landscape that make up a P.E.I. bucket list experience.

The half-day adventure kicks off in the historic port of Georgetown, hopping aboard Perry's comfortable boat. A third-generation fisherman, Perry talks about the lifestyle of fishermen, the seasons, and the challenges they face. On the way out, the boat hauls up three buoys containing a lobster trap, a rock crab pot, and mussel rock. As guests touch and feel each of the species, Perry explains the histories and practicalities of the species, which might not seem like a big deal to islanders, but to someone from Toronto or New York, you may as well be hauling out Martians.

With P.E.I.'s famous red shores in the distance, the boat heads off for a photo-op by Panmure Island, where shutterbugs can capture images of the oldest wooden lighthouse on the Island. If you're lucky, some porpoises might show up.

But our destination is Boughton Island, where Perry's grandfather and father were raised, and where Perry spent many a lobster season. Guests are provided with wetsuits, snorkels, and clam rakes before hopping into chest-high water looking for clams. One of the

60 bald eagles that lives on the island might be soaring overhead. Each rake promises the reward of a palm-sized clam (or bigger — they can get as large as one kilogram). The abundance of clams scooped into a floating plastic bin soon yields enough for a traditional clambake on the beach. As the crew sets everything up, clients can stroll along the sandy beach looking for sea glass or let the kids poke their fingers into tidal pools.

The clams are steamed in seawater and served without condiments — no wine, butter, or garlic. They simply don't need it. Grown in the cold waters of the Atlantic and raked by your own hand, how could these clams not make the best clambake of your life? Perry is all about engaging all five senses — sight, touch, sound, smell, and taste — and experiencing what it's like to live on a small island in Atlantic Canada. His efforts have created a bucket list experience well worth shelling out for.

START HERE: canadianbucketlist.com/clams

CROSS CONFEDERATION BRIDGE

At the birth pang of Canada, when the founding provinces gathered for the Charlottetown Conference, tiny Prince Edward Island was only accessible by ferry. It may have been Canada through and through, but it wasn't physically connected to Canada, and winter ferry crossings could be notoriously dicey. A century later, a debate raged about the merits of building a massive bridge to connect the island to the New Brunswick mainland. The Islanders for a Better Tomorrow argued for the economic benefits of building such a bridge, in terms of both trade and tourism. Friends of the Island felt their lifestyles were under threat and said that not enough research had been done (or indeed could ever be done) to justify the expense. They even tried a legal blockade, but lost when a judge ruled the environmental assessment was adequate. Finally, it came down to a vote in which islanders were asked if they were in favour of replacing the ferries with an unspecified alternative. In January 1988, a resounding 59.4 percent voted yes to the fixed link. Four years and one billion dollars later, the 12.9-kilometre Confederation Bridge opened for traffic.

Many years later, I found myself in a car about to make this remarkable crossing. It was summer, so the fact that this is the world's longest bridge over ice-covered water didn't impress me. Nor did the pricey round-trip toll, although if there's one bridge that doesn't give you much of an option, this is it (ferry service between P.E.I. and New Brunswick was discontinued when the bridge opened). Once I had passed the toll on the East Bridge Approach, the fact that I was on an engineering marvel that once employed over 5,000 people and boosted the province's GDP during construction by 5 percent was kind of lost on me as well. What impressed me deeply was my car cruising at 80 kilometres per hour, surrounded on either side by the cold, dark waters of the Atlantic. The engineers had thoughtfully curved the bridge to ensure distracted drivers like myself would pay attention to the road, and not launch off the bridge to add motor vehicles to the marine life below. The highest curve — known as the Navigation Span — is 60 metres above seawater, which is ample height for cruise ships and tankers to pass underneath, between piers spaced 250 metres apart. For those more nervous than myself, rest easy: there are 22 surveillance cameras, 7,000 drain ports, emergency alarms, strict speed limits, and a surface designed to minimize water spray. The bridge was built to last 100 years, by which time we should be making the crossing in flying cars anyway.

Confederation Bridge is more than just a homegrown mega-industrial project, full of impressive numbers and statistics that hopefully kept you entertained. It's an umbilical cord of national pride, a symbol of democracy, and a fast, efficient way to get to a truly lovely destination.

START HERE: canadianbucketlist.com/confederation

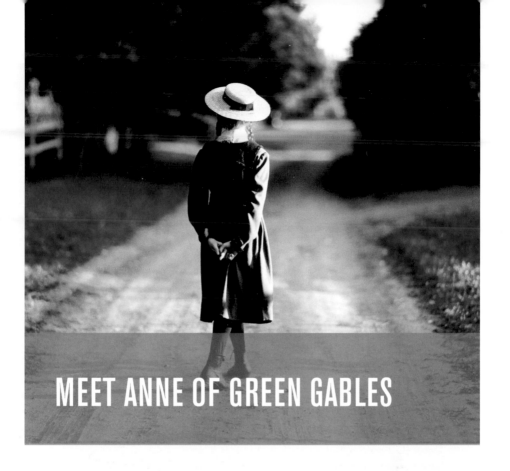

MEET ANNE OF GREEN GABLES

Long, long, long before Harry Potter and *Twilight*, other epic children's book series crossed into the mainstream to become an international publishing phenomenon. It followed the life and misadventures of a red-headed, freckled orphan with sparkling green eyes. Set among the rolling green fields and small-town shenanigans of Prince Edward Island, Lucy Maud Montgomery's *Anne of Green Gables*, and the eight sequels that followed it, immersed readers in the daily lives of early twentieth-century P.E.I. citizens. Written over a period of nearly 15 years, the books follow Anne's evolution from scrappy kid to educated young lady to poised and upright citizen, from age 11 into her late fifties. Anne resonated around the world,

with more than 50 million books sold, numerous accolades for her author, and the distinction of being both a Canadian and a Japanese cultural icon. Montgomery's genius lay not only in the richness of her characters but also in her descriptions of the world in which they operated. Prince Edward Island's allure as a destination is assured with anyone who reads *Anne of Green Gables*, including school kids in Japan who continue to do so. I, too, was required to visit the fields of Cavendish and Avonlea as a student in South Africa. No surprise, then, that thousands of Canadian and international visitors beeline to the inspiration behind the books, along with a range of attractions honouring the Maritimes' most famous literary hero.

Green Gables Heritage Place is just part of Lucy Maud Montgomery's Cavendish National Historic Site. Visitors can explore the original farmhouse, which belonged to cousins of Montgomery's grandfather, along with the Haunted Woods and Lovers Lane that inspired places of the same names in the books. Green Gables continues to receive around 350,000 visitors a year. In the capital, July to September sees the annual production of *Anne of Green Gables — The Musical* at the Charlottetown Festival. Adapted from the book, the musical has been running for five decades and is performed at the Confederation Centre of the Arts. A half-hour drive away you'll find Avonlea: Village of Anne of Green Gables, a historical village that recreates the life and times of Prince Edward Island in the early 1900s. Character actors and horses and buggies roam about the village, with visitors popping into musical kitchen parties, plays from the books, and Anne-branded chocolate factories and ice-cream

parlours. If you get thirsty, grab a bottle of official Anne-branded raspberry cordial, her much-loved bright-red drink.

Yes, enterprising Anne, in the form of the Anne of Green Gables Licensing Authority Inc., is not one to let a merchandising opportunity pass her by. Neither is P.E.I.'s provincial government, which owns half of the corporation, with the other half owned by Montgomery's descendants. Hence the trove of Anne-branded merchandise available at the Anne of Green Gables Store, eagerly snapped up by Japanese tourists. The Japanese love Anne as much as Alice in Wonderland, which is why you'll probably see Japanese tourists hanging about the site of Lucy Maud Montgomery's Cavendish home, some of them in full costume.

If you don't know Anne of Green Gables, or have no interest in the antics of conservative, religious Maritime society, you're free to swap this item for something like, say, a visit to the sweeping Greenwich Dunes in Prince Edward Island National Park. This rare coastal dune system and its adjacent wetlands have beautiful walking trails and a long, white wooden boardwalk that glows with life at sunset. But when it comes to realizing a fantasy world, kudos to P.E.I.'s Anne attractions for living up to our imaginations.

START HERE: canadianbucketlist.com/gables

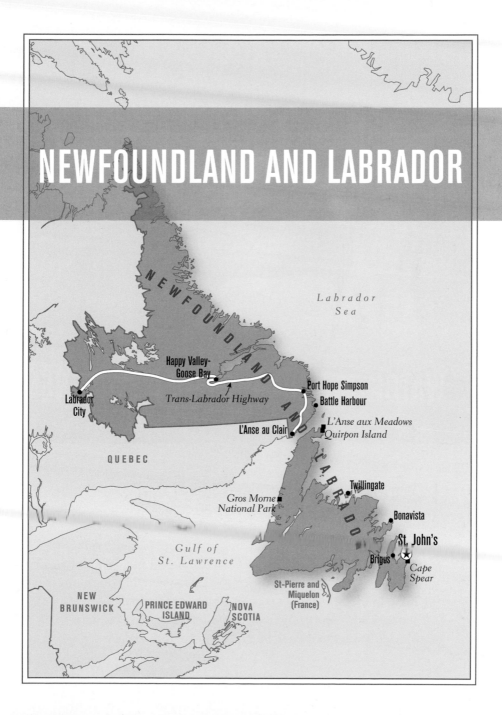

NEWFOUNDLAND AND LABRADOR

Labrador
Sea

N E W F O U N D L A N D   A N D   L A B R A D O R

QUEBEC

Happy Valley-
Goose Bay

Labrador
City

Trans-Labrador Highway

Port Hope Simpson
Battle Harbour

L'Anse au Clair

L'Anse aux Meadows
Quirpon Island

Twillingate

Gros Morne
National Park

Bonavista

St. John's

Brigus

Cape
Spear

St-Pierre and
Miquelon
(France)

Gulf of
St. Lawrence

NEW
BRUNSWICK

PRINCE EDWARD
ISLAND

NOVA
SCOTIA

WATCH THE SUN RISE ON A CONTINENT

Having arrived late the previous evening in St. John's, and with just four pitiful hours of sleep, I awake with a fool's determination to witness the first sunrise in North America. Just 25 minutes' drive away from my hotel is Cape Spear, the most easterly point in Canada and, notwithstanding the technicalities of Greenland, the most easterly point of North America. When you have but one morning in St. John's, you have to make it count.

Sunrises are more glorious than sunsets, because you have to work much harder to witness them. No "relax with a glass of wine"

Wind, Rain, and Fog

Don't be too upset if your sunset is also draped in fog. With 121 foggy days a year, St. John's is Canada's foggiest city, not to mention the windiest. Take comfort that the wind blows away the fog (along with the occasional household pet). ➤

moments here, but just as sunsets seal the day, early morning egg yolk sunrises bring with them the promise of unlimited potential. Excited by this thought, I pull back the curtains at my hotel to see fog so thick you could float a sumo wrestler on it. St. John's is famous for this atmospheric fog, which is great if your life is a film noir mystery but rather inconvenient for sunrise hunters.

Fortified with strong coffee and hope, I hop in the car and direct the GPS toward Cape Spear. The roads at this time of day are desolate. Lonely metal clangs on the big fishing ships along Marine Drive. I follow directions to Water Street and turn left onto Blackhead Road as the car's headlights reflect back at me in the fog. There's a dirty light in the air, as if the sun is feeling ill and doesn't want to get out of bed. The cut painted wooden houses, dispersed farther and farther apart, and just as I begin to relax into the ambience of driving inside a cloud, I catch a movement in the trees up ahead. A large moose jumps out in front of me, causing me to brake hard and wake up everyone within miles with a panicked thumping on my horn. Seriously, Moose, you've got the whole province to roam about in, why throw the tourist a surprise party at dawn?

I'd been warned about moose on the roads in Newfoundland, which appear to toy with cars on purpose, like spiteful teenagers annoying authority. The moose vanishes into the brush, leaving me a shot of early morning adrenalin more powerful than any espresso. Minutes later I arrive at the Cape Spear National Historic Site, the parking lot deserted. Clearly, I'm the only person optimistic enough to believe in a foggy sunrise. The wind is howling, the air is wet, and I'm cursing luck, weather, and moose when I stop dead in my tracks. The full power of the North Atlantic, crashing into the rocks of a major continent, can have that effect. Punishing waves as high as buildings smash into the coast as I gaze upon nature's neverending battle of unstoppable fluid meeting immovable solid. Feeling vulnerable and puny, I notice a warning sign, flattened on the ground up ahead. Walking along the coast, wisely sticking to the trails, I listen to the waves, feeling the atmosphere. There are no icebergs or whales this morning. No, on this day, it's just the Atlantic — the mightiest of all oceans — and one humbled writer, greeting her waves before anyone else on an entire continent. An experience well worth getting up in the morning for.

START HERE: canadianbucketlist.com/capespear

THANK COD FOR BATTLE HARBOUR

Despite the name, there was no conflict in placing Battle Harbour on our Great Canadian Bucket List. I've never been anywhere quite like it. Sure, one can find restored historical villages and picturesque Atlantic fishing towns, but when the two blend together, surrounded by extraordinary subarctic beauty and infused with the comforts of a high-end hotel, the result is just the sort of destination you'll never forget.

The settlement's history has been pounded into every flaking log, so, let's start with the past. Battle Harbour was founded as early as 1750 as a remote cod fishing community on Battle Island off the

southeast coast of Labrador. For nearly two centuries, the community grew some, but not much changed. Abundant cod, seal, and salmon were harvested by schooners and brought into the protected harbour to be salted, packed, and shipped to Europe. The initial settlers were British seamen, and over time some married local women and became livyers (for "live heres"). There were also stationers and floaters, seasonal schooners that would arrive each summer to trawl for the rich bounty of the North Atlantic. Labrador's first Marconi transmitter was set up, and at one point, the island had the largest store in Labrador. In 1909, American explorer Robert Peary used Battle Harbour's transmitter to inform the world about his successful journey to the North Pole, and a small fishing village in Labrador became the focus of the world.

Located nine miles from the remote mainland, Battle Harbour might also have thrived because of the island's lack of biting insects. You don't have to spend too much time on the mainland to understand just what a blessing that is. By the 1970s, the isolated settlement was devastated by the collapse of the Atlantic cod industry. Overfishing combined with new technology sank fisheries by the dozens, along with the coastal towns that supported them. Forced government relocation left ghost villages, as communities moved en masse to towns with services like schools and hospitals.

Today, a smattering of locals return to refurbished old cottages in the summer, but most of the cabins and wharves are splintering with the memories of the past. Battle Harbour was no different until a non-profit historic trust decided to restore the community and transform it into a living museum. As the Iceberg Hunter ferry smashes into waves rolling into Mary's Harbour, I am eager to taste the fruits of their efforts. What will it feel like to stroll on the boardwalk of "them days"?

Grey skies, huge waves, and howling wind make for a memorable ferry crossing, but the protected cove of Battle Island ensures a smooth arrival. Restored clapboard houses face the inlet, a picture-perfect Canada postcard. Overnight guests stay in two inns or a number of historical cottages. Included in the package are all meals, a guided tour, and ferry transport. Bags conveyed to the rooms, I enjoy the most delicious cod cakes I've ever tasted before Captain Jim Jones leads us new arrivals on a tour of the fisheries. Blackened fishing equipment is stacked in original storage sheds, the oldest dating back to 1771. We learn about the catching and curing of cod, the hard life of migrating seamen, shipwrecks, and sailing. Above us is the very room where Peary made his historic announcement. Life-sized photos add to the ambiance. Some of you will love this history; perhaps others will prefer the exhilarating walk to the crest of the island, feeling the cold embrace of the Atlantic's wind, gazing at massive icebergs prowling on the horizon. Walking trails lead in every direction, and the island is too small to get lost in. Soft, spongy terrain invites me to lie down among the blooming bakeapples, chomping on the berries and imagining patterns in the clouds above.

For an establishment in a remote fishing settlement, the Harry Smith Room in the Mercantile Building is as comfortable as any high-end hotel, with soft robes, original paintings, and a lounge. There are, however, no phones, no TVs, and Wi-Fi is only available

in the dining room. There's also no need to lock the doors. Many guests will stay for one night, but I'm grateful I'll be here for two. The morning ferry departs back to the mainland shortly after breakfast, and I'm eager to hike the tundra landscape of Great Caribou Island, a short skip road across the tickle (a local term for channel). The sun's rays break through the clouds, brightening the plump orange bakeapples, shimmering off quartzite rock. The vista reminds me of Iceland, or scenes in a fantasy movie … the ones that look too beautiful to be real. After lunch, Captain Jim takes the Boston Whaler out to Cape Charles, where the bugs of the mainland attack.

"Back home, we call these birds," I tell him, having clapped out another mosquito.

Battle Harbour's bug-free zone is appreciated more than ever. The Whaler skirts around the island, and suddenly we are surrounded by a pod of orcas. Playful and curious, they gift me the best whale-watching

experience I've had in Canada — not for lack of trying. Perhaps the secret lies in the lack of expectations. We didn't expect to see any whales, and that's why they showed up. Delighted by our luck, we take advantage of the last day of the recreational cod-fishing season, and no sooner has my friend Jon lowered a jig than he pulls out a healthy-sized cod. Days like this you want to buy a lottery ticket.

After dinner, I'm standing by the old Marconi towers with Dave Landro, a guest from Edmonton. An egg-yolk sun is setting to our right; an unusually bright "super moon" is rising to our left. On the rocks below, Dave's pre-teen kids are playing with Noah, one of the local Labrador kids who summer on Battle Harbour. It's the sixth year the Landros have made the long journey from Alberta to spend their family holiday on Battle Harbour. They do it for the escape, for the freedom, for the beauty, and for the warm friendships they have struck with locals who breathe life into this historical community. Feeling the beauty and dread of the North Atlantic, watching those opposable orbs balance on celestial string, I make a silent vow to bring my family here one day, too. It's been a magical 48 hours on a little island that truly belongs on everyone's bucket list.

START HERE: canadianbucketlist.com/battleharbour

MAKE AN ICEBERG COCKTAIL

More than just the proverbial tip of an overused metaphor, let us salute the iceberg. Sinkers of unsinkable boats, stalking the oceans in search of prey for ironic disasters, icebergs are one of nature's finest works of art — transient, temporary, and just terrific in a vodka martini. There's a certain panache in mixing millennia-old pure crystal water melted from a roaming iceberg into any beverage. Take St. John's brewery Quidi Vidi's Iceberg beer. The label on its distinctive blue bottle reads: "Made with pure 25,000-year-old iceberg water." If you can apply the term "freshness" to beer, it certainly is one of the freshest beers I've ever tasted. The blue bottle further enhances the feeling you're actually drinking mineral water, until four bottles later you realize you're very drunk.

Thousands of years' worth of heavy, compressed snow break off from glaciers or ice shelves to form icebergs, and Newfoundland's Iceberg Alley is one of the best places in the world to see them — from land, boat, or kayak. Spring and early summer are the best viewing seasons, and so I find myself in the windswept seaside town of Twillingate, where iceberg tourism battles to save its ailing fishing industry. To fortify myself for the adventure ahead, I visit Auk Island Winery, which makes locally sourced wild berry wines. Four of their products are made with iceberg water, and the general manager, Danny Bath, assures me he can taste the difference. Inside their winery, a 6,000-litre tank holds the iceberg water, and if you think that's a lot, you underestimate just how big these ice giants can be. A ship once recorded a 500,000-ton iceberg, while a small 3030-ton berg can provide a year's worth of fresh water for half a million people. You do, however, need a government licence to commercially harvest icebergs, more to protect consumers than for environmental reasons. Icebergs, therefore, don't need to be saved, just avoided should you happen to be captain of, say, a luxury cruise ship. Danny talks about the icebergs that arrive in Twillingate as if they were relatives visiting from Florida. "This one, he was a third of a mile long, I tell you, he was here for five weeks!"

Thirst slaked, I feast on palm-sized fresh mussels at J&J Fishmarket (their fresh seafood platter deserves its own entry on the bucket list) and decide to enlist the help of local skipper Jim Gillard. Since the winds are strong and the rain hard, every operator in town has cancelled their iceberg tours. The friendly folks at the Anchor Inn suggest I call the skipper, and he agrees to take me out on his seven-metre Seabreeze speedboat named *Galactic Mariner*. To find the skipper, all I have to do is drive down Gillard Lane and look for a large observatory.

Skipper Jim, a former meteorological technician for the navy and lifelong fisherman in these waters, was born and raised in Twillingate. He's also an astronomer with a mind-blowing homemade observatory that has a revolving dome (operating on Ski-Doo rails) and a 30-centimetre LX200 Schmidt-Cassegrain telescope. Here's a guy with salt water in his blood and his head in the stars.

We don waterproofs and head out into the bay, rain stinging my eyes. Skipper Jim must have eye shields, for he's comfortably in his element. He talks about his navy days, fishing, the oceans, his kids, grandkids, whales, and icebergs. Skipper Jim's bucket list is telling: finish the shed, lay down the lobster traps, enjoy the stars. Here's a man who has everything he needs, right where he needs it. It takes about 10 minutes before we see our target.

"Ninety percent of the iceberg sits under the water," says the skipper, with that distinctive Newfoundland accent. Icebergs change every day, calving and cracking, with erosion forming distinctive shapes as the ocean and shores gradually wear them down. Our "guest" today is about 20 metres high, with smooth lines, turquoise shades, and sharp peaks. It has also formed a flowerpot, much like the earthy examples on display at the Hopewell Rocks (see page 302). This dry-docked iceberg has the majestic design of a meta-snowflake, a true work of genius.

The skipper keeps his distance. We can hear the ice cracking, which could cause a lower section to roll over and take our boat with

it. He pulls up alongside a floating piece of ice and we haul a chunk on board. It is dense, white, and concrete heavy, unlike clear normal ice, thanks to the rain that has fallen into cracks. I take a knife and stab the top, the ice shattering into large pieces. The seas might be rough and the rain relentless, but I've come a long way to do this, and by golly, you can't let a little weather stand in the way. Not in Canada.

I put the iceberg in a glass and pour some vodka on it. Calving a chunk of iceberg to make a cocktail is something to do before you die, I assure you. The vodka I used: Newfoundland's own Iceberg vodka, made, of course, with authentic iceberg water.

START HERE: canadianbucketlist.com/icebergcocktail

CATCH THE CONTINENTAL DRIFT

Arriving at the Gros Morne National Park Discovery Centre, I am ushered into a modern theatre to watch an introductory film about the region. Picture sweeping helicopter shots of epic landscapes straight out of Lord of the Rings, with attractive couples hiking on the edge of emerald-green cliffs. Cut to a scene that could have been shot in the fjords of Norway, with park interpreters and locals explaining in earnest voice-overs how this land has spirit, and once you experience it, that spirit will stay with you forever.

I'm always a little nervous about these introductory videos. They often set the bar too high, especially when I peer outside the window to see the now-familiar fog and rain. Why is the weather always perfect in these videos?

I walk around the centre, reading exhibits, learning about the geological wonderland of eastern Canada's second-largest park, a UNESCO World Heritage Site, where plate tectonics were first proven as fact. Atlantic Canada's second-largest national park is 1,805 square kilometres in size, encompassing large mountains, forests, shoreline, freshwater fjords, and bog, and yet it's hard to comprehend. Tell me that 500 million years ago the Earth's plates collided, forcing its mantle to split through its crust, resulting in Gros Morne's unique Tablelands, and all I see is

a mountain of stone. Then I meet Cedric and Munju, two of the park's interpreters. We take a short drive to the Tablelands and stroll along its distinctly barren landscape. Cedric picks up a stone, and his French-Canadian accent drools with excitement.

"Each rock has a story, Robin, and the more we know, the more its story comes out." He begins to explain the basics of Gros Morne's importance in the world of science, its sheer uniqueness in our planet's time and space. Picking up a piece of rust-red serpentinite, he shows me how age-old minerals have been deposited on one side like the scales of a snake. Much like a battle plan, he uses rocks to demonstrate how the continents are continuously in flux. As he does so, the clouds begin to lift and the Tablelands loom above us in their glory, a moon mountain on Earth. There's not much time, so we jump in the car and drive to Trout River, a cliché of a small Newfoundland fishing town.

"It's always worth driving through here," says Munju, "just to say hello to the characters." A man is barbecuing fat sausages inside his smoky garage, rain be damned. Gros Morne encompasses several fishing enclaves, where communities live as they have done for centuries. This is not Disneyland, and these are not re-enactors. The hard reality of the Atlantic fishing industry is on display, unusually located within a national park, and as fascinating to a "far away" like myself as the scenic beauty. Cedric takes us to a viewpoint over Trout River, the wind whipping up whitecaps across a freshwater lake. The ruggedness of the mountains and glacier-cut valleys is something to behold. We drop him off to return to his pregnant wife, and Munju invites me for some wine at her place, overlooking the inlet at Woody Point. She's just returned from Halifax after a seven-year hiatus and can't believe her magnificent view for the summer. Some friends arrive, and we head off to the Loft for tasty moose pie. It becomes clear that Gros Morne is more than just a park, it's a community; and yes, that community definitely has a spirit.

I bid my new friends adieu to make the drive to Rocky Point for the night. Since moose were introduced to the park, they have become

Fjord: Go Further

During the last ice age, glaciers created the freshwater fjord of Western Brook Pond, a 30-kilometre-long lake with one of the highest purity ratings for natural water. Boat rides are busy in the summer, so it's worth booking ahead. ➤

quite a handful, especially for motorists. Earlier I had passed a sign on the Trans-Canada Highway that read, rather disturbingly: "660 Moose Collisions." Around the park I'm advised to watch the ditches and pay attention, especially since I'm driving at dusk, when the moose are especially active. After my close encounter in St. John's (see page 389), there's little doubt that moose through the windshield would not be as delicious as moose in a pastry.

After a week of rain, the sun at last breaks through for a glorious morning. Newfoundland has finally upgraded from a black-and-white TV to full-colour 3D. It's a perfect day for the park's signature experience, a two-hour boat cruise up the Western Brook Pond. After I enjoy a relaxing half-hour walk over boardwalk and wild bog, the boat floats up this freshwater fjord between towering 600-metre peaks and cascading waterfalls. The natural beauty rightly stuns everyone on board.

Yet it's not the Western Brook, or the Tablelands, or the great company in Woody Point I'll remember most. It's stopping off at Broom Point, walking 10 minutes on Steve's Trail through a tree tunnel, and emerging at a panoramic view of the aquamarine coast, black mountains, and white beach all to myself. Damn it, that promotional film was right: there is a spirit to this place, and I'll never forget it.

START HERE: canadianbucketlist.com/grosmorne

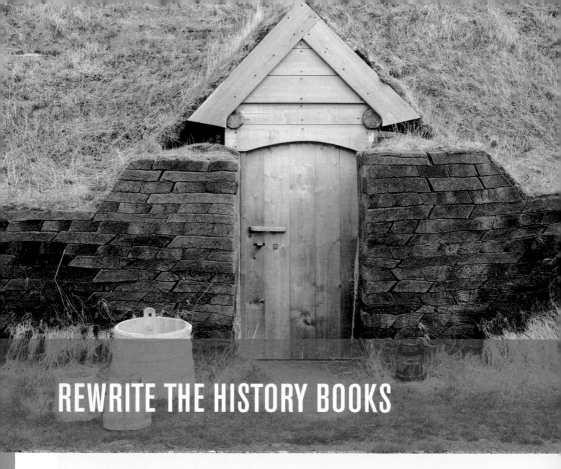

REWRITE THE HISTORY BOOKS

History is written by the victors, conquering their version of events into hard fact. Yet every once in a while the rug gets pulled out from under us, and we're forced to re-evaluate the past. For example: every kid in America knows that Christopher Columbus was the first European to discover the New World, in 1492. Well, thanks to a couple of tenacious Norwegians and a little outpost on the northern tip of Newfoundland, the textbooks have been revised.

The Icelandic Sagas, dating back to the tenth and eleventh centuries, told stories of "Vinland," a land of wild grapes, located in the west beyond Iceland and Greenland. The sagas told how Vinland was visited and settled by Vikings, although there was never any proof to back this up. Some theories suggest that, prior to Columbus, the Chinese traded with Indigenous Americans, and even that Irish seamen traded on the American coast. A lack of physical evidence sinks as many theories as the Atlantic sinks boats. The fact that there exists a Central American pre-Incan deity named Quetzalcoatl who sailed in from the ocean — often described as white and bearded — certainly suggests European influence in the Americas in ages past. Yet without proof, the historical record of Columbus held true.

In the 1960s, Norwegian adventurer Helge Ingstad and his archaeologist wife Anne Stine Ingstad combed the eastern coast of North America searching for physical evidence of Norse settlement. After many red herrings along a coast rich with cod, they happened upon a small, isolated fishing community called L'Anse aux Meadows. When they described to locals what they were looking for, they were surprised to be led to a series of raised mounds. The locals had attributed them to Indigenous people, and the kids who played on them called them the Indian camps. Over the next eight years, the Ingstads' excavations uncovered undeniable proof that this was, in fact, a Norse settlement dating back to 1000 CE — almost 500 years before Columbus. Working in often brutal weather conditions, they discovered eight complete house sites and the remains of a ninth. Parks Canada took over in the 1970s, and when UNESCO awarded its first World Heritage Site to Canada in 1978, the archaeological

Was L'Anse aux Meadows Vinland?

The latest archaeological evidence suggests that Vikings travelled south from L'Anse aux Meadows to the St. Lawrence River and into New Brunswick. Vinland, according to the Norse saga, was a country where wild grapes flourished, and New Brunswick is the northern limit for such grape varieties. Nobody knows why the Norse returned to their shipping base at L'Anse aux Meadows, packed up and sailed away to Greenland, never to return. ➤

and historical significance of L'Anse aux Meadows won the day. "Ya know, you definitely have some Viking in ya," says the colourful site interpreter, Clayton Colborne. My blue eyes and red-tinged beard certainly suggest some interesting breeding in my European Jewish heritage. Clayton was born and raised in the tiny community of L'Anse aux Meadows (population 25) and used to play on the archaeological site as a kid. Today, his bearded, bright-eyed face adorns the Parks Canada pamphlet inside their modern visitor centre.

It's a grey, foggy day, but the drive here from Gros Morne National Park was pretty enough, dotted with fishing communities. The landscape looks like tundra, but Clayton tells me that's only because all the trees close to the road have been cut down. Homes still need a good supply of wood to make it through the long hard winter, and the nearest tree usually does the trick. Despite the solid tourism traffic, Clayton reckons the actual town of L'Anse aux Meadows — dating back to the mid-nineteenth century, when the French ruled the shoreline — will probably disappear. All the young folk have moved on.

After learning about Norse migration and other information from the visitor centre exhibits, we walk along a wooden boardwalk into the field, passing beneath a striking sculpture called *The Meeting of Two Worlds*. "Full circle, ya know," explains Clayton. "When the

Norse arrived and interacted with the locals, it was the first time two branches of humanity met in 100,000 years!"

All that remains of the excavations themselves are mounds, grassed over like burial plots. The Ingstads discovered many artifacts confirming Norse settlement, including a bone knitting needle, a bronze fastening pin, and nails made of a type of iron common in the British Isles. Farther along, Parks Canada has reconstructed a Norse hall, hut, and house out of sod, as they would have looked 1,000 years ago. A re-enactor shares tales around a fire inside, and it isn't hard to imagine the cold, brutal conditions these early settlers had to endure. Perhaps this explains why the settlement was abandoned after a decade's use, the houses burned down. The Norse left, never to return. Perhaps this was only a way station en route to a larger, yet-to-be-discovered community, the Vinland so named because of the wild grapes that grew there. Perhaps it was abandoned because of a hostile relationship with the Native people, since we can agree that Vikings were not the most peace-loving of people.

It's a mystery that remains to be solved. In any event, the only known evidence of European settlement in North America aged into obscurity until a Spaniard arrived hundreds of years later and reintroduced Europe to the "New World." In addition to experiencing the beauty of a stark landscape, and my new understanding of life from another millennia, I depart L'Anse aux Meadows enriched with Clayton's stories and the satisfying feeling that a tiny Canadian village has proudly rewritten North American history.

START HERE: canadianbucketlist.com/lanse

SLEEP IN A LIGHTHOUSE

Paddling along the shoreline, Ed English gives me a lesson about Atlantic storms. "I went over to the West Coast and watched a storm blow in from the Pacific. They told me it was pretty bad, an eight or nine. Well, we kayak in those kind of waves." Clearly, Ed is not your average hotelier, and his four-star Quirpon Lighthouse Inn is not your average hotel. Built in 1922 on the northernmost tip of Newfoundland, the lighthouse overlooks a natural passageway that creates a feeding ground for marine life. Migrating roughly 3,000 kilometres south from Greenland, they're joined by floating hills of solid ice. This is the start of the province's Iceberg Alley, and one of the best places to see these natural marvels drifting on their slow, melting death march.

It's early June — peak iceberg season — as our kayaks skirt the seven-kilometre-long Quirpon Island. Ed bought the lighthouse in 1998, sight unseen, when it was put up for tender by the government. Despite wild weather and other challenges, he's turned it into a hotel that sleeps 25 guests in 11 rooms, from May to October. Quirpon (pronounced kar-poon) has since received rave reviews, especially in international media. "Right now there's a couple from France, Japan, the U.S. … Sometimes I don't see Canadian guests until mid-July."

Gulls are flying above us as the sun tiptoes into view from behind the clouds. We round another corner along the coast and there it is: a single dry-docked iceberg, boxed into the coast like a Viking helmet trapped at the end of a bowling alley. Its two icy peaks tower over us, the middle eroded to reflect water in a bright shade of blue. This mountain of compacted ice looks supernaturally out of place, 10,000 years of frozen water so pure that there's simply no trace of contaminants.

"Keep your distance, Robin. Towers like that crack off all the time, and besides the wave, you don't know how huge this is beneath us."

Icebergs come in all shapes and sizes — tabular, domed, pinnacled, wedged, dry-docked, and blocky — and watching them evolve from day to day is part of the fun. Yet Ed advises me never to turn my back on the ice, shape-shifting as it melts and smashes its way to oblivion on the rocks below. Kayakers should face forward, just in case.

We circle a couple of times, picking up some "bergie bits," small chunks floating in the water. My hands are numb from the cold, so we turn back to the harbour, taking advantage of the favourable wind and current.

Out of our wetsuits, we hop aboard the hotel's Zodiac to see if we can spot some whales. It's still early season, so it's unlikely, but it will give me a better look at the lighthouse from the sea, along with pairs of puffins clumsily flapping about us. It's calm as a lap pool when we leave, but within minutes, we're cresting over three-metre swells. The water is choppy above the Labrador Current, the cold ocean current that flows south from the Arctic. With the icebergs come the whales — humpbacks, orcas, and other species. The bergs herd the fish into the island's coast, allowing guests to watch whales feed literally right below their feet.

Quirpon Island is rocky, mossy, and barren, the lighthouse exposed like a palace guard defending the coast from attacking storms. When storms arrive, guests huddle up in excitement in the dining house, perhaps with hot chocolate and some bakeapple pie. Lighthouses are built to survive hurricane-force gales and monster waves, but the inn's location does present some challenges. Just last week, the wooden dock was smashed against the shore and it is currently being repaired. As Ed points out the heliport, the Zodiac hits a swell and tilts upward at a 45-degree angle. We both pretend not to notice.

It's too early in the season and the wind is picking up, so he gratefully turns the Zodiac back to the small, protected harbour. Jacques Cartier and James Cook charted these very waters, and just up the road is L'Anse aux Meadows, where the continent's first visitors settled. With its history, wildlife, and adventure, Quirpon Island provides welcome shelter in the darkest of storms.

START HERE: canadianbucketlist.com/quirpon

NEWFOUNDLAND AND LABRADOR ↑

GET SCREECHED IN

When Newfoundlanders heard I would be visiting the province for the first time, they didn't ask me if I would explore Gros Morne or track icebergs. They wanted to know if I would be getting screeched in. The fact that this tradition was born out of the St. John's bars on George Street, ready to charge you 12 bucks for the ceremony and certificate, is beside the point. To become an honorary Newfoundlander (not a *Newfie*, for that term is derogatory, unless you're a *Newfie*, in which case it's not), one must get screeched in.

Within a half-hour of my arrival in St. John's, I am at Trapper John's, a block from my hotel, just in time for the barkeep to begin the ceremony. Christian's, another bar in a city that likes its possessive apostrophes, apparently has a more authentic ritual, but they don't

Deed I Is!

Since I assume you'll be "spirited" long before you decide it's a good idea to kiss a puffin's arse, practise the following line to endear yourself to your Newfoundland hosts.

When they ask you: "Is ye an honorary Newfoundlander?"
Reply, with gusto: "Deed I is me ol' cock, and long may your big jib draw!" ➤

do it on Mondays, and this is Monday night. Thus I enter a mostly empty Trapper John's, where a couple from the U.K. and a student's mom are signed up for the evening's screeching. To get screeched in, one must listen to the barkeep's bluster, drink a shot of screech, and then kiss a cod on the mouth — or, in the case of Trapper John's, the behind of a fluffy toy puffin. The "screech" in question is a type of cheap rum that hearkens back to days of yore when the same barrel might carry both rum and molasses. The sediment that remained would be fermented and mixed with grain alcohol to create a drink designed to blind a telescope. *Screech* was a term used for any moonshine, but it is now marketed as rum and consumed with great pride by locals — and by honorary locals, for that matter. It is so named because of the sound one makes after consuming it, or the sound in the flap of the sails on a boat, or whatever you're told by the local who will claim to know these things.

We line up at the bar and the bartender begins his story, which I struggle to understand. It is my first real exposure to the distinctive Newfoundland accent, which rolls like an English barrel, made of Canadian wood, down a Scottish hill. Something about the origins of the rum, aye aye this, ya ya that. We are then asked the following question: "Is ye an honorary Newfoundlander?" To which, we must reply, with enthusiasm: "Deed I is me ol' cock, and long may your big jib draw!"

I shoot back the drink, expecting a harsh burn down my throat, and I'm relieved to find it absent. Back in my university days, I indulged in Stroh rum, which at the time was 80 percent alcohol and could strip the innocence off a club of Girl Scouts. I've also had the misfortune to shoot straight absinthe in Denmark, raki in Albania, and 125-year-old moonshine in Georgia. Screech, by comparison, is palatable.

The toy puffin, representative of the province's official bird, has seen many lips, which the bartender goes to great pains to remind us. At this point, I tell him about the far more intimidating Sourtoe Cocktail in Dawson City (see page 436), which kinda punches a hole in his sails. He must hate travel writers. Still, I gamely kiss the butt of the fluffy puffin, receive a certificate, and that is that. A highlight of Newfoundland it was not, but at least I can tell Newfoundlanders that, yes, I have been screeched in. Despite the potential for hokeyness, every province should have an honorary ritual for visitors. Undeniably, it makes you feel welcome.

START HERE: canadianbucketlist.com/screech

DRIVE THE TRANS-LABRADOR HIGHWAY

"Escaping it all" is an expression we can all relate to. It implies that we're locked away in a prison, behind restrictive high walls we have somehow constructed ourselves. Escape also denotes serious effort, one that is rewarded with invigorated freedom. Still, can this explain why anyone would drive 1,185 kilometres in almost complete isolation on potholed gravel roads renowned for shredding the very soul of an automobile?

The handy *Trans-Labrador Highway Guide*, provided by Labrador's Economic Development Board, has the answer on its front page: "for the adventure of driving through one of the last frontiers in North America. It is on our bucket list as the ultimate road trip." The TLH is the only road that crosses Canada's vast eastern mainland, as large as Japan, yet home to just 26,000 people. The highway has a notorious reputation, although steady roadwork in recent years has made it far more accessible, especially in the summer

months. At least this is what I was telling myself, flying into Labrador City. My plan was to pick up an aptly named Ford Escape, hit the highway, and use the TLH as an excuse to tick off a Labradorean bucket list. I'd come armed with a bug vest, four cans of bug dope, a travel companion with a penchant for meaningful conversation, and USB sticks loaded with music. With no cellphone service, we took advantage of the free loaner emergency satellite phones provided by the government, picked up and dropped off at participating hotels. When the friendly Filipino (there are a lot of Filipinos working in Lab City) at the Wabush Grenville Hotel front desk handed over the sat phone, we weren't sure if we should be comforted or spooked.

Lab City to Goose Bay, it turned out, is mostly paved, curvy blacktop, lacquered across the sprawling buggy boreal landscape. Our first roadside attraction is in Churchill Falls, the second-largest underground power station in the world. Free tours depart daily

The TLH offers limited services, but plenty of highlights.

Point Amour Lighthouse Provincial Historic Site

North along the Straits of Belle Isle and 10 minutes from Forteau is the tallest lighthouse in Atlantic Canada. Explore the maritime exhibits and watch for icebergs from the viewing platform.

Cartwright

Locals Pete and George Barrett offer trips to the 65-kilometre Wonderstands, a beach whose name is inspired by Viking sagas. Explore abandoned clapboard fishing camps in surrounding coves, old graveyards, several short hikes, and stunning coastal views.

Northwest River

A small community located 33 kilometres from Happy Valley–Goose Bay, visit the Labrador Interpretation Centre to learn about the history and people of the region. The Labrador Heritage Museum provides a glimpse of life in the recent past.

Happy Valley-Goose Bay

Load up on deep-fried cod tongues and pop over to the airport to pose with the American T-Bird, Vulcan Low Level Bomber, and Voodoo CF-101 on display

Churchill Falls

Reserve ahead for a guided tour of the world's second-largest underground power station. The sprawling subterranean complex has the ambiance of a Bond villain's lair. ➤

into — location scouts take note — an excellent candidate for a James Bond villain lair. From this unusual company town, we drive east until we hit a 60-kilometre gravel strip before arriving in the double-barrelled city of Happy Valley–Goose Bay. Between the mines and hydro projects, Labrador is enjoying an energy boom. "The province takes our money, but where is our road?" one local asks, referring to the dusty (or icy) reality of the region's transport artery. The state of the Trans-Labrador is a local obsession, although it seemed to please locals that we were crossing it with an urban SUV. Progress may be slow, but at least there is progress.

Labrador's cities have a distinct outpost feel to them. Be it Lab City, with it's booming mines, or Goose Bay, with it's shrinking air force base, locals must bear harsh winters and hot, buggy summers. Visiting the cultural museum in North West River or the aging Military Base Museum in Goose Bay, it's clear locals are desperately trying to preserve a fading historical legacy. Once we're back on the gravel road, I'm hoping the Escape's street tires will preserve their legacy, too, along with that of the windshield: transport trucks machine-gun gravel when they roar past us, although fortuitously, they are rare. Considering how much dust we leave in our wake, there are fortunately not too many cars, either.

Sometimes, it feels like we're competing in the Paris-Dakar Rally. One-pump gas stations are few and far between, necessitating a fill-up at every opportunity. We veer off toward Cartwright, a small fishing community opened to the world with a new branch on the TLH in 2003. Pete and George Barrett's Experience Labrador Tours runs boat trips to surrounding islands and a 65-kilometre-long beach known as the Wonderstrand. Against a backdrop of icebergs and velvet-green coloured hills, we pick sweet bakeapples in Little Packs Harbour, soaking in the Atlantic sun. Colours sharpen in this part of the world, as if your eyes have been tweaked like the viewfinder on binoculars. George reflects on "them days," regaling us with yarns. Understanding the distinctive Labradorean accent takes some practice, assuming you can decipher the local slang.

We backtrack 100 kilometres to the junction and continue toward Port Hope Simpson, now comfortable enough at the wheel to barrel along the gravel. Officially, the speed limit is 70 kilometres per hour, but drivers travel as fast as their nerves can handle. A sign indicates that we've now left the Atlantic time zone and have gained the extra half-hour of Newfoundland time. Several times we stop the car to admire the scenery, although leaving our mobile metal sanctuary brings an onslaught of blood-sucking blackflies. Magnificent sunsets are best enjoyed at the wheel, too. I've seen swallows smaller than Labrador mosquitoes.

The road deposits us in Mary's Harbour for our ferry to Battle Harbour (see page 391), and continues along the coast toward Forteau. Approaching Red Bay, Canada's latest UNESCO World Heritage Site, gravel transforms to blacktop. Hundreds of kilometres of driving dust and noise, and suddenly we're floating on a road that feels as smooth as porcelain. With it, the wild remoteness of Labrador seems to dissipate. Road crews are busy re-paving all summer, and while sections of the road here are in the worst condition of the whole trip, it's smooth sailing all the way to Forteau. We climb the Point Amour Lighthouse (the tallest in Atlantic Canada) and try fly-fishing for the first time with Brad and his dad from Labrador Tours. It's important to make time for something new — even if the fish aren't biting.

Although the ferry to Newfoundland runs on Newfoundland Standard Time, it departs from the Quebec town of Blanc-Sablon. Hey, if trains in Russia can cross five time zones but run on Moscow Time, a rickety old ferry in Quebec can time travel, too. After some challenging fog and wind at the start of our journey, the St. Lawrence is as still as a glass of tap water. I settle down to write in the abandoned ferry bar upstairs, watching a baby humpback ripple the waters in the distance.

Barring incident, you can drive the entire length of the Trans-Labrador Highway in 22 hours, but that would diminish the best attraction of the road — the opportunity to escape to an oft-forgotten corner of Canada, where the characters, history, and landscape add up to a one-of-a-kind bucket list road-trip adventure.

START HERE: canadianbucketlist.com/tlh

DISCOVER THE TWO B'S

Newfoundland and Labrador has no shortage of charming fishing towns, with wooden houses brightly painted against lush green cliffs, sweeping views of the Atlantic, and, if the commercials are anything to go by, unsupervised red-headed kids running about. While there are many wonderful places to visit, the bucket list recommends the two B's: Bonavista and Brigus.

Giovanni Caboto was an Italian explorer, sailing his 50-ton, three-mast ship under a British flag. In 1497, he spotted North America after two months of sailing west on the Atlantic, famously declaring, "O buena vista!" Thus began the long history of an important fishing town, which once swelled to 20,000 souls relying heavily on the Atlantic cod industry. Today, the town and rocky shoreline of Bonavista (population 5,000) is a historic landmark, site of John Cabot's first landing (Giovanni has been anglicized, much like my

real name, Roberto Esrockavinni). Bonavista is known for its heritage buildings, museums, and famously welcoming locals. Wander down Church Road, with its narrow sidestreets, watch for whales and icebergs from the lighthouse, explore the wharves and piers, learn about the salt-fish trade, and hop aboard a full-scale replica of the *Matthew*, Cabot's ship that started it all.

Closer to St. John's is Brigus, a traditional English fishing village with a name derived from the word *brickhouse*. This should give you some indication of the Scottish/Irish-influenced accent in this part of the world. Brigus dates back to 1612, when the town attracted English, Irish, and Welsh settlers. For a small town, it produced many famous Arctic sea captains in its day, such as Captain

Bob Bartlett, whose former home is now the Hawthorne Cottage National Historic Site. Along with other Bartlett family heroes — John, Sam, Robert, Arthur, Isaac, and William — Brigus captains were the first to reach the North Pole, sailing with Admiral Robert Peary, undertaking miracle rescues, and lighting the path for the shipping legacy of the Canadian Maritimes. Other Brigus attractions include the annual Blueberry Festival, Landfall's Kent College, year-round performances at St. George's Anglican Church, Ye Olde Stone Barn Museum, and the Tunnel, where early engineers used steel spikes and gunpowder to blast 24-metre-long holes in solid rock to provide easy access to Abram Bartlett's wharf. You may be in a rush to see Newfoundland, but Brigus wants you to stop, breathe, walk the narrow streets, admire the harbour, and chat with the locals.

Two B's, representing two glimpses into the storied past of Newfoundland. Two places to take your time, feel the ocean breeze, and turn off the modern world.

START HERE: canadianbucketlist.com/bonavista

NEWFOUNDLAND AND LABRADOR ↑

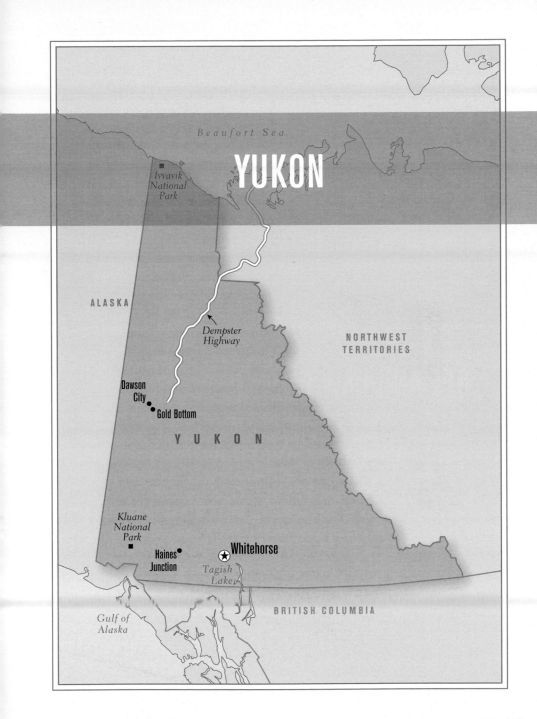

YUKON

Beaufort Sea

Ivvavik National Park

ALASKA

Dempster Highway

NORTHWEST TERRITORIES

Dawson City
Gold Bottom

Y U K O N

Kluane National Park

Haines Junction

★ Whitehorse

Tagish Lake

BRITISH COLUMBIA

Gulf of Alaska

GEE AND HAW ON A DOGSLED

Whitehorse is south of the Arctic Circle, so there is no Arctic night in late November. Still, the Yukon's capital gets light around 9 a.m., dark around 3 p.m., and in between, it's too damn cold to be outdoors anyway — unless you've arrived to go dogsledding, in which case, you'll want to drive 20 minutes outside of town to Muktuk Kennels.

Although he's originally from Toronto, Muktuk's founder Frank Turner is a venerable dogsledding legend in the Yukon. He's the only man to have competed in 23 consecutive Yukon Quests, known as the "toughest race on earth," routinely placing in the top six and winning it once, and he twice received the Vets' Choice Award for his exceptional treatment of his dogs. He's the only Canadian-born person to have won the race in three decades, and he held the record for the fastest time for more than a decade. Joining him for an afternoon dogsled is like having a pond hockey lesson with Wayne Gretzky.

As a dogsledding virgin, I was intrigued, concerned, and ignorant about the concept of harnessing dogs to pull a heavy sled across frozen tundra. When you grow up with apartment dogs, it's difficult to believe that certain breeds thrive in such extreme environments. It instantly became clear that Frank's 125 dogs are treated with as much respect as, if not more than, any suburban poodle — fed the latest naturopathic food, regularly exercised, and treasured like members of a large, mostly canine family. Each Muktuk dog is lovingly named, given a kennel, and cared for by the staff of international volunteers.

The dogs greet me with enthusiastic howls when I arrive shaking off the cold, a low sun still pinking up the sky. The dogs run circles around their kennels amidst a cacophony of barking, making for an exciting welcome. Puppies race excitedly in a large, enclosed, wooden hamster wheel. Muktuk doesn't breed and sell its dogs, and they're made up of various crosses between husky, malamute, wolf, Labrador, and tough-as-bones Yukon mutt. Turner frequently takes in local dogs that are in need of a better home and runs an adoption program for retired sled dogs, but you have to prove yourself a worthy owner first. I inquire how an outdoor sled dog fits into an indoor family home. "Go ahead and ask one," he tells me.

Each dog has its name proudly stencilled on its individual green kennel. I hesitantly approach a husky named Falcon, and I'm surprised to find him as friendly and good-natured as a golden retriever. Most of them are. Turner is confident any one of his dogs would make a loyal, well-trained pet, and treats them as such.

It's time to suit up in the layers of warm gear provided, including military-style snow boots to keep my feet warm and dry. We're heading out to a frozen river in the Takhini Valley, and I'm commandeered

into the team, collecting dogs from their kennels and carrying them to a customized trailer. Turner drops nuggets of advice as we do so. "It's all about teamwork. People think it's the rider in control, but it's all about the dogs. They need to trust you. If the dogs aren't happy, you're not going anywhere." It becomes apparent that despite the spectacular surroundings and the thrill of the sport, dogsledding is more about relationships than anything else.

After a short drive, we arrive at a frozen lake. My eyes become moist, which is not ideal when the temperature is below −30°C. Once unloaded, the dogs eagerly anticipate their run. Frank gives me a brief lesson in dogsledding mechanics: yell "Gee!" for right, "Haa!" for left, and "Whoa whoa!" to stop. Sleds have brakes and footpads to control speed. I have six dogs harnessed to my sled, and, as the saying goes, unless you're the lead dog, the view is all the same.

With a whiplash jerk, the dogs set off into the snow, relishing this opportunity to release their pent-up energy. Dog power is not horsepower. Without my control, my team would run themselves senseless, exhausting their energy and possibly injuring themselves. Frank has to constantly remind me to apply the brake, to find the rhythm and flow. Once I do, the true nature of dogsledding — teamwork —

becomes as clear as the ice crystals clinging to the trees. Watching the effort of each dog, seeing how their muscles pound beneath thick fur and how their individual personalities influence their speed and endurance, makes me appreciate how little effort I need to expend to glide across the lake. With the dogs in their groove, I can look up and truly absorb the jaw-dropping scenery around me.

We spend a couple of hours racing along the snow and ice, and I get accustomed to my team, their personalities, their strengths. Val is a firecracker; Livingston a loyal, steadying force. Incredibly, a healthy Quest pack can travel around 160 kilometres a day, at a speed of around 15 to 20 kilometres per hour, depending on conditions. I imagine Frank's race experiences, wrapped up freezing in the sled as temperatures drop to as low as –70°C, under the bright stars and glowing northern lights. He trains hard all year to prepare his body for the sleep deprivation and physical pounding of the Quest. The unprepared leader puts the team at risk, and the team comes first.

Before the sun sets, we return to the trailers, feed the dogs, and crack out the hot chocolate and thermal warmers, elatedly retreating to Muktuk before the dark afternoon shadows flash-freeze our bones. With a new appreciation for life in the North, you'll be hard pressed to find happier animals — people or dogs — than on a dog-sled adventure.

START HERE: canadianbucketlist.com/dogsled

CAMP IN THE HIGH ARCTIC

"Hypothetically speaking, who would win in a death battle between a grizzly and a gorilla? Or what about a wolverine up against a Tasmanian devil?" I'm asking these questions of my increasingly bemused hiking group as we continue our trek along the alpine ridges to a lookout called Halfway to Heaven. Wolverines are on my brain, because we'd just seen one scrambling across the mountainside, an event that solicited tremendous excitement. This is because nobody has ever actually seen a wolverine before, not even Terry, an Albertan who has worked in forestry for 25 years. Terry owns a company called Wolverine IRM.

"I don't even know a single person who has ever actually seen one," he tells us elatedly, "except you guys!" Judging by the reaction of our group, one would think we'd have had a better chance of spotting Hugh Jackman brandishing titanium claws above the Arctic poppies. This is but one example of the moments that inspire visits to Canada's North, and in particular, Ivvavik National Park.

Every year, more people summit Mount Everest than visit Ivvavik National Park. Located in northern Yukon, although accessed via the western territorial centre of Inuvik (see page 472), Ivvavik stretches 16,000 square kilometres across a region protected as the calving grounds of the porcupine caribou (*Ivvavik* translates as "a place for giving birth" in the Inuvialuit language). It is also the first national park in Canada created through an Aboriginal land claim agreement. As remote as it is, I am surprised to learn we will not be camping in pristine, untouched wilderness, but rather in the remains of an abandoned gold mining camp. What's more, my vision of seeing more than 100,000 caribou mowing tundra in one of the planet's great animal migrations was not realistic, as the caribou migrate in June, and due to unpredictable weather, Parks Canada only offers hosted services during the month of July. It's a relatively new direction for this vital national agency, enticing hikers with hot showers, flush toilets, hot cooked meals, and on-site cultural guides and naturalist interpreters. Still, fewer than 200 people will make the journey each summer, because we are talking about the remote western Arctic, which is neither cheap nor easy to access. But when you do, well … we'll get to that.

Flying in the North can be touch and go. I missed my chance to visit Torngat Mountain National Park in northern Labrador because of foul weather. If it's not the weather, it might be smoke from summer wildfires, creating a sepia-toned Martian sky. I was, therefore, delighted that Aklak Air's Twin Otter made it into the sky, and even

more so that the low-altitude flight over the magnificent Mackenzie Delta turned out to be one of the most stunning flights of my career. Waterways cut in every direction, occasionally marked by traditional whaling and fishing camps. I see a moose and some tundra swans, but most of all, I see a landscape strikingly different from any I've seen before. Our Parks Canada interpreter, Cassandra, has an E.B. White quote on her bag. It reads, rather serendipitously: "Always be on the lookout for wonder."

We make three passes over the runway. Sheep Creek "International Airport" is little more than a patch of open space, and we land with a jolt on the rocky track. Swapping out with the previous week's guests, they all assure us we're in for a treat. Our group consists of seven hikers, two park interpreters, and an Aboriginal escort, with two cooks already at base camp. Among us are a retired couple from Whitehorse, a newly married couple from Alberta, an ER nurse from Halifax, and a doctor from Edmonton, prompting a visible sigh of relief to have lucked out with our very own medical unit. We will come to know one another very well in the next four days. There will be long conversations about the environment, trail songs, and feisty games of cribbage; meals with "Scotch" coffee, traditional Inuit sewing lessons, patio tales, and short walks to the swimming hole. The camp is encircled by a protective electric bear fence, which admittedly takes the edge off, although the fence does little to stop the real menace of the region: the mosquitoes.

Female mosquitoes need blood to nourish their eggs. In the one week or so they're alive, these insects lay up to 500 eggs, and in the short Arctic summer, mosquitoes get very hungry, indeed. This circle of life comes to an abrupt end with each mosquito I crush with the palm of my hand. *Splat! Splat! Splat!* Most Canadian outdoor adventures are accompanied by biting insects, though they seldom show up in the tourism brochures. You also won't read much about horseflies, which the locals in Inuvik call bulldogs, flying about as they do with the menace of a predator drone. There's a dream catcher in the window, and I find myself thinking about a dream catcher/bug zapper combo, until a mosquito lands on my wrist. "In South Africa, we would call this a hummingbird," I tell the group, squashing the bug with my other palm, "although our humming-birds aren't vampires."

"There's still gold in this creek," says Don, a retired geologist from Whitehorse. He's enthusiastically furnishing details about the land we find ourselves in, a land that rather unusually was not glaciated during the last ice age. Evidence of this is found in the unique banks of the gemstone Firth River and the rocky tors that crest the surrounding alpine ridges like plates on a stegosaurus. Beneath a midnight sun that burns through the smoke blowing in from the Alaskan wildfires, the taiga blushes with purple wild crocus, yellow poppies, and Arctic cotton. Not too hot and not too cold makes for fine hiking weather, and as the only humans to be found in about 91,500 protected square kilometres (including the adjacent Vuntut National Park and Arctic National Wildlife Refuge), our foot-bound mode of transport reveals to us but a fraction of the area. Hikers in Ivvavik primarily stick to the area

around base camp at Sheep's Creek. With four days on the ground, we will tackle four outstanding day hikes.

It's a relief to scramble over the bumpy tussocks up into the hills, escaping the willow and sagebrush to bask in bug-free streams of mountain wind. It makes the longest hike, to Wolf Tors, all the more enjoyable as we eat sandwiches at Inspiration Point with the world at our feet. There are wolves in the area (caught on the motion-sensor camera located just outside of our camp), but the view from this rocky outcrop has me howling across the valley. We arrive back in camp with throbbing feet and a healthy appetite for Louisa's homemade bread, bannock, and barbecued chicken.

Having grown up with lions and zebras, I'm not what one would call "bear-aware." This is my first experience with bear bangers, bear spray, and understanding bear behaviour. If the bear is attacking, run … don't play dead … make yourself look bigger … but don't forget to cower! I'm told of one clueless European visitor who actually fumigated his tent with bear spray. On our hike to Inspiration Point, a large adult grizzly heads our way just outside of camp. I'm too stricken to reach for my camera. Ambling upwind, it finally notices our group, and bolts in the opposite direction. "That's how most bear encounters go," explains our Parks guide, Nelson. But you never know.

Past the disintegrating remains of a trapper camp, Terry pulls out his fishing rod while the group relaxes on the gravel alongside the turquoise Firth River. Satiated on sandwiches, protected by my bug net, and exhausted from the hike, I doze into a dreamy state, awakened by the yells of "I've got one!" as Terry hauls in a four-kilogram Dolly Varden, the largest fish Nelson has ever seen pulled from the

The DEW Line

Flying to Ivvavik National Park, you'll notice some unusual radar stations in the Delta. Resembling giant golf balls, these are the relics of the Distant Early Warning (DEW) Line, Arctic military bases built to detect a Soviet invasion during the Cold War. Since the shortest route for a Soviet missile attack was through the Arctic, the DEW stations would allow the United States to scramble its missiles and bombers as early as possible. Most stations were deactivated in the early 1990s, although some are still operational as the DEW Line's successor, the North Warning System. ➤

river, especially at this time of year. "That's one beautiful fish," he says admiringly.

It put up a great fight, and it will make a great dinner once it's hauled back to Louisa's kitchen. In the world of fishing, this is as good as it gets.

"That's the highlight of his trip," remarks his wife, Cyara. Terry is beaming.

Fittingly, our final hike falls on Canada Day. Halfway to Heaven kicks off with a steep ascent up the ridge behind base camp, traversing along several ridges (there's the wolverine!) until it reaches a limestone peak with rock windows that face out over the valley, over the layered hills that fade into the lavender haze. It's a bucket list moment, further accentuated by the sheer amount of effort it took to reach this spot and the knowledge that so few others have been here before us.

The vast amount of space offered in Canada's northern national parks is intimidating. With limited backcountry experience, and no idea where to start, the opportunity to fly into a remote camp with hot showers, meals, and experienced guides is a real plus. Exploring the beauty of the valleys, rivers, and mountains of the western Arctic by foot is a shoe-in for the bucket list. And as for the Tasmanian devil; well, it doesn't stand a chance.

START HERE: canadianbucketlist.com/ivvavik

YUKON ↑

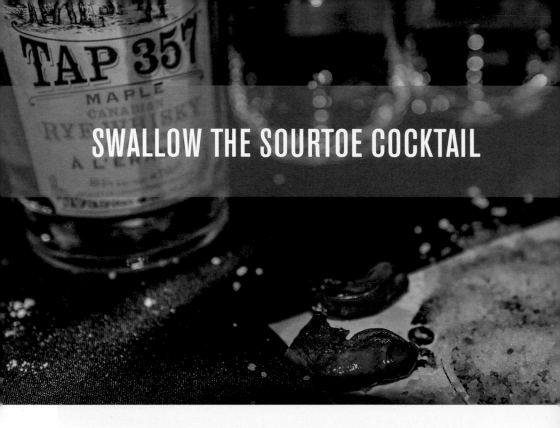

SWALLOW THE SOURTOE COCKTAIL

When you're constantly dealing with different cultures, it's easy to put your foot in it. A friend had told me that a bar in Dawson City serves the most disgusting drink in the world, and I told him he was one stick short of a kebab. Live baby mice in China, boiled spiders in Cambodia, fertilized duck eggs in the Philippines — you generally have to head east to find the tattered fringes of exotic world cuisine; and besides, everyone knows that Canada's beaver tails are not made from real beavers. I had belittled my friend because this "Sourtoe Cocktail" could not possibly be real, with its special ingredient found nowhere on Earth. Actually, it's available everywhere on Earth — it's just very, very odd.

"I'm telling you," he told me, "they drop a severed human toe into a drink."

Really, I just didn't think Canada had it in her.

Dawson City boomed as a major centre of the short-lived Klondike gold rush. Between 1896 and 1898, the population swelled to 40,000, making it the largest city north of San Francisco. By 1902, the gold had dried up, along with dreams of fame and fortune. Dawson City quickly turned into a small outpost with sinking wooden storefronts, population 1,300. In 1973, a local eccentric wanted to capitalize on the summer tourist traffic heading to the Top of the World Highway. Captain Dick, as he is known, had found a severed toe in an old log cabin. Now, when the temperature plum-

mets to –55°C, hard men are known to do strange things, including, as poet Robert Service famously suggested, setting themselves on fire. Captain Dick dropped the shrivelled toe into a glass of champagne and called it the Sourtoe Cocktail. He started a club, crowning himself the Toe Captain. To join it, all you had to do was order the drink and let the toe touch your lips. Word caught on; a legend was born.

Four decades later, I walk into the Downtown Hotel, chilled to my bones. It's winter, and the icy streets of Dawson are deserted. Captain Al, tonight's Toe Captain, is awaiting new customers at the bar. Behind the counter sits the eighth reincarnation of the original toe, preserved in a jar of salt. Over the years, toes have been stolen, lost, and, in some unfortunate cases, swallowed. My toe for the evening is a sickeningly big appendage donated by an American who lost it in a lawn-mower accident. Every customer gets the same toe. I pay five dollars for the tumbler of Yukon Jack whisky (long since

An Expensive Toe

On August 24, 2013, a young man by the name of Joshua Clark walked into the Downtown Bar and ordered the Sourtoe Cocktail. Suspiciously, he placed 500 dollars in cash on the table, the exact amount one is fined should something unfortunate happen to the toe. After the usual ceremony, the man slugged back the drink, toe and all. Recorded for YouTube, the night's Toe Captain, Terry Lee, could only stare in disbelief. This was the big toe! Since the incident, the fine has been raised to $2,500. If someone walks into the bar and slaps down the cash on the bar, at least this time the Toe Captain will know what to expect. In the meantime, the new toes are smaller digits, which makes the Sourtoe Cocktail just a little easier to swallow. ➤

replacing the more expensive champagne) and five dollars to join the club. There's no doubting the authenticity of the digit: it's yellowed and pickled by the salt, and a broken nail crests the top. My stomach lurches as Captain Al launches into a well-rehearsed ritual:

"Drink it fast or drink it slow, but either way, your lips must touch this gnarly looking toe!"

I arch my neck, taste the sweet bourbon, and indulge in this ceremony of cocktail cannibalism. Not too bad. Perhaps a little too much toe jam on the high notes.

Captain Al tells me the club has more than 40,000 members. Anyone of drinking age can join, and since the Downtown Hotel is not responsible for what you put in your drink after it's purchased, the health authorities are powerless to do much about it. Tourists now visit Dawson City specifically to go toe to toe with this challenging libation, much as Captain Dick anticipated. With my name logged in a book, I receive a card confirming membership in the Sourtoe Cocktail Club. I immediately email my friend to apologize for having dismissed his story about a drink with a dismembered human appendage. In my defence, it had been one tough story to swallow, but I should know better than to step on anybody's toes.

START HERE: canadianbucketlist.com/sourtoe

YUKON

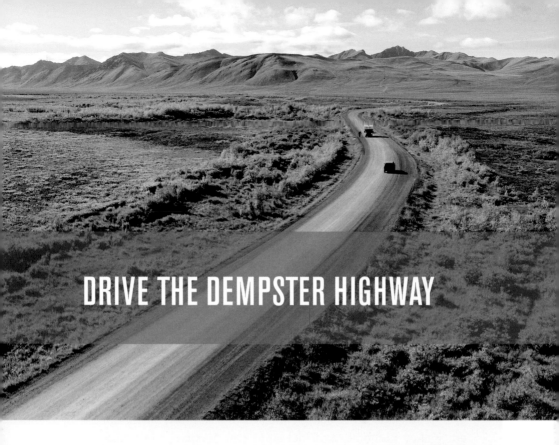

DRIVE THE DEMPSTER HIGHWAY

There are road trips, and then there are adventures. The Dempster Highway, a ghost road built for an oil and gas boom that never came, certainly belongs in the latter category. It begins 40 kilometres east of Dawson City and runs north on a narrow gravel strip for some 750 kilometres before eventually reaching Inuvik, in the Northwest Territories. By this stage, most motorists have turned back, happy to reach the Arctic Circle, just over 400 kilometres into the journey. Considering that many will already have driven 500 kilometres from Whitehorse just to get to the starting junction, we'll forgive them.

Decades ago, when the oil trucks abandoned the road, they left a pathway through a land of pristine mountains, valleys, plateaus, and tundra. Call it the Serengeti of the North, substitute bears for lions,

The World's Smallest Desert

Crossing the Yukon by car, you might want to pop into the aptly named Carcross, located on the South Klondike Highway between Whitehorse and Alaska's Skagway. At just 260 hectares, the nearby Carcross Desert claims to be the world's smallest desert, although geologists prefer to call it the sandy remains of an ancient glacial lake. Either way, the fine grain and terrific views make it ideal for the very desert-like sport of sandboarding. ➤

muskox for wildebeest, caribou for antelope, and wolves for hyenas. You'll also find Dall sheep, wild horses, and some 200 species of birds.

The landscape and wildlife are a perk, but the main priority is getting in and getting out in one piece. This is not the road for just one spare tire. Motorists tell tales of four blowouts in a matter of miles, leaving you stranded as close to the middle of nowhere as you'd ever want to get. Sharp shale shreds tires, and three or even four spares are recommended for the journey. There are no emergency pull-outs, and fuel stops can be spaced hundreds of kilometres apart. The name of the highway itself serves as a warning for the unprepared: Corporal Dempster was an RCMP officer who found an RCMP patrol frozen to death after getting lost without a First Nations guide.

Parks Canada has supplied some spartan campgrounds along the way, with no electricity, and pit toilets. They're a welcome refuge, but they won't save you from the relentless bugs in summer. Pitching a tent can be more trouble than it's worth; what with the bears and wolves, so many drivers opt to sleep in their cars. The road unfolds over a landscape that does, however, yield its rewards: epic views of mountains, rivers, and valleys; wildlife crossing the road; fireweed exploding at the end of the short summer. The few motels and gas stations cater to passing traffic, pearls of survival on the endless gravel string. Fresh water is trucked in, and accommodation can fill up quickly. The gravel road surface is soon replaced by thick mud, with dreaded punctures just a speedometer click away. No wonder so many drivers turn back at the Arctic Circle, their adventure quotient filled to the brim.

If you keep going, the mountain roads become even more challenging, aided by weather that threatens visibility and sticky mud waiting like flycatchers for cars. In summer, there are ferry services over several rivers, while winter allows cars to drive directly over the ice, including those braving the legendary Alcan 5000 Rally race. The final stretch to Inuvik consists of a couple of hundred kilometres of tundra before the highway connects to a paved road. After days of dicey gravel, it feels as if the car is floating on air.

So why is such a gruelling road trip on the Great Canadian Bucket List? For starters, it's a lifeline through some of the most desolate and remote scenery you'll find anywhere in the world — a personal challenge of skill, perseverance, and sense of adventure. Canada's North, and all its creatures, await you on a rocky road you'll never forget.

START HERE: canadianbucketlist.com/dawson

YUKON ↑

CLIMB THE GOLDEN STAIRS

G-O-L-D — a substance that historically has driven people to the very edge of their mental and physical limits. When gold was discovered in Yukon's Klondike region, it attracted more than 100,000 prospectors, insects to a golden flame (and even more likely to be toasted by it). Unlike the San Francisco gold rush a half-century prior, the Klondike was not nearly as accessible. Prospectors had just two options to get to the headwaters of the Yukon River: hike the White Pass route from Skagway, Alaska, or take on the shorter, steeper, and cheaper Chilkoot Trail. Since nobody wants to dawdle when there's gold to be found (it is a gold *rush*, after all), the Chilkoot Trail from Dyea, Alaska, became known as the Poor Man's Route to the Klondike.

Before the Gold

The Tlingit were the first to use the Chilkoot Trail as one of five trade routes into the interior. Different clans would manage the trade routes, with the Raven clan in charge of the Chilkoot. The Tlingit traded furs, fish, and clothing with the interior tribes, until European fur traders arrived and became valuable new trading partners. The U.S. Navy later negotiated with the Tlingit so that prospectors could use the trail, with the Tlingit initially profiting from packing services before being unable to keep up with demand. ➤

Many of these prospectors had more ambition than sense. After several tragedies, the North-West Mounted Police insisted that prospectors (also known as "stampeders") only enter Canada if they had at least one ton of gear. Pack mules, aerial tramways, and porters were utilized to schlep this gear from campsite to campsite, crossing coastal rainforest and treacherous high alpine passes to get to the valley below. With some 40 cache drops, it was tough going. Leading up to the Chilkoot Pass, the trail elevated almost 300 metres in the final 800 metres alone. These were the intimidating Golden Stairs, 1,500 steps cut into the ice and snow, leading to riches or misery. The mere sight of the pass was enough to send many a defeated stampeder retreating in the opposite direction. In April 1898, unstable weather caused avalanche conditions, and despite warnings from trail guides, prospectors insisted on moving forward. A series of avalanches claimed the lives of more than 60 people in just one day. The following year, the trail became obsolete with the introduction of a railway running along the White Pass. That year also signalled the end of the Klondike gold rush, as prospectors in Dawson City found no opportunities, and the media hype shifted to the Spanish American War. The boom was over, but the Chilkoot Trail was far from finished.

Each summer, the 53-kilometre trail attracts hikers from around the world, drawn to the spectacular scenery, a rugged challenge,

YUKON

and the enduring draw of history. It constitutes the largest National Historic Site in the country, and in partnership with the United States, is known as the Klondike Gold Rush International Historic Site. Maintained by Parks Canada and the U.S. National Parks Service, just 50 hikers are allowed to enter the trail each day, and due to high demand, reservations are essential. In the ghostly wake of shoddy tent cities are well-maintained campgrounds, interpretative signs, and warden patrols. Noting its slippery, snow-covered rocky terrain, Parks Canada leaves no doubt this is a demanding trail: **"The Chilkoot should only be attempted by persons who are physically fit and experienced in hiking and backpacking."** They bold that, to show they're serious.

The Dyea trailhead is accessed via Skagway (a three-hour drive from Whitehorse), with hikers collected at the Bennett, B.C., trailhead by the White Pass and Yukon Route Railway, or by charter plane. It generally takes between three to five days to hike the trail, depending on your pace. Taking on the Golden Stairs and crossing the pass from Sheep Camp to Happy Camp is typically a 12-hour haul. Once you're over the pass, it gets warmer as you enter the boreal forests, arriving at the gem-coloured Lake Lindeman, and onto Bare Loon Lake and finally Bennett. Today's Chilkoot Trail attracts hikers chasing a different type of gold, although one that I'd argue is no less precious. The gold of the great outdoors, the gold of a physical challenge, and the gold of ticking off an unforgettable experience on the Great Canadian Bucket List.

START HERE: canadianbucketlist.com/chilkoottrail

SKATE ON A CRYSTAL LAKE

Hopefully, you've noticed that the items that make up the Great Canadian Bucket List rely on things that you can actually do, as opposed to fantasy scenarios that are fun to imagine and all but impossible to experience. This is why you will not find the following:

- Watch two walrus bulls battle under an eclipse.
- Go narwhal hunting on an ice floe with Leonardo DiCaprio.
- Watch the Toronto Maple Leafs win the Stanley Cup (ouch!).

When I saw a YouTube clip of a bunch of guys shooting a puck to each other on a mirror-ice lake, surrounded by mountains and with fish swimming beneath them, I had to wonder: Can you really do this? Yes, you can. Or, more cleverly, yes, Yu-kon. Granted, the conditions have to be Goldilocks, and this does not happen every year. It has to be early winter, when the temperature drops for weeks, the lakes freeze up, but the snow is yet to fall. Alternatively, snow has fallen but heavy wind has scattered the flakes before they can scratch up the smoothness of the lake surface. Every three years or so, you'll find these conditions at one of several lakes not far from Whitehorse: Kluane Lake, in the national park; Fish Lake; Kusawa Lake; and, the scene of the video that went viral and dropped jaws around the world, Windy Arm on Tagish Lake, part of a chain of lakes that form the headwaters of the Yukon River, framed by dramatic mountains that create a tunnel for the wind to barrel through — hence its name.

Local photographer Peter Maher takes his family out every year searching for this type of magic. He'll arrive at the shore and check the ice. Just 10 centimetres will do it, since trucks can drive on 15 centimetres and thrill-seekers might go out on as little as five. Strong winds keep snow off the ice and the surface as smooth as freshly cut glass. Once you're skating, it's a window that reveals schools of grayling or trout swimming beneath you, or bottom-feeders drifting along the sandy depths. Ice bubbles create beautiful art in the ice, smooth pockets of air suspended like frozen thought balloons. You can skate for miles on this pond-hockey rink of dreams, although strong winds might blow you farther than you intended. Peter might have someone drive the car 10 kilometres

Gather Round, Ye Sourdoughs

You can't just show up in Whitehorse and call yourself a sourdough. The term dates back to the Klondike gold rush, when the name of the hard, fermented bread eaten by locals was bestowed on those who managed to stick around from the freeze of fall to the thaw of spring. Everyone else, well, they were just a bunch of *cheechakos*, a Chinook word for a newcomer. ➤

down the road to avoid the family having to skate against the wind, which I'm sure his three kids appreciate. He'll whip out his camera and take some remarkable photos.

Once word gets out, locals start showing up with their skates and sticks. There used to be dozens of people, but with Facebook and YouTube spreading the good news, these days there might be hundreds, not to mention people coming in from farther away. Of course, on a lake that stretches over 100 kilometres, there's plenty of room for everyone, with games of pond hockey featuring 20 or 30 players, all bundled up, carrying Thermos flasks with hot chocolate (or something stronger), gliding on their reflections in a real-life fantasy.

"This is one of the things that makes being a Canadian so special," says Peter. And while you may not be able to show up and do this every winter, it's special enough, distinctly Canadian enough, and real enough to make it onto the Great Canadian Bucket List

START HERE: canadianbucketlist.com/windyarm

CHEER AT THE ARCTIC GAMES

Every two years, participants from northern Canada, Greenland, northern Scandinavia, Alaska, Iceland, and the Russian province of Yupa gather for a chillier alternative to the Winter Olympics. Founded in 1970, the Arctic Games was designed to "furnish the opportunity through sport, the social and cultural meeting of Northern peoples regardless of language, race, or creed."

Regional and territorial trials whittle down the field until only the best athletes compete in different sports across three categories: major sports (such as hockey, volleyball, indoor soccer, cross-country skiing), traditional sports (including Inuit and Dene events, dog-mushing, snowshoeing), and emerging sports (such as snowboarding and table tennis). A new location hosts the March event biennially, proudly drawing upwards of 1,500 athletes from

more than 100 towns, villages, hamlets, and communities across the Arctic. The Inuit sports include the thrilling one-foot and two-foot high kick, the knuckle hop, sledge jump, and one-hand reach, all involving impressive strength, agility, and skill. I tried a one-foot kick once, attempting to tap the high-hanging target and land on the same foot. My testicles have never forgiven me. Dene sports include the finger pull, pole push, and the snow snake, a spear-tossing game inspired by caribou-hunting techniques. It's a festive atmosphere throughout, with medallists awarded a distinctive Arctic Games ulu-shaped medal and a colourful closing ceremony celebrating the very best of life in the North. You might not find yourself in Nuuk, Greenland, or Fairbanks, Alaska, but when the games once again visit Whitehorse, Yellowknife, or other Canadian host towns, come on up to support the Olympics of the North.

PAN FOR GOLD

The Klondike gold rush of 1898 was a boom that could be heard around the world. Although it was short-lived, you can still hear the faint whispers of its allure — the seductive promise of instant wealth — with a visit to Dawson City and a half-hour drive to Gold Bottom. Once a town of 5,000 people, Gold Bottom has just five residents these days, all still involved in active gold mining. During the summer months (−40°C weather doesn't draw too many visitors), you can sign up for a panning tour and sift through real pay dirt, with the bonus of being able to keep whatever you find.

Tips for Panning for Gold

1. Fill your pan halfway to three-quarters of the way to the top with silt. Pick out the bigger rocks, looking for nuggets as you do so.
2. Find a spot where the river flows strongly enough to carry away the silt from your pan. Sit on a log or rock unless you're particularly bendy.
3. Dip your pan in the water, using your fingers to sort the dirt and moss. Heavy gold will sink to the bottom of your submerged pan.
4. Shake the pan while it's submerged, breaking up the silt even more, allowing any gold to sink and silt to rise to the top.
5. Tilt the pan downward, shaking the pan some more.
6. Submerge the pan again, shaking it up and down and left to right, allowing the river to wash away the lighter material. Tilt occasionally, rinse, and repeat. Keep checking to see if any gold has sunk to the bottom.
7. Use tweezers or a wet finger to extract your treasure.
8. Cash it in, and blow it all at the local saloon. ➤

As you slip on your rubber boots and load your metal pan with rocks and gravel, spare a thought for the hardened prospectors who came before you. When word finally got out about streams of gold discovered up north, some 100,000 people flocked to the Yukon in search of glory. Dawson City, a ramshackle outpost, became the largest Canadian city west of Winnipeg. The boom was such that a single room in Dawson might rent for $100 a month, when a four-bedroom apartment in New York City could be had for only $120. Only 40,000 people accomplished the 400-kilometre journey through the rugged winter landscape. To stake a claim on the Klondike and surrounding rivers, they had to bring everything with them and face months of dirty, back-breaking work. Unfortunately, by the time the majority of prospectors arrived, most of the claims had been staked, the gold extracted, poems written, and fortunes made. It didn't take long for booming Dawson to sink back into the ghost towns of history, its proud saloons literally sinking into the permafrost.

YUKON ↑

Parks Canada and the government came to the rescue in the 1960s, restoring the town as a National Historic Site, preserved for the thousands of tourists who visit each year. People come from around the world for the history, the quirks (see Sourtoe Cocktail, page 436), the scenery, the drives, and the boom-time legends, people such as Chris Johansen, a miner on Hunker Creek, who offered one Cecile Marion her weight in gold if she would be his wife — an offer that cost him $25,000 when the 61-kilogram beauty agreed.

It was the same Hunker Creek where David Millar is now bent over and facing upriver, explaining how to pan the pay dirt. His family has been operating the Gold Bottom mining camp for more than three decades, expanding it with rustic log cabins and daily tours, rain or shine. Calf-deep in the muddy brown water, he fills the pan with water, shaking it gently at first while picking out the big rocks. Dipping the pan at a 45-degree angle, he adds more water; the pan is spun and shaken, the gravel slowly rinsed and discarded. Gold is 19 times heavier than water, so you'll know you've got something when you spot tiny flakes resting at the bottom of the pan. It's a slow process for first-timers, and you might walk away with anywhere between one and ten flakes.

In the meantime, expect to learn about the entire process, hear about the gold rush, and even see mammoth bones, teeth, and tusks that have been discovered by miners digging into the permafrost. There's an eight-centimetre nugget on display in the mine's Gold Lodge, and enough value in the area to keep several mines in profitable operation. As you walk away with a vital keepsake, your hard-won treasures certainly won't be worth much in value, but panning at Gold Bottom, unlike prospecting in the nineteenth century, is all about the experience.

START HERE: canadianbucketlist.com/goldpan

FLY OVER KLUANE NATIONAL PARK

About two hours' drive from Whitehorse along the famed Alaska Highway lies the sleepy little town of Haines Junction. There's not a heck of a lot going on, besides hikers and climbers hanging out at the bakery and an impressive new cultural museum celebrating the life and times of the region's Champagne and Aishihik people. The town receives a fair amount of passing traffic made up of RVs, motorbikes, and cars making their way north, enjoying hour after hour of snow-capped mountains, valleys, and glaciers, as well as the occasional moose or elk. From the road, you simply have no idea what lies beyond those first peaks — the striking and magnificent wilderness comprising the 22,000-square-kilometre Kluane National Park and Reserve. And although you can stop for a hike around crystal-clear Kathleen Lake and even climb a nearby peak, there are limits to where your legs can take you.

Which is why I'm sitting in a six-seat Cessna 205 operated by Sifton Air, embarking on a one-hour flightseeing tour. Call me a Robin with a bird's-eye view of the world's largest non-polar ice caps, the continent's tallest mountains, and an alien world of rock and ice.

The altimeter wobbles at 6,000 metres when we first see the Kaskawulsh Glacier, a massive river of moving ice that S-curves through a chain of mountains, carving out a valley with all the patience in the universe. Eighty-two percent of Kluane's surface area consists of mountain and ice. The scale of this natural beauty even has our pilot reaching for his camera, a man who flies this route daily during the summer tourist season. In the context of endless ice, giant rockfalls, and serrated granite peaks, our plane feels as small as a gnat and my adjectives as thin as toothpicks. We fly up the glacier, hoping for a glimpse of Mount Logan to the east. Almost six kilometres tall, the largest mountain in Canada also boasts the largest base circumference of any mountain on earth, including the giants found in the Himalayas. The tallest peak on the continent, Denali, takes up residence farther north, in Alaska, and considered together with other peaks in the area over 5,000 metres, it's clear why climbers have been coming here for decades.

Today, fortunately, is not one for ropes and harnesses, clinging to life by my fingertips. Although the Cessna bounces around in the thermals, rattling and roller-coastering, I've learned that such turbulence presents as much of a problem for planes as small bumps in the road do for cars. Even though it's a crisp summer day, Mount Logan is hidden in the clouds, so we bank left and make our way toward Kluane's most impressive wall of ice, the 70-kilometre-long, 5-kilometre-wide Lowell Glacier. When moist Pacific air collides with these Arctic air masses, it results in huge amounts of snow, compacted over time into glaciers. Lowell's surges and ice dams have

Canada's Highest Mountain

Located within Kluane National Park is Canada's Mount Logan, towering at 5,959 metres. Even if it does take second place to Alaska's Denali, North America's highest mountain, Logan is still higher than any mountain in Africa, Europe, or Oceania. It has the largest base circumference of any non-volcanic mountain on Earth. ➤

resulted in devastating floods, with local legends recalling whole villages being washed away by tsunamis of mountain water.

Down below I see deep crevices, cut like scars into the ice, and pools of ice-blue water, some of the purest drinking water on earth. We trace the glacier, watching it break apart into braided streams and muddy silt, and continue the journey over stunted forests of aspen, spruce, and poplar. I'm keeping my eyes peeled for bear and moose, and spot a half-dozen white Dall sheep, the park's most abundant mammal, perched impossibly high atop a mountain.

The hour-long flight is almost complete, and I've seen just a fraction of this vast open space, the flora and fauna hidden below like secrets. Most of Kluane is accessible only by air, hence the flightseeing options available in Haines Junction. Hop on board a plane or helicopter and witness the blue ice and black rock brush strokes on a truly spectacular Canadian canvas.

START HERE: canadianbucketlist.com/kluane

YUKON ↑

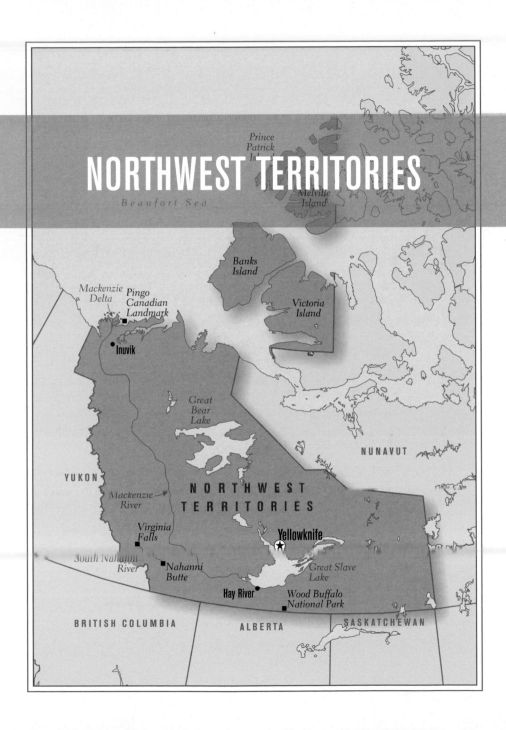

NORTHWEST TERRITORIES

Beaufort Sea

Prince Patrick Is.

Melville Island

Banks Island

Victoria Island

Mackenzie Delta

Pingo Canadian Landmark

• **Inuvik**

Great Bear Lake

NUNAVUT

YUKON

Mackenzie River

NORTHWEST TERRITORIES

Virginia Falls

• **Yellowknife**

South Nahanni River

■ **Nahanni Butte**

Great Slave Lake

Hay River •

Wood Buffalo National Park

BRITISH COLUMBIA

ALBERTA

SASKATCHEWAN

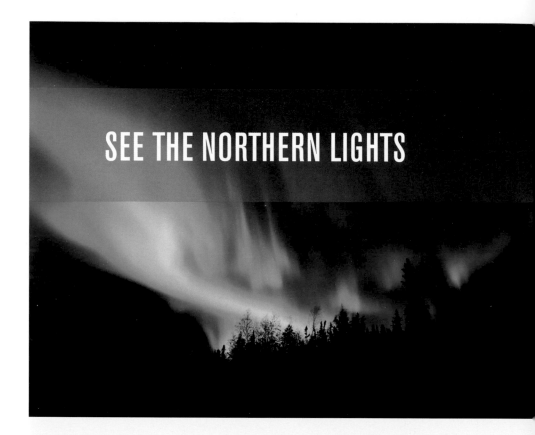

SEE THE NORTHERN LIGHTS

It's my tenth failed attempt to see the northern lights, and here's my conclusion: when you live in cold, sparsely populated northern climes, surrounded by unimaginable amounts of space, your mind begins to untangle. Your unwinding brain fires relaxing neurons into the backs of your eyeballs, resulting in beautiful hallucinations that can best be described as "lights dancing across the sky." When a traveller arrives from out of town with hopes of experiencing such a phenomenon, here's what he'll hear:

1. You should have been here last week, they were incredible!
2. You should be here next week, they'll be incredible!

Being here right now, on the other hand, results in clear skies with no dancing lights, or foggy skies with no dancing lights, or rainy nights with 12 Japanese tourists looking glumly toward the sky. This was my experience when I spent two weeks in Alaska. Ditto for a week in the Yukon. Likewise a week in northern Saskatchewan, and now, during a week in the best place to view the alleged natural light show, right below the aurora belt in Yellowknife.

Adding to my misery is the fact that my dad has flown up from Vancouver to join me, as viewing the aurora borealis has been the number-one item on his bucket list ever since he saw an awful eighties movie called *St. Elmo's Fire*, which does not actually feature the aurora borealis but does contain the light going out of Ally Sheedy's acting career. Bucket lists are personal, and I'm not one to question, but we still pass on Grant Beck's offer to visit his comfortable Aurora Watching cabin on a cold, rainy night when Yellowknife is consumed by a permanent cloud. Grant, a champion dog musher who also runs mushing tours, is being wonderfully optimistic.

"Sometimes the clouds break, and we get a beautiful show!" he tells us. You can almost hear those nerves crackling behind his retinas.

We would spend the night with a dozen Japanese tourists, who visit Yellowknife in the belief that procreating beneath the northern lights ushers in extremely good luck for any resulting babies. Of course, they're not seeing the lights if they're actually procreating, at least not in front of us.

Northerners tell us that the fabled northern lights are the result of electrical storms caused by solar flares smashing into Earth's magnetic field. Yellowknife sits directly under the aurora oval, where these lights can be seen at their most brilliant, attracting tourists from around the world in the hope that they, too, will share in this mass hallucination. Every local I meet is eager to share a story of the sky exploding in luminous shades of green, red, and blue, "like, just last week, on the day before you arrived."

The rain continues to fall, but it doesn't dampen the spirits of Carlos Gonzalez at Yellowknife Outdoor Adventures. After all, we've just spent the day fishing on Great Slave, and Carlos has seen the skies part like the Red Sea before. Just not tonight. The weather forecast is looking fantastic, however, for the day after we leave.

Thanks to Buffalo Air, we are now in Hay River. It's cloudy, of course, which makes for poor (that is, impossible) aurora viewing. Before retiring for the night at the town's Ptarmigan Inn, we ask the friendly receptionist, half-heartedly, to call us if he notices, oh, a natural fireworks display in the sky. Imagine, then, our reactions when the hotel phone wakes us shortly after midnight with exciting news! The sky, would you believe, is absolutely clear — but there are no lights in it. Seriously, guy?

At 2 a.m., the phone rings again. Something about lights in the sky. My dad is at the door before I open my eyes, and I meet him in the parking lot. He looks somewhat perplexed, repeatedly asking: "Where, where, where?" I direct his attention to a faint glow above us and the fact that we're standing under a rather bright street light. We walk a couple of blocks to the river, where there's less light pollution, and sure enough, a huge green band is glowing in the sky. To our right, spectacular bolts of lightning are firing on the horizon. To our left, a bright, half-crescent yellow moon bobs in the purple sky. My dad puts his arm around me, a huge smile on his face.

"Will you look at that!" he says in amazement.

Yep, I can see it clearly.

Unless we've officially spent too much time in the North, and now we're starting to hallucinate, too.

START HERE: canadianbucketlist.com/aurora

Your Pilot May Look Familiar

From *The Deadliest Catch* to *Ice Road Truckers* to *Flying Wild Alaska*, TV audiences love the extreme lifestyles and personalities of men and women of the North. With its retro colours, larger-than-life characters, and dangerous working environment, it was just a matter of time before Buffalo Airways flew high in the world of television. Originally produced for the History Channel by Vancouver-based Omni Film (the same company that produced my own series called *Word Travels*, using many of the same crew), *Ice Pilots* has been seen on networks including National Geographic around the world, making stars of its very authentic owners, managers, pilots, and maintenance crew. There's even an *Ice Pilots* roller coaster in Denmark's Legoland Park. When these old birds are flying, though, you can rest assured the folks at Buffalo Airways are more concerned with service and safety than with television ratings. ➤

Justin shows me around the interior of a powerful Lockheed Electra, as well as Buffalo's water bombers (sorry, Mordecai Richler's ghost, but it's impossible for a bomber to suck up a swimmer in a lake). I'm itching to get in the air, and it's time for the 4:30 p.m. departure to Hay River. While Buffalo operates according to the same regulations as any commercial airline in Canada, the age of its planes and the attitudes of its crew are distinctly different. "We've got little interest in modern aviation. That's like sitting in a doctor's office," explains Mikey. "Most pilots want to be in a suit walking through a terminal. Our guys love adventure."

The formalities are minimal, on the understanding that passengers know how to operate a seat belt, and won't do handstands in the aisles during turbulence. How refreshing to see pilots in jeans. The props roar to life, and in a surprisingly short takeoff the DC-3 tilts forward and gently floats into the big northern sky. It's a smooth ride at 1,500 metres above the lake, and with the pilot's permission, passengers can poke their heads into the cockpit, perhaps even take the jump seat and ask some questions. The 45-minute flight to the small transport hub of Hay River is fun, fascinating, and, I suppose, what flying used to be like.

Fortunately, Buffalo's influence now extends to ensuring there's something to do in Hay River when you get there. Together with her husband, Fraser, and stepson Spencer, Kathy McBryan has launched Hay River's first tour operator, 2 Seasons Adventures. Guests can spend the night in a yurt or cabin on the sandy beaches of Great Slave; hop aboard an ATV; go fishing; ski, snowmobile, and ice-fish in the winter; take a jet boat to Louise Falls; party on a barge; spend the night watching the northern lights; or enjoy a barbecue on a boat as they float up the Mackenzie River. "There's so much to do here," says hunky Spencer as he cuts a Polaris ATV into the forest. All you need are locals with the right toys, toys that 2 Seasons has in abundance.

Back in Yellowknife, the distinctly green DC-3 lands on the runway. Nobody is quite sure what possessed Joe to adopt the colour, and four decades of aviation life in the northern extremes have blurred fact and myth, even for the founder. Maybe it's because he was born on St. Patrick's Day, or perhaps it was to remember the first green planes he ever flew. One thing's for sure: it makes for memorable merchandise in the gift shop. "People would come and demand souvenirs, and it's just grown from there," explains Peter, as we stand in the merchandise store. Everyone's wearing something that says "Buffalo," and by the end of my visit, it's hard to distinguish who's a passenger, a visitor, a pilot, or a member of the crew.

For making flying fun again — on the ground, in the air, and on TV, too — Buffalo Airways buzzes the Great Canadian Bucket List.

START HERE: canadianbucketlist.com/buffaloair

EXPLORE CANADA'S LARGEST NATIONAL PARK

Wood Buffalo National Park, straddling Alberta and the Northwest Territories, has an area of 44,807 square kilometres. In Europe, they might call that a country, a country the size of Denmark, and bigger than Switzerland. Wood Buffalo, I might add, has no people living in it.

Established in 1922 as northern Canada's first national park, and still the country's largest, Wood Buffalo is a massive stretch of land that protects, among other creatures, the last free-roaming wood bison herds in the world. Bison were once prolific, roaming in boreal forests from Saskatchewan to British Columbia and all the way north to the Yukon, Alaska, and the Northwest Territories, but unchecked hunting and severe winters took them to the very brink of extinction. At the end of the nineteenth century there were fewer than 250 animals left. Thanks to the efforts of conservationists and Parks Canada, their numbers have rebounded to around 10,000, with half of those living in Wood Buffalo National Park.

Joining them in this vast expanse of wilderness are bears, moose, wolverines, beavers, otters, and the world's largest wolves. Fortuitously, the park also provides protection for a migratory flock of whooping cranes, another species flying back from the brink. In 1941, there were just 21 left in existence. Today, Wood Buffalo is home to some 300 whooping cranes, nesting in a remote corner of the park. Birdwatchers rejoice!

I drive the long road in from Hay River, carving through dense forests of aspen, poplar, spruce, and Jack pine, hoping to see some animals. Canadian wildlife can be painfully shy at the best of times, never mind in the country's biggest national park. Still, I catch a glimpse of a black bear, and a sassy red fox welcomes me to Fort Smith, Wood Buffalo's nearest town.

Here, I meet Parks Canada's Richard Zaidan, who takes me on an introductory visit into this vast, protected wilderness. Our first stop is the Salt River Day Area, the trailhead for five popular hikes, where we stroll the 750-metre Kartsland Loop. Gypsum and limestone have created an extensive cave system beneath our feet, of special benefit to our slithery friend, the red garter snake. Similar to the dens in Narcisse, Manitoba (see page 164), hundreds of snakes hibernate in these sinkholes and cracks for the winter. Next we drive to Salt Plains and Grosbeak Lake, finding mineral-rich mud with a dusting of white salt, the landscape looking distinctly Martian. Glaciers deposited thousands of rocks in the copper-red mud, mud that is ideal for capturing our footprints along with those of other recent visitors — bison, wolf, and human. Then we visit the public campsites at Pine Lake, where algae have turned the water a rich shade of aquamarine. Easy to see why it's so popular in the summer months, but it's the drive home that introduces us to the park's star attraction.

Three large bulls stand on the side of the dirt road, each hulking body carrying an enormous head. If the bugs are bad enough to necessitate us donning bug nets at times, these beasts have no chance. Clouds of blackflies surround them, forcing one to rub itself in the dust for relief. Just metres away, their bulk is intimidating, even from the relatively safe confines of the pickup truck. It's quite the moment, staring down some of the biggest wild bison in the world, here in Canada's biggest national park. Wood Buffalo has a space on the bucket list, and it's a very large space indeed.

START HERE: canadianbucketlist.com/woodbuffalo

SHELL OUT FOR FISH AND CHIPS AT BULLOCKS

After years in the ho-hum-drum, Canada's food scene has blossomed. We've got some of the finest restaurants on the continent, operated by rock star chefs of wildly diverse backgrounds. When a restaurant becomes synonymous with a provincial capital, it demands investigation — especially when reports range from "essential" to "avoid at all costs." Such is the case with Bullocks Bistro, a ramshackle fish shack in Old Town Yellowknife. With a reputation for serving the most expensive fish 'n' chips in Canada, and an open kitchen run by a legendary local character, it demanded a culinary investigation.

Established by husband and wife Sam and Renata Bullock in 1989, the bistro has grown from a simple wooden fish shack into a larger wooden fish shack, covered in bumper stickers, notices, and the satisfied scrawling left by decades of happy customers. The potato chipper is against the wall, the cold beers are in the fridge, and the place has the feel of a warm, frat-house family kitchen. The menu consists of northern seafood delights — pickerel, whitefish, lake trout, Arctic char — grilled, pan-fried, or deep-fried. For the serious carnivore, there are also grilled caribou, muskox, and bison steaks. No chicken, no beef, only food you can find in the North, all served with a fresh salad and homemade fries. The fish is particularly fresh, with most of it caught in Great Slave Lake just a block away. There's a wisecracking chef on the other end of the long wooden counter,

unhurriedly carving huge hunks of meat, prepping, grilling, frying, and chatting with the customers. It is packed with Japanese tourists and enthusiastic locals.

"Nothing in Yellowknife comes close to this sort of quality," enthuses a mining consultant. Quality and quantity, for the portions are noticeably large. Slabs of meat cover the dinner plates, while fish fillets are as large as a basketball player's hands. A patron next to me receives her dish, with the chef adding another large piece of fish because her huge portion didn't look huge enough.

I order Arctic char sashimi to start, a lovely salmon-like fish best enjoyed up north. Next up is the pan-fried pickerel. It is cooked with

so much butter that it isn't so much fried as poached, and is accompanied by a sweet-spicy garlic herb mix that hits all the right notes. The salad is fresh and simple, with the choice of house-made vinaigrette or a rich, creamy feta cheese dressing. Crispy fries taste like real potatoes.

The secret is the cold waters of Great Slave. The colder the water, the sweeter and fresher the fish. With a dozen meals on the go, Renata chats away, somehow finding time to show some tourists where the bathroom light is. The meat is medium rare, the fish melts in your mouth. Enjoying a cold Pilsner from the fridge, I read the bumper stickers:

Do you know why divorce is expensive? Because it's worth it!
Mall Wart: Your Choice for Cheap Plastic Crap.
Prices Subject to Customer Attitude.

I'd been forewarned about the cost of visiting Bullocks. A meal for two typically costs around $125. Renata shrugs it off. This is Yellowknife, the nearest big city is 1,700 kilometres away. The fish is as fresh as it gets (the Arctic char is flown in daily), and as Renata herself once reminded me, "If you want an experience, it's gonna cost you!"

An experience is right. Some people might balk at the prices, others at the attitude. The Bullocks retired in 2016, but the sale of the bistro came with conditions: almost nothing can change. New owners Mark Elson and Jo-Ann Martin are fully committed to keeping Bullocks Bistro's unique ambience and legendary quality. A good thing, too. Having eaten in hundreds of restaurants around the country, I can say with confidence that few meals are as synonymous with their city, or as memorable, as Bullocks Bistro.

START HERE: canadianbucketlist.com/bullocks

EAT THE MUKTUK

I'll be the first to admit that Inuit-inspired dishes are unlikely to find their way to your local mall's food court. There's no Inuit curries, noodles, or hot cheese. While the North certainly offers delightful dishes prepared with unusual local ingredients (spruce tip jelly! morels!) the Inuvialuit and Gwich'in feast on delicacies that one might call an acquired taste (and they'll be the first to admit that, too). When poor weather cancelled my day's excursion to see the pingos outside the small hamlet of Tuktoyaktuk, the owners of Inuvik's Up North Tours, Kylik Kisoun-Taylor and his formidable uncle,

Life in a Northern Town

Inuvik, the last stop on the Dempster Highway, was built in the 1960s as a regional centre for the western Arctic. In summer, it sees a steady traffic of RVs and tour bikes, and it is home to the region's only hospital. An excellent visitor centre explores the cultural and natural history of the western Arctic.

A curious note: the local liquor store has the best prices for Scotch I've seen anywhere in the country. Dining is limited, but don't miss the fish tacos and reindeer chilli at Alestines, served out of an old yellow school bus. Supplies can be procured at the NorthMart supermarket. Given the distances they have to travel, some things are understandably expensive, and others surprisingly reasonable. While the town once boasted half a dozen pubs, at the time of writing, there is only the Legion, Shivers, and the notorious Trappers, which has the ambiance of a Wild West saloon. With a major new road being constructed to Tuktoyaktuk, there are hopes that tourism will increase in the area, which is serviced by a small but impressive airport and a welcoming community of characters. ➤

Jerry Kisoun, warmly invited me to their kitchen to sample some local flavours. Although dining options are limited in the town, I'd already been impressed with the muskox and brie burger I'd devoured at the Mackenzie Hotel, and the fresh and flavourful whitefish tacos served out of a yellow schoolbus at Alestines. Tonight's menu, however, would be a different kettle of dehydrated fish altogether.

Dried meats and fish form a large part of the northern diet, with Kylik slicing thin strips of both on a cardboard cutting board and placing them in an electric dehydrator. Let's start with whale meat. It looks not unlike jerky, but tastes like the meat of a cow fed a strict diet of sardines. The fishy-meaty taste doesn't exactly roll off the taste buds. Next to the whale is a plate with similar-looking dried beaver, which tastes exactly how you'd imagine a large aquatic rodent to taste, sprinkled with the special flavour of guilt that accompanies eating any national animal on the menu. The dried reindeer is more recognizable, tasting like venison — lean and gamey. More appealing is the boiled tundra swan, which is deliciously ducky, while dried strips of whitefish are suitably complemented by large wads of butter. Dried seal meat also looks like jerky but with a fatty, pungent fishiness to it as well. I guess mammals truly are what they eat. The star of the show, besides Jerry's stories, is traditional muktuk; that is, raw baby beluga whale. Cut into small pieces, it is very rich in vitamin C (in case you were wondering why Indigenous northern people don't get scurvy) and looks very much like … well, the skin of a raw baby beluga. Since my toddler has subjected me to hour upon hour of Raffi's classic hit "Baby Beluga," the song spins its notes in my head as I reach for a firm, spongy square. Jerry suggests less chewing and more swallowing, especially with the cartilage texture. Swim so fine and you swim so free … Raffi is killing me. I plop the piece in my mouth and instantly realize that muktuk is a dish best left to those who can appreciate it, like family friends who pop over for a visit and take great delight in the smorgasbord on offer. Jerry further explains that muktuk must be served right or else one risks contracting botulism. This particular whale was hunted last season and only sees light outside the freezer on special occasions. It's a tough whale to swallow. With enough time, one can acquire a taste for whale, although, as comedian Jackie Mason once remarked, one never has to acquire a taste for french fries.

My favourite dish of the evening is frozen Arctic char, served raw to melt in my mouth like ice-cream sashimi. Somewhere between salmon and trout, char is the northern cuisine's most sought-after fish. The evening is also memorable for the traditional clothing. At one point, I try on a seal jacket, polar bear mitts, beaver hat, and wolf boots. Wool and Gore-Tex don't stand a chance. It is easy to understand why animals play such a vital role in Arctic Aboriginal culture.

The weather never does ease up for my visit to Tuktoyaktuk, which, along with Herschel Island, belongs on my Great Canadian Bucket List. It does, however, allow time for a boat ride up the extraordinary Mackenzie Delta, listening to Jerry's stories of growing up in the region, taking his team of dogs out in the winter to trap, hunt, and visit family in the delta. With a Gwich'in mom and

Inuvialuit dad, Jerry knows both worlds, pointing out places from his childhood in the labyrinth of waterways. I see more than a dozen beaver, slapping their tails at our approach. Graceful tundra swans rest on the grassy banks. The mosquitoes are pretty fierce, but this is life in an Arctic summer. Jerry gets a sparkle in his eye recalling the dog teams that gave him so much freedom as a child, and as an adult, too. A peachy sun radiates a special glow at midnight; the purity in the light has to be experienced at least once in one's life. As for snacks on board: delicious homemade cookies, courtesy of Jerry's wife — sweet, buttery, and agreeably muktuk-free.

START HERE: *canadianbucketlist.com/inuvik*

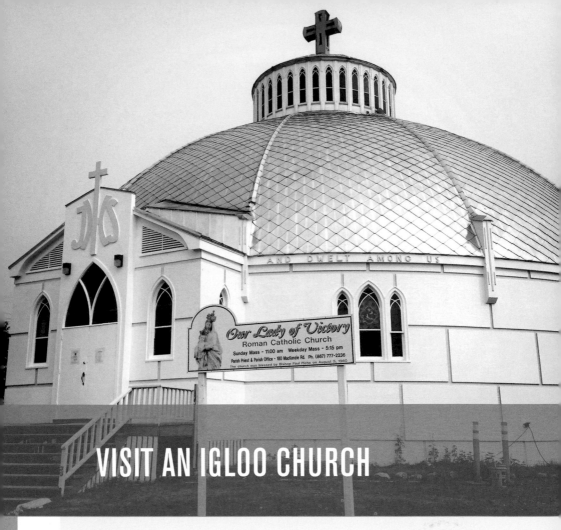

AND DWELT AMONG US

Our Lady of Victory
Roman Catholic Church
Sunday Mass - 11:00 am Weekday Mass - 5:15 pm
Parish Priest & Parish Office - 180 MacKenzie Rd. Ph. (867) 777-2236
The church was blessed by Bishop Paul Piche on August 5, 1960

VISIT AN IGLOO CHURCH

The first time I visited Europe, I suffered from church fatigue. It happens to the best of tourists, visiting one soaring cathedral after another. In Southeast Asia, they call it temple fatigue, and they also use the phrase "Same Same but Different" to describe the repetition of menus, or souvenirs, or temples. I mention this because it is exceedingly rare to encounter a church that doesn't look like any other church on earth. Such is the case with Our Lady of Victory in Inuvik, more popularly known as the Igloo Church.

Nunavut Has One, Too

In Iqaluit, it was Queen Elizabeth II who broke ground with a silver spade on a similar igloo-shaped Anglican church in 1972. Built by Inuit carpenters, St. Jude's Cathedral featured a rotund base beneath a spire and cross. In 2005, the church was destroyed by arson, although many of the interior artifacts were fortunately salvaged from the fire. After years of fundraising, the igloo church was rebuilt and opened in 2012 at a cost of eight million dollars. The Anglican Diocese of the Arctic is the largest in the world, covering an area of four million square kilometres. ➤

No, it is not made of ice.

In 1958, Inuvik was emerging atop the permafrost as the new capital of the western Arctic. The government had decided to base itself here due to its position on a stretch of flat land and sheltered from the wind. Nearby Aklavik, which actually had a local population, was considered too vulnerable to flooding in the Mackenzie Delta. The Catholic Church sent a priest from Quebec named Brother Maurice Larocque, who was inspired to build a church that reflected the arctic environment, a building that would be simple yet meaningful. A skilled carpenter, he designed the Igloo Church without a blueprint, just a guide of a few lines on a piece of plywood. Timber was boated almost 2,000 kilometres down the Mackenzie River from Fort Smith, along with gravel to create an insulation bed.

It took two years to build the striking exterior, complemented with stained-glass windows, embossing, and interior religious artwork by a young artist named Mona Thrasher. Sharing a namesake with the iconic Notre Dame cathedral in Paris, Our Lady of Victory officially opened in 1960, and today it's the most photographed attraction in town. Each Christmas, the church holds a popular concert in English, Gwich'in, and Inuvialuktun, as well as a performance from a local Filipino choir, reflecting the shifting demographics of the region. Tagalog carols in an Arctic igloo church? Now that's different.

START HERE: canadianbucketlist.com/igloochurch

NORTHWEST TERRITORIES ↑

RAFT THE NAHANNI

Hell's Gate, Deadmen Valley, Funeral Range, Headless Creek: rafting the South Nahanni River sounds lawless, wild, and untamed. It's certainly attracted its fair share of adventurers, from crusty prospectors and Pierre Trudeau to today's modern bucket lister. Awaiting all is 500 kilometres of untouched Northwest Territories, comprising vast mountain chains, 1,400-metre-high canyons, evergreen forests, and twisting waterways. It's not easy to get there: first you have to get to Yellowknife, then fly or drive to Fort Simpson, and from there charter a float plane over the Nahanni mountain range to the base of Virginia Falls. It's quite the starting

Hikeable, If Not Climbable

Beyond the rafting adventures, Nahanni National Park Reserve gives one an opportunity to hike to an imposing semicircle of peaks christened by a group of American rock climbers as the "Cirque of the Unclimbables." Granite walls 2,740 metres high dramatically face each other, forming an imposing amphitheatre. Kicking off from Glacier Lake, day-trippers to the "Unclimbables" can get dramatic views by hiking up to a viewpoint. You will also encounter Rabbitkettle Lake, the largest tufa hot springs in Canada. Incidentally, rock climbers do visit from around the world to conquer the now climbable "Unclimbables." ➤

line: a spectacular 96-metre-high waterfall, almost twice the height of Niagara Falls. Early explorers wrote how they could hear its thunder from more than 30 kilometres away. Bucket listers — as opposed to hard-core rafters, who might start much farther up the river — typically employ the services of professional raft operators who take care of the logistics, portages, cooking, and rafting. All you have to do is go along for the ride, and although you'll pass rapids (including one eight-kilometre stretch and a particular churning soup called the Figure Eight, or Hell's Gate), professional help means the excursion is manageable for virgin rafters.

Each morning of the week-long trip presents a scenic jewel, as you float with the current down a series of four spectacular canyons. Within the stunted tundra, there is also hope of spotting some northern wildlife: bears, Dall sheep, caribou, wolves. Passing through a hairpin known as Big Bend, you'll begin to encounter the more sinister aspects of the Nahanni, such as Headless Creek, where the decapitated skeletons of two prospecting brothers were found in 1908. Wrote R. M. Patterson in his seminal journals exploring the region in the late 1920s: "a country lorded over by wild mountain men ... the river fast and bad." Lured by a gold rush but forewarned of treacherous conditions, especially travelling upriver, many prospectors

perished — hence the morbid place names. All of that is in contrast to the modern experience, as you drift in a protected national park reserve recognized by UNESCO as one of its four earliest World Heritage Sites. Operators such as Nahanni River Adventures make sure their clients are well fed on gourmet snacks, dozing in the 22 hours of daily summer sunshine as the world passes by.

After travellers bathe in the Kraus Hot Springs, the rafts gradually make their way to the islands of the Nahanni Delta, an area known as the Splits or, less kindly, Bug Hell Island. The hordes of awaiting mosquitoes are legendary, rendering bug suits essential. These are mosquitoes that take to DEET like toddlers to apple juice. But they don't seem to bother the locals in the only settlement you'll see all week, the small community of Nahanni Butte. This is where most raft journeys conclude, a welcome float plane or van waiting to return tired, sunburned, bitten, and fully inspired rafters back to civilization. Budget some time to adjust after completing one of Canada's great outdoor adventures.

START HERE: canadianbucketlist.com/nahanni

And Pingo Was Its Name-O!

Bucket lists are suckers for unusual natural land formations. Atlantic Canada has its rocky flowerpots and sea arches, and western Canada its badlands hoodoos, but the North has the coolest (*ahem*) formation of them all. A pingo is a mound of frozen earth that can rise up to 70 metres high and up to 600 metres in diameter. It's also a fun word to add to your vocabulary, coming from the Inuvialuktun word for "small hill." Alaska has the world's tallest pingo, but Tuktoyaktuk, in the Mackenzie Delta, is the best place to see these frozen upside-down teacups, with 1,350 hills in the area. Pingo National Landmark protects eight of them (including Ibyuk, the world's second-tallest pingo). The pingos dominate the flat landscape here, with some being more than 1,000 years old. The Inuvialuit have traditionally used the pingos as navigational landmarks or as vantage points from which to spot animals during hunts, although, due to their fragile nature, they are protected from visitors, who are not allowed to walk on them. There is a boardwalk trail and viewing point at the Parks Canada–managed landmark site, with the pingos best accessed via boat tour (20 minutes on the Beaufort Sea from Tuktoyaktuk) or a flightseeing excursion from Inuvik. Pingo!

START HERE: canadianbucketlist.com/pingo ➤

Attend a Northern Festival

Toonik Tyme, Iqaluit
Each April, as the days finally start getting longer, Iqaluit gathers for a week of games, music, and feasting. With temperatures still well below zero, the festival brings the community together, showcasing Inuit traditions and skills. Events include sealing, igloo building, dog team races, fishing, and traditional outdoor games.

Caribou Carnival, Yellowknife
Held annually since 1955, the Caribou Carnival is a celebration of life in the North, which evolved from a trappers gathering into a spring celebration that attracts thousands of people from around the region. Catch fiddle parties, survival games, and dogsled derbies, and eat off your hangover at the pancake breakfasts.

Yukon Sourdough Rendezvous, Whitehorse
With Whitehorse enduring freezing temperatures each winter, this gold rush–inspired festival is a chance to squash the cabin fever and release some energy. Participate or support competitors at the flour-packing competition, axe toss, chainsaw chuck, and log-splitting. Wisely, there are separate activities at the Kidsfest.

Dawson City Music Festival, Dawson City

A weekend music jam in 1979 has grown into one of the highlights of the Yukon summer, drawing artists from around the country to an intimate, rollicking festival. With performances taking place in multiple venues in town, the fest features family-friendly daytime programming, a New Age market, and a Midnight Dome fun run/walk.

Folk on the Rocks Festival, Yellowknife

Billed as the biggest party under the midnight sun, Yellowknife slices into summer with twenty-four hours of cultural programming on six stages, a traditional food fair, beer garden, and kids' programs. There's a battle of the bands, free outdoor performances, and headline acts from northern and national artists.

Nunavut Arts Festival, Rankin Inlet

Celebrating the rich art and culture of Nunavut, this annual festival brings together the most talented artists from the territory's 26 incorporated communities, showcasing their talents with exhibitions, performances, and workshops.

↑

NORTHWEST TERRITORIES

HOOK A NORTHERN PIKE

Life is too short not to do what you're passionate about, which, in Carlos Gonzalez's case, is fishing, cooking, and introducing visitors from around the world to the beauty and bounty of Great Slave Lake. His log cabins rest on its shores, his boats zip about its rocky islands, and Carlos loves nothing more than catching-and-releasing the prize trophy in the world's ninth-largest lake, the great northern pike.

Great Slave (the name has nothing to do with slavery, but is attributed to the Slavey First Nation) covers an area of 27,000 square kilometres, a very big lake for very big fish. The largest of them all, sitting at the top of its underwater food chain, is the great northern pike. Dark green

Freedom on Great Slave Lake

It's certainly not the most digestible name for a lake, but you can relax: Great Slave Lake has nothing to do with slavery. *Slave*, in this case, should be pronounced *Slavey*, after the indigenous people who lived there when English explorer Samuel Hearne stumbled upon the lake in 1771. It is fed by Slave River, which should also consider adding an accurate and innocuous *y* to its name. ➤

with yellow spots, they can grow up to 1.5 metres, weigh as much as 30 kilograms, and are prized by sport fishers for their aggressive, fighting nature. With teeth as sharp as a shark's, northern pike (also known as jackfish) patrol the waters preying on trout, whitefish, and other unlucky creatures. Over the years, Carlos has seen some monsters, but he runs a strict catch-and-release operation. Such is his respect for the pike that if someone is after a trophy, he's happy to lose the revenue.

Kitted out in rain gear, we speedboat out of his base in Old Town Yellowknife. Back to the wind, Carlos manoeuvres us through the dozens of islands that dot the north arm of Great Slave. It's easy to see how treacherous these channels can be, the shallow rocks lurking beneath the waters like predators. After 45 minutes, he finds a quiet spot, hands our small group some rods, and instructs us how to cast, reel, and jerk for pike. There's no time to sit back and drink beer. We stand on one side of the boat, repeatedly casting our lines, with no bait and a single hook. Within minutes, Jason from Korea snags a beauty! "That's Emily," says Carlos, holding the fish up so Jason can pose for photographs. No sooner has he released the fish back into the water than my dad snags his first of the day, introduced by Carlos as "George." Next up is Jennifer, Samuel (my first catch), and Big Bertha, a beast of a beauty, about one metre in length. By the time we break for lunch, we have caught and released a total of eight pikes, have let a dozen get away, and are well satisfied with our accomplishments.

NORTHWEST TERRITORIES ↑

485

Fishing is only half the fun. With his background in restaurants, Carlos takes shore lunches seriously. Although he has picnic tables and firepits on various islands, we head to the comfort of the warm, fully stocked cabin for a barbecue of lake trout marinated in olive oil, basil, garlic, and lemon fusion.

"Some friends of mine amassed small fortunes and always said they'd do things when they retired, but then they started dropping dead, literally," says Carlos. What's it all for if you're not doing what you want with it? From a small fishing operation set up in 1991 to keep him busy during the summers, his Yellowknife Outdoor Adventures has grown into one of the region's top outfitters, offering aurora viewing at the cabin, snowmobile adventures, and trips to Nahanni National Park. Having moved north from Montreal 30 years ago to "escape the traffic," he's clearly enjoying himself — and so are we.

The biggest fish I've ever caught on one of the most spectacular lakes I've ever seen — now that's one for the bucket list.

START HERE: canadianbucketlist.com/pike

About Those Mosquitos

They are, among many other nuisances, Canada's dirty summer secret. *Diptera: Culicidae* is a buzz-winged, syringe-nosed space invader that attacks victims with all the tenacity of a Mongol horde (minus the civility and manners). Too small to be captured in the sweeping brochure photos of northern landscapes, mosquitoes nevertheless warrant attention because, each summer they are a topic that sits on everybody's minds (and arms, and necks, and uncovered skin).

For northerners, mosquitoes are as natural as the midnight sun or northern lights (although understandably less appreciated). As with the midnight sun or northern lights, ferocious biting insects are not something most southerners have much experience with (well, us southerners who live in large, bug-free urban centres, at least). But they are certainly a wonder of the North, as in: "I wonder how many I can kill in a single hand-clap," or, "I wonder how that mosquito managed to nonchalantly fly off after I dropped a phone book on it."

The truth is, one does make peace with the northern mosquito. We can walk out with a white flag and a big smile, and … they'll still riddle us with bite-bullets and breed on the corpses of our scabs. Still, Canadian mosquitoes are polite enough not to carry any horrible diseases like malaria. Basic mosquito precautions include long clothing and repellent or nets, although in Ivvavik National Park, I watched an Arctic mosquito bite through two layers of clothing (and a mosquito net) with all the resistance of a titanium drill entering papier mâché. A guy on that trip slathered himself in military-grade 95 percent DEET. The usual repellent brands do suffice, but this is not always the case with natural mosquito repellents. If you were to examine the mosquitoes chewing on my arm, you'd see them licking the citronella like one licks the celery-salt rim off a Caesar (both acts followed by the enthusiastic swallowing of red liquid).

But let's be serious. Bug season peaks and then settles. The initial shock of entering a cloud of bugs subsides, too. For all their annoyance, we are talking about insects that cannot stand up to a breeze. Employ common sense, basic precautions, perhaps a head net, and rest assured we can share the remarkable beauty of the Arctic wilderness with all the creatures that inhabit it — bright and beautiful, great, annoying, and small. ➤

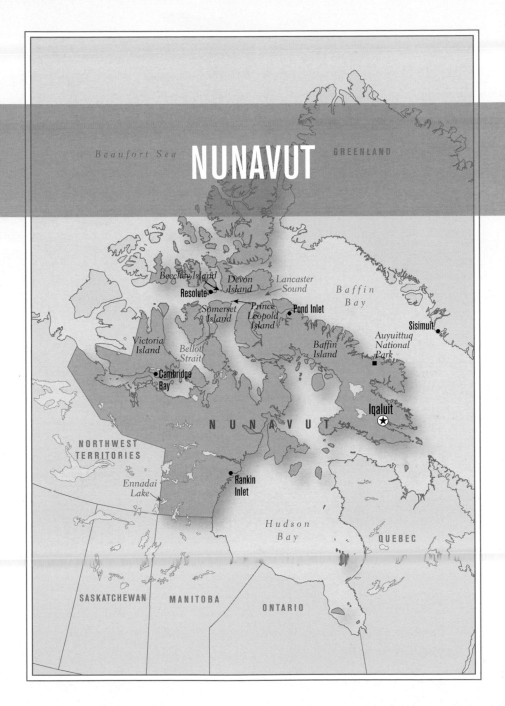

NUNAVUT

Beaufort Sea

GREENLAND

Beechey Island
Devon
Island
Lancaster
Sound
Baffin
Bay
Resolute
Somerset
Island
Prince
Leopold
Island
Pond Inlet
Sisimuit
Victoria
Island
Bellot
Strait
Baffin
Island
Auyuittuq
National
Park
Cambridge
Bay
N U N A V U T
Iqaluit
NORTHWEST
TERRITORIES
Ennadai
Lake
Rankin
Inlet
Hudson
Bay
QUEBEC
SASKATCHEWAN
MANITOBA
ONTARIO

GOING NUTS FOR NUNAVUT

Before we get to the bucket list for Nunavut, it's helpful to put a few things in perspective. There is a country in Europe called Macedonia, sometimes confused with macadamia, which is itself a type of nut. Macedonia occupies an area of roughly 25,000 square kilometres, with a population of over two million people. Somerset Island, where you'll find Arctic Watch (page 508), is roughly 25,000 square kilometres. Permanent population: zero.

Just how big is Nunavut? Well, it's bigger than the three largest mainland U.S. states — California, Texas, and Montana — combined. It's bigger than Western Europe, bigger than the secrets of the Cold War, bigger than the appetite of a wolverine. It's 1.8 million square kilometres of land, shaped like a hammer pounding into Canada's Great White North. A hammer that's bigger than Mexico and its 112 million people. Big enough to make you go macadamias.

Just 37,000 people live in "Our Land," as it is called in the Inuktitut mother tongue. If you're looking to get away from it all, you've come to the right place.

CRUISE THE NORTHWEST PASSAGE

In those Northwest Voyages
Where navigation must be executed
In exquisite sort.
— John Davis, 1594

It suspends from the roof of the world, an intricate chandelier of a frozen archipelago, illuminating the wind-burned faces of those in search of adventure. A desolate landscape of ice and rock that, nevertheless, promises wealth and glory, or, like any light burning too bright, doom for those who don't pay heed. The Northwest Passage connects Europe and Asia across the Arctic. A safe, reliable passage could double the speed and halve the cost of traditional shipping routes. Explorers of legend first sailed in search of its discovery as early as the sixteenth century, finding themselves in a forbidding and unpredictable polar wasteland, home to strange creatures, curious "natives," desolate storms, and labyrinthine icy passages trapping boats like bugs in a spider's web. It didn't stop them coming, sea-dog captains whose

NUNAVUT ↑

491

names we still recall hundreds of years later: Frobisher Bay, Davis Strait, McClintock Channel, Baffin Island, Fort Ross — legends of Arctic exploration, and yet the most famous of all has no great islands or bays named after him. Sir John Franklin even casts a shadow over the first man who successfully found his way through, the Norwegian Roald Amundsen. The fate of Franklin's expedition (see page 501) remains a mystery, the scarred and scattered bones found on several islands suggesting foul depths of human misery. Today, from the comfort of an ice-strengthened expedition ship, we can follow Franklin's footsteps, at least to the point where they fade away.

Anyone can attempt the Northwest Passage now in a manner of comfort early explorers could never have imagined. It attracts passengers from around the world, some of us here for the history, others for the landscape and wildlife. All are aware that we are embarking on a true northern adventure into an astonishing part of the world that very few people will ever see. Bundle up, bucket listers. Bring your cameras, your books, and your appetite for curiosity. The charter flight from Ottawa to Kangerlussuaq, Greenland, is taxiing down the runway. Awaiting us is One Ocean Expedition's 117-metre-long, 18-metre-wide *Akademik Sergey Vavilov*. Awaiting us is a once-in-a-lifetime Arctic adventure.

Eighty-four passengers, 66 crew, 10 Zodiacs, and almost 2,000 nautical miles to sail in 12 days if we hope to return home via

a charter flight from Cambridge Bay to Edmonton. We begin in Greenland, the world's biggest island and least densely populated country, because Franklin's final voyage passed through here, too, filling up on supplies and sending five unfit (but ultimately lucky) men home before the ships crossed Baffin Bay and promptly vanished. A thick ice-sheet blankets most of Greenland, with a small, primarily Inuit population clinging to the narrow shorelines. There is not a tree to be found anywhere, but farther up the coast, in the town of Sisimiut, it is anything but drab. Houses are painted bright colours, modern supermarkets sell fresh produce, and locals are stylishly Scandinavian, as befits a nation still officially governed by Denmark.

Life in Greenland is distinctly different from life in the Canadian Arctic, even though, culturally, the Inuit communities are similar. As we wander the town, finding healthy Icelandic horses grazing in a field of Arctic poppies and dozens of boisterous barking huskies, the passengers sniff each other out. There is a large group from the Vancouver Aquarium, media from New York and Germany, a museum director who happens to have been the last Canadian to circumnavigate North America, scientists, artists, photographers, writers, families, couples, and, of course, travellers like yourself.

More than just a cruise ship, the *Vavilov* will conduct important Arctic research, transform into a floating museum, and host presentations and exhibits that include original maps from the 1850s and relics from the *Erebus*, one of Franklin's recently discovered ships (see page 502). We are, after all, on the same vessel that was instrumental in the discovery of Franklin's flagship in September 2014. While One Ocean staff is comprised of cheery North Americans, the ship's working crew is Russian. Our rooms are basic yet comfortable, but the meals are outstanding: a Scotch bar is well stocked, fine wine will flow. There's a Finnish sauna and a hot tub on the upper deck. But if you're thinking a glitzy floating hotel can take on the Northwest Passage, think again. Due to heavy sea ice and prowling icebergs, there's no guarantee that even our expedition ship will make it. This is a journey of discovery on the icy fringes of adventure tourism. When the highlights include grave markers of dead sailors on one of the bleakest islands you can imagine, nobody is here for the tan and Jimmy Buffett's "Margaritaville."

Crossing the Davis Strait north toward Baffin Island brings monstrous 10,000-year-old icebergs, lurking for unsuspecting boat hulls and maritime disasters. We take the Zodiacs into a jigsaw puzzle of glacial ice and cruise about this frozen sculpture garden, admiring the formations and alien-blue colours, the seabirds standing guard atop each berg like sentinels. Icebergs in the shapes of sea dragons, ducks, archways, mushrooms, flowerpots, plateaus, wedges, and a five-storey crown for Poseidon's head. So many shapes, and this just the tip of a proverbial metaphor!

From the ship's bridge, a quiet, serious place that is nonetheless open to passengers, I watch the *Vavilov* cautiously push aside growlers and dense, heart-of-glacier black ice. This is an ice-strengthened vessel, not an icebreaker. Fortunately, a high-pressure zone has calmed the seas for our two-day ocean crossing. Fascinating presentations about Franklin, marine biology, and life in the Arctic and beyond keep us busy. When a polar bear is spotted on some sea ice many miles from shore, I understand why *Ursus maritimus* is classified as a marine mammal.

Beyond the staggering views and intriguing history, any Northwest Passage crossing is a journey of people — the passengers who share meals and excursions and late nights at the bar, the people of the Arctic we encounter in remote northern towns like Pond Inlet. Residents here demonstrate their sport, throat singing, dancing, and drumming, at the Cultural Centre. I ask one of them what she thinks about us tourists arriving en masse.

"It's a little like a human zoo," she tells me. "We get to see people from all over the world."

"Wait a second," I ask. "You mean, we are the ones in the cage?"

"Of course!" She laughs. The Inuit sense of humour is legendary.

Harsh realities are never too far away in the Arctic. We discover during our brief visit that a local family have been seriously injured in a tent fire. Without a resident doctor in Pond Inlet, our ship doctor, Thandi Wilkinson, rushes to help. She spends the next 12 hours frantically trying to save lives, making national news in the process, and receiving a formal letter of gratitude from the Nunavut government. Guests are more than willing to halt our itinerary and put the lives of strangers first. One Ocean's polar commitment to leave only footprints transcends environmental responsibility. It extends to Arctic communities, too.

Later, a shore excursion at Dundas Harbour on Devon Island shows us just how far those communities stretch into the past. Hiking along the coastline, we encounter the remains of an RCMP camp from the 1920s, sunken stones from 500-year-old Thule settlements, and evidence of the Dorsets, who colonized the central and eastern Arctic two millennia ago. Highlighter-orange lichen, lime-green mosses, and yellow poppies thrive in the sunshine. Light this far north has a rejuvenating quality, as if Mother Nature has just learned Photoshop. Some life, yes, but death is never far behind. The landscape becomes a rocky desert, leading up to the almost century-old graves of two RCMP offers, overlooking a barren bay. As we sail farther into Lancaster Sound, the surrounding islands exude an alien starkness. No wonder NASA tested its Mars Rover on Devon Island.

"The chewed bones of Franklin's men are rolling in the permafrost," I tell some new friends as we blissfully drink beer in *Vavilov*'s upper deck hot tub. We have just sailed past the most spectacular iceberg I've ever seen, its two blue-ice peaks shimmering, taller than the ship. The more we learn about the tribulations of early Arctic explorers, the more we become aware of the ship's comforts, from the cappuccino machine, infused cocktails, and reading lamps to the onboard massage therapist. Despite the modern technology, the GPS and radar and stabilizers, ships still sink or get grounded in the Northwest Passage. The seriousness of the officers on the bridge is reassuring, even if our Russian captain's real name, and I'm not making this up, is Captain Valeriy Beluga.

Visitors to Beechey Island feel Arctic frost pile up on their bones. The Franklin expedition overwintered on this small spit of an island, as bleak a frozen wasteland as you'd ever want to visit. Case in point: wooden grave markers where three of Franklin's men are buried. When the bodies were exhumed for study in the 1980s, the death mask of 20-year-old John Torrington made world news, giving a 12-year-old boy in South Africa nightmares. Twenty-five years later, I'm standing above the permafrost-preserved grave of Torrington, and I still can't get his blond locks, peeled eyelids, and shrunken lips out of my head. Survival suits, provided to all *Vavilov* passengers for each excursion, may be designed for the elements, but they are vulnerable to thoughts of desperate men boiling human bones to suck out the marrow. Real-life horror blows icy chills down your neck, no matter what you're wearing. We walk up the rocky beach to memorial cairns, finding rusted tins discarded from unsuccessful rescue missions. Beechey Island doesn't even feature in the atlas back in the ship's library. For those on the trail of Franklin, its significance is undeniable.

"Ah for just one time, I would take the Northwest Passage,
to find the hand of Franklin reaching for the Beaufort Sea,
Tracing one warm line through a land so wide and savage,
and make a Northwest Passage to the sea."
— Stan Rogers, "Northwest Passage" ➤

There is no web access on the *Vavilov*. No world news, no Facebook, no email. It adds to the sense of isolation, our separation from work, loved ones, and the rest of wired-up humanity. When the ship repositions alongside the imposing table-flat cliffs of Prince Leopold Island, it feels like we've entered a location in a fantasy novel. This seasonal home for hundreds of thousands of migratory birds looks as if the ghost of Jackson Pollock has splattered white streaks of guano on the almost 300-metre-high limestone cliffs.

Despite the impressive array of camera lenses on board, nobody's gotten a great picture of a whale yet. Marine mammals continue to be frustratingly scarce. Fortunately, nobody got a photo of me slipping off the outdoor stairway on the stern, either. Making my way from the hot tub to the sauna, I found myself spread-eagled on the cold metal, bruised and bashed but miraculously in one piece. It hurt to laugh, but laugh I did. Would Peary, Amundsen, or the mighty John Rae have been impressed that I'd somehow managed to clutch onto the can of Heineken? I made a joke to a nearby Russian sailor that my meat had been tenderized. Given the history of cannibalism in the Arctic, I don't think he found it funny.

If there's a climax when crossing the Northwest Passage, we find it in the Bellot Strait, a hairline fracture on a map, just under a kilometre wide at its narrowest point. Our evening crossing must be perfectly timed to stem the tide. With the Arctic sun sparkling on lake-smooth water, the Atlantic finally meets the Pacific. On our left (port side) is the northernmost point of continental North America, on the right (starboard) are the first landforms of the Arctic

Archipelago. Two polar bears swim along either side of us, cutting a triangle wake in the calm water. Seals swim up ahead and we get swept up in the moment, some of us singing with the ghost of Stan Rogers, others gratefully eating hot blueberry crumble brought to the frigid upper deck. I have cruised around the Galapagos, Antarctica, and in the Caribbean and South China Seas. Crossing the Bellot Strait under a midnight sun on a clear, icy evening is as memorable an ocean experience as one can have.

"Em, I think that bear is eating a beluga whale!"

Our Zodiacs are invading Conningham Bay on the eastern shore of Prince Edward Island (the Arctic version, not the Maritimes one). Skirting through sea ice, two large adult male bears are feasting on five baby belugas, the bears comfortable with our presence as we gently drift toward them in muted silence. Shallow waters in the bay often trap belugas when the tide recedes, resulting in a buffet for local hunters and hungry bears. A large snowy owl gazes down on us as our Zodiacs putter deeper into the bay, where we encounter more than a dozen young belugas that survived the tide. The Arctic is not the Serengeti. Animals that live north of 66 degrees are hunted, and therefore skittish. As rare as wildlife encounters may be, there's a purity in the moment, the triumph of having worked for it, even if the wind is cold enough to strip the paint off a Zamboni. A century after Amundsen, and 60 years after Canada's St. Roche found the first deep-water Northwest Passage, fewer than 300 registered ships have successfully navigated the Northwest Passage. Is our

crossing with the *Vavilov* among them? Some might argue our east-to-west passage doesn't count, that we didn't travel from Baffin Bay to the Beaufort Sea. "I think you can legitimately call it the Northwest Passage. It's nitpicking to say our trip didn't cover the critical stuff. We've done the best bits." This from the mouth of Tony Sopar, an Arctic legend who has sailed the passage eight times and written the region's bestselling guidebooks. He's aboard with us, too, along with so many wonderful people who have once again demonstrated that any passage is only as meaningful as the people you share it with. Eating the muktuk (this time, raw narwhal) that Graydon procured in Greenland, learning how to smile with my eyes from Leslie, our onboard Inuit interpreter, the Scots teaching me about Scotch, the aquarium folks about marine conservation, the photographers how to frame a good story. Everyone has a warm story to share. Canadians, Australians, Americans, Brits, Germans, Russians, and Dutch … there are cruise ships, expedition ships, battleships, and cargo ships, but every sailor worth his or her salt knows the most important of them all are friendships. Forgive me there if I went overboard with the sentimentality.

For all the history, there's murkiness when it comes to the future of the Arctic. Climate change is leading to potential ice-free summers, and with the possibility of a reliable passage revolutionizing the shipping industry, nations are sharpening their claws and planting their flags. As for the opportunity to explore the Northwest Passage onboard One Ocean's *Akademik Sergey Vavilov*? No murkiness about this one. It's a bucket list experience as clear as ice.

START HERE: canadianbucketlist.com/northwestpassage

Franklin: The Arctic's Most Enduring Mystery

It is one of the greatest and most shocking of all maritime mysteries. How did two ice-strengthened ships, captained by polar veterans and stocked with the latest and greatest in shipping technology, vanish into the ice of the Northwest Passage, with all 129 men on board? From the moment the expedition left England in May 1845, the fate of the Royal Navy bomb vessels *Erebus* and *Terror* has captured the public imagination.

Franklin, a controversial choice to command the expedition, was widely seen as being too old for the challenge ahead. His notoriety today has more to do with his wife Lady Jane Franklin's tireless efforts to learn the fate of her husband. For all their hype, the two ships did not get very far into the passage before being trapped in sea ice. Although they had enough food for three years, five with rationing, it is presumed that all the men starved to death, scattered among several islands after abandoning the ships as early as September 1846. Like victims in an Agatha Christie novel, the mysterious North picked them off one by one. Shocking initial evidence of cannibalism on skeletons were largely dismissed until proven as fact by forensic scientists as late as 2015.

Theories for the disaster abound. Thousands of tin cans of sub-par and spoiled food could have resulted in lead poisoning, starvation, disease, and mutiny. Most historians agree that the expedition suffered greatly from the British navy's arrogance about their technology and prowess, ignoring Inuit Arctic survival techniques, mucked in weak leadership, and mired in antiquated Victorian formalities. The search for Franklin resulted in many more lives and boats lost, as the Royal Navy and private expeditions wrestled with misleading and scant information, and punishing, unpredictable Arctic weather. In 1859, an expedition discovered a cairn on King William Island with a note that

£20,000
REWARD
WILL BE GIVEN BY
Her Majesty's Government
TO ANY PARTY OR PARTIES, OF ANY COUNTRY, WHO SHALL RENDER EFFICIENT
ASSISTANCE TO THE CREWS OF THE
DISCOVERY SHIPS
UNDER THE COMMAND OF
SIR JOHN FRANKLIN,

1.—To any Party or Parties who, in the judgment of the Board of Admiralty, shall discover and effectually relieve the Crews of Her Majesty's Ships "Erebus" and "Terror," the

£20,000.

OR

2.—To any Party or Parties who, in the judgment of the Board of Admiralty, shall discover and effectually relieve any of the Crews of Her Majesty's Ships "Erebus" and "Terror," or shall convey such intelligence as shall lead to the relief of such Crews or any of them, the Sum of

£10,000.

OR

3.—To any Party or Parties who, in the judgment of the Board of Admiralty, shall by virtue of his or their efforts first succeed in ascertaining their fate,

£10,000.

W. A. B. HAMILTON,
Secretary of the Admiralty.

revealed Franklin had died in June 1847, along with 23 other men. The ships had been abandoned and the men were sledging south on foot in hopes of survival. Dozens of skeletons and relics have been found since, with the *Erebus* and *Terror* finally discovered through the combined efforts of Parks Canada, the Royal Canadian Geographic Society, One Ocean Expeditions, and several other partners. Franklin's grave has never been located.

Inuit oral history told of a group of starving men pulling a boat and supplies, dying of starvation and exhaustion, and the ships then sinking.

Dr. John Rae, an exceptional Hudson's Bay Company explorer admired by the Inuit, first brought the brutal tales of cannibalism to the public's attention. An affront to high-minded British sensibilities, Rae was largely discredited and subsequently never knighted. It took years before Inuit testimonial was finally taken seriously, which led directly to the trail of bodies and eventually the sunken ships.

Despite Lady Franklin's efforts (some say to ensure her Royal Navy pension), Franklin's folly was finally pushed aside by the heroic and successful efforts of Norwegian explorer Roald Amundsen and his successful conquering of the Northwest Passage in 1906. Yet interest in the Franklin expedition never abated. Northwest Passage itineraries offered by operators like One Ocean immerse guests in the history, hardship, and ultimate triumph of Arctic naval exploration.

SEE UNICORNS FROM THE ICE FLOE

The jury is still out on why an Arctic whale sprouts a long spiral tusk more familiar from fantasy posters of unicorns. More certain is the fact that the tusk of the narwhal inspired the mythical unicorn. Some historians believe that whalers deliberately withheld information about the narwhal, a rare and prized whale found only in the Arctic, in order to increase the value and mystery of its tusk. Primarily found in males, the tusk typically extrudes from the upper left canine, and can grow up to three metres in length. Marine scientists still don't know what purpose the tusk fulfils, although it is generally believed to distinguish males for mating purposes. There is no evidence that narwhal hunt or fend off predators with the protrusions.

The trade of unicorn horn is tightly regulated in Canada and illegal in the United States, but it is perfectly acceptable and you are thoroughly encouraged to visit Pond Inlet, connect with an operator like Co-op Outfitting or Tagak Outfitting, and head out to the floe edge to see this remarkable creature in action. If the weather co-operates, it's about a two-hour snowmobile ride on the sea ice. Finding leads in the ice during the spring months, narwhal families (some of them up to 1,000 strong) swim north in search of rich marine feeding grounds. While you're in Pond Inlet, contact the local Parks Canada office to arrange a visit to the stunning glaciers and migratory bird sanctuary in Sirmilik National Park.

NUNAVUT ↑

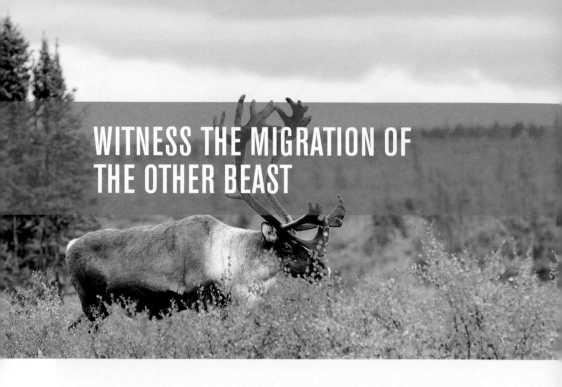

WITNESS THE MIGRATION OF THE OTHER BEAST

Just about everyone knows about the annual migration of the wildebeest in East Africa. Indeed, the largest movement of land animals on the planet is on many a bucket list. The North has its own incredible migration, although it is far less well known. Every year, hundreds of thousands of caribou migrate across the Arctic. The Porcupine caribou herd migrate between Ivvavik National Park (page 431) and the Alaska Wildlife Reserve, while the Beverly and Qamanirjuaq herd migrate north to south on the Barren Lands west of Hudson Bay. Much like the great wildebeest trek between the Masai Mara and Serengeti, the sheer volume of one species attracts volumes of others. In the case of the Arctic, this includes some of the most elusive creatures on a wildlife lover's checklist: wolves and wolverines.

Arctic Haven is a remote lodge located at the treeline on the 84-kilometre-long Ennadai Lake, one of the great lakes in Nunavut's

was refashioned as a wildlife station in 2013, allowing visitors to finally witness the remarkable caribou migration. Each spring and fall, up to 300,000 caribou migrate along the eskers and lakes of the Barren Lands, directly in the path of the post-and-beam lodge. There are activities for both warmer and cooler weather, including snowmobiling, dogsledding, tundra hiking, boating, kite skiing, and fishing for trophy-sized lake trout, northern pike, and grayling. If luck is on your side, it's also a great spot to see the northern lights.

Ennadai Lake was the original home and hunting grounds of the Ahiarmiut people, who were forced to relocate by the government in 1949. Today, the lodge is partly owned by a pair of Nunavut entrepreneurs, and respect for the environment and landscape is impressive (the entire lodge is solar-powered). One doesn't expect gourmet meals, hot showers, wine, and Wi-Fi connections in the Arctic wilderness. Given the location, you can expect to pay what you would for a luxury safari lodge in the Serengeti. What you walk away with, on the other hand, is a one-of-a-kind wildlife and wilderness experience, guaranteed to blow the Tilley hat off of even the most experienced safari nut.

START HERE: canadianbucketlist.com/arctichaven

NUNAVUT

VISIT A NORSE GOD

Thor, the powerful god of Thunder (lately a hunky blond super-hero sharing screen time with the Hulk, Captain America, and Iron Man) has traditionally wielded his mighty hammer in the mythical kingdom of Asgard. What if I were to tell you that both Thor and Asgard are located in "a land that never melts" right here in Canada? Auyuittuq was the first national park established in Nunavut, located on the east coast of Baffin Island. Carved by glaciers, some 85 percent of the park consists of rock and ice, a stark landscape that nevertheless attracts hikers and climbers from around the world. Each summer, with its proximity to Iqaluit, Auyuittuq becomes the most accessible park in Nunavut, and, therefore, its most affordable.

Sorry, Darling, England Needs Me

It was the most expensive stunt of its time, and perhaps the most daring opening sequence for a Bond film ever. In *The Spy Who Loved Me*, Roger Moore leaves a beautiful double-crossing blond agent in a remote ski cabin. Suddenly, half a dozen armed bad guys are chasing him in a thrilling ski chase, their bullets somehow missing Bond's eighties yellow jumpsuit. They corner him down on the edge of an enormous cliff. Bond skis right off the lip, the music pausing, along with our breaths, for a long twenty seconds. Finally, Bond opens a Union Jack parachute (of course), and the iconic James Bond theme kicks in on all cylinders. A close-up of Roger Moore, clearly against a studio backdrop, has him looking quite unperturbed. Stuntman Rick Sylvester successfully performed the ski/base jump stunt off Mount Asgard in what is now Auyuittuq National Park. Only James Bond can ski downhill for three minutes and arrive at the top of a mountain. ➤

The star attraction is undoubtedly Thor Peak, the highest uninterrupted rock face on Earth. Looming over the Weasel River Valley, Thor reduces its visitors to mere specks on the landscape. We are mortals in the presence of a geological wonder, an awe-inspiring granite god of the natural world. If you hike farther along the Akshayuk Pass, you will stumble beneath the twin shadows of mighty Mount Asgard, two imposing cylindrical towers of granite separated by a saddle. If the God of Thunder existed beyond cartoon panels and summer blockbusters, Mount Asgard would be the perfect spot for him to live.

START HERE: canadianbucketlist.com/auyuittuq

NUNAVUT

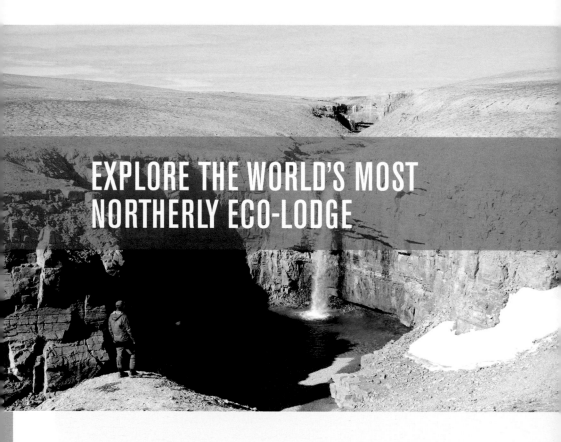

EXPLORE THE WORLD'S MOST NORTHERLY ECO-LODGE

Arctic Sunwest Charters' de Havilland Dash 8 takes off from Yellowknife on the 1,500-kilometre journey north into the neighbouring territory of Nunavut. On board are tourists from Connecticut, New Mexico, Scotland, New York, and California, along with a group of Canadian geologists and some marine scientists from Mystic Aquarium. Our destination is Arctic Watch, a unique beluga whale observation post and eco-lodge located 800 kilometres north of the Arctic Circle.

As a launch pad for a once-in-a-lifetime Arctic safari, the Watch boasts several attractions: the most comfortable remote facilities in the High Arctic (private tented cabins, gourmet meals, internet), a

variety of tundra toys, an impeccable location, and the fact that it is owned and operated by Richard Weber and his family. Weber is the most travelled North Pole explorer on the planet, the first man to trek to the North Pole six times, including unsupported expeditions that have never been equalled. His wife, Josée, has led six expeditions herself, and both have also trekked to the South Pole (Richard kite-sledded out). Both sons are in the business as well: Tessum holds the distinction of being the youngest person to trek to the North Pole, while Nansen is an accomplished wildlife photographer. These are people who live and love the Arctic, sharing this passion with others at their summer camp overlooking the purple inlet of the Cunningham River. During the short summer months, when the sun burns 24 hours a day, a charter flight lands once a week on the tundra runway. It switches over the week's guests, bringing with it a load of fresh food and supplies. I'm as north as I've ever been, nigh an elf toss from Santa. The desolate tundra looks like the moon, and fittingly, a moon buggy is waiting to greet us.

WATCH BELUGAS PLAY AT YOUR FEET

Arctic Watch's new arrivals pile into the back of a bright-yellow Unimog, a 50-year-old four-by-four truck that somehow weathers one of the harshest climates on the planet. It's a short drive to the lodge, comprising a large dome-shaped communal dining tent, bathrooms, hot showers, a fully equipped restaurant-grade kitchen, and an equipment room. Individual living quarters, with double beds, sinks, and marine toilets, sit outside like adjacent milk chocolate Hershey kisses. Every summer, up to 2,000 beluga whales gather at the mouth of the Cunningham River for a natural body wash and to feed on rich nutrients in the flowing Arctic meltwaters. We excitedly put on rubber boots and walk over the rock and estuaries to the river mouth, drawn to the water boiling with life up ahead.

We're in luck: ice at the mouth of the inlet has finally cleared and the whales have arrived, hundreds of them, arching their backs, popping their heads out of the water, rolling and rubbing their bodies on the gravel below. Belugas, among the most social of all whales, cackle and chirp with delight as marine scientists tell us their exfoliating gravel skin rub is actually pleasurable. I can almost hear David Attenborough's voice narrating the phenomenon of these Arctic ghosts, and you can if you watch BBC's *Frozen Planet*, which filmed a beluga segment right here at Arctic Watch. Fittingly, it turns out that two of the guys on my plane are actually BBC nature filmmakers. I love nature documentaries and often wonder: "Where in the world is that?" What a remarkable feeling when you realize that it is right in front of you.

SLEEP UNDER THE MIDNIGHT SUN

Considering the nearest grocery store is 1,500 kilometres away, chef Jeff Stewart and the staff at Arctic Watch serve up magnificent fare: roast lamb, braised ribs, pickled Arctic char, adobo chicken, butter-smooth tenderloin, fresh salads, and vegetables. There is homemade bread, mayonnaise, and yogourt. Much like my experience at Skoki Lodge in Banff, I'm eating like royalty in the wilderness.

We're introduced to the Webers – doyens of the Canadian Arctic — and their young, attractive staff. It's easy to make yourself at home when it feels like a home, complete with Josée, the nurturing mom. Our groups span a wide range of ages (eight to 70) and interests (birders, scientists, hikers, photographers), and Arctic Watch does its best to make sure everyone is accommodated. We're chatting in the main lodge, getting to know one another, when I make two rather dumb comments:

What not to say in the High Arctic summer, Part 1: **Damn, I just realized I forgot my headlamp!**

What not to say in the High Arctic summer, Part 2: **Wow, we're so remote, the stars are going to be epic tonight!**

ON THE BUCKET LIST: David Suzuki

You should visit Pond Inlet, Nunavut, have an Inuit guide take you on the ice floe. I couldn't believe it, there were narwhal everywhere! When we got back, there were polar bear prints right through our camp.

David Suzuki
Science Broadcaster,
Environmentalist

There are no stars, of course, for the same reason I won't need to worry about a flashlight. This far north, the sun wheels across the sky, roughly 15 degrees every 15 minutes. It never sets, and so the sky never gets so much as mildly dusky. The midnight sun is disorienting but energizing. Still, with the white fabric of our sleeping tents, I quickly realize:

What not to say in the High Arctic summer, Part 3: "I forgot my eye mask!"

The comfortable beds have heavy duvets and warm fleece sheets. Yet high winds shake the tents, and polar bears stalk my dreams. I awake constantly on my first night, panicking that I've overslept for the morning's activities. It's okay, it's only 2 a.m., bright as day. Sleeping without night is an early afternoon nap that never ends.

SWIM IN AN ARCTIC WATERFALL

Tessum Weber greets me with a freshly made cappuccino in the morning. Each day, the youngest man to trek to the North Pole is my personal barista. After a hearty breakfast, we go for a walk to some local waterfalls. The tundra is sweeping, a desert of shale skipping stones and crushed limestone — desert, that is, were it not for the bright blue streams, mineralized with rock flour into shades of green and turquoise. The local waterfall is a 15-metre beauty, surrounded by sharp-cut canyon walls. Farther up, a series of smaller but just as striking cascades invite a swim. If God put us on Earth to endure supermarket lineups and mortgages, he wanted us to take Arctic waterfall showers, too.

I strip down and take a refreshing dip in water pure enough to bottle and sell to Fiji. Thanks to warming temperatures and shrinking Arctic ice, mosquitoes have invaded the island for the first time. They're as big as oil rigs and ready to drill, but fortunately, their small numbers are nothing compared with bug net hell down south.

We continue our walk, familiarizing ourselves with the landscape. Although the island is covered in a sheet of ice for much of the year, life stubbornly resists in the form of small plants, flowers, and white candy balls of Arctic cotton. We walk through a valley, giving a wide berth to a sandpiper protecting her nest. A hot lunch awaits, the ATVs are fuelled, and there just might be a larger form of life lurking 16 kilometres away, at Polar Bear Point.

ATV TO ICEBERGS AND ANCIENT RUINS

The Watch is as small as a poppy seed on a basketball court. To get around, we need the Unimog, rafts, and tough ATVs built for such terrain. I salute our opposable thumbs, which gave humanity the dexterity to evolve beyond the apes, build tools, text message, and accelerate on ATVs.

We drive up along the coast, crossing streams and crunching rocks, past an old scientific observation cabin and slowly toward the famed Northwest Passage. The path is lined by inukshuks, piled stones used by Inuit for millennia as a form of communication and guidance. The stone guardians ensure we are travelling in the right direction. In the distance are icebergs, along with floating crusts of slowly melting sea ice.

Tessum stops off at a small circular mound of rocks, explaining that these are the archaeological remains of 1,000-year-old Thule hunting stations. Dozens of similar stations line the coast, where Inuit ancestors hunted whales and seals. We can still see the heavy bones of bowhead and beluga whales. I tell Tessum I've seen UNESCO World Heritage Site status awarded for less, but he says such remains are fairly common up the coast, where many of the stations have not been excavated.

We continue to the point, racing along the beach, slaloming between beached chunks of ice. Two large icebergs are drifting just off shore. We stop to observe the ice, hopping between the giant floating slabs. Steve from Santa Fe spots something through his binoculars, and sure enough, it's a polar bear. One of the staff always carries a rifle, just in case, and we're given bear spray in case we decide to wander off. But since the lodge opened in 2000, there has never been any problem with the bears. In fact, in all of Richard Weber's expeditions to the North Pole, he has never even seen a bear, although he has come across their tracks. They're out here, but with this much space, no two species have to cramp each other's style.

HIKE IN THE TUNDRA

Eight thousand years ago, the vast plains of the tundra that buttress Cunningham Inlet were under the sea. We can see this as we hike among the fossils and shells on its distinctly seabed landscape. Once past the rocks that have been gathered downstream by the river, the ground becomes soft and spongy with moss, sprouting tufts of grass like hair on the face of a teenage boy. A finger-thick branch of Arctic willow, growing low to the soil, might be a century old. Only the hardiest of life can survive here. Alpine sorrel (with leaves that taste like strawberry), Arctic poppies, and glossy yellow buttercups whisper a fragile beauty in this unforgiving starkness.

We hike along the blue river that cuts through Gull Canyon, spotting boisterous Arctic hares on the mossy green slopes. There's no need to carry a water bottle; we simply drink from the streams. Mucks, the insulated rubber boot of choice at Arctic Watch, prove invaluable across this terrain. At one point, they magically keep water

NUNAVUT ↑

Five Arctic Creatures that Turn White for Winter

For greater warmth and protection against predators, animals in the Arctic go through a remarkable transformation in the winter.

Arctic hare: brown and black during summer months
ermine: world's smallest weasel flips brown to white
Arctic fox: nature's most northerly fox is brown-grey in summer
barren ground caribou: predominantly brown in summer, predominantly white in winter
rock ptarmigan: moults brown to white in winter, keeping its brown or black tail

out after a river crossing that went up to my knees. I haven't had such appreciation for a product since I discovered the iPod.

We walk to Sunday Lake ("because we used to visit here on Sundays," explains Josée) across a badlands landscape, discovering the scattered remains of bowhead whales miles inshore. Arctic fox cubs were spotted in a nearby den a few weeks ago, but today it is abandoned. The white skull of a baby fox on the tundra is a reminder that life is tough in the wild, and only the strongest survive. We walk past more bones. "Members of the Franklin expedition?" I joke, recalling the ill-fated British mission to discover the Northwest Passage, a mission that scattered the frozen, scurvy-ridden, and emaciated remains of 129 men throughout the region (see page 501).

A strong, biting breeze is picking up, so we return to the Watch, appreciating the hot roasted veggies and sweet desserts more than ever. Some primeval instinct has given me a huge appetite, as if it expects no further supply planes to arrive.

PADDLE A CRYSTAL CLEAR ARCTIC STREAM

Canada is baking in a mid-July heat wave, but the Arctic turns on us. Gale force winds rock our tents and stinging rain attacks the windows of the lodge as the temperature plummets and snow begins to fall. We huddle up in the lodge with coffee and hot chocolate as the Mystic marine scientists give a presentation about beluga behaviour and Richard Weber takes us on a journey to the North Pole.

For his pioneering work as a polar explorer and conservationist, Richard has received numerous awards and honours, most recently the Order of Canada. Listening to tales of Richard's military-like preparation and experience is fascinating, a battle against the harshest elements on the planet. The keys to his success are efficiency, the right caloric intake, correct walking distances, body-fat ratio, gear, equipment, and attitude. His words are efficient, too, an Arctic general with no time or energy to waste.

Next up, Jeff Turner and Justin Maguire show us an Attenborough-narrated BBC documentary they filmed in British Columbia. They captured wolves attacking a grizzly and spent months waiting for those jaw-dropping shots you see on TV. One guest is a bestselling photographer, another a bond trader obsessed with great migrations. Everyone is having a bucket list sort of week.

Although it's still chilly and grey, by the following day, the weather has softened enough to allow us to head upstream on the Unimog to meet river rafts and a kayak. The river is as smooth as glass, so after a lunch in the field (heartwarming borscht), I hop in the kayak with a Belarusian named Rus and expertly snap the steering pedal. We head over some gentle rapids backwards, but the current is generous and smooth, and so, straightening up, it shepherds us along the canyon under the watchful gaze of a rough-legged hawk. The others follow us in the rafts, berthing on the gravel after someone spots a muskox. Although they've been hunted for their fur and meat, today we stalk these shaggy beasts of the tundra with our cameras.

With another storm blowing in, we retreat to base, where the brave decide to bear the icy winds to spend more time with the belugas. I opt for beluga-shaped ice cubes in a glass of Iceberg vodka with a teaspoon of honey. It keeps the Arctic chill at bay.

FISH FOR ARCTIC CHAR

Freezing rain or shine, there is one day left in our Arctic Watch adventure to head deeper into the tundra, on rugged Bombardier all-terrain vehicles. I've ridden ATVs before, but never on a landscape so complementary to their capabilities: muddy, rocky, wet, no trees for thousands of kilometres. Warned never to underestimate the Arctic, I layered up to the point of absurdity (three pairs of socks, two layers of merino wool long underwear). Our destination, Inukshuk Lake, is a three-hour ride away, where we will pull out rods and attempt to catch some tasty Arctic char. Similar to salmon, Arctic char is lighter, whiter, and rarer to find on your plate.

Just minutes outside the Watch, I'm once again feeling the isolation, desolation, and striking beauty of the tundra. We cross rivers and estuaries, and ride on the spines of ridges, even as a light snow begins to fall. Tessum stops up ahead and points out two muskoxen in the valley below. They appear to be running toward us, disappearing on the slope before popping up 30 metres away. They're not snorting or stamping their feet, but it's unusual for these huge Arctic creatures to get so close. They trot along onto the path in front of us, and for the next 10 minutes, they clear our way, like squad cars leading a motorcade. Finally, they vanish into a valley below, leaving us elated from the encounter.

After roller-coastering up and down muddy banks and rocky hills, we arrive at the lake. Low cloud hovers on the hills, draining all colour from the landscape. Then the sun breaks through for a moment, pouring turquoise dye into the water. Sven (Arctic Watch's shaggy-haired handyman) and Tessum prepare the rods, and after soup, sandwiches, and coffee, we're casting our lines from the shore. Landlocked char grow slowly, and a strict quota is in place. Our goal is to catch four medium-sized fish for the kitchen and catch-and-release the rest. It's Sven who reels in the first couple of char. As for me, let's just say if you teach this man to fish, he's still not going to catch anything.

On the long ride back (when did you last spend six hours on an ATV?), with my right thumb on the throttle, I find myself zoning out. Life seems very simple: get back to the warmth of the Watch, eat, survive. This is the way of the Arctic north.

Considering its size, I explored but a fraction's fraction of Nunavut. I did not get the opportunity to spend time with its Inuit people or visit their towns and settlements. Yet as small as my Arctic dosage was, it was in the company of people who love it, explore it, and are devoted to introducing us southerners to its wonders. Nunavut before you die? You'd be a macadamia not to.

START HERE: canadianbucketlist.com/arcticwatch

Beaufort Sea

ALASKA

Somerset
Island

Victoria
Island

NUNAVUT

YUKON

Dempster
Highway

Kluane
National
Park

⊛ Whitehorse

Great
Bear
Lake

NORTHWEST
TERRITORIES

Virginia Falls
South Nahanni River
Nahanni
Butte

Great Slave
Lake

⊛ Yellowknife

Wood Buffalo
National Park

Great Bear
Rainforest

Haida
Gwaii

Athabasca Sand Dunes
Provincial Wilderness Park

PACIFIC
OCEAN

BRITISH
COLUMBIA

ALBERTA

SASKATCHEWAN

MANITOBA

Vancouver
Island

Jasper National Park

Icefields
Parkway

Banff National Parkt

● Calgary

⊛ Edmonton

Prince Albert
National Park

Lake
Winnipeg

● Vancouver

Okanagan

● Saskatoon

Bloodvein
River

⊛ Victoria

Porcupine
Hills

● Regina

Lake
Manitoba

Grasslands
National Park

Winnipeg ⊛

UNITED STATES

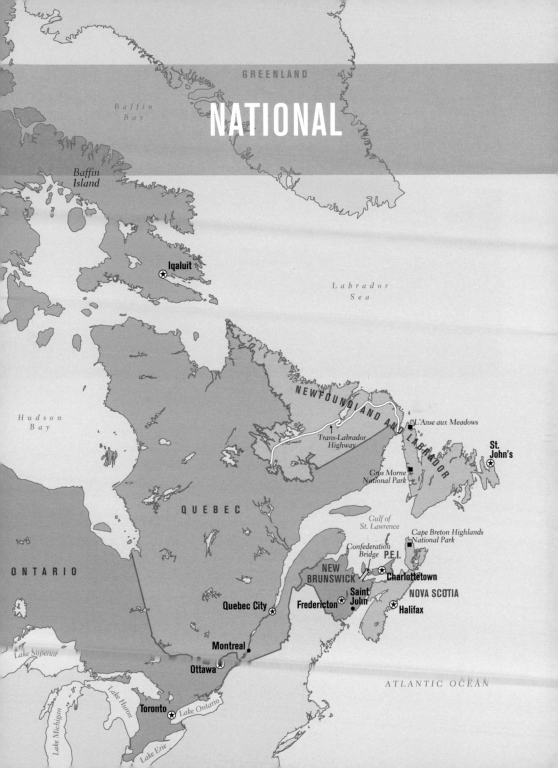

NATIONAL

GREENLAND

Baffin Bay

Baffin Island

Iqaluit ✪

Labrador Sea

Hudson Bay

NEWFOUNDLAND AND LABRADOR

L'Anse aux Meadows

Trans-Labrador Highway

St. John's ✪

Gros Morne National Park

QUEBEC

Gulf of St. Lawrence

Cape Breton Highlands National Park

ONTARIO

Confederation Bridge

P.E.I.

NEW BRUNSWICK

Charlottetown ✪

Quebec City ✪

Fredericton

Saint John

NOVA SCOTIA

Halifax

Montreal

Ottawa ✪

Lake Superior

Lake Huron

Toronto ✪

Lake Ontario

Lake Michigan

Lake Erie

ATLANTIC OCEAN

SEE CANADA FROM THE *CANADIAN*

I've been fortunate to experience some of the world's great, and not so great, train journeys. The Trans-Siberian, the Trans-Mongolian, the Tazara from Zambia to Dar es Salaam, Tanzania. Trains across Croatia, Poland, and Hungary. Trains through Western Europe and India. I find long train journeys a pleasant mode of transport — far less stressful than driving, far more comfortable than buses, much slower than airplanes but with the benefit of actually seeing something other than the seat in front of you. VIA Rail's *Canadian* is a 4,466-kilometre journey that slices the country from east to west, and vice versa. The four-night, three-day passage is rightly regarded as one of the world's great train voyages, and if people from around the world are boarding, it certainly demands investigation for the bucket list.

It's 8 p.m. on a Friday night in June at Pacific Central Station in Vancouver. My wife and I arrive in a typical West Coast downpour,

the summer determined to hide no matter how much everyone seeks it. Like other passengers in the waiting room, we each have a carry-on piece of luggage, with larger items checked in along with pets, bikes, and equipment. We're shown to our Touring Class cabin, which features two bunks, a basin, storage, and a toilet. The two classes of sleeping cars are named after English settlers or French explorers. Car 213 is called Bliss Manor, not for the state of mind it will later induce but for a commissary in the Revolutionary War and New Brunswick settler named Daniel Bliss.

This week's configuration of the *Canadian* consists of 21 cars, which measure a total of 644 metres long and together weigh 1,540 tons. We have two engine machines: one to pull the train and one to power the cars. Configurations might vary depending on demand, but expect panoramic-view cars and double-storey domed viewing cars, dining cars, activity cars, and a wonderfully retro Park Car at the back, complete with a bar and view of the tracks left behind. The showers and toilets are clean, the food outstanding, and activity coordinators hold beer and wine tastings, movies, games, and interpretation sessions. During the 11 days I spent on a train in Russia, I could only have dreamt of such facilities and services, confined as I was to a sleeper car with stale noodles, dirty washrooms, and rough attendants showing all the hospitality of aggravated vampire bats.

Despite many renovations over the years, VIA Rail's cars still carry the pastel colours, industrial carpets, stainless steel, and boxiness of the 1950s glory days, before airfares were affordable and the Trans-Canada Highway was complete. The cross-country journey was

initially offered by two competing railway companies on Canadian Pacific Railway's *Canadian* and Canadian National Railway's *Super Continental*. As passenger numbers declined, Canadian Pacific Railway (CPR) hoped to discontinue the service, forcing the federal government to take over with its VIA Rail Crown corporation. In 1990, the train moved from the CPR route through Calgary and Regina to the CN route via Edmonton and Saskatoon. While trainspotters will no doubt love all this information, my wife and I were simply looking forward to some quality time together, enjoying the soporific effect of the world passing us by and the opportunity to see Canada's landscape transform before our eyes.

It takes a night or two to get used to sleeping on a train — the rocking, the sounds, the feeling of hurtling forward at 130 kilometres per hour with your eyes closed. I wake up shortly before dawn to find the tracks running alongside semi-arid cliffs and a swollen Thompson River. Heavy rains have resulted in the river breaching its banks in some areas, and the water level seems alarmingly high. As dawn breaks, an American tourist, enthusiastically taking photos out the front of the dome car, joins me. We high-five like kids after skirting a particularly steep cliff and when exiting especially long and dark tunnels.

I return to the cabin for a few hours of sleep and wake for an excellent breakfast (crab hollandaise eggs Benedict) and a day touring through the most dramatic part of the journey: the Coastal Range, Selkirks, and Canadian Rockies. It's my third visit to the Rockies this year, but the expressions on the faces of my fellow passengers remind me of the impact these mountains have on those from afar. The viewing cars come into their own.

In the course of its journey, the *Canadian* will make 10 major stops for servicing and changing of crew and engineers. Additional stops take place in small towns such as Clearwater, B.C., Unity, Saskatchewan, and Winnitoba, Manitoba, if there are passengers or cargo to service. Stops range from 15 minutes to stretch your legs on a dusty platform to an hour or more to explore the town of Jasper or the Forks in Winnipeg. With a good book, a bottle of wine, a comfortable bed, tons of writing to do, and a lovely wife to spend time with, I never feel bored. The only responsibility we have is to show up for the three daily meals in the dining car. Time on a train is time in movement, literally barrelling through boreal forests, mountains and prairies. Just to prove its time is so malleable, the Canadian goes through four time zones. And yet everything runs like clockwork. The attendants are helpful and friendly, the meals consistently excellent and varied (rosemary lamb chops, pan seared scallops, quinoa

salad with goat cheese). Crossing Siberia, all I had to feast on was cheap instant noodles, cheaper vodka, and a never-changing landscape of farmland.

Out our window, we see the world in perpetual green motion blur, forest and fields punctuated by urban development, marshes, or copper-brown lakes reflecting Simpsonesque clouds against a sunny blue sky. When we step outside in Hornepayne, Ontario, we're attacked by blackflies; gratefully, they cannot penetrate the heavy steel doors of our comfortable air-conditioned bubble. Occasionally the attendants will announce a moose or bear sighting, the animals visible only for the briefest of moments. From time to time, I spot trucks and cars on the Trans-Canada Highway, and I feel fortunate I can pass them without having to keep my eyes on the road. Wherever they're going, we're Canadians on the move inside the *Canadian*, perpetually on the move, too.

As I write these words in the activity car, a lady opposite me begins to chat. She's come up from Florida with her husband, and together they've been overwhelmed by the size, beauty, and nature of the Canada we have experienced outside the window. I ask her why, of all the options available to them, they decided to hop on board the *Canadian*.

"Travel by train lets you actually see a country," she says. "Really, this should be on everyone's bucket list."

She has no idea just how much I agree with her.

START HERE: canadianbucketlist.com/Canadian

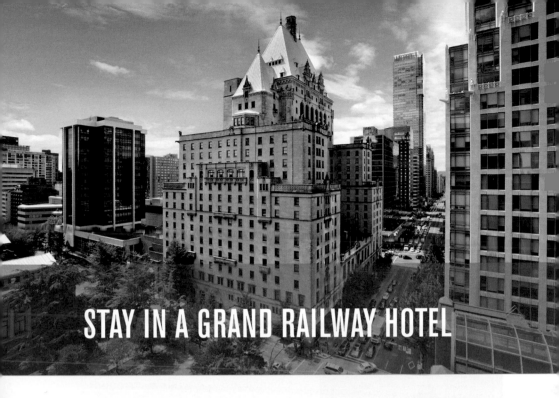

STAY IN A GRAND RAILWAY HOTEL

With the completion of the Grand Pacific Railway in 1885, Canada opened up to the masses. The challenge facing the rail companies: how to incentivize settlers, generate revenue, and get tourists on board. The solution was as ambitious as the railway itself: build opulent, luxury castle-like hotels to spike interest. For the first time, Canada was marketed abroad as an outdoor-lover's paradise, and for the first time, the Rockies were seen as a holiday destination as opposed to barriers to settlement. Paying homage to the design of Scottish castles and French chateaus, turreted hotels sprouted in the mountains as well as key urban centres along railway routes. Over the years, several hotels burned down or were demolished. Today, Canada's remaining grand railway hotels are treasured national landmarks and continue to transport celebrities, royalty, head of states and everyday bucket listers to a storied era of old-world luxury charm.

- **The Empress (Victoria):** Opened in 1908; high tea overlooking the Inner Harbour is a Victoria must.
- **The Fairmont Hotel Vancouver:** Opened in 1888; enjoy cocktails in the people-watching piano bar.
- **The Fairmont Banff Springs:** Opened in 1888; soak in the mineral hot springs of the stunning Willow Stream spa.
- **The Fairmont Chateau Lake Louise:** Opened in 1911; explore the Mountain Adventure Program for unique all-season activities.
- **The Fairmont Jasper Park Lodge:** Opened in 1922; wildlife surrounds the lodge and its acclaimed Stanley Thomson golf course.
- **The Fairmont Palliser Calgary:** Opened in 1914, watch the Stampede Parade from Calgary's oldest hotel.
- **The Fairmont Hotel Macdonald Edmonton:** Opened in 1915 with architecture inspired by six-teenth-century French castles.
- **The Bessborough (Saskatoon):** Opened in 1935; the city's best-known landmark was modelled on a Bavarian castle.
- **The Hotel Saskatchewan (Regina):** Opened in 1927 as a tow-ering, less ostentatious landmark to reflect more modern tastes.

- **The Fort Garry Hotel (Winnipeg):** Opened in 1913 one block from Union Station as the city's premier hotel.
- **The Fairmont Royal York (Toronto):** Opened in 1929 on Front Street, it continues to host the Queen during state visits.
- **Fairmont Chateau Laurier (Ottawa):** Opened in 1912, the Château overlooks Parliament and the Rideau Canal.
- **Fairmont Le Chateau Frontenac (Quebec City):** Opened in 1893, it dominates the city's skyline with sweeping views of the St. Lawrence River.
- **The Westin Nova Scotian (Halifax):** Opened in 1930, this was CNR's answer to rival CPR's Lord Nelson Hotel.

SHOP THE COUNTRY'S BEST URBAN MARKETS

Granville Island Market, Vancouver: In the 1970s, a former industrial site was transformed into one of Vancouver's most popular tourist attractions. Overlooking False Creek, the island features a busy food market, art galleries, an eponymous microbrewery, boutique distilleries, flashy restaurants, two theatres, various bars, a hotel, a water park, and gift shops. There are more than 300 stores, with the toy-like Aquabus ferrying visitors along the creek. Stroll around the market for fine cheeses, chocolates, fruit, baked goods, condiments, and artisan gifts. Listen to buskers while you have a snack on the outdoor deck (but watch out for the turkey-sized gulls!) For a harbour adventure, hire a motorboat, or rent a stand-up

paddleboard or a kayak. Little ones will lose their marbles inside the Kids' Market, which has a four-level indoor Adventure Zone and an old-fashioned arcade.

St. Lawrence Market, Toronto: *National Geographic* once called the St. Lawrence Market "the world's best food market." Toronto's largest indoor market has been located on Front Street for more than two centuries, although portions of the buildings were destroyed by fire and rebuilt. The two-storey South Market has more than 120 specialty vendors, with fresh produce, meat, fish, baked goods, and artisan cheese. You'll also find various restaurants and cafés. Retail businesses are located in the St. Lawrence Hall, where you can also find exhibitions, concerts, and rental space. The market is a short distance from other Toronto must-do's, and is well serviced by buses and streetcars.

ByWard Market, Ottawa: Conveniently located close to Ottawa's primo attractions (Parliament! The Rideau Canal! The National Gallery!), ByWard gets its unusual spelling from the area's original surveyor, John By, and the ward in which the market was located. Attracting some 50,000 people each summer weekend, the original market building has produce and retail stores surrounded by boutiques, restaurants, galleries, and gift shops. Open-air vendors sprout up on George and

NATIONAL ↑

York Streets, too, and buskers add to the lively atmosphere. Don't miss the warm, sweet Beaver Tails on the corner of George and William, the fine coffee at various establishments, the Obama-inspired baked goods at Moulin de Provence, and a taster flight at the Clocktower or Lowertown craft breweries.

The Forks, Winnipeg: There are several terrific urban markets in the Prairies — Saskatoon's and Regina's farmers' markets come to mind — but only one of them has 6,000 years of Aboriginal history and is a National Historic Site to boot. The area at the confluence of the mighty Assiniboine and Red Rivers once attracted hunters, traders, pioneers, and settlers. Today, tourists hunt for souvenirs and locals gather up gourmet treats. There's a theatre, children's museum, boutique hotel, and a provincial tourism exhibit. It's also just a short walk from the Canadian Museum for Human Rights (see page 192). When the Assiniboine River freezes over in winter, out come the skating trails, Olympic-sized rink, and the popular RAW:almond, a pop-up restaurant. Parks Canada operates an adjacent area with walking trails, a prairie garden, outdoor amphitheatre, and canoe beach. The Oodena Celebration Circle, with its eight steel arms pointing toward specific constellations, is another highlight for visitors.

TAKE AN EPIC CANADIAN ROAD TRIP

Wide, open roads, beautiful scenery, charming towns — road trips take us to places we'd otherwise miss, connecting us to the power of the journey itself. We've already looked at the stunning Icefields Parkway (page 84), the Dempster Highway (page 439), the Cabot Trail (page 354), and the Trans-Labrador Highway (page 415). Here are several more routes to put on your bucket list.

Sea to Sky Highway, B.C.: A stunning 133-kilometre drive on Highway 99 takes you from Vancouver to Whistler (although it's strongly suggested to tack on the additional 130 kilometres and continue to Lillooet). Trace the curvaceous coastline of North America's most southerly fjord, packing in scenic showstoppers like Shannon Falls, views of the Tantalus Range, and Paradise Valley. Stop at Brackendale Eagles Provincial Park to see the largest congregation of wintering bald eagles, Squamish for the gondola, and Whistler for the year-round attractions.

Viking Trail, Newfoundland and Labrador: The largest themed road trip in Newfoundland and Labrador, the Viking Trail cuts from the west coast of Newfoundland through to southern Labrador, with two UNESCO World Heritage Sites (and bucket list attractions) along the way. Gros Morne National Park and L'Anse aux Meadows National Historic Site are natural highlights, but don't drive past Arches Provincial Park without stopping, and spend time in the vibrant coastal communities of Rocky Harbour, Woody Point, or Cow Head. Fishing along the Viking Trail is legendary, too.

Alaska Highway, Yukon: Built during World War II to transport U.S. soldiers to bases in Alaska, this epic road (also known as the ALCAN Highway) begins in Dawson Creek, B.C., running north for over 2,000 kilometres to Delta Junction, Alaska. Although its length and remoteness can be challenging, the highway itself is in relatively good shape, paved all the way with occasional potholes or construction due to constant upgrading. Weather conditions can be treacherous, however, so it's wise to plan ahead. Most people continue on to Fairbanks Alaska, and complete the drive in seven to 10 days.

Saint John River, New Brunswick: New Brunswick is a province seemingly designed for road trips, and the tourism board has obliged by routing out some great trips: The Fundy Coastal Drive, the Acadian Coastal Drive, the Appalachian Range Route, and my favourite, the River Valley Scenic Drive. Follow the wide Saint John River for some 400 kilometres alongside tranquil fields, picturesque barns, and several old covered bridges (including the Hartland, see page 318). Pop into the historic old town of Fredericton, and stay overnight in the small town of Sussex just to see local history wonderfully painted on murals around town.

Brandon to Spruce Woods Provincial Park, Manitoba: *National Geographic* picked this prairie road trip in western Manitoba as one of the best on the continent. Ramble by rich farmland, river valleys, and highlands. Enjoy that big prairie sky and vast sense of space, along with some interesting stops along the way: the Chapman Museum looks at the region's pioneering history; the Canadian Fossil Discovery Centre has the remains of a huge marine lizard discovered in the area; or just enjoy the beauty of the International Peace Gardens, celebrating the relationship between the U.S. and Canada. The drive ends at Spruce Woods Provincial Park, where you can look for wildlife or venture into the meadows and sand dunes.

The Gaspésie Tour, Quebec: Here's a 1,442-kilometre road trip that starts in Montreal, explores the surrounding region, and then makes it way to Bas-Saint-Laurent and the Quebec Maritimes. Leaving Montreal, you'll head south to Chambly, before continuing on Route 223 through the Richelieu Valley. Passing Fort Lennox, make your way toward Quebec's wine route near the U.S. border, continuing to the lovely Eastern Townships. From here, the route takes you through towns like Abbaye de Saint-Benoît-du-Lac, Sherbrooke, Ulverton, Drummondville, Trois-Rivières, and Lac Saint-Pierre. Like all the best road trips, this weeklong adventure blends scenery, history, and culture.

Prince Edward County, Ontario: Once off the beaten track, Prince Edward County is attracting more and more road-trippers with its vineyards, artisans, and a gorgeous scenic drive along the Loyalist Parkway, also known as Highway 33. The route runs along the shores of Lake Ontario and through the countryside, passing by redbrick farmhouses, bucolic pastureland, and pioneer cemeteries. Since it's just a two-hour drive from Toronto, I suggest you stop at the beaches of North Beach Provincial Park or, 40 kilometres further down the road, the more popular Sandbanks Provincial Park. To enjoy the region's renaissance, visit the towns of Wellington and Picton, which have lots of history to share.

GAZE UPON CANADA'S BEST WATERFALLS

Something inside us resonates when we see a large quantity of water falling through the air — the velocity, the volume, the height, the sheer power. Whatever drenches your fancy, tick these exceptional waterfalls off your Canadian bucket list.

Helmcken Falls, B.C.: Located in Wells Gray Provincial Park, Helmcken is an impressive cascade in summer, and even more so in winter, when the water spray at the bottom of the falls freezes, creating a massive ice cone up to 50 metres tall.

Grand Falls-Grand Sault, New Brunswick (see page 323)

Niagara Falls, Ontario (see page 244)

Virginia Falls, Northwest Territories: With a 30-storey drop, Virginia Falls is twice the height of Niagara Falls. One hundred million tons of water crash over the falls every day. Fly-over day tours are available from Fort Simpson.

Della Falls, B.C.: Located near Port Alberni on Vancouver Island, Della's 440-metre drop is considered by many to be the tallest waterfall in Canada. It will entail a multi-day canoe and hiking adventure to find it, though.

Athabasca Falls, Alberta: One of Jasper National Park's most popular attractions, Athabasca Falls make up for a short 23-metre drop with the fiercest volume in the Rockies. Various paved trails and wheelchair viewing platforms allow everyone to hear the roar.

Takakkaw Falls, B.C.: Thundering with glacier run-off each summer, Takakkaw (which translates roughly as "magnificent" in Cree) drops 384 metres in total. It's easy to access from mid-June to mid-October; drive through a series of switchbacks to find a mostly paved walkway to the base.

NATIONAL ↑

541

Montmorency Falls, Quebec:
Explore Quebec's most famous waterfall (proudly 30 metres higher than Niagara Falls) by foot, cliffside rail car, suspension bridge, *via ferrata* or zipline. Each winter, a "Sugar Loaf" cone of ice forms at the bottom, beautifully lit up for nighttime visitors.

Pissing Mare Falls, Newfoundland and Labrador: A highlight on the Western Brook Pond boat cruise in Gros Morne National Park, this beauty cascades 250 metres in one vertical drop, with spray blowing in the wind.

Cameron Falls, Alberta: Located inside the town site of Waterton Village in Waterton Lakes National Park, access these falls with a short (wheelchair- and stroller-friendly) walk on a paved trail. A popular year-round attraction, the falls are just as spectacular at night as they are in the day.

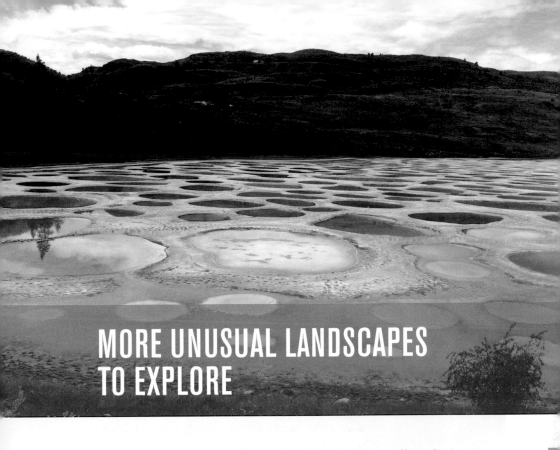

MORE UNUSUAL LANDSCAPES TO EXPLORE

If you liked Crooked Bush (see page 127), the Hopewell Rocks (see page 302), and the Athabasca Sand Dunes (see page 136), consider these bizarre Canadian landscapes.

Spotted Lake, B.C.: Canada has over three million lakes, but just of outside of Osoyoos, B.C., is one of the strangest. Hundreds of circular spots stretch across the aptly named Spotted Lake, containing highly concentrated minerals that often paint the pools in different colours. These are more visible in the summer, when water evaporates, leaving behind pools so dense in magnesium, calcium, and other minerals that they were once used to make ammunition during the First World War. Although the lake is located on private property, it can be easily seen from Highway 3, west of Osoyoos.

NATIONAL ↑

Balancing Rock, Nova Scotia: Canada's balancing rocks defy gravity and inspire wonder. The Savona Balancing Rock on the shores of Kamloops Lake, B.C., is impressive, but my favourite is the large, upright basalt column precariously perched on the coast of Long Island in St. Mary's Bay, Nova Scotia. Easily accessible via a 2.4-kilometre trail, the nine-metre-high column has been standing tall for over 200 years, literally hanging over the water's edge. While it looks like a whisper could blow it over, the Balancing Rock continues to stand up to winds and storms that hit the Bay of Fundy.

The Hoodoos Trail, Alberta: Over millions of years, the soft sandstone near Drumheller in southern Alberta has been worn away by wind and erosion. When it's capped with a harder, less erosive rock, the result is a hoodoo — four- to seven-metre-high red rock pillars that have become a symbol of the province's badlands. Cree and Blackfoot attributed stories and legends to these imposing fairy chimneys, which can be seen in various shapes and sizes. To access the Hoodoo Trail, head out of Drumheller on Highway 10 and play "spot the hoodoo."

Cheltenham Badlands, Ontario: Ontario's contribution to our list is a landscape as red as blood, and just as eerie. Located on the Niagara Escarpment north of Brampton, the Cheltenham Badlands are the

result of over-farming in the past, stripping a protective outer rock layer to expose a soft shale at the mercy of punishing erosion. Rich in iron-oxide, the red shale looks like the surface of Mars, framed with lush trees and bush. Although the Bruce Trail runs through the badlands, there is no public access to this endangered area, but there is a viewing area from the road and parking lot.

Manicouagan Crater, Quebec: You have to get high to appreciate this one. On the ground, a 70-kilometre-long circular lake is unusual, but from space, it looks like someone punched Earth with a bottle

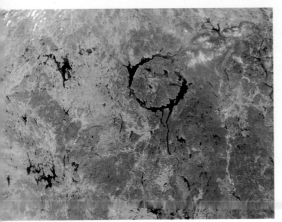

cap. The Manicouagan Crater is one of the world's oldest impact craters, the result of an asteroid hit some 213 to 215 million years ago. Stretching 100 kilometres across, the outer ring of water surrounds an inner island, giving it the distinct shape of an eyeball. No wonder it is known as the "Eye of Quebec." The crater is located 300 kilometres north of the city of Baie-Comeau.

EXPLORE MORE NATIONAL PARKS

once hiked across the South Pacific island of Rarotonga with an elder named Pa, who traipses barefoot across the island every day. He dropped many nuggets of wisdom that morning, and I'll always remember this one: "If someone is not well, physically or mentally, just put them in nature, and leave them alone for 15 minutes."

I wonder if this is what the founders of Parks Canada were thinking in 1911 when they launched the world's first national parks service. With 7,200 employees deeply committed to conservation, Parks Canada continues to govern our 46 national parks, 171 national historic sites, and four national marine conservation areas. Anyone who spends any time in these vast spaces is bound to feel *something*:

an appreciation for Canada's abundant natural beauty; delight with a wildlife encounter; elation during a physical pursuit like hiking, climbing, paddling, or biking; or best of all, a reconnection to the forests, mountains, rivers, tundra, and plains that existed long before Canada. It's no accident that many bucket list items in this book take place in a national park, and it wouldn't be amiss to place every national park on a Canadian bucket list.

Let's learn about a few more:

Yoho, B.C.: Located on the western slope of the Rockies and straddling the Continental Divide, Canada's second-oldest park is a haven for mountain wilderness. Highlights include the Takakkaw Falls, the Natural Bridge over Kicking Horse River, Emerald Lake, and Lake O'Hara.

Waterton Lakes, Alberta: Sharing borders with B.C., and Montana, Waterton is famed for having the deepest lakes in the Rockies, windswept mountain vistas, and great summer weather. Check out the Red Rock Canyon, the Prince of Wales Hotel, and the scenic Waterton Village.

Riding Mountain, Manitoba: The core of a UNESCO biosphere reserve, Riding Mountain is a green lung of parkland and boreal forest, located on the escarpment of south-central Manitoba. Camp in Parks Canada's oTENTik (a cross between an A-frame cabin and a prospector tent) and explore the town site of Wasagaming and the park's extensive trail system.

Thousand Islands, Ontario: The first park established east of the Rockies comprises more than 20 islands (all that remains of worn-down mountain tops), about 90 islets, marshlands, and channels. Popular with paddlers, it has long served as an important corridor for humans and wildlife. Look for wildlife along the Jones Creek Trail, a network of accessible trail loops.

La Mauricie, Quebec: Halfway between Montreal and Quebec City, La Mauricie protects 536 square kilometres of pristine valleys, lakes, and forest. It's popular with paddlers, campers, and hikers. Swim in the Cascades waterfalls, canoe camp on the shores of Wapizagonke Lake, or simply drive along the parkway to enjoy the various viewpoints.

Kouchibouguac, New Brunswick: Named for the Mi'kmaq word meaning "river of long tides," this park along New Brunswick's eastern shore protects bogs, salt marshes, rivers, lagoons, and forest. The most popular attractions include the 25-kilometre-long Barrier Islands dune system, Kellys Beach, and the park's Dark Sky Preserve programs.

Sable Island, Nova Scotia: There are not many places in the world where you can see free-roaming feral horses. Remote Sable Island, accessible only by air or sea, has hundreds of them. Harsh weather conditions around the island have caused more than 350 shipwrecks in the area, but it also helps to create a unique treeless world.

Torngat Mountains, Newfoundland and Labrador: Located on the northern tip of Labrador, this protected area set up by Parks Canada is for visitors eager to explore the tundra, mountains, wildlife, and fjords each summer. Journey through this spiritual place with your Inuit cultural hosts.

Vuntut, Yukon: A lot more people summit Everest every year than visit Vuntut, which was established to protect migrating Porcupine caribou and half a million migratory birds. Since it has no facilities of any kind, only experienced backcountry adventurers need apply.

Tuktut Nogait, Northwest Territories: Another one of North America's most isolated and challenging national parks, this 16,340-sqare-kilometre area protects the calving grounds of the Bluenose West caribou. Expect striking red canyons, sprawling tundra, waterfalls, and a wilderness untouched by modern man. Extensive logistical preparation is advised.

Qausuittuq, Nunavut: On the Northeast of Bathurst Island, you're deep in Northwest Passage territory (page 491), with the nearest community being Resolute. Broad, rocky, and treeless valleys are home to endangered Peary caribou, polar bears, and only the hardiest of Arctic flora and fauna.

TICK OFF CANADA'S UNESCO SITES

We've already visited a dozen Canadian UNESCO World Heritage Sites in this book, places that have been recognized by the United Nations as having "cultural, historical, scientific, or some other form of significance." Countries prepare an inventory of heritage destinations, which are put on a "tentative" list. After intense amounts of paperwork, much debate, and hopefully the popping of champagne corks, new UNESCO sites are added. At time of writing, Canada has 18 UNESCO World Heritage Sites, but our 2004 tentative list had 11 potentials, of which five have since been inscribed. Below are some of the UNESCO sites we didn't get to, along with six potentials waiting in the wings.

Bothriolepis canadensis
350,000,000 d'années
(Devonien)
Miguasha, Québec

Head-Smashed-In-Buffalo Jump, Alberta: Located at the foothills of the Rockies, the site, with an interpretive centre and museum, bears testimony to more than 6,000 years of communal hunting.

Waterton Glacier International Peace Park, Alberta/Montana: The union of Canada's Waterton Lakes National Park and the United States' Glacier National Park is the centrepiece of a unique biosphere, and the "Crown of the Continent" ecosystem.

Miguasha National Park, Quebec: Located on the Gaspé Peninsula, the park holds the world's greatest paleontological record of fossils from the Devonian period, a crucial time during the evolution of life on Earth.

Joggins Fossil Cliffs, Nova Scotia: Coastal exposure of Coal Age rocks has created the most complete terrestrial fossil record of the Carboniferous period, attracting scientists, palaeontologists, and tourists.

Landscape of Grand-Pre, Nova Scotia: An exceptional example of early European settlement on the North Atlantic coast, this site is a memorial to the Acadian way of life and the Great Expulsion of 1755 to 1764.

Red Bay Basque Whaling Station, Newfoundland and Labrador: The discovery of three galleons and four chalupas from a Basque whaling station on the southern tip of Labrador was a major archaeological discovery.

Mistaken Point, Newfoundland and Labrador: Canada's most recent UNESCO site is found on the southern tip of the Avalon Peninsula and contains the oldest known evidence of multi-cellular life on the planet. It was inscribed in July 2016.

On the UNESCO "Tentative" List:

Gwaii Haanas, B.C.: Already containing the inscribed SGang Gwaay Haida Village, the archipelago of 138 islands is uniquely protected from ocean floor to mountain top, preserving the rich heritage of the Haida people (see page 3).

Áísínai'pi, Alberta: Located about 100 kilometres from Lethbridge, this area encompasses Writing-on-Stone Provincial Park, which contains the largest concentration of Great Plains rock art. It is sacred to the Blackfoot and other Aboriginal tribes.

Ivvavik/Vuntut/Herschel Island, Yukon: These 15,500 square kilometres of protected wilderness on Yukon's coastal plain was never glaciated, becoming a key area in the history of human settlement in North America, and home to 10 percent of the world's caribou (see page 432).

Quttinirpaaq, Nunavut: The "Top of the World" is located at the northernmost tip of Canada, with the highest concentration of precontact sites in the High Arctic, the highest mountain in eastern North America, and vast areas of Arctic desert.

The Klondike, Yukon: Encompassing the Chilkoot Trail (page 442), Dawson City (page 437), Native fishing camps, and the Klondike gold fields, the site pays tribute to the world's most famous nineteenth-century gold rush.

Pimachiowin Aki, Manitoba and Ontario: A protected biosphere spanning two provinces and 33,400 square kilometres of boreal forest, this ancestral home of five First Nations tribes was almost inscribed by UNESCO in 2016. The nomination was withdrawn by the government when one of the First Nations withdrew support for "the land that gives life."

EPILOGUE

It is said that Canadians define themselves by what they are not. They are *not* Americans. They are *not* overly proud or boastful. They would never beat their chests to proclaim they live in the best country in the world, with wonders ready to dazzle any local or visitor with the curiosity to seek them out. Although I am an immigrant, I feel a tremendous connection to this unassuming, vast, and frequently surprising country. Canada is not perfect, but it is industrious, progressive, and deeply invested in a positive future. As Bono once said, "The world needs more Canada." For as the range of bucket list experiences in this book demonstrate, Canada itself is one of a kind.

"I never met a Canadian I didn't like." It's a common phrase I hear around the world. Canadians are recognized as friendly, generous, polite, and accepting of each other's cultural differences. We enjoy freedom of press, religion, the right to vote, the right to fair trial, and the right to tell our neighbouring province that their hockey team can't skate. Canadians invented insulin and IMAX, the electron microscope, the electric wheelchair, the zipper, ginger ale, basketball, and the baseball mitt. A Canadian invented Superman. Our six time zones encompass 10 percent of the world's forests, 10 percent of its renewable freshwater supply, and some two million lakes. We mine over 60 minerals inside the world's tenth-largest economy, but have a deep and healthy respect for nature and the outdoors. *Unless* it's freezing the carrot off a snowman, in which case, we are known to enjoy our underground heated shopping malls.

The nickname of our one dollar coin is a synonym for insane. Canadian players in U.S. teams listen to the U.S. anthem, while Scandinavians on Canadian teams fire up to our anthem, "O Canada." We print everything in French and English, drive in kilometres, but weigh in pounds. We gave the world Bryan Adams, Leonard Cohen, Shania Twain, Joni Mitchell, Neil Young, Nickelback, and Justin Bieber (and people *still* like us). Comedy and acting legends from Dan Aykroyd and Mike Myers to Seth Rogan and Russell Peters. Business legacies like the Bronfmans, Reichmanns, Aspers, and the guy who founded Cirque du Soleil. Writers like Mordecai Richler, William Gibson, Alice Munro, Margaret Atwood, and Douglas Coupland. Architects and doctors and actors and scientists — Canadians have made a big impact on the world, even as we quietly let our neighbours south of the 49th take the ticker parade. To be Canadian is to perfect the art of understatement. Case in point: we have wolf, cougar, bear, moose, eagle, wolverine, and orca, all of which would make an imposing impression at a conference of costumed national animals. Yet Canadians are not about bearing fangs, flashing claws, or shouting loud, flashy names. Like our humble beaver, we get the job done, usually while standing quietly on the podium of the UN Human Development Index for Highest Quality of Life. We have one of the world's highest levels of education, life expectancy, literacy, and health. There's a reason why the poor, destitute, and hungry dream of Canada. We are a nation that appreciates our legacy, luck, and good fortune, and we open our borders and hearts to refugees. We are sensitive to those who can only dream of our opportunities.

Over the years researching this book, I asked many people about their Canadian bucket list — where they want to go and what they want to do before they proverbially kick the bucket. It's a deeply personal question, and everyone is different. This book, after all, comprises activities and destinations I personally found interesting, given my experience and profession. Skipper Jim in Newfoundland told me his bucket list included finishing his shed, which I thought was as admirable an answer as any I'd heard.

My Great Canadian Bucket List is expansive, but it is also a living document. You met many people and learned about destinations you may not have known existed. Details will no doubt change and new items will be added, which is why all the practical information, reading guides, galleries, and maps sit on canadianbucketlist.com, where it is easier to update. Despite some cynicism in the media, I believe that the bucket list trend is a force for good. These are the dreams that drive us forward, inspire us to aspire to new adventures, and evolve with our age and interests.

Regardless of whether you tick off adventures from *The Great Canadian Bucket List*, finally build the shed, spend time with the kids, or simply finish reading this book, it's never too late, or early, to fill your bucket with the rich experiences that make living worthwhile.

Robin Esrock
Vancouver, B.C.

ACKNOWLEDGEMENTS

Researching the adventures, experiencing them, and surviving to write this book would not have been possible without the support, help, participation, enthusiasm, and vision of many people and organizations across Canada. With URLs provided after each item, I encourage you to find out more about these one-of-a-kind destinations, characters, and activities. Behind the scenes, I'd like to thank, in no particular order:

BRITISH COLUMBIA: Destination British Columbia, Janice Greenwood-Fraser, Andrea Visscher, Lana Kingston, Susan Hubbard, Liz Sperandeo, Teresa Davis, Josie Heisig, Luba Plotnikoff, Geoff Moore (#thanks), Heidi Korven, Cindy Burr, Mika Ryan, Nancie Hall, B.C. Ferries, Howard Grieve, Morgan Sommerville, Holly Wood, Robin Baycroft, Dee Raffo, Sarah Pearson, Jeremy Roche, CMH guides Rob, Mikey and Bob, heli-ski buddies (Natman, David, Dave, Mike, Jimm, and Larita), Greg McCracken. The WCT crew: Kyle, Jarrod, Robbie, Andrew, Chris, and James. Amber Sessions, Jorden Hutchison, Sonu Purhar, Tourism Vancouver. Also Randy Burke, David Suzuki, Feet Banks, Monica Dickinson, Jeff Topham, Eagle Rider Kamloops, James Nixon, Masa Takei, Michael Hannan, Rusty Noble, Juliette Recompsat, Jeff and Dianne Pennock, Teneille McGill, Sam Olstead, Graham Bell, Holly Lenk, Katie Dabbs, Lee Newman, T.J. Watt, and Bhaskar Krishnamurthy.

ALBERTA: Travel Alberta, Jessica Harcombe-Fleming, Anastasia Martin-Stilwell, Amy Wolski, Hala Dehais, Vanessa Gagnon, Charlie Locke, Tricia Woikin, Mary Morrison, Tessa Mackay, Doug Lentz, ski instructors John Jo and Kaz, Go RVing, Neil English and Isabel, Nancy Dery, Bin Lau, Ralph Sliger, and Ian Mackenzie.

SASKATCHEWAN: Tourism Saskatchewan, Jonathan Potts, Shane Owen, Jodi Holliday, Carla Bechard, Jenn Smith Nelson, Corporal Dan Toppings, the RCMP, Tyrone Tootoosis, Gord Vaaderland, Aviva Zack, Alexandra Stang, Tourism Saskatoon, Tourism Regina, Gary Kalmek, and Parks Canada.

MANITOBA: Travel Manitoba, Cathy Senecal, Julia Adams, Jillian Reckseidler, Linda Whitfield, Gillian Chester, Tourism Winnipeg, Tricia Schers, Lynda Cunter, Neil Mumby, Maureen Fitzhenry, Shel Zolkewich, Parks Canada, and Robert and Kristen Baron

ONTARIO: Ontario Tourism Marketing Partnership, Jantlue Van Kregten, Kattrin Sieber, Vanessa Somarriba, Ann Swerdfager, Melanie Wade, Melanie Coates, Michael Braham, Henriette Riegel, Irene Knight, Sue Mallabon, Niagara Parks, the Toronto Maple Leafs, Paul Pepe, Ian McMillan, Cathy Presenger, Larry Lage, Steve Kristjanson, Helen Lovekin, John Langford, and Matt Rothwell.

QUEBEC: Tourisme Québec, Gillian Hall, Patrick Lemaire, Paule Bergeron, Magalie Boutin, Catherine Binette, Pierre Bessette, Gilbert Rozon, Lola Burke, Lucas Aykroyd, Suzie Loiselle, Nancy Donnelly, the Adventure Travel Trade Association, and everyone who joined me for Winter Carnaval and on the *via ferrata*.

NEW BRUNSWICK: Tourism New Brunswick, Alison Aiton, Margaret MacKenzie, Heather MacDonald-Bosse, Lynn Meehan, Joan Meade, Kurt Gumushel, Jocelyn Chen, and the kind officer who pulled us over at 166 km/h and didn't ruin our day.

PRINCE EDWARD ISLAND: Tourism Prince Edward Island, George Larter, Joe Kalmek, Keri May, Nathalie Gaultier, Keri May, Caroline Mongrain, Ryan and Stacey Evans, Pat Deighan, Brenda Gallant, Isabel McDouggal, Robert Ferguson, Eza Paventi, and Pamela Beck.

NOVA SCOTIA: Nova Scotia Tourism Agency, Destination Cape Breton, Pam Wamback, Randy Brooks, Gregory Gallagher, Angelo Spinazzola, Gregory Gallagher, Wolfgang Gicharr, Ludovic Bischoff, Parks Canada, and Monica MacNeil.

NEWFOUNDLAND AND LABRADOR: Newfoundland and Labrador Tourism, Destination Labrador, Gillian Marx, Keith Small, Randy Letto, Jon Rothbart, Laura Walbourne, Janice Goudie, Ford Canada, Sarah Sullivan, Monica MacNeil, Nunatsiavut Group of Companies, Tour Labrador, Peter Bull, the Anchor Inn, Munju Ravindra, and that moose for not killing me.

YUKON: Travel Yukon, the one-of-a-kind Jim Kemshead, Denny Kobayashi, Peter Mather, Marten Berkman, Frank Turner, Terry and Cyara Dodge, Parks Canada, Helena Katz, Guy Theriault, and Peter Maher.

NORTHWEST TERRITORIES: Northwest Territories Tourism, Julie Warnock, Kylik Kisoun-Taylor, Barb Cote, Eva Holland, Tundra North Adventures, Carlos Gonzalez, Ash Mohandas, and Parks Canada.

NUNAVUT: One Ocean Expeditions, Aaron and Cathy Lawton, Elyse Mailhot, Jeff Topham, the staff, crew, and passengers of the Akademik Sergey Vavilov, Ryan Bray, Sara Acher, Richard Weber, Tessum Weber, Nansen Weber, Josée Auclair, and everyone at Arctic Watch, Ruslan Margolin, Prisca Campbell, Graham Dickson, Nunavut Tourism, Parks Canada, Leslie Qammaniq, Tamara Tarasoff, and Paul Scriver, who gave me the shirt off his back.

Thanks to everyone who has attended one of my speaking events and/or and registered on canadianbucketlist.com!

SPECIAL THANKS: Jaclyn Hodsdon, Margaret Bryant, Kirk Howard, Carrie Gleason, Karen McMullin, my patient editor Allison Hirst, Synora van Drine, Cheryl Hawley, Catherine Dorton, Courtney Horner, Laura Boyle, and all at Dundurn Press. Hilary McMahon and all at Westwood Creative Artists. Cathy Hirst, Jackie Miller, Mark Mizzoni and all at the Lavin Agency. Gloria Loree, Deidre Campbell, Helen de Faye and all at Destination Canada. Matt Drennan-Scace, Lauren More, Michelle Lee-Gracey, Josh Norton, and whoever figured out how to make a Ford Escape survive the Trans-Labrador Highway.

Thanks to Ann Campbell, Randall Shirley, Linda Bates, the late Ron Barker, Ian Mackenzie, Ken Hegan, the Travel Media Association of Canada,

ACKNOWLEDGEMENTS ↑

560

the Vancouver and Burnaby public libraries, Heather Taylor, Katherine Beatty, and all at Keen Footwear. Nathalie Gauthier, Kerri May, Caroline Mongrain, and all at Great Canadian Trails. Chris Lee, Minty Thompson, Kimberley Morton, Elyse Mailhot, Karen Margolese, Jon Rothbart, Jarrod Levitan, Marc Telio, Sherill Sirrs, Patrick Crean, and everyone else who helped me shape an unlikely career over the past decade. My thanks to David Rock for his invaluable help with producing our bucket list videos and website. My thanks to Mary Rostad for the wonderful maps.

Several stories were researched while filming the TV series *Word Travels*, which taught me how to travel hard, write hard, and chase a good story. A big shout-out to Heather Hawthorne-Doyle, Julia Dimon, Leah Kimura, Caroline Manuel, Sean Cable, Deb Wainwright, Mike Bodnarchuk, Mary Frymire, Peter Steel, Zach Williams, Ian Mackenzie, Paul Vance all at Omni Film, and the visionary Patrice Baillargeon.

SPECIAL THANKS TO THE FOLLOWING, WITHOUT WHOM THERE WOULD BE NO COMPANION WEBSITE OR SPEAKING TOURS: Ford Canada, Destination Canada, Parks Canada, Travel Manitoba, Tourism Saskatchewan, Tourism New Brunswick, Great Canadian Trails, Spectacular NWT, and KEEN Footwear.

My family has supported me since the beginning of my travel writing career, holding me up when I was sworn in as a Canadian citizen, battered and bruised from my accident the previous day. They provided the much-needed encouragement and space to prove I could make a living travelling the world. With love to Bradley, Staci, Gary, Abby, Erin, Bobba, Cecile, Alex, and Ian. My late grandfather once told me that he'd always wanted to see the world, but by the time he could afford to, he was too old. I got the message, Abie Esrock.

Finally, deep gratitude for my parents and part-time roadies, Joe and Cheryl Kalmek (without whom there would be no Robin Esrock), my ever-supportive wife, Ana Carolina, and my inspiring children, Raquel and Galileo. Daddy's coming home.

PHOTO CREDITS

PHOTO CREDITS